ARCO

Reading Lists for

COLLEGE-BOUND STUDENTS

3rd Edition

Doug E
Michel
Patri

ARCO
THOMSON LEARNING™

Australia • Canada • Denmark • Japan • Mexico • New Zealand • Philippines
Puerto Rico • Singapore • South Africa • Spain • United Kingdom • United States

3rd Edition

An ARCO Book

ARCO is a registered trademark of Thomson Learning, Inc., and is used herein under license by Peterson's.

About Peterson's

Founded in 1966, Peterson's, a division of Thomson Learning, is the nation's largest and most respected provider of lifelong learning online resources, software, reference guides, and books. The Education Supersite℠ at petersons.com—the Web's most heavily traveled education resource—has searchable databases and interactive tools for contacting U.S.-accredited institutions and programs. CollegeQuest℠ (CollegeQuest.com) offers a complete solution for every step of the college decision-making process. GradAdvantage™ (GradAdvantage.org), developed with Educational Testing Service, is the only electronic admissions service capable of sending official graduate test score reports with a candidate's online application. Peterson's serves more than 55 million education consumers annually.

Thomson Learning is among the world's leading providers of lifelong learning, serving the needs of individuals, learning institutions, and corporations with products and services for both traditional classrooms and for online learning. For more information about the products and services offered by Thomson Learning, please visit www.thomsonlearning.com. Headquartered in Stamford, Connecticut, with offices worldwide, Thomson Learning is part of The Thomson Corporation (www.thomson.com), a leading e-information and solutions company in the business, professional, and education marketplaces. The Corporation's common shares are listed on the Toronto and London stock exchanges.

For more information, contact Peterson's, 2000 Lenox Drive, Lawrenceville, NJ 08648; 800-338-3282; or find us on the World Wide Web at: www.petersons.com/about

ISSN: 1530-0013
ISBN 0-7645-6101-4

Printed in Canada

10 9 8 7 6 5 4 3 2 1 02 01 00

To those who taught me the fine balance between work and play. To them I owe my professional happiness: Edwin R. Estell, Richard Blough and Dale E. Graham.

—DOUG ESTELL

To my parents Jim and Ruth Shaffer who launched my love of reading, and my sons Matt and Andy Satchwell who continue to share it.

—MICHELE SATCHWELL

To Lloyd Wright—who was always adding another bookcase to our house and with whom I shared many a book.

—PATRICIA WRIGHT

Acknowledgments

Our gratitude to former student Tim Padgett whose knowledge and insight are clearly shown in the foreword to our new edition. His writing skills have outstripped his teachers'.

Our thanks to those who shared their thoughts about reading with us: Michael Agnes, Michael Drexler, Hans Gundersen, Lesley Kleiser, Mary Palecek, Sherri Pankratz, Deborah Pearlstein, Charles Phillips, Dana Rapp, Matt Satchwell, Jim Shaffer, Craig Sowder, and Jim Streisel.

Our appreciation to our colleagues at Carmel High School for their encouragement.

And to Jodi and Russ who are supportive in all our endeavors.

Finally, our most effusive thanks to our editor Stephanie Hammett. Her enthusiasm made writing this edition a fulfilling experience.

Contents

Preface

The third edition of *Reading Lists for College-Bound Students* reflects a major rewrite from the previous two editions. This edition contains not only lists from new contributors, but a number of updated favorites. Many of our lists were provided by the institution's faculty while others were compiled from information provided in the university's web page and current course catalog. These lists can and will change over time and should be regarded as close approximizations, not official requirements.

The third edition also contains several new, exciting tools to help college-bound students. You'll find brief biographical descriptions of the ten authors whose books are most frequently recommended by colleges: William Shakespeare, William Faulkner, Charles Dickens, Ernest Hemingway, Jane Austin, Homer, Mark Twain, Sophocles, Nathaniel Hawthorne, and F. Scott Fitzgerald. These individuals have made a lasting impact in the world of literature and we felt it important you get to know them a bit.

We've added suggested reading lists for students who have particular interests in any of the sciences, business, education, music, philosophy, political science, or history. For example, if you have an interest in science, you'll find suggestions on the list that include *A Brief History of Time: From the Big Bang to Black Holes* by Stephen Hawking, Charles Darwin's *Origin of Species* and *The Sea Around Us*, or *Silent Spring* by Rachel Carson.

There are six lists of literary prize winners: the Nobel Prize for Literature, the Pulitzer Prize, the National Book Award, the National Book Club Critics Award, the PEN/Faulkner Award, and the Whitbread Award. These lists are a great tool to help you stay on top of the best contemporary literature available. Recent prize winners have included the now-famous likes of Toni Morrison, John Updike, Annie Proulx, Charles Frazier, and Rita Dove.

Scattered throughout the book you'll find commentaries from book-loving individuals describing how reading affected their lives. It's inspiring to see how people with different lives and backgrounds view reading and its life-long value.

Finally, we've taken a look at hundreds of applications used by colleges and universities nationwide and pulled out the most often used reading-related essay questions students are currently asked. Among other things, you may be asked to describe a book that's been especially significant to you or a character you have particular respect for. Regardless of the specific question, your essay will be stronger if you can support your ideas with examples from your reading.

Over the last 10 years, we've learned that there's still no better way to succeed in college than to be well read. We've appreciated your comments on the first two editions, and we've tried to make this edition even more valuable for you.

Foreword

With all due respect to filmmakers, orators or painters, reading is still the most precious medium that we have, because it is the only genuinely active means of engaging the human mind. Everything else is ultimately a passive exercise, and simply doesn't hold the intellect to the same sparking grindstone that the printed word does.

As a result, I'm a big believer in reading lists as the maps that guide us to the best texts—that is, as long as those lists are as historically, geographically and culturally complete as a fine world atlas. Narrow-minded politics, sadly, has played too large a role in forming college canons over the past few decades, leaving students with the absurd impression that they somehow have to choose between Charles Dickens and Toni Morrison—who are probably my two favorite authors.

When I was a college student, I read Dickens' *A Christmas Carol* for the first time as literature instead of sentimental holiday fare; and it affirmed then, and continues to affirm today, my decision to be a journalist. When the Ghost of Christmas Present opens his robe and reveals to Scrooge the two wretched children he calls Ignorance and Want, Dickens writes, "Where angels might have sat enthroned, devils lurked, and glared out menacing. No change, no degradation, no perversion of humanity, in any grade, through all the mysteries of wonderful creation, has monsters half so horrible and dread." That passage rings in my ears every time I confront children in similar conditions during my reporting in Latin America, and drives me to convey to readers at least some measure of the rich indignation with which Dickens—who began his career as a journalist—wrote it.

By the same token, I'm not drawn to Morrison because reading an African-American novelist is politically correct. I do value her epics of black struggle for making me more aware as a white American. But, as a native of the U.S. heartland, I've discovered that Morrison does that so effectively for me in large part because she's also a great Midwestern novelist—a writer who bridges racial gaps by elegantly weaving common regional experiences, like watching the "theatrical" change of seasons. In her best book, *Beloved,* autumn arrives in Ohio "with its bottles of blood and gold," and snow falls "fat enough and heavy enough to crash like nickels on stone. It always surprised him how quiet it was. Not like rain, but like a secret." Those probably aren't the sort of passages that either conservatives or liberals expect a reader to glean from Morrison—which is precisely why ideologues have no business peddling reading lists. Morrison is my favorite modern American writer because, by evoking parts of my own childhood for me, she moves me to sympathize more genuinely with the black experience.

A book's ability to move, teach and inspire is something a reading list doesn't advertise. But if it's a good list, it will at least, like a good map, lead a student to what Evelyn Waugh called the "low door in the wall," which opens to the truths we're always laboring to find out about ourselves and our world. This book contains a variety of lists—some you'll embrace, others you'll question—but from their cumulative sum you will build your own. Doug Estell, Michele Satchwell, and Pat Wright have helped generations of Carmel High School students, including me, build broad, solid and sometimes delightfully offbeat reading repertoires that enhanced our college careers and our adult lives. They know that standards like *The Great Gatsby* ought to be complemented with surprises like *Siddhartha.* In other words, they're the kind of teachers who have every business peddling reading lists—and, for students, this edition is one of the best guides available to the grindstones that await them in college.

—TIM PADGETT
Miami Bureau Chief, *Time* magazine

CHAPTER 1

Why You Need This Book!

Looking into your college future is at the same time both exciting and frightening. As you anticipate living on your own, going to parties, making new friends, and taking stimulating classes, your excitement may be balanced by your fear of choosing the best college, fitting in socially, and surviving academically. One thing that can tip the scales in your favor and alleviate some of your worries about survival is to prepare yourself by being well read. Here finally is a book that helps you to develop a reading plan that prepares you for the rigors of college academia. This book will give you:

- **Suggested reading lists from representative American colleges** Take a look at the lists submitted by colleges you're interested in (or colleges that share a similar profile to your top picks) to get a feel for what's important to the university.
- **A reading list of the 100 most recommended books and the 10 most recommended authors from these college lists** We've looked at each of the college lists and compiled a list of the 100 most recommended books and the 10 most recommended authors. These authors and works should form the backbone of your pre-college reading plan.
- **A plan for making your personal reading list** Facing the hundreds of recommended works in this book can be overwhelming when your reading time is limited; this book helps you make a personal reading plan that is comprehensive *and* manageable.
- **Tips for better reading skills** These will help you remember and use what you have read.

- **Some special interest lists** Not everyone wants to major in English Literature, so these lists of books are particularly useful for students of natural sciences, political science, fine arts, and many other disciplines.
- **Reading-related essay questions from college applications** Many college applications contain essay questions that require applicants to write on book-related topics. Look for the essay writing icon and spend a few minutes considering how you'd answer the question if it were posed to you today.
- **Commentaries on reading** Various individuals who love reading have expressed the impact reading has had on their lives. We've included their words in the hopes you'll be inspired to make reading a priority in your life.

READING IS ESSENTIAL IN COLLEGE PREPARATION

Your success in college depends on your reading:

- It improves your vocabulary.
- It makes you a better writer.
- It helps you understand yourself and others, as well as the past and present societies you will be studying.
- It provides you with the background to succeed in college.

Let's look at each of these ideas.

Improve Your Vocabulary

Have you ever talked with a person whose way of speaking is very different from your own? Some examples might be a Southerner if you are from the North, an Easterner if you are from the West, or a person from a social class different enough from yours that his or her choice of words sounds strange to you. If you are around people from other environments long enough, you will pick up some of their words and even their patterns of speech.

That's how you began to accumulate your vocabulary, isn't it? For your first few years your words—*mama, cookie, baby,* and so on—came mainly from those who raised you. You weren't born with these words in your mind. You heard them. Books can have the same effect on you. If you live for a while with authors such as Dickens or Shakespeare or Melville, you will begin to add their words to your vocabulary—and you won't have to look up each new word you encounter. When you hear words in your mind often enough, you begin to understand them and finally to use them—just as you did when you were a child.

Spend a moment reading a passage from Herman Melville's *Moby-Dick.* If you're not familiar with the book, it's a story about a mad sea captain, Ahab, and his enemy, the white whale Moby-Dick.

> *But at this critical instant a sudden exclamation was heard that took every eye from the whale. With a start all glared at dark Ahab, who was surrounded by five dusky phantoms that seemed fresh formed out of air. The phantoms, for so they then seemed, were flitting on the other side of the deck, and, with a noiseless celerity, were casting loose the tackles and bands of the boat which swung there. This boat had always been deemed one of the spare boats, though technically called the captain's, on account of its hanging from the starboard quarter. The figure that now stood by its bows was tall and swart, with one white tooth evilly protruding from its steel-like lips. A rumpled Chinese jacket of black cotton funereally invested him, with wide black trousers of the same dark stuff. But strangely crowning this ebonness was a glistening white plaited turban, the living hair braided and coiled round and round upon his head. Less swart in aspect, the companions of this figure were of that vivid, tiger-yellow complexion peculiar to some of the aboriginal natives of the Manillas—a race notorious for a certain diabolism of subtlety.*

Weren't you able to feel the rising fear in this passage? Yet perhaps some of the words were new to you. In the middle of an exciting scene, you don't always need to turn to a dictionary to understand the meaning of a word. You can use context clues: the emotion in the passage, the meaning of the words around the unknown word, or the subject matter of the passage. Even though you may not know the meaning of the word "celerity" in the third sentence of Melville's passage, you can get its meaning (swiftness) from the vivid image created by the passage.

If you encounter new words often enough in reading—and take the time to figure them out—they become part of your vocabulary. Knowing them will help you perform better on college entrance tests, in college courses, and on the job later in life.

Become a Better Writer

Even before you enter college you will need to show your skill as a writer. As you apply to colleges, you'll find you're often required to write a college application essay, and many times, these essays ask you to discuss something from your reading. The Common Application, which is printed and distributed on behalf of participating colleges by the National Association of Secondary School Principals and accepted by hundreds of colleges and universities, has the following as one of its four essay choices: "Describe a character in fiction, an historical figure, or a creative work (as in art, music, science, etc.) that has had an influence on you, and explain that influence." Recently one of Notre Dame's questions asked for a discussion of Martin Luther King's famous "I Have a Dream" speech. Frequently the University of Pennsylvania has prospective students list four or five of their favorite books and discuss one of them. Stanford University often asks applicants to choose a favorite quotation and comment on its significance. Barnard College has its applicants list the books they have read during high school, saying, "the most diverse lists are the most attractive on an application." Many other colleges have questions that ask applicants to write essays on book-related topics, and in this book you can find some of these questions where prompted by the writing icon. If colleges do not ask specific literary questions, they may instead ask you to "describe yourself" or to write and answer your own essay question. Your essay will be stronger if you can support your ideas with examples from your reading.

Once you get to college, the list of writing assignments will be almost endless. Most schools say that above all else, you should leave college with the ability to write and express yourself well—and they make sure you get adequate practice by incorporating writing exercises wherever possible. Don't be surprised if even your math class requires some type of regular writing assignment!

Reading helps you become a better writer by enlarging your vocabulary and introducing you to more complex sentence patterns and expanded ideas. How does this work? As a child you began by imitating other people's sentence patterns. At first it was just one word, perhaps "bye-bye," "cookie," or "mama." Gradually you advanced to simple sentences: "Go bye-bye," "Want cookie." And then to more complex structures: "Please give me a cookie." "May I go to the store with you?" As you grew, your prolonged exposure to "adult" speech patterns changed the way you spoke.

Professor Martha Rainbolt of DePauw University says that works of 19th-century British fiction help show readers "the 'right' way to write sentences." In Henry James's horror tale "The Turn of the Screw" there is a wonderful sentence about young children trying to mollify their caretaker with loads of kindness. A governess senses something menacingly evil about her young charges, yet they are able at least momentarily to "polish"away her fears. She says, "They had never, I think, wanted to do so many things for their poor protectress; I mean—though they got their lessons better and better, which was naturally what would please her most—in the way of diverting, entertaining, surprising her; reading her passages, telling her stories, acting her charades, pouncing out at her, in disguises, as animals and historical characters, and above all astonishing her by the 'pieces' they had secretly got by heart and could interminably recite." Today we would say they really "laid it on." But can't you see what they were up to? James's sentence includes so much description, so much action, that you can actually visualize the scene. As you read for college you will be building a foundation for the kind of expression expected by university professors. Unconsciously you absorb the patterns in what you read and you become a better writer.

No matter how elegant your sentences are, however, your writing will not impress your professors unless you have something interesting to say. Through reading you'll be exposed to a variety of people, ideas, and attitudes.

You'll develop critical-thinking skills that allow you to form opinions and make value judgements. You'll start to make connections between the things you read and the things you see on the evening news. In short, you'll be better prepared to form an opinion—or thesis—for your writing if you've surrounded yourself with the various ideas and opinions of others. Just think how impressed your European History professor would be if you compared a passage from Dante's *Inferno* to World War II Nazi propaganda in your midterm paper. With a wide and varied reading plan, you'll have a solid foundation of ideas from which to draw as you craft the countless essay, papers, and theses required in your classes.

Better Understand Yourself and Others

Books can help you understand your own feelings, ideas, opinions and those of others. You've probably already experienced this. Did you read *A Separate Peace* or *The Catcher in the Rye*? Haven't you had some of the problems those young people faced? Experienced some of their feelings? Shared some of their opinions? Isn't it nice to know that someone out there is a little like you? The more you read, the more you will find this is true, and the more help you will get in thinking through your own ideas and emotions. Now and then you may even change your mind or your heart. Books on the college and university lists such as Hesse's *Siddhartha*, Sophocles' *Antigone*, and Twain's *The Adventures of Huckleberry Finn* are about some of the problems young people face.

Wide reading also familiarizes you with people, places, and cultures different from your own. When you have read Harper Lee's *To Kill a Mockingbird*, you begin to understand the emotions of those involved in the civil rights movement of the 1960s. After reading *The Pearl* by John Steinbeck, you come to understand how greed can corrupt people in a society. From Victor Hugo's *Les Misérables* you learn about the poverty and despair that bred revolt in 19th-century France. Reading allows you to travel across the world and through time without ever leaving the comfort of your room.

Succeed in College

Most colleges will either give you credit or exempt you from classes on the basis of tests you take that demonstrate your mastery of a subject. You may be familiar with Advanced Placement programs, which offer such tests while you are in high school. When you have selected your college, contact the admissions officer to find out if that university offers the College-Level Examination Program (CLEP) or similar programs. These programs can save you (and your parents) lots of money and time. How can you best prepare for these tests? READ.

Whether or not you will be able to test out of classes, reading will help you get the most out of the classes you do take. Let's look into your future. It is the second semester of your freshman year. You have three chapters to read in sociology, two in world history, two in trigonometry (plus the problems at the end of the chapters), and your freshman lit teacher wants you to read *The Iliad* by Friday. Can you feel the panic rising? If you had already read *The Iliad* last year and were familiar with it, all you would have to do is review it, not start from scratch. And if your world history professor assigns an essay asking you to discuss the Trojan War, well, you'll have it made. There are so many demands on your time when you are in college that reading now can give you the head start you may need to survive.

More than anywhere else, college is the place to share and explore ideas. If you have read lots of books before you get there, you will have more to share—both with your professors and with your friends.

CHAPTER 2

How to Use This Book

THE LISTS IN THIS BOOK

At first glance, the hundreds of pages of lists in this book can be overwhelming. If you're getting close to the start of college you may think there's no way you can accomplish even one of those lists, let alone all 100. But take heart, we've simplified things for you. Chapter 3, "The Most-Often Recommended Authors and Works," contains a list of the 100 most-often recommended books on college lists. Each book is annotated to give you an idea of what it is about, when it was written, and the nationality of the author. This list is indispensable when forming your own comprehensive reading plan.

For those of you looking for diverse reading suggestions, Chapter 4, "The College and University Lists," contains lists from representative colleges and universities across the nation. Some are pre-college reading lists prepared by the colleges and universities themselves; others include selections from freshman-sophomore syllabi, first year seminars, course descriptions, or required core programs. As you scan this section, don't limit yourself only to the colleges you recognize. Professors from many institutions have given interesting tips on what to read and how to read.

Finally, in Chapter 5, "Special Interest Lists and Major Literary Awards," you'll find two additional types of lists: the "if" lists and the prize-winner lists. The "if" lists center around specific disciplines. If you plan to study science, business, education, the arts, philosophy, history, or AP English, these lists suggest reading suited to your interest. The second set of lists identifies national prize winners for literature. Here you'll find books that knowledgeable organizations have honored for their excellence.

MAKING A PERSONAL READING LIST

If you're like many students and your time is limited, start your reading with the 10 or 20 books that sound most interesting. Choosing what you are going to read is like filling your plate at a Thanksgiving buffet. Like Thanksgiving food, all the books listed are good—but in different ways. Some are filling and nutritious and others are delicious and fattening. As you're filling your plate, try to select a variety. Vonnegut's *Slaughterhouse Five* and Orwell's *Animal Farm*, even though they satirize serious matters, are delicious and fattening. Conrad's *Heart of Darkness* and Thoreau's *Walden* are filling and nutritious. The first leads you on an increasingly frightening river journey into the heart of Africa, and the second gives you ideas on being an individual—"marching to a different drummer."

Read as many kinds of books as possible. Don't limit yourself to one particular style, country, or time period, or to only male or female authors. The most important thing is that you have lots of variety in your reading. A little bit of fiction, a little bit of drama, a little bit of poetry—you should try them all to feed your brain!

There are no hard and fast rules for selecting the right books for your reading list, and you should be flexible with the works you choose. If you think the book listed for a particular writer is too long or too difficult for the moment, choose another of his or her titles. For example, if wading into Melville's *Moby-Dick* seems to be more than your schedule can handle right now, try one of his other classics such as *Billy Budd.*

On the following pages you will find a sample reading list and a blank list that you may use. Notice that in the sample list every category is filled with at least one work. When you have completed your reading, make sure that you, too, have read something from each category. Have fun with this list; remember to tailor it to fit your needs, your interests, and your busy schedule.

SAMPLE PERSONAL READING LIST

Fiction

American Novel

Fitzgerald, *The Great Gatsby*

Updike, *Rabbit, Run*

British Novel

Orwell, *Animal Farm*

Austen, *Emma*

World Novel

Camus, *The Stranger*

Flaubert, *Madame Bovary*

Male Author

Hemingway, *The Sun Also Rises*

Crane, *Red Badge of Courage*

Female Author

Brontë, *Jane Eyre*

Cather, *My Antonia*

Pre-18th C. Works

Bible: "Job," "Genesis"

Chaucer, *Canterbury Tales* (Prologue and Wife of Bath's Tale)

18th C. Novel

Swift, *Gulliver's Travels*

Fielding, *Tom Jones*

19th C. Novel

Twain, *Huckleberry Finn*

Dickens, *Great Expectations*

20th C. Novel

Morrison, *Sula*

Salinger, *Catcher in the Rye*

Short Stories (American)

Faulkner, "The Bear"

Poe, "Fall of the House of Usher"

Short Stories (World)

Kafka, "Metamorphosis"

O'Connor, "A Good Man Is Hard to Find"

SAMPLE PERSONAL READING LIST *(continued)*

Drama

Classical Drama

Sophocles, *Antigone* __________

Aristophanes, *Lysistrata* __________

British Drama

Shakespeare, *Hamlet* __________

Shaw, *Pygmalion* __________

American Drama

Miller, *Death of a Salesman* __________

Williams, *Glass Menagerie* __________

World Drama

Ibsen, *A Doll's House* __________

Poetry

Lyrical

Emily Dickinson __________

Walt Whitman __________

Robert Frost __________

Epic

Homer, *The Odyssey* __________

Dante, *Inferno* __________

Non-Fiction

Biography

Franklin, *Autobiography* __________

Philosophy/Religion

Plato, *Apology* __________

History

Thoreau, *Civil Disobedience* __________

Science

Darwin, *Origin of Species* __________

PERSONAL READING LIST

Fiction

American Novel

____

____

British Novel

____

____

World Novel

____

____

Male Author

____

____

Female Author

____

____

Pre-18th C. Works

____

____

18th C. Novel

____

____

19th C. Novel

____

____

20th C. Novel

____

____

Short Stories (American)

____

____

Short Stories (World)

____

____

PERSONAL READING LIST *(continued)*

Drama

Classical Drama

____

____

British Drama

____

____

American Drama

____

____

World Drama

____

____

Poetry

Lyrical

____

____

____

Epic

____

____

____

Non-Fiction

Biography

____

Philosophy/Religion

____

History

____

Science

____

REMEMBERING WHAT YOU'VE READ

One way to keep track of what you've read is to keep a reading diary. What should it include?

Author

When keeping track of what you've read, it helps to find some information about the author—when and where he or she was writing and any other interesting personal information. Books are not written in a vacuum. They reflect the influence of the author's surroundings on his or her particular thoughts, attitudes, and emotions.

Theme

It is also important to be aware of the main idea of the work itself. If you're reading fiction, you may want to jot down the main elements: character, plot, setting. If your book is nonfiction, be sure to list the support for the author's main idea. In poetry you should note the word pictures that are most vivid.

Overall Impressions

After you've finished your reading, be sure to note what was unforgettable about the work. What made it different from other books you've read? What made it similar? Overall, did you like the book? Write down all of your evaluations. Often writing will help you crystallize your impressions of the work and will make it easier to recall key information if you need to in later years.

On the following page you will find a sample format for a reading diary. Just remember to adapt it to fit your needs.

READING DIARY

TITLE ______________________ **When written** ______________________

AUTHOR ______________________ **Nationality** ______________________

____

____

____

____

TYPE OF WORK (Fiction, non-fiction, poetry, etc.)

____

____

MAIN IDEA ____

____

____

____

____

____

____

____

____

IMPORTANT ELEMENTS

EVALUATION

Reader's Guides: Proceed with Caution!

Once you have made your personal reading list, you may be tempted to skip the books and use *Cliffs Notes*, *Monarch Notes*, or some other type of reader's guides. DON'T! There is no substitute for the real thing. You cannot get a feel for the author's use of language, the speech patterns of the characters, or the vividness of the descriptive passages from reading ABOUT the book. Just as hearsay is not admissible as evidence in a court of law, knowing a book only through secondhand information from a reader's guide is not admissible in the college classroom.

Reader's guides, however, can help you if you are experiencing difficulty in understanding a particular book. If you have trouble understanding the main idea, isolating the theme, or interpreting the characters, a reader's guide often can point you in the right direction, or at least give you a point of departure. Your librarian can also help you find literary criticism that gives profiles of an author's life and synopses and critiques of his or her works.

CHAPTER 3

The Most-Often Recommended Authors and Works

THE 10 MOST RECOMMENDED AUTHORS

The authors most frequently mentioned by all the colleges are listed and briefly described below. These authors, playwrights, and poets represent "the best of the best," so you should try to include some of their works in your personal reading list.

1. **William Shakespeare** (British, 1564–1616) Many considered this poet and dramatist the greatest of all playwrights. Best known are his tragedies: *Romeo and Juliet, Julius Caesar, MacBeth, King Lear, Othello* and *Hamlet*; his comedies: *Twelfth Night, As You Like It*; the tragicomedies: *The Winter's Tale* and *The Tempest*; and the histories: *Richard II* and *Henry V*.
2. **William Faulkner** (American 1897–1962) Faulkner's best-known novels explore the problems of the South after the Civil War. Most famous of his works are *The Sound and The Fury, The Reivers, The Hamlet*, and *Absalom, Absalom!*.
3. **Charles Dickens** (British, 1812–1870) The most popular writer of his time, Dickens's works include the short story "A Christmas Carol" and novels *A Tale of Two Cities, Great Expectations, Oliver Twist, David Copperfield, The Old Curiosity Shop, Nicholas Nickleby, Hard Times, Bleak House*, and *Martin Chuzzlewit*.

4. **Ernest Hemingway** (American, 1899–1961) Hemingway's machismo and no-frills journalistic style influenced many other American writers of his time. His works include the novels *A Farewell to Arms, The Sun Also Rises,* and *For Whom the Bell Tolls*; the novella *The Old Man and the Sea*; and many short stories like "The Killers" and "The Snows of Kilimanjaro."
5. **Jane Austen** (British, 1775–1817) Mostly about young women in pursuit of suitable husbands, Austen's novels are comedies of manners. They include *Pride and Prejudice, Sense and Sensibility, Emma,* and *Mansfield Park.* Her *Northanger Abbey* is an early Gothic novel.
6. **Homer** (Greek, before 700 BC) Said to be blind, Homer is the first great European poet. Two epic poems are ascribed to him: *The Iliad,* about a great battle in the Trojan War, and *The Odyssey,* about Odysseus' ten year journey home after the fall of Troy.
7. **Mark Twain** (American, 1835–1910) Mark Twain's humor is as fresh today as it was in the 19th century. His best known novels are *The Adventures of Tom Sawyer* and *The Adventures of Huckleberry Finn.* His children's novel *The Prince and the Pauper* and the satire *A Connecticut Yankee in King Arthur's Court* are also widely read.
8. **Sophocles** (Greek, c. 496–406 BC) Sophocles wrote some 123 tragedies; seven survive. They include *Antigone, Oedipus Rex* (or *Oedipus Tyrannus*) and *Oedipus at Colonus.*
9. **Nathaniel Hawthorne** (American, 1804–1864) One of America's first great writers, Hawthorne explored the moral and spiritual conflicts of his day. His novels *The Scarlet Letter* and *The House of the Seven Gables* are well known, as are his short stories in *Twice-Told Tales.*
10. **F. Scott Fitzgerald** (American, 1896–1940) Fitzgerald's life and his novels reproduce Jazz Age America for the modern reader. His most famous novel *The Great Gatsby* is about the corruption of the American dream. His others are *Tender Is the Night, This Side of Paradise, The Beautiful and the Damned, In Our Time,* and *The Last Tycoon* (unfinished).

THE 100 MOST RECOMMENDED WORKS

This list of the 100 works most frequently recommended by colleges and universities is compiled from the pre-college reading lists, freshmen syllabi, and core programs detailed in Chapter 4, "The College and University Lists." The annotations will help you decide which books you'd like to read first.

The author's nationality and the date of publication are in parentheses before each annotation. If you are interested in other works by the same author, alternate suggestions that were consistently mentioned by the colleges appear in parentheses at the end of the annotation.

Novels and Short Stories

Austen, Jane, *Pride and Prejudice* (British, 1813): A novel about love and marriage among the English country gentry of Austen's day. The hero's pride in his social class conflicts with the heroine's prejudice against him based on first impressions. (*Emma*)

Baldwin, James, *Go Tell It on the Mountain* (American, 1953): This semi-autobiographical novel about a 14-year-old black youth's religious conversion is based on Baldwin's experience as a young storefront preacher in Harlem. (*Notes of a Native Son*)

Bellow, Saul, *Seize the Day* (American, 1956): In this novella, a son grapples with his love and hate for an unworthy father. When he won the Nobel Prize in 1976, Bellow was cited for "the human understanding and the analysis of contemporary culture that are combined in his work." (*Henderson the Rain King*)

Brontë, Charlotte, *Jane Eyre* (British, 1847): This romantic novel introduced a new type of heroine to English fiction. Jane Eyre is an intelligent, passionate, and not especially beautiful young woman who falls in love with a strange moody man tormented by dark secrets.

Brontë, Emily, *Wuthering Heights* (British, 1847): One of the masterpieces of English romanticism, this is a novel of love and revenge. The demonic passion of the hero-villain Heathcliff destroys his beloved Catherine, her family, and eventually himself.

Camus, Albert, *The Stranger* (French, 1942): An existential novel in which a young man, observing rather than participating in life, commits a senseless murder. While in prison awaiting execution, he comes to value life. Camus won the Nobel Prize in 1957.

Carroll, Lewis, *Alice's Adventures in Wonderland* (British, 1865): A fantasy in which Alice follows the White Rabbit to a dream world. The characters she encounters (the Mad Hatter, the Queen of Hearts, and others) are part of the adult world she must deal with. Sir John Tenniel's illustrations have become as classic as Lewis Carroll's story. (*Through the Looking Glass*)

Cather, Willa, *My Antonia* (American, 1918): A realistic novel about immigrant pioneers as they strive to adapt to the Nebraska prairies. It is the story of the struggles of Antonia and other women who are strengthened by the harsh realities of life. (*Death Comes for the Archbishop*)

Cervantes, Miguel de, *Don Quixote* (Spanish, 1605, 1615): A novel in which an eccentric old gentleman setting out as a knight goes "tilting at windmills" to right the wrongs of the world. This work, made up of twelve stories, "has been translated into more languages than any other book except the Bible" (L. H. Hornstein).

Chopin, Kate, *The Awakening* (American, 1899): This is the story of a New Orleans woman who abandons her husband and children to search for love and self-understanding. A controversial book when it was published because of the character's extramarital affair, the book was virtually ignored for 50 years.

Conrad, Joseph, *Heart of Darkness* (British, 1902): A probing psychological novel that explores the darkness in the soul of each man. Conrad's narrator Marlow makes a journey into the depths of the Congo where he discovers the extent to which greed can corrupt a good man. (*The Secret Sharer, Lord Jim*)

Crane, Stephen, *The Red Badge of Courage* (American, 1895): This Civil War novel, which Crane called "a psychological portrayal of fear," reveals the grim aspects of war in the life of an ordinary soldier. Henry Fleming joins the army full of romantic visions of battle, which are shattered by combat.

Defoe, Daniel, *Robinson Crusoe* (British, 1719): Based on the true story of Alexander Selkirk's sea experiences, this novel is about the adventures of a man who spends 24 years on an isolated island. With the help of an islander whom he names Friday, Crusoe shows courage and ingenuity in meeting the challenges of his predicament.

Dickens, Charles, *Great Expectations* (British, 1860–61): A novel about Pip, a poor boy, who is made rich by a mysterious benefactor, sets out to realize his "great expectations," and finally becomes a man of worth and character. As in all his works, Dickens populates this novel with memorable and eccentric characters. (*David Copperfield, A Tale of Two Cities*)

Dostoevski, Feodor, *Crime and Punishment* (Russian, 1866): A psychological novel about a poor student who murders an old woman pawnbroker and her sister. After the crime, his conscience bothers him until he confesses. He is sent to Siberia, and finally becomes truly repentent. (*The Brothers Karamazov*)

Eliot, George, *The Mill on the Floss* (British, 1860): The Victorian world of male supremacy is the background for this novel of a stormy relationship between a brother and sister. Maggie Tulliver's life is miserable because her brother Tom disapproves of her choices of romances. (*Middlemarch*)

Ellison, Ralph, *Invisible Man* (American, 1947): "I am an invisible man," begins this novel of an unnamed black man's search for identity as an individual and as a member of his race and his society. This story goes beyond one man's search and chronicles every man's struggle to find himself.

Faulkner, William, *The Sound and the Fury* (American, 1929): The theme for this Nobel Prize–winning author's novel is the decline of the Southern family. Presented through four points of view, it examines the deterioration of the Compson family. ("The Bear," *As I Lay Dying, Light in August, Absalom, Absalom*)

Fielding, Henry, *Tom Jones* (British, 1749): A humorous novel about the adventures of an amorous young man whose impulsiveness often leads him into difficult situations. (*Joseph Andrews*)

Fitzgerald, F. Scott, *The Great Gatsby* (American, 1925): A novel in which a young man corrupts himself and the American Dream in order to regain a lost love. *The Great Gatsby* "belongs not only to American but to world literature...to the tragic predicament of humanity as a whole" (A. E. Dyson).

Flaubert, Gustave, *Madame Bovary* (French, 1857): A realistic novel in which a young wife is bored with her husband. In her extramarital affairs, she seeks unsuccessfully to find the emotional experiences she has read about in romantic novels.

Forster, E.M., *A Passage to India* (British, 1924): A pessimistic novel about man's inhumanity to man. A young English woman in British-ruled India accuses an Indian doctor of a sexual assault; her accusation causes racial tension between the British and Indian communities and destroys the young man's career. (*A Room with a View, Howard's End*)

García Márquez, Gabriel, *One Hundred Years of Solitude* (Columbian, 1967): This Latin American novel portrays seven generations in the lives of the Buendia family. García Márquez employs a technique called magic realism—the use of magic, myth, and religion to intensify reality.

Golding, William, *Lord of the Flies* (British, 1954): In this novel a group of English schoolboys who are stranded on an island without adults become savages. This moral fable implies that defects in society are caused in part by defects in individuals.

Hardy, Thomas, *Tess of the D'Urbervilles* (British, 1891): A Victorian novel in which the happiness and marriage of Tess and her husband are destroyed because she confesses to him that she bore a child as the result of a forced sexual relationship with her employer's son. (*The Return of the Native*)

Hawthorne, Nathaniel, *The Scarlet Letter* (American, 1850): A novel about an adulterous Puritan woman who keeps secret the identity of the father of her illegitimate child. Her sin and the secret sin of the father are dwarfed by the vengefulness of her husband.

Hemingway, Ernest, *A Farewell to Arms* (American, 1929): In this semiautobiographical novel, which takes place during World War I, an American lieutenant falls in love and runs away with the woman who nurses him to health. Hemingway, winner of the 1954 Nobel Prize, is known for his journalistic style. (*The Sun Also Rises*)

Hurston, Zora Neale, *Their Eyes Were Watching God* (American, 1937): A novel about a woman's search for a happy life. "The image of the black woman as the mule of the world becomes a metaphor for the roles that Janie requdiates in her quest for self-fulfillment..." (Sherley Williams).

Huxley, Aldous, *Brave New World* (British, 1932): In this bitter satire about the future, Nobel prize–winner Huxley conceives a world controlled by advances in science and social changes. Individuals are no longer important and their lives are planned out for them.

James, Henry, *The Turn of the Screw* (American, 1898): This novella is a study of good and evil in which the children are "the arena and the victim" (Hortense Calisher). A governess in charge of two children discovers they are under the evil influence of ghosts and attempts to save them. (*Portrait of a Lady*)

Joyce, James, *A Portrait of the Artist as a Young Man* (Irish, 1916): A novel about a young man growing up in Ireland and rebelling against family, country, and religion to become an artist. Joyce's use of stream-of-consciousness has influenced many modern writers. (*Ulysses, The Dubliners*)

Kafka, Franz, *The Trial* (Czechoslovakian, 1925): In this novel a man is tried for a crime he knows nothing about, yet he feels guilty and is executed. W. H. Auden described Kafka as "the author who comes nearest to bearing the same kind of relation to our age [that] Dante, Shakespeare, and Goethe bore to theirs..." (*Metamorphosis*)

Lawrence, D.H., *Sons and Lovers* (British, 1913): An autobiographical novel about a youth who is torn between a dominant working-class father and a possessive genteel mother. "Lawrence has been one of the most influential figures in Anglo-American literature and life of this century" (Martin Seymour-Smith). (*Women in Love*)

Lewis, Sinclair, *Babbitt* (American, 1922): A satirical novel about a middle-class businessman in an average midwestern city. Babbitt becomes a pathetic yet comical character because of his exaggerated sense of his importance. Lewis was the first American to win the Nobel Prize. (*Main Street*)

Malamud, Bernard, *The Assistant* (American, 1957): A novel in which a Gentile hoodlum "out of a compelling pity" goes to work for a Jewish grocer whom he has robbed. Finally taking the grocer's place, he becomes a Jew himself and accepts all that is Jewish.

Mann, Thomas, *Death in Venice* (German, 1912): In this novella an author becomes aware of a darker side of himself when he visits Venice and fantasizes a love for a young boy he sees there. This story alludes frequently to Greek literature and mythology.

Melville, Herman, *Moby-Dick* (American, 1851): A complex novel about a mad sea captain's pursuit of the White Whale. To Clifton Fadiman, "as we turn the pages, our hands close about an imaginary harpoon…in our ears rings the cry: 'There she blows!'"

Morrison, Toni, *Sula* (American, 1973): A novel about the lifelong friendship of two vastly different women who become estranged when one causes the other's husband to abandon her. "Its humor is earthy and delightful, and its dialogue is especially sharp" (Jonathan Yardley). (*Beloved*)

O'Connor, Flannery, *A Good Man Is Hard to Find* (American, 1955): A triad of short stories set in Georgia. The title story is about the deadly confrontation between a religious grandmother and a mad murderer. O'Connor's characters "hold their fears at bay with a rustic religiosity that is as functional as their speech or dress" (James Greene).

Olsen, Tillie, *Tell Me a Riddle* (American, 1956–60): A group of short stories including a novella about the problems of aging. An old man and woman quarrel bitterly about whether to stay in their own home or to move to the Haven, a retirement home.

Orwell, George, *Animal Farm* (British, 1945): The classic satire of communism in which the pigs lead the other farm animals in a revolution against the humans, setting up their own government where "All animals are equal, but some animals are more equal than others." (*1984*)

Paton, Alan, *Cry, the Beloved Country* (South African, 1948): A novel about a black minister in South Africa who goes in search of his children and finds them corrupted and destroyed by white society. The roots of both the generational and racial conflicts of black South Africans are explored in this story.

Poe, Edgar Allan, *Great Tales and Poems* (American, 1839–45): Poe is considered the father of detective stories and a master of supernatural tales. The stories most often recommended are "The Fall of the House of Usher," "The Purloined Letter," "The Cask of Amontillado," "The Pit and the Pendulum," and "The Tell-Tale Heart."

Salinger, J. D., *The Catcher in the Rye* (American, 1951): A novel in which a prep school dropout rejects the "phoniness" he sees all about him. *Catcher* is "one of those rare books that influenced one generation after another, causing each to claim it as its own" (Adam Moss).

Scott, Sir Walter, *Ivanhoe* (British, 1820): A story of chivalry in which the Norman hero Wilfred finally wins his true love, the Saxon Rowena, with the help of the Black Knight (Richard the Lion-Hearted in disguise) and brings about a temporary peace between the Normans and the Saxons. (*Heart of Midlothian*)

Shelley, Mary, *Frankenstein* (British, 1818): A gothic tale of terror in which Frankenstein creates a monster from corpses. Because everyone who sees him fears him, the monster despairs and turns on his creator.

Steinbeck, John, *The Grapes of Wrath* (American, 1939): A historical novel by the 1962 Nobel Prize winner about the desperate flight of tenant farmers from the Midwest during the Depression. Members of the Joad family struggle to retain their humanity and dignity in the face of the hostility they find in California. (*Of Mice and Men, Cannery Row, The Pearl*)

Swift, Jonathan, *Gulliver's Travels* (British, 1726): A satire on mankind in which an 18th-century Englishman visits foreign lands populated by bizarre creatures who illuminate many of the vices and weaknesses of his society.

Thackeray, William Makepeace, *Vanity Fair* (British, 1847–48): A novel of 19th-century upper-middle-class British society that portrays 20 years in the lives of two young women very opposite in character: gentle, sentimental Amelia and lively, cunning Becky.

Tolstoy, Leo, *War and Peace* (Russian, 1865-69): A historical novel of the Napoleonic Wars that celebrates the Russian spirit and shows the effect of war and peace on every social class in Russian society. (*Anna Karenina*)

Turgenev, Ivan, *Fathers and Sons* (Russian, 1862): In this novel two young men experience difficulty in their relationships with their parents and with their women friends. "The aspirations of Russia's liberal youth are pitted against those of the conservative landowning gentry..." (R. Freedman).

Twain, Mark, *The Adventures of Huckleberry Finn* (American, 1886): In this novel Huck takes a trip down the river with a runaway slave and learns the worth of life. According to Ernest Hemingway, "All modern American literature comes from one book by Mark Twain called *Huckleberry Finn*."

Updike, John, *Rabbit, Run* (American, 1961): The first of the Rabbit Angstrom novels in which an immature young man still longing for the lost glory of his youth runs away from his responsibilities and abandons his wife and child.

Voltaire, *Candide* (French, 1759): A satire against those who complacently accept life's disasters. This bitter criticism is disguised as a rollicking travel story in which Candide is puzzled because everything bad happens to him in this "best of all possible worlds."

Vonnegut, Kurt, *Slaughterhouse Five* (American, 1969): A semi-autobiographical novel about the firebombing of Dresden in World War II. In the story a time traveler, Billy Pilgrim, finds peace in a future world where he is "grateful that so many of those moments are nice." (*Cat's Cradle*)

Walker, Alice, *The Color Purple* (American, 1982): A novel that focuses on "the role of male domination in the frustration of the black woman's struggle for independence" (Mel Watkins). In this story a young black girl sees herself as property until another woman teaches her to value herself.

Welty, Eudora, *Thirteen Stories* (American, 1965): A collection of short stories about people and life in the deep South. Most often mentioned by colleges are "Why I Live at the PO," "The Worn Path," and "The Petrified Man."

Wharton, Edith, *The Age of Innocence* (American, 1920): A novel about a couple condemned to a loveless marriage by the conventions of their social class. "Wharton's work formed a bridge from the 19th-century novel to the magazine fiction of the present" (Louise Brogan). (*The House of Mirth, Ethan Frome*)

Woolf, Virginia, *To the Lighthouse* (British, 1927): Written in stream-of-consciousness, this semi-autobiographical novel describes the Ramsey family's life in their country home. The lighthouse they see from the window is a symbolic goal for them all. (*A Room of One's Own*)

Wright, Richard, *Native Son* (American, 1940): In this novel Bigger Thomas, a young black man from the Chicago slums, lashes out against a hostile society by committing two murders. The book is based partly on Wright's experiences, partly on an actual murder case.

DRAMA

Aeschylus, *Orestia* (Greek, 458 BC): A triad of plays in which a son seeks revenge against his mother for the murder of his father. In the final play he is exonerated for killing his mother by a tribunal of Athenian judges and the goddess Athena.

Aristophanes, *Lysistrata* (Greek, 411 BC): In this comedy the women of warring Athens and Sparta go on a marital strike until their men end their fighting. "Aristophanes made in this play a last appeal, half farcical, half serious, for peace" (Sir Paul Harvey).

Beckett, Samuel, *Waiting for Godot* (Irish, 1952): A Theater of the Absurd play in which two tramps sit endlessly waiting for someone named Godot, who never arrives.

Brecht, Bertolt, *Mother Courage and Her Children* (German, 1941): In this anti-war play set during the Thirty Years War, Mother Courage moves her wagon from battlefront to battlefront peddling her wares. One by one her three children are killed even though she seeks to profit from war, not become personally involved in it.

Chekhov, Anton, *The Cherry Orchard* (Russian, 1904): The members of an aristocratic family in this play are unwilling and unable to face the loss of their property. Their plight depicts the decline of the powerful Russian landowners following the end of the feudal system in 1861. (*The Three Sisters*)

Euripides, *Medea* (Greek, 431 BC): In this tragedy of vengeance, Medea is a passionate woman whose love turns to hate when her husband deserts her. It climaxes with her killing their two sons. (*The Bacchae*)

Goethe, Johann von, *Faust, Part I* (German, 1808): A play about the legendary scholar who sells his soul to the devil. In this poetic drama, Faust is attracted to a young peasant girl. The devil's plans for his soul are temporarily defeated because Faust's lust for her turns to love.

Ibsen, Henrik, *A Doll's House* (Norwegian, 1879): In this drama the main character slams the door and walks out on a marriage based on inequality. Her revolt against her marriage to a selfish, hypocritical man who treats her as a doll rather than an individual gave impetus to the fight for women's rights.

Marlowe, Christopher, *Doctor Faustus* (British, 1604): In this play, Faust is torn between his lust for knowledge as a means to power and his awareness of the sinfulness of his desires. Because the legend of Faust appears so frequently in the arts, the term *Faustian* has come to mean a willingness to sacrifice spiritual values in return for knowledge or power.

Miller, Arthur, *Death of a Salesman* (American, 1949): A Pulitzer Prize–winning play in which a traveling salesman "riding on a smile and a shoeshine" realizes that his dreams will never be real and, unable to cope with the failures of his life, commits suicide.

Molière, *The Misanthrope* (French, 1666): Alceste, the leading character in this comedy, is admirable in hating the hypocrisy in his society. In his zeal for complete honesty, however, he succeeds in becoming a complete fool. (*Tartuffe*)

O'Neill, Eugene, *Desire Under the Elms* (American, 1924): A naturalistic drama about love, lust, and greed that contrasts a sensitive, emotional son with his severe, puritanical father. (*The Emperor Jones, The Hairy Ape*)

Shakespeare, William, *Hamlet* (British, 1600): A great tragedy in which a prince is troubled by his inability to act to avenge the "murder most foul" of his father. William Hazlett says the play "abounds most in striking reflections on human life..." (Many colleges urge students to read as much Shakespeare as possible—at least one tragedy, one comedy, and one history.)

Shaw, George Bernard, *Pygmalion* (British, 1913): A play in which a professor of phonetics interferes with the social order by teaching a Cockney girl to act and speak like a duchess. (*Saint Joan*, *Arms and the Man*)

Sophocles, *Oedipus Rex* (Greek, 430 BC): The tragedy of a king who unwittingly has killed his father and married his mother. When he discovers what he has done, he blinds himself for "there is nothing beautiful left to see in this world." (*Antigone*)

Wilde, Oscar, *The Importance of Being Earnest* (British, 1895): A worldly and cynical farce about a confusion of identities that ends happily when the real Earnest turns out to be a long-lost infant whose nurse had absent-mindedly misplaced him. (*Lady Windermere's Fan*)

Wilder, Thornton, *Our Town* (American, 1938): In this Pulitzer Prize–winning play the stage manager speaks directly to the audience from a set bare of props. The play tells the story of two families as they experience daily life, love and marriage, and death.

Williams, Tennessee, *The Glass Menagerie* (American, 1945): The mother in this play dwells on the past and longs to find "a gentleman caller" for her crippled daughter who has withdrawn into the world of her glass animals. As in many of Williams' plays, the characters live in a world of unfulfilled dreams. (*A Streetcar Named Desire*)

POETRY

Allison, Alexander, Ed., *Norton Anthology of Poetry* (Shorter Edition): A collection of poetry by American and British poets. The poets most frequently recommended by the colleges are William Blake; Robert Browning; Emily

Dickinson; T. S. Eliot; Robert Frost; John Keats; William Shakespeare (the sonnets); Alfred, Lord Tennyson; William Wordsworth; and William Butler Yeats.

Anonymous, *Beowulf* (British, c. 700 AD): In this adventurous Old English epic poem, Beowulf overcomes monsters and slays a fire-breathing dragon. The poem is based on Norse legends and historical events of the sixth century.

Anonymous, *Sir Gawain and the Green Knight* (British, c. 1350–1400): "The jewel of medieval English literature" (M. Gaston Paris), this Arthurian tale is about the ordeals an ideal knight undergoes to prove his courage and his virtue. The two main episodes are Gawain's beheading of the terrible Green Knight and his efforts to resist the advances of a beautiful lady.

Chaucer, Geoffrey, *Canterbury Tales* (British, c. 1387–1400): In this poetic narrative, Chaucer presents a colorful group of medieval travelers on their way to a religious shrine. On their journey they tell each other tales—some amusing, some serious, some ribald. (Many colleges suggest reading only the prologue and one or two tales.)

Dante, *Inferno* (Italian, c. 1320): In this first book of *The Divine Comedy*, Dante's journey through Hell reveals the medieval view of sin. As he travels through the different levels of the Underworld, he witnesses the punishments for sin.

Homer, *The Odyssey* (Greek, c. 9th century BC): The epic of Odysseus' ordeals after the Trojan War as he tries for ten years to return home to Ithaca. On his journey he faces the dangers of the Cyclops, the Sirens, Circe, and others. Many other writers have used the character and the journey of Odysseus (Ulysses) in their works. (*The Iliad*)

Milton, John, *Paradise Lost* (British, 1667): Considered the greatest epic in any modern language, this poem tells of Satan's temptation of Adam and Eve, their expulsion from the Garden of Eden (Paradise), and the promise of their eventual salvation by the Son of God.

Vergil, *The Aeneid* (Roman, c. 18 BC): This epic poem recounts the troubled journey of Aeneas as he leads the survivors of Troy to Italy where they become the founders of Rome.

Whitman, Walt, *Leaves of Grass* (American, 1855): In his use of free verse and his emphasis on the importance of the individual, Whitman was a forerunner of modern poetry. In these twelve untitled poems he wanted to "elevate, enlarge, purify, deepen, and make happy the attributes of the body and soul of man."

MISCELLANEOUS

Aristotle, *Poetics* (Greek, 4th century BC): A treatise on literary principles. The theories of tragedy in this work still influence Western drama. Called by Dante "the master of those who know," Aristotle is one of the world's greatest philosophers.

Augustine, Saint, *Confessions* (Italian, 397–401): A spiritual autobiography of St. Augustine's early life and his conversion to Christianity. His is "the only detailed account of the childhood of a great man which antiquity has left us" (Maynard Mack).

Bible: A collection of the sacred literature of Judaism and Christianity. Much of our Western writing alludes to the language and the stories in the Bible. Many colleges suggest the King James Version for literary study.

Darwin, Charles, *Origin of Species* (British, 1859): Darwin's book on his theories of natural selection and of evolution was a sellout the day it was issued and caused a storm of controversy that still continues today. (*The Voyage of the Beagle*)

Emerson, Ralph Waldo, "The American Scholar" in *Essays* (American, 1837): An address at Harvard in which Emerson urged Americans to declare intellectual independence from Europe, to be thinkers and "not parrots of other men's thought." ("Self-Reliance")

Franklin, Benjamin, *Autobiography* (American, 1867): An account of Franklin's life and achievements during the first 51 years of his life. In it Franklin appears "as a universal genius…the embodiment of what we like to call the American spirit" (S. E. Morrison).

Freud, Sigmund, *Civilization and Its Discontents* (German, 1930): A book about the conflict between the human desire for personal freedom and the demands of society. Freud writes that "The price we pay for our advance in civilization is a loss of happiness through the heightening of the sense of guilt." (*Dora*)

Hamilton, Edith, *Mythology* (American 1940): A collection of Greek, Roman, and Norse myths and legends that are often alluded to in the language and literature of the Western world.

Machiavelli, Niccolò, *The Prince* (Italian, 1532): A treatise giving the absolute ruler practical advice on ways to maintain a strong central government. The term *Machiavellian* has for generations meant "ruthless and deceitful," because Machiavelli theorized that politics are above moral law.

Marx, Karl, *Communist Manifesto* (German, 1848): Written with Friedrich Engels as the official platform of the International Communist League, this short book expresses Marx's belief in the inevitability of conflict between social classes and calls on the workers of the world to unite and revolt.

Montaigne, Michel de, *Selected Essays* (French, 1580): The creator of the personal essay, Montaigne wrote about many subjects—cannibals, friendship, women, books, prayer. Though the entire work is a self-portrait, this book about one man is "really a book about all men" (Walter Kerr).

Plato, *Republic* (Greek, c. 370 BC): In this dialogue Plato creates an ideal society where justice is equated with health and happiness in the state and in the individual. Echoing Omar about the Koran, Ralph Waldo Emerson said of the *Republic*, "Burn the libraries, for their value is in this book." (*Apology*)

Thoreau, Henry David, *Walden* (American, 1854): In this book Thoreau, an extreme individualist, advised "a man is rich in proportion to the number of things he can afford to let alone." *Walden* is about the 26 months he spent alone in the woods to "front the essential facts of life." (*Civil Disobedience*)

CHAPTER 4

The College and University Lists

The University of Alabama
P.O. Box 870132
Tuscaloosa, AL 35487-0132
(205) 348 6010
http://www.ua.edu

In a letter to college-bound students planning to attend the university, Professor Robert W. Halli, Jr. writes that he hopes the following list will be "interesting and helpful." But he offers it with "a fistful of warnings," saying "it is not complete or definitive because it is deliberately short enough to be feasible."

Reading the books on the list, he says "won't automatically make you into an educated or cultured person, nor will it guarantee you an A in Freshman English. So, what is it good for? Reading the works on this list, mostly drawn from English and American literature, will give you a background, a direction, a springboard that will be of value to you in a number of ways, some related to your academic course work and some not.

"But, perhaps most of all, reading literature, such as the works on this list, should help establish a life-long pleasure in reading. And those who read effectively and with enjoyment tend to 'do' well and 'live' well (not necessarily the same thing)."

SUGGESTED READING LIST FOR HIGH SCHOOL STUDENTS

Poetry anthology with selections from **W.H. Auden; William Blake; Robert Browning; Samuel Taylor Coleridge; Emily Dickinson; John Donne; T.S. Eliot; Robert Frost; Thomas Hardy; George Herbert; Robert Herrick; John Keats; Robert Lowell; Edgar Allan Poe; Alexander Pope; Theodore Roethke; William Shakespeare** (sonnets); **P.B. Shelley; Wallace Stevens; Sir Philip Sydney; Alfred, Lord Tennyson; Walt Whitman; William Wordsworth; Sir Thomas Wyatt; W.B. Yeats.**

Austen, Jane	*Pride and Prejudice*
Bellow, Saul	*Humboldt's Gift*
Chaucer, Geoffrey	*The Canterbury Tales* (selections, perhaps in translation)
Conrad, Joseph	*Heart of Darkness*
Defoe, Daniel	*Robinson Crusoe*
Dickens, Charles	*Great Expectations* or *Hard Times*
Faulkner, William	"The Bear"
Fielding, Henry	*Joseph Andrews* or *Tom Jones*
Fitzgerald, F. Scott	*The Great Gatsby*
Fowles, John	*The French Lieutenant's Woman*
Hardy, Thomas	*The Return of the Native*
Hawthorne, Nathaniel	*The Scarlet Letter*
Hemingway, Ernest	*A Farewell to Arms*
Homer	*The Iliad* and/or *The Odyssey*
James, Henry	*The American* or *The Portrait of a Lady*
Joyce, James	*Dubliners*
Lewis, Sinclair	*Babbitt* or *Main Street*
Miller, Arthur	*Death of a Salesman*
Milton, John	*Paradise Lost* (selections)
Paton, Alan	*Cry, The Beloved Country*
Shakespeare, William	A comedy such as *Midsummer Night's Dream*; a history such as *Richard II*; a tragedy such as *Hamlet* or *King Lear*
Shaw, George Bernard	*Arms and the Man*
Sophocles	*Oedipus Rex*

Thoreau, Henry David	*Walden*
Twain, Mark	*The Adventures of Huckleberry Finn*
Vergil	*The Aeneid*
Vonnegut, Kurt	*Slaughterhouse Five*
Waugh, Evelyn	*A Handful of Dust*
Wright, Richard	*Native Son*

Alaska Pacific University
4104 University Drive
Anchorage, AK 99508
(907) 564-8288
http://www.alaskapacific.edu

According to Professor Aubrey Nixon, Faculty of Humanities, Arts, and Communication, the following is a general list of the texts required in several of Alaska Pacific's introductory English courses.

Approaches to Literature

Diyanni, Robert	*Literature: Reading Literature, Poetry, Drama, the Essay*

World Literature

	Gilgamesh (Mason, tr.)
	Mahabarata (Buck, tr.)
	"Exodus" from the *Bible*
Aeschylus	*Oresteia*
Dante	*The Inferno* (Mandelbaum, tr.)
Shikibu, Murasaki	*The Tale of Genji*

British Literature

Blake, William	*The Marriage of Heaven and Hell*
Butler, Samuel	*Erehwon*

Shakespeare, William	*The Tempest*
Swift, Jonathan	*Gulliver's Travels*

Genres in Literature: The Novel

Brontë, Emily	*Wuthering Heights*
Burgess, Anthony	*A Clockwork Orange*
Conrad, Joseph	*Heart of Darkness*
Flaubert, Gustave	*Madame Bovary*
Hardy, Thomas	*Tess of the D'Urbervilles*
Hemingway, Ernest	*A Farewell to Arms*
Mack, Maynard, et al., eds.	*Norton Anthology of World Masterpieces,* Vol. 1, 5th ed.
Lawrence, D.H.	*Women in Love*
Tolstoy, Leo	*Kreutzer Sonata*

Medieval Literature

	Beowulf (Raffel, tr.)
	The Maginogi (Ford, tr.)
	Parzifal (Hatto, tr.)

Genres in Literature: The European Novel

Austen, Jane	*Pride and Prejudice*
Balzac, Honoré de	*Lost Illusions*
Dickens, Charles	*Oliver Twist*
Flaubert, Gustave	*A Sentimental Education*
Stendhal	*The Red and the Black*
Thackeray, William Makepeace	*Vanity Fair*

Themes in Literature: Northern Literature

Carter, Marilyn	*Legends, Tales & Totems of Alaska*
Cornberg, David	*Liquid Mirrors*
McPhee, John	*Coming into the Country*

Amherst College
South Pleasant Street
Amherst, MA 01002
(413) 542-2000
http://www.amherst.edu

Amherst's course *Writing About Reading* is primarily intended for freshmen and sophomores. It is an introduction to a variety of texts and the reading problems they pose. Writing is frequent—at least one short paper every week. The course includes the following works:

Bender, Robert and Charles Squier, eds.	*Sonnet: An Anthology*
Jacobs, Harriet	*Incidents in the Life of a Slave Girl*
Middleton, Thomas (Patricia Thomson, ed.)	*The Changeling*
Morrison, Toni	*Beloved*
Omang, Joanne, ed.	*Psychological Operations in Guerrilla Warfare*
Pynchon, Thomas	*The Crying of Lot 49*

The supplemental texts that may be included are

Barthes, Roland	*Camera Lucida: Reflections on Photography*
Berger, John	*Ways of Seeing*
Kawabata, Yasunari	*Snow Country*
McLuhan, Marshall	*Understanding Media: The Extensions of Man*
Miller, Frank	*Batman: Year One or The Dark Knight Returns*
Molière	*The Misanthrope* (Wilbur, tr.)
Spiegelman, Art	*Maus: A Survivor's Tale*

The College of Wooster: Discuss a creative work that has some special meaning or has influenced you in a profound way. This piece can be literature, film, art, scientific theory, or another significant influential idea.

Arizona State University
Tempe, AZ 85287
(480) 965-9011
http://www.asu.edu

First-year students at Arizona State University are required to take two semesters (or the equivalent) of writing courses in which students develop multiple critical reading, thinking, and writing strategies that will serve them in a variety of academic and professional settings.

In these courses, students are encouraged to understand writing as a way of knowing and acting in the world, and reading and writing as interdependent activities that require different kinds of approaches depending on the rhetorical situation in which they take place. Students may elect to enroll in computer-mediated communication sections of writing courses. Specific texts for Arizona's first-year writing courses are selected from the following:

Rhetorics

Lunsford, Andrea and John Rusziewicz	*Everything's an Argument*
Ramage, John and John Bean, eds.	*The Allyn and Bacon Guide to Writing*, 2nd ed.
Axelrod, Rise and Charles Cooper	*The St Martin Guide to Writing*, 5th ed.

Computer Mediated Communication Textbooks

Holeton, Richard	*Composing Cyberspace: Identity, Community, and Knowledge in the Electronic Age*
Hawisher, Gail and Cynthia Selfe	*Literacy, Technology, and Society: Confronting the Issues*

Readers

George, Diana, and John Trimbur	*Reading Culture: Contexts for Critical Reading and Writing*
McCormick, Kathleen	*Reading Our Histories, Understanding Our Cultures*

Optional Handbooks

Hairston, Maxine, John Ruszkiewicz, and Christy Friend	*The Scott, Foresman Handbook for Writers*
Lunsford, Andrea and Robert Connors	*Easy Writer: A Pocket Guide*

Auburn University
Auburn University, AL 36849-5145
(334) 844-4000
http://www.auburn.edu

The Freshman English Committee at Auburn precedes its pre-college reading list with the following "Preliminary Word to Consumers":

> *While we have had in mind the college-bound high school student in producing this list, it is more, perhaps, "a list for all seasons," as much for during and after college as it is for pre-college. The works in this list, we want to make clear, do not constitute an exhaustive or absolute listing of any kind...They are, rather, simply our suggestions for some valuable, meaningful reading...*

> *Two other points should be made briefly. First, because we do want the list to be a helpful guide, we have made specific recommendations for your reading. For example, W.B. Yeats is not simply named, but some Yeats poems are specifically suggested. This does not mean that these are the only or all the "good" poems by Yeats, but they are good poems and poems good for providing an introduction to Yeats' work...Our specific recommendations, then, are not intended to be absolute evaluations, but reasonable, helpful suggestions for valuable reading...*

A glance at the list will show, too, that we have excluded writers who have only recently come into prominence. We hope that there will be some reading of contemporary works, but not enough time has elapsed at this point to test how really valuable or significant these works are…

Pre-College Reading List

(An * designates works of a high level of difficulty for pre-college readers.)

American Novels

Crane, Stephen	*The Red Badge of Courage*
Ellison, Ralph	*Invisible Man*
Faulkner, William	*The Unvanquished*
Hawthorne, Nathaniel	*The Scarlet Letter*
Hemingway, Ernest	*A Farewell to Arms*
James, Henry	*The Portrait of a Lady**
Melville, Herman	*Moby-Dick**
Steinbeck, John	*The Grapes of Wrath*
Twain, Mark	*The Adventures of Huckleberry Finn*
Wright, Richard	*Native Son*

British Novels

Austen, Jane	*Pride and Prejudice*
Brontë, Emily	*Wuthering Heights**
Defoe, Daniel	*Robinson Crusoe*
Dickens, Charles	*David Copperfield; A Tale of Two Cities*
Eliot, George	*Adam Bede*
Fielding, Henry	*Joseph Andrews*
Hardy, Thomas	*The Return of the Native*
Orwell, George	*1984*
Swift, Jonathan	*Gulliver's Travels*
Thackeray, William Makepeace	*Vanity Fair*

International Novels

Camus, Albert	*The Stranger**
Cervantes, Miguel de	*Don Quixote*
Dostoevski, Fyodor	*Crime and Punishment**
Flaubert, Gustave	*Madame Bovary*
Kafka, Franz	*The Trial*
Stendhal	*The Red and the Black*
Tolstoy, Leo	*The Cossacks*; *War and Peace**
Turgenev, Ivan	*Fathers and Sons*

American Short Stories

Anderson, Sherwood	*Winesburg, Ohio*
Faulkner, William	"A Rose for Emily," "Barn Burning"
Hawthorne, Nathaniel	"The Minister's Black Veil," "Rappaccini's Daughter," "Young Goodman Brown"
Hemingway, Ernest	"The Killers," "The Snows of Kilimanjaro," "The Short Happy Life of Francis Macomber"
James, Henry	"The Beast in the Jungle," "Europe," "The Turn of the Screw"
Poe, Edgar Allan	"The Cask of Amontillado," "The Fall of the House of Usher," "The Purloined Letter"

British Short Stories

Conrad, Joseph	"The Lagoon," "The Secret Sharer," "Typhoon"
Joyce, James	*Dubliners*
Stevenson, R.L.	"Dr. Jekyll and Mr. Hyde"

International Short Stories

Chekhov, Anton P.	"The Kiss," "Misery"
Kafka, Franz	"The Hunter Gracchus," "Metamorphosis," "Jackals and Arabs"
Mann, Thomas	*Death in Venice*, "Disorder and Early Sorrow"
Maupassant, Guy de	"A Piece of String"

American Poetry

Bradstreet, Anne	"Verses Upon the Burning of Our House"
Crane, Hart	"Proem: To Brooklyn Bridge," "The River" (both from *The Bridge*), "Repose of Rivers," "Royal Palm"
cummings, e.e.	"anyone lived in a pretty how town," "a man who had fallen among thieves," "my father moved through dooms of love," "next to of course god america i," "pity this busy monster, manunkind"
Dickinson, Emily	Numbers 49, 67, 214, 216, 303, 341, 435, 449, 465, 650, 712, 986, 1737 (from *The Complete Poems of Emily Dickinson*)
Eliot, T.S.	"The Journey of the Magi," "The Love Song of J. Alfred Prufrock," "Sweeney Among the Nightingales"
Frost, Robert	"After Apple-Picking," "Birches," "Death of the Hired Man," "Departmental," "Desert Places," "Mending Wall," "The Road Not Taken"
Hughes, Langston	"Afro-American Fragment," "As I Grew Older," "Harlem," "The Negro Sings of Rivers," "Theme for English B"
Lindsay, Vachel	"Abraham Lincoln Walks at Midnight," "The Congo"
Pound, Ezra	"The Garden," "Portrait d'une Femme," "The River Merchant's Wife: A Letter," "Salutation"
Ransom, John Crowe	"Bells for John Whiteside's Daughter," "Blue Girls," "Dead Boy," "The Equilibrists," "Janet Waking," "Prelude to an Evening," "Winter Remembered"
Robinson, Edwin A.	"Miniver Cheevy," "Richard Cory"
Stevens, Wallace	"Anecdote of the Jar," "Poems of Our Climate," "The Snow Man," "Sunday Morning"
Taylor, Edward	"Meditation Eight"
Whitman, Walt	"Out of the Cradle Endlessly Rocking," "Song of Myself," "When Lilacs Last in the Dooryard Bloom'd"

British Poetry

	"The Seafarer"
	"The Wanderer"
	Ballads "Barbara Allan," "Edward," "Lord Randall," "Sir Patrick Spens"
Arnold, Matthew	"Dover Beach," "Thrysis"
Auden, W.H.	"In Memory of W.B. Yeats," "Lullaby," "Musée des Beaux Arts," "The Unknown Citizen"
Blake, William	"The Chimney Sweeper," "The Lamb," "London," "The Tyger"
Browning, Robert	"My Last Duchess," "Porphyria's Lover," "Soliloquy of the Spanish Cloister"
Byron, George Gordon	Canto III from *Childe Harold's Pilgrimage*; Cantos I and II from *Don Juan*; "Prisoner of Chillon," "She Walks in Beauty"
Chaucer, Geoffrey	The General Prologue and two or three tales (such as "The Nun's Priest's Tale") from *The Canterbury Tales*
Coleridge, Samuel Taylor	"Christabel," "Kubla Khan," *The Rime of the Ancient Mariner*
Donne, John	"The Flea," "A Hymn to God the Father," Holy Sonnets: 7, 10, 14; "The Relic," "Song," "A Valediction: Forbidding Mourning"
Hopkins, Gerard Manley	"God's Grandeur," "Spring and Fall," "Thou Art Indeed Just, Lord"
Keats, John	"Bright Star," "The Eve of St. Agnes," "La Belle Dame Sans Merci," "To Autumn," Odes: "On a Grecian Urn," "On Melancholy," "To a Nightingale"
Milton, John	Book I of *Paradise Lost*; "When I Consider How My Light Is Spent"
Pope, Alexander	"The Rape of the Lock"
Shakespeare, William	Sonnets 18, 29, 55, 71, 106, 116, 129, 130, 138, 144, 146
Shelley, Percy Bysshe	"Hymn to Intellectual Beauty," "Mutability," "Ode to the West Wind," "Ozymandias," "To a Skylark"

Spenser, Edmund	Canto I, Book I of *The Faerie Queene*
Tennyson, Alfred Lord	"The Lady of Shalott," "Ulysses"
Thomas, Dylan	"And Death Shall Have No Dominion," "Do Not Go Gentle into That Good Night," "Fern Hill"
Wordsworth, William	"Intimations of Immortality," "London, 1802"
Yeats, William Butler	"Easter, 1916," "In Memory of Major Robert Gregory," "Lapis Lazuli," "Nineteen Hundred and Nineteen," "The Second Coming," "When You Are Old," "The Wild Swans at Coole"

American Drama

Miller, Arthur	*Death of a Salesman*
O'Neill, Eugene	*Desire under the Elms**
Williams, Tennessee	*The Glass Menagerie*

British Drama

Goldsmith, Oliver	*She Stoops to Conquer*
Shakespeare, William	*As You Like It*; *Hamlet*; *Henry IV Part 1*; *MacBeth*; *Romeo and Juliet*
Shaw, George Bernard	*Major Barbara*

International Drama

Aeschylus	*Oresteia**
Brecht, Bertolt	*The Caucasian Chalk Circle**
Euripides	*Medea*
Molière	*Tartuffe*
Sophocles	*Antigone*; *Oedipus Rex*

Miscellaneous

	Beowulf
	Bible
	Sir Gawain and the Green Knight
Boswell, James	*Life of Samuel Johnson* (1737–1760 and 1763)
Cellini, Benvenuto	*Autobiography*

Dante	*The Inferno*
De Quincey, Thomas	*Confessions of an English Opium Eater*
Emerson, Ralph Waldo	Essays: "The American Scholar," "Self-Reliance"
Frank, Anne	*The Diary of a Young Girl*
Franklin, Benjamin	*Autobiography* (especially boyhood and youth portions)
Hamilton, Edith	*Mythology*
Homer	*The Iliad*; *The Odyssey*
Lamb, Charles	*The Essays of Elia*
Montaigne, Michel de	"Of Friendship," "Of Idleness," "Of Solitariness"
Plato	*Apology*
Plutarch	"Antony," "Cicero," "Pompey," from *Lives of the Noble Greeks & Romans*
Russell, Bertrand	*Unpopular Essays*
Thoreau, Henry David	*Walden*
Vergil	*The Aeneid*

Colby-Sawyer College: Discuss a literary or artistic work which has had a special impact on you.

Ball State University
2000 University Avenue
Muncie, IN 47306
(800) 482-4278
http://www.bsu.edu

The Ball State English Department prefaces its suggested reading list for pre-college students with this comment: "Though most teachers of literature at the college level feel that the quality of reading is more important than the specific works read by college-bound high school students, the works listed below represent the literary tradition in our culture that well-prepared students should be acquainted with when they enter college. While many entering students will, of course, only have read a few of the works listed below, we hope that they will bring an understanding of and respect for the heritage that they represent."

SUGGESTED READING LIST IN LITERATURE FOR COLLEGE-BOUND STUDENTS

Classical Literature

The Epic

Homer	*The Iliad* or *The Odyssey*
Vergil	*The Aeneid*

Tragedy

Aeschylus	*Agamemnon* or *Prometheus Unbound*
Euripides	*Medea* or *The Trojan Woman*
Sophocles	*Antigone* or *Oedipus Rex*

Philosophy

Aristotle	Discussion of tragedy in *The Poetics*
Plato	One of the Socratic Dialogues

Poetry

Sappho	Selections

Biblical Literature

Readings in both the Old and the New Testaments, including "Genesis," "Psalms," "Job," and at least one of the gospels.

Medieval Literature

	Beowulf or *The Song of Roland*
	Everyman
	Selected medieval ballads
Chaucer, Geoffrey	Selections from *The Canterbury Tales*

Dante	Readings in *The Divine Comedy*
Julian of Norwich	Selections
Marjorie à Kempis	Selections

Renaissance Literature

Drama

Marlowe, Christopher	*Doctor Faustus*
Shakespeare, William	Two tragedies, one comedy, one history play

Poetry

Shakespeare, William	Selections from the sonnets

Novel

Cervantes, Miguel de	*Don Quixote* (Part 1)

Philosophy

Erasmus	*In Praise of Folly*
Machiavelli, Niccolò	*The Prince*
More, Thomas	*Utopia*

17th-Century

Drama

Milton, John	"Comus"
Molière	Two comedies

Poetry

Donne, John	Selections
Dryden, John	Selections

Prose

Phillips, Catherine	Selections

18th-Century

Drama

Goethe, Johann W. von	*Faust* (Part 1)
Goldsmith, Oliver	*She Stoops to Conquer* (or another representative comedy)
Voltaire	*Candide*

Poetry

Selections from the poetry of **William Blake**, **Robert Burns**, **Oliver Goldsmith**, **Alexander Pope**, and **Edward Taylor**.

Novels

Burney, Fanny	*Evelina*
Defoe, Daniel	*Robinson Crusoe*
Fielding, Henry	*Joseph Andrews*
Swift, Jonathan	*Gulliver's Travels*

Prose

Franklin, Benjamin	*Autobiography*
Wollstonecraft, Mary	*A Vindication of the Rights of Women*

19th-Century

Drama

Ibsen, Henrik	*A Doll's House*
Shaw, George Bernard	*Major Barbara*
Wilde, Oscar	*The Importance of Being Earnest*

Poetry

Selections from the works of the following poets: **Matthew Arnold; Emily Brontë; E.B. Browning; Robert Browning; George Gordon; Lord Byron; Samuel Taylor Coleridge**: "Christabel," *Lyrical Ballads* (especially "The Rime of the Ancient Mariner,"); **Emily Dickinson; John Keats; Christina Rossetti; Percy Bysshe Shelley; Alfred, Lord Tennyson; Walt Whitman; William**

Wordsworth (including "Ode: Intimations of Immortality" and *Lyrical Ballads*)

Novels

(At least one by the following writers)

Austen, Jane	*Pride and Prejudice*
Brontë, Emily	*Wuthering Heights*
Dickens, Charles	*Great Expectations*
Dostoevski, Fyodor	*Crime and Punishment*
Douglass, Fredrick	*Narrative of the Life of Fredrick Douglass*
Eliot, George	*The Mill on the Floss*
Flaubert, Gustave	*Madame Bovary*
Hardy, Thomas	*Tess of the D'Urbervilles*
Hawthorne, Nathaniel	*The Scarlet Letter*
James, Henry	*The Turn of the Screw*
Melville, Herman	*Billy Budd*
Rowson, Susanna	*Charlotte Temple*
Shelley, Mary	*Frankenstein*
Stowe, Harriet Beecher	*Uncle Tom's Cabin*
Tolstoy, Leo	*Anna Karenina*
Twain, Mark	*The Adventures of Huckleberry Finn*

Short Stories

Representative selections from **Kate Chopin**, **Mary Wilkins Freeman**, **Nathaniel Hawthorne**, **Sarah Orne Jewett** ("The Country of the Pointed Firs"), **Edgar Allan Poe**, **Mark Twain.**

Prose

Carlyle, Thomas	"Characteristics"
Emerson, Ralph Waldo	"Self-Reliance"
Mill, John Stuart	Essay: "The Subjection of Women"
Thoreau, Henry David	"Civil Disobedience" or *Walden*
Wordsworth, Dorothy	*Journals*

20th-Century

Drama

Beckett, Samuel	*Waiting for Godot*
Brecht, Bertholt	*Mother Courage and Her Children*
Eliot, T.S.	*Murder in the Cathedral*
Hellman, Lillian	*The Children's Hour* or *Toys in the Attic*
MacLeish, Archibald	*J.B.*
Miller, Arthur	*Death of a Salesman*
O'Neill, Eugene	*The Emperor Jones* or *The Hairy Ape*
Stoppard, Tom	*Rosencrantz and Guildenstern Are Dead*
Williams, Tennessee	*The Glass Menagerie*

American Poetry

Selections from the works of the following poets: **e.e. cummings**, **Paul Laurence Dunbar**, **T.S. Eliot** ("The Love Song of J. Alfred Prufrock," "Old Possum's Book of Practical Cats"), **Robert Frost** ("Birches," "Death of the Hired Man," "Mending Wall), **Langston Hughes**, **Amy Lowell**, **Claude McKay**, **Sylvia Plath**, **Adrienne Rich**, **W.C. Williams.**

British Poetry

Selections from the following poets: **W.H. Auden**, **A.E. Housman**, **Stevie Smith**, **William Butler Yeats.**

American Fiction

Baldwin, James	*Another Country*
Bellow, Saul	*Seize the Day*
Cather, Willa	*0 Pioneers!*
Cleaver, Eldridge	*Soul on Ice*
Faulkner, William	"The Bear," "That Evening Sun," *Light in August*
Fitzgerald, F. Scott	*The Great Gatsby*
Hemingway, Ernest	*A Farewell to Arms*
Hurston, Zora Neale	*Their Eyes Were Watching God*
Momaday, Scott	*The Way to Rainy Mountain*
Oates, Joyce Carol	A novel

Plath, Sylvia	*The Bell Jar*
Roth, Henry	*Call It Sleep*
Steinbeck, John	*Of Mice and Men*, "The Red Pony"
Wharton, Edith	*The Age of Innocence* or *Summer*
Wright, Richard	*Native Son*

British Fiction

Burgess, Anthony	*A Clockwork Orange*
Donleavy, J.P.	*The Gingerman*
Greene, Graham	A novel
Huxley, Aldous	*Brave New World*
Joyce, James	*Dubliners*
Lawrence, D.H.	"Odour of Chrysanthemums," *Sons and Lovers*
Orwell, George	*Animal Farm*
Waugh, Evelyn	A novel
Woolf, Virginia	"The Mark on the Wall," "A Room of One's Own"

Other Fiction

Achebe, Chinua	*Things Fall Apart*
Beauvoir, Simone de	*The Second Sex*
Camus, Albert	*The Stranger*
Colette	A novel
Hesse, Herman	*Siddhartha*
Kafka, Franz	"The Metamorphosis"
Paton, Alan	*Cry, The Beloved Country*

Non-Fiction

Camus, Albert	"The Myth of Sisyphus"
Eisley, Loren	*The Immense Journey*
Frank, Anne	*Diary of a Young Girl*
Gould, Stephen Jay	A selection
Russell, Bertrand	A selection
Sagan, Carl	A selection
Strachey, Lytton	*Queen Victoria*
Tuchman, Barbara	*A Distant Mirror*
Wiesel, Elie	*Night*

Barnard College, Columbia University
3009 Broadway
New York, NY 10027-6598
(212) 854-5262
http://www.barnard.columbia.edu

Professor Cary H. Plotkin has appended comments to the following list of texts from the syllabus of a year-long introductory survey course and to a list of classical literature he feels students would profit from reading.

Introductory Survey Course

	Beowulf
	"The Dream of the Rood"
	Piers Plowman (excerpts)
	"The Seafarer" (tr. Ezra Pound)
	The Second Shepherd's Play
	Sir Gawain and the Green Knight
	Selections from 16th-century lyrics
Arnold, Matthew	"Dover Beach"
Austen, Jane	*Northanger Abbey*
Beckett, Samuel	*Waiting for Godot*
Behn, Aphra	*The Rover*
Brontë, Emily	*Wuthering Heights*
Browning, Robert	"Andrea del Sarto," "Childe Roland to the Dark Tower Came," "Fra Lippo Lippi," "My Last Duchess," "Rabbi Ben Ezra," "Soliloquy of the Spanish Cloister"
Coleridge, Samuel Taylor	"The Eolian Harp," "Frost at Midnight," "Kubla Khan," "The Rime of the Ancient Mariner"
Collins, William	"Ode to Evening"
Congreve, William	*Love for Love*
Chaucer, Geoffrey	*The Canterbury Tales* (The whole thing, if you can. Otherwise, the general prologue, The Miller's Tale, and The Wife of Bath's Tale are suggested.)

Defoe, Daniel	*Moll Flanders*
Dickens, Charles	*Great Expectations*
Donne, John	Satires
Dryden, John	*Absalom* and *Achitophel*
Eliot, T.S.	*The Waste Land,* and other selections
Fielding, Henry	*Joseph Andrews*
Hardy, Thomas	*Jude the Obscure*
Heaney, Seamus	Poems
Hopkins, Gerard Manley	"As Kingfishers Catch Fire," "Carrion Comfort," "God's Grandeur," "The Leaden Echo and the Golden Echo," "No Worst, There Is None," "Pied Beauty," "That Nature Is a Heraclitean Fire and of the Comfort of the Resurrection," "Spelt from Sibyl's Leaves," "Thou Art Indeed Just," "The Windhover"
Johnson, Samuel	*Rasselas*
Jonson, Ben	*Volpone*
Joyce, James	*A Portrait of the Artist as a Young Man*
Julian of Norwich	from *A Book of Showings*
Keats, John	"The Eve of St. Agnes," "Ode on a Grecian Urn," "Ode to a Nightingale," "To Autumn"
Kempe, Margery	from *The Book of Margery Kempe*
Layner, Aemilia	"To the Doubtful Reader," "To the Virtuous Reader," (*Pilate's Wife Apologizes for Eve)*
Marlowe, Christopher	*Dr. Faustus,* "The Passionate Shepherd to His Love," *Tamburlaine the Great* (Part 1)
Marvell, Andrew	"Bermudas," "An Horatian Ode," and his mower eclogues
Milton, John	"Lycidas," *Samson Agonistes, Paradise Lost*
Pepys, Samuel	from *The Diary*
Philips, Katherine	"A Married State," "On the Death of My First and Dearest Child," "The World"
Pope, Alexander	"A Discourse on Pastoral Poetry," "An Essay on Man," "The Rape of the Lock," "Windsor Forest"
Raleigh, Sir Walter	"The Nymph's Reply to the Shepherd"
Rossetti, Christina	"The Goblin Market," "Winter: My Secret," "Sleeping at Last"

Shakespeare, William	*As You Like It*; *A Comedy of Errors*; *Hamlet*; *Henry V*; *King Lear*; *A Midsummer Night's Dream*; *Timon of Athens*
Shelley, Percy Bysshe	"Hymn to Intellectual Beauty," "Mont Blanc," "Ode to the West Wind," "To a Skylark"
Sidney, Sir Philip	"Ye Goatherd Gods"
Spenser, Edmund	*The Faerie Queene*, "A Letter of the Authors," and "October" from *The Shepheardes Calendar*
Sterne, Laurence	*Tristram Shandy*
Swift, Jonathan	*Gulliver's Travels*; "A Modest Proposal"
Tennyson, Alfred Lord	From *Idylls of the King*: "The Coming of Arthur," "Lancelot and Elaine," "The Last Tournament," "The Passing of Arthur"; *In Memoriam A.H.H.*
Walcott, Derek	Poems
Wilde, Oscar	*The Importance of Being Ernest*
Woolf, Virginia	*To the Lighthouse*
Wordsworth, William	"Lines Written in Early Spring," *The Prelude*, "Tintern Abbey"
Wroth, Mary	from *The Countess of Montgomery's Urania*
Yeats, William Butler	"The Second Coming," and other poems

Classical List

	Bible (King James Version). Old Testament: "Genesis"; "Exodus" (through the 10 Commandments); "Deuteronomy" (the death of Moses); "Joshua" (through the fall of Jericho); "Judges" (Deborah, the story of Joel, Samson); "I & II Samuel"; "I Kings" (through Ahab); "Job"; "Psalms" 1, 8, 19, 22, 23, 24, 91, 100, 104, 123, 137, 139; "Proverbs" 1–7, 22, 24–29, 31; "Ecclesiastes"; "Song of Solomon"; "Jeremiah"; "Isaiah"; "Ezekiel"; "Daniel"; "Jonah". New Testament: The Four Gospels; "Romans"; "Ephesians"; "Hebrews"; "Revelation"
Aeschylus	*The Oresteia*
Aristophanes	*The Birds*; *Lysistrata*
Aristotle	*Poetics* (a minimum)

Augustine, Saint	*Confessions*
Boccaccio, Giovanni	*The Decameron*
Catullus	*Carmina* iii, v, lxii, lxx, lxxxv, cl
Dante	*The Divine Comedy* (Mandelbaum tr.)
Euripides	*Electra*; *Medea*; *The Bacchae*
Homer	*Iliad*; *Odyssey* (Fitzgerald, tr.)
Homeric Hymns	"Hymn to Demeter"
Horace	*The Art of Poetry* and a couple of odes and satires
Ovid	*Metamorphoses* (Humphries, tr.)
Plato	*Ion*; *Meno*; *Phaedrus*; *Republic:* Books 2, 3, 6, 7, 10; *Symposium*; *Timaeus*
Sappho	Selected lyrics
Sophocles	*Antigone, Oedipus Rex*
Vergil	*The Aeneid* (Mandelbaum, tr.)

Baylor University
Waco, TX 76798
(800) 229-5678
http://www.baylor.edu

In its brochure, "An Invitation: Voyage of Discovery," the Baylor College of Arts and Sciences Committee for Suggested Reading presents the following list. They preface it with "any list of recommended books, including this one, is incomplete and, to some extent, arbitrary. The books suggested here many have read with profit and pleasure. Therefore, we offer this list, which represents a variety of topics and points of view, not as an end, but as a beginning of a voyage of discovery."

Arts and Letters

Cather, Willa	*The Professor's House*
Cervantes, Miguel de	*Don Quixote*
Dostoevski, Fyodor	*The Brothers Karamazov*

Melville, Herman	*Moby-Dick*
Tolstoy, Leo	*Anna Karenina*
Woolf, Virginia	*A Room of One's Own*
Wright, Richard	*Native Son*

The Sciences

Darwin, Charles	*The Voyage of the Beagle*
Eiseley, Loren	*The Immense Journey*
Freud, Sigmund	*Character and Culture*
Kuhn, Thomas S.	*The Copernican Revolution*
Skinner, B.F.	*Beyond Freedom and Dignity*
Thomas, Lewis	*The Medusa and the Snail*

Philosophy

Gandhi, M.K.	*Autobiography*
Hughes, Robert	*The Shock of the New*
James, William	*The Varieties of Religious Experience*
Marx, K. and Friedrich Engels	*The Communist Manifesto*
Mill, John Stuart	*On Liberty*
Niebuhr, H. Richard	*Christ and Culture*

History

Boorstin, Daniel	*The Discoverers*
Burckhardt, Jacob	*The Civilization of the Renaissance in Italy*
Catton, Bruce	*Civil War Trilogy: The Coming Fury; Terrible Swift Sword; Never Call Retreat*
Hofstadter, Richard	*Anti-Intellectualism in American Life*
Spence, Jonathan	*The Gate of Heavenly Peace*
Tuchman, Barbara	*The Proud Tower*

In a Baylor literature course open to freshmen and sophomores the following novels are recommended:

Agee, James	*A Death in the Family*
Austen, Jane	*Emma; Mansfield Park; Pride and Prejudice*

Bellow, Saul	*Dangling Man, Henderson the Rain King; Seize the Day*
Bowden, Elizabeth	*The Death of the Heart*
Bradford, Richard	*Red Sky at Morning*
Brontë, Charlotte	*Jane Eyre*
Brontë, Emily	*Wuthering Heights*
Butler, Samuel	*The Way of All Flesh*
Cather, Willa	*Death Comes for the Archbishop; My Antonia*
Conrad, Joseph	*Lord Jim; Nostromo*
Dickens, Charles	*Dombey and Son; Great Expectations; Hard Times*
Eliot, George	*The Mill on the Floss*
Faulkner, William	*As I Lay Dying; The Reivers*
Fitzgerald, F. Scott	*The Great Gatsby*
Golding, William	*Lord of the Flies*
Hardy, Thomas	*Mayor of Casterbridge; Return of the Native; Tess of the D'Urbervilles*
Hemingway, Ernest	*A Farewell to Arms; For Whom the Bell Tolls*
Huxley, Aldous	*Brave New World*
James, Henry	*The American; Washington Square*
Kesey, Ken	*One Flew over the Cuckoo's Nest*
Knowles, John	*A Separate Peace*
Lawrence, D.H.	*Sons and Lovers*
Lewis, Sinclair	*Babbitt; Main Street*
Miller, Walter	*A Canticle for Leibowitz*
Norris, Frank	*The Octopus*
Orwell, George	*Burmese Days; 1984*
Porter, Katherine Anne	*Ship of Fools*
Scott, Walter	*Waverley*
Sinclair, Upton	*The Jungle*
Steinbeck, John	*The Grapes of Wrath*
Styron, William	*Lie Down in Darkness*
Trollope, Anthony	*Barchester Towers*
Wolfe, Thomas	*Look Homeward, Angel*
Wright, Richard	*Native Son*

Reading has everything to do with exposure. We are forever changed by our chance encounters with books and the people who live between the bindings. Our experiences with reading also lay bare the fact that we know much less than we think.

Dr. Dana Rapp
Ashland College, Associate Professor

Bloomsburg University of Pennsylvania
400 E. Second Street
Bloomsburg, PA 17815-1301
(570) 389-4000
http://www.bloomu.edu

Professor Louis F. Thompson of the Bloomsburg Department of English suggests the following as a "useful list from which college-bound students may select works for summer reading." He says that "all of these works are indisputably part of our literary heritage; they both reflect and propound ideas fundamental to Western civilization." The Bloomsburg English Department brochure in its section on high school preparation points out that works such as these "have achieved immortality because each is unique and excellent as a literary production, has had a powerful influence on later writers, and is a source of ideas and perceptions of life that remain important even to this day."

	Bible
Arnold, Matthew	Essays (especially "Function of Criticism at the Present Time"); poems ("Buried Life," To Marguerite," "Dover Beach")
Baldwin, James	Selections
Bulfinch, Thomas	*Mythology*
Bunyan, John	*Pilgrim's Progress*

Carlyle, Thomas	*Sartor Resartus* (chapters on "Everlasting Nay," "Center of Indifference," "Everlasting Yea")
Cervantes, Miguel de	*Don Quixote* (Putnam tr., in *Viking Portable Cervantes*)
Chaucer, Geoffrey	*The Canterbury Tales*
Chopin, Kate	*The Awakening*
Conrad, Joseph	*Heart of Darkness*
Dickens, Charles	*Great Expectations*
Dickinson, Emily	Poetry selections
Dostoevski, Fyodor	*Crime and Punishment*
Emerson, Ralph Waldo	Essays (especially "Self-Reliance," "The American Scholar")
Faulkner, William	"The Bear"
Fielding, Henry	*Joseph Andrews*; *Tom Jones*
Fitzgerald, F. Scott	Selections
Hansberry, Lorraine	*A Raisin in the Sun*
Hardy, Thomas	*The Mayor of Casterbridge*
Hawthorne, Nathaniel	*The Scarlet Letter*; short stories
Hemingway, Ernest	*A Farewell to Arms*; *For Whom the Bell Tolls*
Homer	*The Iliad* and *The Odyssey* (Rouse, tr.)
Ibsen, Henrik	*Ghosts*
Kafka, Franz	Stories
Koestler, Arthur	*Darkness at Noon*
Matthew, Saint	*Matthew: Christ's Sermon on the Mount*
Melville, Herman	*Moby-Dick*
Meredith, George	*The Ordeal of Richard Feverel*
Morrison, Toni	A novel
Orwell, George	*1984*
Shakespeare, William	*Henry IV, Part 1*; *King Lear*; *Midsummer Night's Dream*; *Twelfth Night*
Shaw, George Bernard	*Man and Superman*
Sophocles	*Antigone*; *Oedipus at Colonus*; *Oedipus Rex*
Swift, Jonathan	*Gulliver's Travels*
Thoreau, Henry David	*Walden*
Thurber, James	Selections

Toomer, Jean	Selections
Twain, Mark	Selections
Vergil	*The Aeneid* (Humphries, tr.)
Walker, Alice	Selections

Boston College
140 Commonwealth Avenue
Chestnut Hill, MA 02467
(617) 552-8000
http://www.bc.edu

Fr. William B. Neenan, S.J., Academic Vice President and Dean of Faculties at Boston, has composed a reading list that is given to incoming freshmen at the college. A letter prefaces the list:

> *Welcome to Boston College!*
>
> *During your college years, you will enjoy opportunities for leisure such as most likely you will never have again. Hence, I encourage you to develop the habit of reading good books. The attached list may assist you. It represents responses I might make to the question, "Have you read a good book recently?"*
>
> *These titles are not necessarily my candidates for the "Great Books" category. They are simply books I have read over the course of many years and for various reasons remain memorable. Absent from the list are the Classics, Dante, and Shakespeare—no need to state the obvious—as well as books of poetry. But don't spurn the poets. Other books are absent either because I have not read them, they didn't impress me or because they have slipped my mind.*
>
> *And your list? What will it look like in four years? In twenty years?*

The Dean's List

Agee, James	*A Death in the Family*
Amis, Kingsley	*Lucky Jim*
Ashe, Arthur	*Days of Grace*
Bernanos, George	*Diary of a Country Priest*
Bolt, Robert	*A Man for All Seasons*
Brokaw, Tom	*The Greatest Generation*
Camus, Albert	*The Fall*
Fitzgerald, F. Scott	*The Great Gatsby*
Greene, Graham	*The Power and the Glory*
Hillesum, Etty	*An Interrupted Life*
Joyce, James	*Portrait of the Artist as a Young Man*
Junger, Sebastian	*The Perfect Storm*
Ladd, Florence	*Sarah's Psalm*
McCullough, David	*Truman*
McDermott, Alice	*Charming Billy*
Morris, Charles	*American Catholic: The Saints and Sinners Who Built America's Most Powerful Church*
Naylor, Gloria	*Women of Brewster*
Nouwen, Henri	*The Return of the Prodigal Son*
O'Malley S.J., John	*The First Jesuits*
Pelikan, Jaroslav	*Jesus Through the Centuries*
Petry, Ann	*The Street*
Robinson, Marilynne	*Housekeeping*
Shaara, Michael	*The Killer Angels*
Stegner, Wallace	*Collected Short Stories*
Undset, Sigrid	*Kristin Lavransdatter*
Warren, Robert Penn	*All the King's Men*
Winchester, Simon	*River at the Center of the World*

Brandeis University
415 South Street
Waltham, MA 02454-9110
(781) 736-2000
http://www.brandeis.edu

According to Professor Mitsue Miyata Frey, all entering Brandeis freshmen must take a two-step program of University Studies in the Humanities. Step 1 courses include a Homeric text, a selection from the Old Testament and the New Testament, in addition to other texts that the individual faculty members choose. For Step 2, instructors select works from two of the following authors: Dante, William Shakespeare, Denis Diderot, Jane Austen, Emily Dickinson, Sigmund Freud, Franz Fanon, as well as other readings.

In Step 1, authors and their works have included:

	Bhagavad Gita
	Bible ("Genesis," "Exodus," "I & II Samuel," "Job," "Proverbs," "Jonah," "Matthew," "Luke," "John," "I Corinthians," other Pauline letters)
	Enuma Elish
	The Gilgamesh Epic
	Upanishads
Aeschylus	*The Oresteia*
Apuleius	*The Golden Ass*
Aristophanes	*The Birds*; *The Clouds*
Aristotle	*Nicomachean Ethics*
Cicero	*De Officiis*
Euripides	*The Bacchae*; *Iphigenia in Aulis*; *Medea*; *Electra*; *Hippolytus*; *Ion*
Hesiod	*Theogony*; *Works and Days*
Homer	*The Odyssey*; *The Iliad*
Morrison, Toni	*Beloved*
O'Brien, Tim	"How to Tell a War Story"

Petronius, Gaius	*Satyricon*
Plato	*Dialogues: Apology, Crito, Euthyphro to Phaedo*
Plutarch	*Lives*
Pritchard, James B., ed.	*The Ancient Near East I*
Procopius	*Secret History*
Sappho	*Sappho: A New Translation* (Barnard, tr.)
Sophocles	*Trachineae*; The Oedipus Cycle: *Oedipus Rex, Oedipus at Colonus, Antigone*
Theognis of Megara	*Poetry*
Vergil	*The Aeneid*

In the second semester, authors and their works have recently included:

	Beowulf
	The Cid
	The Elder Edda
	The Nibelungenlied
	One Thousand and One Nights
	Song of Roland
Achebe, Chinua	*Things Fall Apart*
Anouilh, Jean	*Antigone*
Ayer, Sir Alfred Jules	*Language, Truth, and Logic*
Augustine, Saint	*Confessions*
Austen, Jane	*Emma; Pride and Prejudice*
Baldwin, James	"Sonny's Blues"
Baudelaire, Charles	*The Flowers of Evil*
Bellah, Robert N., et al.	*Habits of the Heart*
Brontë, Charlotte	*Jane Eyre*
Calderón de la Barca, Pedro	*Life Is a Dream*
Camus, Albert	*The Stranger; The Plague*
Cesaire, Aimé	*A Tempest*
Conrad, Joseph	*Heart of Darkness*
Dante	*Inferno; Vita Nuova*
Descartes, René	*Meditations*
Dickens, Charles	*Hard Times*

Diderot, Denis	*Rameau's Nephew*; *The Supplement to Bougainville's Voyage*
Dostoevski, Fyodor	*Crime and Punishment*; "White Nights," "The Dream of a Ridiculous Man"
Ellison, Ralph	*Invisible Man*
Erasmus, Desiderius	*The Praise of Folly*
Fanon, Frantz	*The Wretched of the Earth*
Ferdowsi, Aboe-Quasem	*Shahname*
Fitzgerald, F. Scott	*The Great Gatsby*
Flaubert, Gustave	*Madame Bovary*
Forster, E.M.	*A Passage to India*
Frankl, Victor	*Man's Search for Meaning*
Freud, Sigmund	*Civilization and Its Discontents*; *Dora*; *Wit and Its Relation to the Unconscious*
Gaskell, Elizabeth Cleghorn	*Mary Barton*
Gilman, Charlotte P.	"The Yellow Wallpaper"
Gottfried, V. Strassburg	*Tristan*
Hardy, Thomas	*The Mayor of Casterbridge*
Hardy, G.H.	*A Mathematician's Apology*
Hegel, Georg	*Phenomenology of Spirit*
Heine, Heinrich	*Germany: A Winter's Tale*
Hoffman, E.T.A.	*The Golden Pot*
Hsi-Yu Chi	*Monkey* (selections)
Hume, David	*An Inquiry Concerning the Principles of Morals*
Hurston, Zora Neale	*Their Eyes Were Watching God*
Huysmans, Joris K.	*Against Nature*
Jacobs, Harriet	*Incidents in the Life of a Slave Girl*
James, William	"The Will to Believe," "The Moral Philosopher and the Moral Life," essays on pragmatism
Kafka, Franz	"A Hunger Artist," *Metamorphosis*
Kant, Immanuel	*Metaphysics of Virtue*
Kauffman, Walter	*Existentialism from Dostoevsky to Sartre*
Kerouac, Jack	*The Dharma Bums*
Kipling, Rudyard	*Kim*

Kraus, Karl	*The Last Days of Mankind*
Machiavelli, Niccolò	*The Prince*
Malcolm X and Alex Haley	*The Autobiography of Malcolm X*
Mann, Thomas	*Death in Venice*
Marx, Karl and Friedrich Engels	*The Communist Manifesto*
Mill, John Stuart	*Utilitarianism; On Liberty*
Miller, Arthur	*Death of a Salesman*
Mishima, Yukio	*The Sailor Who Fell From Grace With the Sea*
Molière	*Tartuffe*
Montaigne, Michel de	*Essays*
Moore, George Edward	*Principia Ethica*
Morrison, Toni	*Sula; The Bluest Eye; Beloved*
Murdoch, Iris	*The Sovereignty of Good*
Nabokov, Vladimir	*Lolita*
Nietzsche, F.W.	*The Genealogy of Morals*
Pascal, Blaise	*Pensées*
Paton, Alan	*Cry, the Beloved Country*
Petronius, Gaius	*Satyricon*
Poe, Edgar Allan	Selected short stories
Rabelais, François	*Gargantua and Pantagruel*
Rojas, Fernando de	*The Spanish Bawd; Celestina*
Rousseau, Jean Jacques	*Discourse on Inequality*
Sartre, Jean-Paul	*Existentialism and Humanism*
Shakespeare, William	*King Lear; The Tempest; Hamlet*
Shelley, Mary	*Frankenstein*
Steinbeck, John	*The Grapes of Wrath*
Swift, Jonathan	*Gulliver's Travels*
Tanizaki, Junichiro	*Some Prefer Nettles*
Tolstoy, Leo	*Death of Ivan Illych; Master and Man*
Twain, Mark	*The Adventures of Huckleberry Finn*
Voltaire	*Candide*
Wright, Richard	*Almost a Man; Native Son*

It was clear to me soon after my first semester had begun that reading was going to be integral to my success. Even in classes such as chemistry, which in high school traditionally did not entail much outside reading, I found myself constantly reading the textbook as well as supplementary texts in order to stay caught up and to better understand class material. In history, English, or social science courses, it is not unusual to purchase five to ten fairly large books. Not only is more reading assigned in college, but my own reading also greatly increased. Whereas in the past I had been able to slide by not always staying caught up on readings for my classes, I have found it extremely difficult to understand class material or excel in college without keeping up with assigned reading.

My advice to high school students, as a college freshman at a challenging university, is to read as much and as wide a variety of material as is possible. Increasing your exposure to literature through plays, novels, poetry, journals, short stories, reviews, essays, epics, and even the newspaper will improve your chances of success in college. You will see the benefits as you reach college and are better acquainted with expected reading requirements, increase your vocabulary, and are a better writer. Reading and writing are inseparable skills, especially in college. Even if you are not assigned to, write down some reactions or thoughts after reading something. It will polish your reading skills and prepare you for the countless reading-writing assignments in college. Increased reading will almost always lead to better quality of writing, and that is an invaluable skill to possess coming into college.

Mary Palecek
Freshman, DePauw University

Bucknell University
Lewisburg, PA 17837
(570) 577-2000
http://www.bucknell.edu

All first-year students at Bucknell may choose from a number of foundation seminars, small classes of about 15 students. According to the university, the seminars "are offered by many different faculty and focus on a wide variety of subjects. Whatever the topics, they are designed to cultivate the attitudes, skills, and knowledge necessary for students to benefit maximally from a Bucknell education and to negotiate the complexities of the modern world...These courses address foundational skills in reading, writing, listening, and speaking."

The following are examples of some of the seminars and the authors or books they may require:

Myth, Reason, Faith

This course is designed to introduce students to important works in the Western intellectual tradition. Major writers from Homer to Dante are studied.

Art, Nature, Knowledge

A continuation of "Myth, Reason, Faith," this course introduces students to important artists, writers, musical composers, and texts in the humanities. Selections from some of the following are included: **Martin Luther**, **William Shakespeare**, **Galileo**, **René Descartes**, **Johann Sebastian Bach**, **Sir Isaac Newton**, **David Hume**, **Wolfgang Mozart**, **Percy Bysshe Shelley**, **Charles Darwin**, **Karl Marx**, **Paul Cezanne**, and **Fyodor Dostoevsky**.

The Wild

The purpose of this seminar about the wild and experiences of wilderness is to help students understand how definitions and values related to "nature" and "the wild" change from age to age. Readings can include

	Narratives from Cherokee, Seneca, and Hopi
	Bible ("Genesis," "Exodus," "Job")
Abram, David	The Spell of the Sensuous: Perception and Language in a More Than Human World
Bradford, William	*History of Plymouth Plantation*; *The Journals of Lewis and Clark*
Cabeza de Vaca, Alvar Núñez	*Adventures in the Unknown Interior of America.*
Darwin, Charles	Darwin's visions of the wild
Emerson, Ralph Waldo	Essays
Freud, Sigmund	Freud's visions of the wild
Krakauer, Jon	*Into the Wild*
Keats, John	Selected poems
London, Jack	London's visions of the wild
Plato	Selections
Shakespeare, William	*Tempest*
Shelley, Percy Bysshe	Selected poems
Snyder, Gary	*The Practice of the Wild*
Thoreau, Henry David	*Essays*

Studied also may be music such as Igor Stravinsky's "The Rites of Spring" and Jimi Hendrix's "Electric Ladyland."

Darwin, Marx, Nietzsche, Freud

In this seminar students read and discuss the principal writings of Karl Marx, Nietzsche, and Freud, whose ideas were influenced by Charles Darwin's *On the Origin of Species by Means of Natural Selections* (1859). In addition to Darwin, the texts included are Marx and Engels, *Selected Works in One Volume* (Lawrence & Wishart); Friedrich Wilhelm Nietzsche, *Portable Nietzsche* (Viking Penguin); and Sigmund Freud, *Freud Reader* (Norton).

Our Choices Affect Our Lives

The readings for this seminar are from popular books mostly of student's choosing within the guidelines of the assignments.

Animal Cognition

The readings for this seminar, which is concerned with the ability of animal life to think, reason, and communicate, include Donald Griffin on animal cognition, original research reports regarding primate communication, Joel Wallman's "Aping Language," and a monograph on what young chimpanzees understand.

Freshmen at Bucknell are required to take a writing course in addition to their Foundation Seminars. There are several literature and composition courses from which they may choose.

Literature and Composition 101.1

In this course students consider the subjects of communities and outsiders. Texts may include

Cheever, John	*Oh What a Paradise It Seems*
Faulkner, William	*As I Lay Dying*
Melville, Herman	"Bartleby"
Morrison, Toni	*Sula*
Wharton, Edith	*Ethan Frome*

The course also uses a packet including works by **Nathaniel Hawthorne**, **George Washington Carver**, and **Flannery O'Connor**.

Literature and Composition 101.2

In this course, students read an assortment of stories and poems and Shakespeare's *Hamlet* and Mary Shelley's *Frankenstein* to help them improve their writing and get practice in various techniques of literary analysis.

Literature and Composition 101.3

Texts in this course include

Behn, Aphra	*Oroonoko*
Hacker, Diana	*A Writer's Reference*
Jacobs, Harriet	*Incidents in the Life of a Slave Girl*

Johnson, Charles	*Middle Passage*
Melville, Herman	"Benito Cereno"
Shakespeare, William	*The Tempest*
Styron, William	The Confessions of Nat Turner
Whitman, Walt	*Leaves of Grass*

Butler University
4600 Sunset Avenue
Indianapolis, IN 46208
(800) 368-6852
http://www.butler.edu

During the first semester of Butler's two-term freshman English course, students are normally working with readings from texts such as *The Harper & Row Reader* (Booth and Gregory), *Theme and Variations: The Impact of Great Ideas* (Behrens and Rosen), or *Audiences and Intentions: A Book of Arguments* (Bradbury and Quinn). For the second semester, instructors choose the works they wish to use for their individual sections. A list of typical selections would include these ancients and moderns:

Barth, John	"Lost in the Funhouse"
Blake, William	Selected poems
Brontë, Charlotte	*Jane Eyre*
Brontë, Emily	*Wuthering Heights*
Brooks, Gwendolyn	Selected poems
Chaucer, Geoffrey	*The Canterbury Tales*
Conrad, Joseph	*Heart of Darkness*; *Lord Jim*
Dickens, Charles	*Bleak House*
Dickinson, Emily	Selected poems
Dostoevski, Fyodor	*Crime and Punishment*
Euripides	*Medea*
Faulkner, William	"The Bear"
Fitzgerald, F. Scott	*The Great Gatsby*

Hawthorne, Nathaniel	Short stories
Hardy, Thomas	*Tess of the d'Urbervilles*
Heaney, Seamus	Selected poems
Hemingway, Ernest	*For Whom the Bell Tolls*
Homer	*The Odyssey*
Joyce, James	*A Portrait of the Artist as a Young Man*
Lawrence, D.H.	*Sons and Lovers*
Levertov, Denise	Selected poems
Orwell, George	*1984*
Poe, Edgar Allan	*Tales*
Pope, Alexander	*The Rape of the Lock*
Shakespeare, William	*Othello; King Lear; Hamlet*
Shaw, George Bernard	*Candida; Major Barbara*
Sophocles	*Antigone; Oedipus the King*
Swift, Jonathan	*Gulliver's Travels*
Twain, Mark	Selections
Vonnegut, Kurt	*Slaughterhouse Five*
Wolfe, Thomas	*Look Homeward, Angel*
Wright, Richard	*Native Son*
Yeats, William Butler	Selected poems

University of California, Berkeley
Berkeley, CA 94720
(510) 642-6000
http://www.berkeley.edu

Freshman seminars in a number of academic areas are offered at Berkeley. Readings assigned in recent seminars offered by the Anthropology, Astronomy, Classics, Comparative Literature, English, History, and Philosophy Departments have included:

Austen, Jane	*Pride and Prejudice*
Chernyshevsky, Nikolai	*What Is to Be Done*
Dostoevsky, Fyodor	"Notes from the Underground," "The Double," "Notes from the House of the Dead"
Euripides	*Medea*
Fitzgerald, F. Scott	*The Great Gatsby*
Greene, Brian	*The Elegant Universe*
Leon-Portilla, Miguel	*Fifteen Aztec Poets*
Tedlock, Dennis, ed.	*Quiche Maya Popol Vuh*
Turgenev, Ivan	*Fathers and Sons*
Wideman, Edgar	*The Cattle Killing*

In the English Department's Reading and Comprehension courses, some of the works studied have included:

Atwood, Margaret	*The Handmaid's Tale*
Austen, Jane	*Emma*
Beckett, Samuel	*Waiting for Godot*
Blake, William	*Songs of Innocence and Experience*
Brontë, Charlotte	*Jane Eyre*
Burton, Maria Amparo Ruiz de	*Who Would Have Thought It*
Camus, Albert	*Resistance, Rebellion, and Death*
Carroll, Lewis	*Alice's Adventures in Wonderland*
Crews, Fredrick	*The Random House Handbook*
Dickens, Charles	*Great Expectations*
Dundes, Alan	*Cinderella: A Casebook*
Gordimer, Nadine	*Six Feet of Country*
Hopkins, Winnemucca	*Life Among the Paiutes*
Hurston, Zora Neal	*Moses, Man of the Mountain; Their Eyes Were Watching God*
Jacobs, Harriet	*Incidents in the Life of a Slave Girl*
James, Henry	*The Turn of the Screw*
Joyce, James	*The Portrait of the Artist as a Young Man*

Kerouac, Jack	*On the Road*
Morrison, Toni	*Sula*
Nabokov, Vladimir	*Lolita*
O'Connor, Flannery	"A Good Man is Hard to Find"
Orwell, George	*The Orwell Reader*
Pynchon, Thomas	*The Crying of Lot 49*
Rowson, Susanna Haswell	*Charlotte Temple*
Rhys, Jean	*Wide Sargasso Sea*
Stoker, Bram	*Dracula*
Swift, Jonathan	*Gulliver's Travels*
Tan, Amy	*The Joy Luck Club*
Thompson, Hunter S.	*Fear and Loathing in Las Vegas*
Twain, Mark	*Roughing It*
Woolf, Virginia	*To the Lighthouse*

The most immediately helpful works I read in high school were by Shakespeare. Not only did I get a head start on much of what would be assigned in college, but a solid background in Shakespeare's works also helped my lateral understanding of other texts, in that many allusions and basic themes are linked to his literature. I was also fortunate enough to have a great literature teacher my senior year in high school who introduced me to many works that have helped me in college. Hemingway, Steinbeck, Hesse, Rand, and Huxley, in addition to being some of my favorite authors, have also been those that taught me to think in ways most similar to the way I must think through much of my collegiate reading assignments. Overall, I would say that developing good reading skills in high school, and even before, is the most valuable skill you can take with you to college.

Matt Satchwell
Freshman, Washington University in St. Louis

University of California, Davis
Davis, CA 95616
(530) 752-1011
http://www.ucdavis.edu

The English faculty at University of California, Davis, invited senate and federation faculty to list their favorite works of fiction, non-fiction, poetry, or drama, either in or out of their areas of expertise. The result is the following recreational reading list for English majors as well as for non-majors and prospective majors.

	Beowulf
	Sir Gawain and the Green Knight
Achebe, Chinua	*Things Fall Apart*
Albee, Edward	*The Zoo Story*
Allende, Isabel	*Paula*
Anaya, Rudolfo	*Bless Me, Ultima*
Atwood, Margaret	*The Handmaid's Tale*
Austen, Jane	*Emma, Pride and Prejudice*
Austin, Mary	*Land of Little Rain*
Barker, Pat	*Regeneration*
Barrett, Andrea	*Ship Fever*
Barth, John	*Lost in the Funhouse*
Bass, Rick	*Winter: Notes From Montana*
Behn, Aphra	*Oroonoko*
Bester, Alfred	*The Stars My Destination*
Birkerts, Sven	*Gutenberg Elegies*
Bishop, Elizabeth	*Collected Poems*
Brontë, Charlotte	*Jane Eyre; Villette*
Brontë, Emily	*Wuthering Heights*

Bryson, Bill	*The Lost Continent; The Mother Tongue*
Butler, Octavia	*Dawn*
Byatt, A.S.	*Possession*
Cairncross, Frances	*Costing the Earth*
Calasso, Roberto	*The Marriage of Cadmus & Harmony*
Calvino, Italo	*Italian Folk Tales*
Canin, Ethan	*The Palace Thief*
Capote, Truman	*In Cold Blood*
Carver, Raymond	*Where I'm Calling From*
Castellanos, Rosario	*The Book of Lamentations*
Cather, Willa	*My Antonia*
Catton, Bruce	*A Stillness at Appomattox*
Chandler, Raymond	*The Long Goodbye*
Chaucer	*The Canterbury Tales*
Coe, Jonathan	*The Winshaw Legacy: or, What a Carve Up!*
Conrad, Joseph	*Lord Jim; Nostromo*
Cooper, J. California	*A Piece of Mine*
Coover, Robert	*The Public Burning*
Cross, Amanda	*Death in a Tenured Position*
Dante	*Inferno; Purgatorio; Paradiso*
Danticat, Edwidge	*Breath, Eyes, Memory*
De Bernieres, Louis	*Corelli's Mandolin*
Dick, Philip K.	*The Man in the High Castle*
Dickens, Charles	*Bleak House; Great Expectations*
Didion, Joan	*Slouching Towards Bethlehem*
Dillard, Annie	*Pilgrim at Tinker Creek*
Dixon, Stephen	*Interstate*
Dostoevski, Fyodor	*The Gambler*
Douglass, Frederick	*The Narrative of the Life of Frederick Douglass*
Dove, Rita	*The Darker Face of the Earth*
Drabble, Margaret	*The Waterfall*

DuBois, W.E.B.	*The Souls of Black Folk*
Ehrlich, Gretel	*A Match to the Heart*
Eliot, George	*Middlemarch; The Mill on the Floss*
Eliot, T.S.	*The Waste Land*
Ellison, Ralph	*Invisible Man*
Equiano, Olaudah	*The Interesting Narrative of Olaudah Equiano*
Erdrich, Louise	*Love Medicine*
Faulkner, William	*The Sound and the Fury*
Fitzgerald, F. Scott	*Tender is the Night; The Great Gatsby*
Flaubert, Gustave	*Madame Bovary*
Foote, Shelby	*The Civil War*
Forché, Carolyn	*The Country Between Us*
Ford, Ford Madox	*The Good Soldier*
Forster, E.M.	*A Passage to India; A Room with a View; Howard's End*
Franz, Marie-Louise von	*Shadow & Evil in Fairy Tales*
Frazier, Charles	*Cold Mountain*
Frost, Robert	*Collected Poems*
Fussell, Paul	*Abroad*
Gaines, Ernest	*A Lesson Before Dying*
García Márquez, Gabriel	*One Hundred Years of Solitude*
Garrard, Apsley Cherry	*The Worst Journey in the World*
Gibbons, Stella	*Cold Comfort Farm*
Godwin, Gail	*Father Melancholy's Daughter; The Good Husband*
Guterson, David	*Snow Falling on Cedars*
Hammett, Dashiell	*The Maltese Falcon*
Hardy, Thomas	*Far from the Madding Crowd; Tess of the D'Urbervilles; Poems*
Harper, Frances E.W.	*Iola Leroy*
Harrison, Jim	*The Shape of the Journey: New and Selected Poems*
Harrison, Tony	*Poetry*
Hass, Robert	*Twentieth Century Pleasures*
Hawthorne, Nathaniel	*The Blithedale Romance; The House of the Seven Gables*
Heaney, Seamus	*Poetry*

Hegi, Ursula	*Stones from the River*
Heller, Joseph	*Catch 22*
Hemingway, Ernest	*Collected Stories; The Sun Also Rises*
Herr, Michael	*Dispatches*
Hirshfield, Jane	*The October Palace*
Hogg, James	*Private Memoirs and Confessions of a Justified Sinner*
Homer	*The Iliad*
Housman, A.E.	*A Shropshire Lad*
Houston, James	*Continental Drift; In the Ring of Fire*
Houston, Pam	*Cowboys Are My Weakness*
Hughes, Edan Milton	*Artists in California 1786–1940*
Hurston, Zora Neale	*Their Eyes Were Watching God*
Inchbald, Elizabeth	*A Simple Story*
Jacobs, Harriet	*Incidents in the Life of a Slave Girl*
James, Henry	*Daisy Miller; The Wings of the Dove*
Joyce, James	*Ulysses* or *A Portrait of the Artist as a Young Man*
Jessup, Helen Ibbitson and Thierry Zephir, eds.	*Sculpture of Angkor and Ancient Cambodia: Millennium of Glory*
Johnson, Diane	*Le Divorce*
Johnson, James Weldon	*The Autobiography of an Ex-Colored Man*
Joyce, James	*Dubliners*
Jung, Carl	*Memories, Dreams, Reflections*
Junger, Sebastian	*The Perfect Storm*
Kaplan, Alice	*French Lessons*
Kerouac, Jack	*Dharma Bums*
Landon, Letitia E.	*Selected Poetry*
Lansing, Alfred	*Endurance*
Larsen, Nella	*Quicksand*
Lawrence, D.H.	*Sons and Lovers; Women in Love*
LeGuin, Ursula K.	*The Earthsea Trilogy; The Left Hand of Darkness*
Lessing, Doris	*The Golden Notebook*
Lodge, David	*Nice Work, Paradise News and other Lodge novels*
Maclean, Norman	*A River Runs Through It*
Mahfuz, Naguib	*Palace of Desire; Palace Walk; Sugar Street*
Mailer, Norman	*The Executioner's Song*

Malory, Sir Thomas	*Le Morte D'Arthur*
Mandela, Nelson	*Long Walk to Freedom: The Autobiography of Nelson Mandela*
Mansfield, Katherine	*Stories*
McBride, James	*The Color of Water*
McEwan, Ian	*The Child in Time*
McPhee, John	*Coming into the Country*; *Survival of the Bark Canoe*
Melville, Herman	*Moby-Dick*; *Pierre*
Merrill, James	*Divine Comedies*
Merwin, W.S.	*The Vixen*
Middleton, Thomas	*Women Beware Women*
Milton, John	*Paradise Lost*
Morrison, Toni	*Beloved*; *The Bluest Eye*
Nabokov, Vladimir	*Pale Fire*
Naylor, Gloria	*Mama Day*
O'Brian, Patrick	The Aubrey-Maturin novel series
O'Brien, Tim	*In the Lake of the Woods*; *The Things They Carried*
O'Connor, Flannery	*The Complete Stories*
Ovid	*Metamorphoses*
Owens, Louis	*Dark River*; *Nightland*
Pessoa, Fernando	*Always Astonished*; *The Poems of Fernando Pessoa*
Poe, Edgar A.	*Narrative of Arthur Gordon Pym*
Pope, Alexander	*Rape of the Lock*
Porter, Katherine Anne	*Pale Horse, Pale Rider*
Proulx, E. Annie	*The Shipping News*
Reisner, Marc	*Cadillac Desert*
Robertson, David	*Real Matter*
Robinson, Kim Stanley	*Red Mars*
Robinson, Marilynne	*Housekeeping*
Roth, Philip	*The Ghost Writer*
Roy, Arundhati	*The God of Small Things*
Rushdie, Salman	*Midnight's Children*

Salinger, J.D.	*The Catcher in the Rye*
Saramago, Jose	*Blindness; Baltasar and Blimunda*
Sayers, Dorothy	*Gaudy Night*
Shakespeare, William	*Hamlet; Measure for Measure; Midsummer Night's Dream; Much Ado About Nothing; Othello; Romeo and Juliet; The Tempest*
Shelley, Percy Bysshe	*A Defense of Poetry*
Silko, Leslie Marmon	*Yellow Woman and a Beauty of the Spirit; Ceremony*
Smiley, Jane	*Moo*
Smith, Charlotte	*Desmond*
Snyder, Gary	*Practice of the Wild*
Steinbeck, John	*In Dubious Battle; The Grapes of Wrath*
Stowe, Harriet Beecher	*Uncle Tom's Cabin*
Tabucchi, Antionio	*Pereira Declares*
Tennyson, Alfred	*In Memoriam*
Thoreau, Henry David	*Civil Disobedience*
Traven, B.	*The Rebellion of the Hanged; The Treasure of the Sierra Madre*
Trollope, Anthony	*The Way We Live Now*
Twain, Mark	*A Connecticut Yankee in King Arthur's Court; The Adventures of Huckleberry Finn*
Tyler, Anne	*Earthly Possessions; The Accidental Tourist*
Updike, John	*The Centaur*
Vidal, Gore	*Lincoln*
Webster, John	*Duchess of Malfi*
West, Nathaniel	*Miss Lonelyhearts*
Wharton, Edith	*Age of Innocence; Ethan Frome; The House of Mirth*
Whitman, Walt	*Leaves of Grass*
Williams, Terry Tempest	*Refuge*
Woolf, Virginia	*A Room of One's Own; Mrs. Dalloway; The Waves; To the Lighthouse*
Wordsworth, William	*The Prelude*

California Institute of Technology
1200 East California Boulevard
Pasadena, CA 91125
(626) 396-6811
http://www.caltech.edu

Freshmen entering Caltech are required to take two terms of freshman humanities. Depending on the particular course, European, American, and Asian literature are studied. The content of the prescribed reading material is up to the individual instructor; however, some of the humanities courses typically teach certain works.

Homer and **Aristotle,** for example, are among the Greeks taught in Humanities 1, Greek Civilization. In Humanities 3, Early European Literature, the selections are usually English literature, but **Dante, Molière,** and **Rabelais** are also frequently taught.

Humanities II, Literature and Psychology, introduces the student to "literature and psychology considered as parallel investigations of such essential human issues as development of a sense of self, the nature of dreams, levels (conscious and unconscious) of communication." Works studied include, among others, those by **Samuel Taylor Coleridge**, **Fyodor Dostoevski**, **Thomas Mann**, and **Robert Louis Stevenson**.

New York University: Select a creative work—a novel, a film, a poem, a musical piece, a painting, or other work of art—that has influenced the way you view the world and the way you view yourself. Discuss the work and its effect on you.

Centenary College, Louisiana
2911 Centenary Blvd.
PO Box 41188
Shreveport, LA 71134-1188.
http://www.centenary.edu

First-year students at Centenary College take at least one course in a two-semester sequence First Year Experience. The faculty for the course is drawn from the departments of English, Geology, Geography, German, Health and Exercise Science, History and Political Science, Music, Philosophy, Religion, and Sociology.

The course has a unifying theme that varies annually. One year's theme, Forbidden Knowledge, focused on "how we construct knowledge: what we choose to limit and value." Writers that students encounter in First Year Experience include **Aristotle**, **Francis Bacon**, **Frederick Douglass**, **Sigmund Freud**, **Martin Luther King, Jr.**, **Carl Jung**, **Niccolò Machiavelli**, **Karl Marx**, **Plato**, **William Shakespeare**, **Sophocles**, and **Henry David Thoreau**.

Another introductory course first year students may take, which is not a part of the First Year Experience, has them learn about philosophy through the conception of an examined life. **Robert Nozick**'s *The Examined Life* is the first work studied. The course then considers the lives of three intellectuals: **Socrates**, **Charles Darwin**, and **Noam Chomsky**. Specific texts studied are **Darwin**'s *The Descent of Man*, **Edward Hermann** and **Noam Chomsky**'s *In Manufacturing Consent*, and **Stanley Karnow**'s *Vietnam*.

Clarkson University
PO Box 5605
Potsdam, NY 13699
(315) 268-6400
http://www.clarkson.edu

Great Ideas in Western Culture is the title of the core program at Clarkson. Required reading for its courses include four of the following books each semester of the academic year, plus one additional work of the faculty member's choice.

	Bible, Oxford Study Edition (New English translation, annotated)
Austen, Jane	*Pride and Prejudice*
Camus, Albert	*The Stranger*
Dante	*Inferno*
Darwin, Charles (Appleman, ed.)	*Darwin*
Freud, Sigmund	*Civilization and Its Discontents*
Homer	*The Odyssey*
Locke, John	*Second Treatise on Government*
Machiavelli, Niccolò	*The Prince*
Marx, Karl (Tucker, ed.)	*The Marx-Engels Reader*
Plato	*The Last Days of Socrates*
Shakespeare, William	Any play
Sophocles	*The Oedipus Cycle*
Voltaire	*Candide* and other writings

Colby College
4000 Mayflower Hill
Waterville, ME 04901-8840
(207) 872-3000
http://www.colby.edu

There are a variety of works used to provide inspiration for writing in Colby's freshman English course. Some of the sections read, discuss, and write about works by **Henry David Thoreau**, **Mark Twain**, **Annie Dillard**, **Norman MacClean**, **Robert M. Pirsig**, **Helen Keller**, **Roland Barthes**, and **Salman Rushdie**. Describing his section, Professor John R. Sweney says, "As Samuel Johnson reminds us, 'What is written without effort is in general read without pleasure.' But what is it that pleases readers, and how and where do we focus our efforts as writers?" The following are some of the works considered in the various sections of English 115 at Colby College:

Brecht, Bertolt	*Plays*
Cassill, R.V.	*Norton Anthology of Contemporary Fiction*
Colombo, Gary, et al., eds.	*Rereading America: Cultural Contexts for Critical Thinking and Writing*
Dorsen, Norman, ed.	*The Rights of Americans*
Eagleton, Terry	*Literary Theory*
Fante, John	*Wait Until Spring, Bandini*
Freud, Sigmund	*Three Case Histories*
Henley, Beth	*The Wake of Jamey Foster*
Kazin, Alfred	*A Walker in the City*
Kingston, Maxine Hong	*Woman Warrior*
Lurie, Nancy O., ed.	*Mountain Wolf Woman, Sister of Crashing Thunder: The Autobiography of a Winnebago Indian*
Marius, Richard	*Writing on History, A Writer's Companion*
Mathabane, Mark	*Kaffir Boy in America*
Scholes, Robert	*Textual Power: Literary Theory and the Teaching of English*
Scholes, Robert and Nancy Comley	*The Practice of Writing*

Sontag, Susan	*AIDS and Its Metaphors*
Woolf, Virginia	*A Room of One's Own*
Wycherley, William	*The Country Wife*
Ziff, Linda	*The Responsible Reader*

Colorado College
14 East Cache La Poudre Street
Colorado Springs, CO 80903
(719) 389-6000
http://www.coloradocollege.edu

According to Professor George Butte of the Department of English at Colorado College, the college has no set list of recommended titles nor a common freshman reading list, but the following are the works required in several of the entering-level courses:

English 201: Introduction to Literature

Bain, C.E., et al., eds.	*The Norton Introduction to Literature,* 3rd ed.
Chekhov, Anton	*The Three Sisters*
Dickens, Charles	*A Tale of Two Cities*
Durrenmatt, Friedrich	*The Visit*
Aristophanes	*The Birds*
Malamud, Bernhard	*The Natural*
Pinter, Harold	*The Dumb Waiter*
Shakespeare, William	*Twelfth Night*
Soyinka, Wole	*Death and the King's Horseman*

Recommended:

Holman, C. Hugh	*Handbook to Literature*

And students must choose one of the following:

Fugard, Athol	*Master Harold and the Boys* or *Siswe Banzi is Dead*
Morrison, Toni	*Sula*
Orwell, George	*Animal Farm* or *Road to Wigan Pier*

Short fiction read in the course includes:

Anderson, Sherwood	"The Egg"
Baldwin, James	"Sonny's Blues"
Bambara, Toni Cade	"My Man Bovanne"
Chekhov, Anton	"The Lady with the Dog"
Doyle, Sir Arthur Conan	"The Adventure of the Speckled Band"
García Márquez, Gabriel	"A Very Old Man with Enormous Wings"
Hawthorne, Nathaniel	"Young Goodman Brown"
Hemingway, Ernest	"The Short Happy Life of Francis Macomber"
Kafka, Franz	"The Hunger Artist"
Lawrence, D.H.	"Odour of Chrysanthemums"
Le Guin, Ursula	"The Ones Who Walk Away from Omelas"
Lessing, Doris	"Our Friend Judith"
O'Connor, Flannery	"The Artificial Nigger"
Olson, Tillie	"O Yes"
Richler, Mordecai	"The Summer My Grandmother Was Supposed to Die"
Twain, Mark	"The Celebrated Jumping Frog of Calaveras County"

Poetry selections include:

	Ballads: "Lord Randall," "Sir Patrick Spens"
Blake, William	"The Sick Rose"
Brooke, Rupert	"The Soldier"
Browning, Robert	"Soliloquy of the Spanish Cloister"
Chasin, Helen	"Joy Sonnet"
Donne, John	"A Valediction: Forbidding Mourning," "Batter My Heart"
Eliot, T.S.	"The Love Song of J. Alfred Prufrock"
Giovanni, Nikki	"Poetry"
Harper, F.E.	"Dear John, Dear Coltrane"
Knight, Etheridge	"The Idea of Ancestry"
Marvell, Andrew	"To His Coy Mistress"
Owen, Wilfred	"Dulce Et Decorum Est"
Plath, Sylvia	"Lady Lazarus"

Pound, Ezra	"In a Station of the Metro"
Rich, Adrienne	"Diving Into the Wreck"
Shakespeare, William	"Th' Expense of Spirit"
Tennyson, Alfred Lord	"Break, Break, Break"
Thomas, Dylan	"Do Not Go Gentle Into That Good Night," "Fern Hill"
Wordsworth, William	"London, 1802"
Yeats, William Butler	Selections

Composition-Literature 100: Theory and Practice of Literature

Harari, Josue V.	*Textual Strategies*
Hulme, Keri	*The Bone People*
Mann, Thomas	*Marlo the Magician*
Molière	*Tartuffe*
Morrison, Toni	*Sula*
Plato	*Phaedrus*
Puig, Manuel	*Pubis Angelical*
Tutuola, Amos	"Homecoming," "Tra-la-la"

Comparative Literature 100

Aristophanes	*The Birds*
Conrad, Joseph	*Lord Jim*
Freud, Sigmund	*Dora*
Hesiod	*Theogony; Works and Days*
Shakespeare, William	*Twelfth Night*
Shelley, Mary	*Frankenstein*

English 203: Convention and Change

The Nature of Comedy

Aristophanes	*The Clouds* (Arnott, tr.)
Amado, Jorge	*The Two Deaths of Quincas Watervell*
Austen, Jane	*Pride and Prejudice*
Beckett, Samuel	*Waiting for Godot*
Boëll, Heinrich	*The Clown*

Faulkner, William	*As I Lay Dying*
Freud, Sigmund	*Jokes and Their Relation to the Unconscious*
Heller, Joseph	*Catch-22*
Homer	*The Odyssey* (Fitzgerald, tr.)
Shakespeare, William	*Twelfth Night*
Shaw, George Bernard	*Pygmalion*
Stoppard, Tom	"Jumpers," "The Real Inspector Hound," "The Real Thing"

Drew University: For each category below, identify your favorite. A. book (with author) B. movie or play C. academic subject D. period in history.

University of Colorado at Boulder
Boulder, CO 80309
(303) 492-7115
http://www.colorado.edu

Professor Mary Klages, Director of Undergraduate Studies, English Department, University of Colorado at Boulder states, "It doesn't matter so much WHAT you read as (1) THAT you read and (2) HOW you read." Her colleagues in the department suggested the following for students preparing for college:

1. Read widely. Sample everything, not just genres you like.
2. Read closely. Learn to pay attention to how language works, in prose and in poetry. Read out loud, especially poetry. Work to develop an ear for the rhythm and sound of words, just as you would for music.
3. Read critically. Think about what you read. Figure out why an author did what s/he did—why this word, why this paragraph

structure, why did this character do this, why this symbol? Ask yourself questions about what you read. Talk to other people who have read the same story, book, or poem about what they thought. Get beyond "I liked it." Ask WHY.

4. Learn the English language. Study grammar. Learn how the various parts of speech work. Learn how sentences are put together. Learn punctuation and how it functions.
5. Write. Practice writing sentences that make sense, paragraphs that hang together, essays that make a sound argument.

These are skills that will help any college-bound student do well in whatever field or discipline he or she chooses to study.

Columbia College, Columbia University
212 Hamilton Hall
New York, NY 10027
(212) 854-2441
http://www.columbia.edu/co/college

Since 1919, Columbia College has had a required core curriculum made up of Literature Humanities, Contemporary Civilization, Music Humanities, and Art Humanities courses. Required and recommended works for the Literature Humanities and Contemporary Civilization sections are listed below.

Literature Humanities (Fall Semester Assignments)

Aeschylus	*Aeschylus I: Oresteia* (Lattimore, tr.)
Aristophanes	*Aristophanes: Four Comedies* (Arrowsmith, tr.)
Aristotle	*Nichomachean Ethics* (Ross, tr.); *Poetics* (Janko, tr.)
Euripides	*Euripides I* (Warner, tr.) *Medea*; *Euripides V* (Arrowsmith, tr.) *Bacchae*
Homer	*The Iliad* (Lattimore, tr.); *The Odyssey* (Lattimore, tr.)
Homeric Hymns	*Homeric Hymns* (Athanassakis, tr.), "Homeric Hymn to Demeter"

Plato	*Apology* (Grube, tr.) "Trial and Death of Socrates"; *Republic* (Grube, tr.); *Symposium* (Hamilton, tr.)
Sappho	Selections
Sophocles	*Sophocles I: Oedipus the King* (Grene, tr.); *Antigone* (Wyckoff, tr.); *Oedipus at Colonus* (Fitzgerald, tr.)
Thucydides	*Peloponnesian War* (Warner, tr.)
Vergil	*Aeneid* (Fitzgerald, tr.)

Literature Humanities (Spring Semester Assignments)

	Bible: Old and New Testaments, Revised Standard or King James Version
Augustine, Saint	*Confessions* (Pine-Coffin, tr.)
Austen, Jane	*Pride and Prejudice*
Boccaccio, Giovanni	*The Decameron* (McWilliam, tr.)
Dante	*Inferno* (Mandelbaum, tr.)
Descartes, René	*Discourse on Method*; *Meditations on First Philosophy* (Cress, tr.)
Goethe, Johann W. von	*Faust, Part I* (Salm, tr.)
Lafayette, Mde. de	*Princesse de Cleves* (Mitford/Tancock, tr.)
Montaigne, Michel de	*Essays* (Cohen, tr.)
Shakespeare, William	*King Lear*

Contemporary Civilization (Fall Semester)

Section I: The Greek and Roman World

Required:

Plato	*Republic* (Lee, tr.)

Recommended:

Plato	*The Last Days of Socrates*
Aristotle (Barker, ed.)	*The Politics*

Recommended:

Aristotle	*Nichomachean Ethics*

Required:

Garrety and Gay, eds.	*Columbia History of the World* chapters 18–21

Recommended:

Cicero	*On the Good Life* (Grant, tr.)
Epictetus	*The Handbook of Epictetus*
Livy	*History of Rome* (Selincourt, tr.)

Section II: The Sources of the Judeo-Christian Tradition

Required:

Bible. Hebrew Bible: "Exodus," "Isaiah." New Testament: "Matthew," "Acts" (selections), and "Galatians" or "Romans"

Section III: The Middle Ages

Required:

Aquinas, Saint Thomas (Sigmund, ed.)	*Aquinas on Ethics and Politics*
Augustine, Saint	*City of God*
Garrety and Gay, eds.	*Columbia History of the World* chapters 32–33, 35

Recommended:

Medieval Political Philosophy (Lerner, ed.)	"Alfarabi," "Maimonides"

Section IV: Renaissance and Reformation

Required:

Braudel, Fernand	"European Expansion and Capitalism, 1450–1650" in *Chapters in Western Civilization* 3rd ed., Vol. 1
Calvin, John	*Institutes* Book IV, Chapter 20
Garrety and Gay, eds.	*Columbia History of the World* chapters 39–44
Hillerbrand, H.J., ed.	*Protestant Reformation*
Machiavelli, Niccolò	*The Prince* and *Discourses*
More, Thomas	*Utopia*

Section V: The New Science

Required:

Bacon, Francis	*The New Organon*
Galileo	*Discoveries and Opinions*
Descartes, René	*Discourse on Method* or *Meditations on First Philosophy*

Recommended:

Garrety and Gay, eds.	*Columbia History of the World* chapter 59

Section VI: New Philosophy and the Polity

Required:

Garrety and Gay, eds.	*Columbia History of the World* chapter 48
Hobbes, Thomas	*Leviathan*
Locke, John	Two Treatises on Government

Contemporary Civilization (Spring Semester)

Section I: The Enlightenment and the French Revolution

Required:

Rousseau, Jean-Jacques	"Discourse on the Origin of Inequality" and "The Social Contract"

Recommended:

Rousseau, Jean-Jacques	*émile* (entire text recommended)
Wollstonecraft, Mary	*A Vindication of the Rights of Women*

Required

Hume, David	Selection from "Inquiry Concerning the Principals of Morals" in *Introduction to Contemporary Civilization in the West*, Vol. 1

Recommended:

Hume, David	"Inquiry Concerning Human Understanding," "Inquiry Concerning the Principles of Morals," "Treatise on Human Nature." *Essays: Moral, Political and Literary*

Required:

Garrety and Gay, eds.	*Columbia History of the World* chapters 64, 65, 66 (on American and French Revolutions); documents on the French Revolution; Federalist Papers #10, #51
Kant	*Grounding for Metaphysics of Morals* and "What is Enlightenment"

Recommended:

Burke, Edmund	*Reflections on the Revolution in France*

Section II: Economy, Society, and the State

Required:

Garrety and Gay, eds.	*Columbia History of the World* chapters 72, 73, 74
Hegel, Georg	"Ethics" from *The Philosophy of Right* (C.J. Friedrich ed.), *The Philosophy of Hegel* 3rd part, or *Reason in History*
Marx, Karl (R. Tucker, ed.)	Selections from *Marx-Engels Reader*
Mill, John Stuart	"On Liberty," "The Subjection of Women," selections from "On Representative Government," in *Three Essays*

Recommended:

Bentham, Jeremy	"Principles of Legislation" in *Introduction to Contemporary Civilization in the West,* Vol. II

Section III: Darwin, Freud, Nietzsche

Required:

Darwin, Charles	"Descent of Man" or "Origin of Species" in *Darwin* (Appleman, ed.)
Freud, Sigmund	*Civilization and Its Discontents; Three Essays on the Theory of Sexuality* or *Selections from Introductory Lectures*
Nietzsche, Friedrich	*Genealogy of Morals*

Recommended:

	"Illustrations of Universal Progress" in *Introduction to Contemporary Civilization in the West,* Vol. II
Appleman, ed.	"Social Darwinism, Gender, and Race" in the *Darwin Reader,* Part V

Section IV: Modernity and Its Discontents (Tentative)

Science and Revolutions in the 20th Century

Arendt, Hannah	*On Violence; The Origins of Totalitarianism*
Gramsci, Antonio	*The Modern Prince*

Habermas, Jurgen	*Toward a Rational Society*
Lenin, V.I.	"Imperialism" or "The State and Revolution"
Merleu-Ponty, Maurice	*Humanism and Terror*
Weber, Max	"Science as a Vocation" and "Politics as a Vocation" in *Essays in Sociology*

The Ambiguities of Integration: Class, Race, and Gender

Beauvoir, Simone de	*The Second Sex*
Fanon, Frantz	*The Wretched of the Earth*
Harrington, Michael	*The Other America*
Mahowald, Mary B., ed.	*Philosophy of Women*
Malcolm X and Alex Haley	*The Autobiography of Malcolm X*
Rawls, John	*A Theory of Justice*
Snitow, Ann, ed.	*Powers of Desire*
Supreme Court	*Brown vs. Board of Education* (1954); *Serrano vs. Priest* (1971); *San Antonio School District vs. Rodriguez* (1973); *De Funis vs. Odegaard* (1974); *University of California Regents vs. Bakke* (1978)

Wabash College: In 350 words or more, discuss a quotation or creative work that has had a significant impact on you. Be sure to express yourself as carefully and clearly as you can.

Cornell University
Information & Referral Center
Day Hall Lobby
Ithaca, NY 14853-2801
(607) 254-4636
http://www.cornell.edu

Most freshmen at Cornell must take first-year writing seminars. To fulfill this requirement, the John S. Knight Writing Program gives them a choice of more than 125 different courses offered by over 30 departments and programs.

Each seminar is limited to 17 students. The reading assignments of 75 pages or fewer a week may be in the humanities, social sciences, expressive arts, or sciences depending upon the department that is offering the seminar. Examples of readings in a few of the seminars follow:

African Studies

The Black Experience in Writing; African American Women Writers

This seminar provides a unique opportunity to explore the visions, values, themes, characters, and settings presented by African American women writers. Probing the rich worlds of **Harriet Jacobs**, **Zora Neale Hurston**, **Alice Walker**, and **Toni Morrison**, students engage in dialogue—both written and oral—for the stimulating exchange of ideas. Literary themes of self-knowledge are studied in conjunction with essays and other works by authors of diverse backgrounds. Through written and oral communication, students face the challenge and the privilege of understanding the significance of literary themes as they relate to broader issues of society, and to their personal lives as well.

Asian Studies

Mother Buddha of the Clouds

An old text says that the first Buddha to appear in the territory of what is now northern Vietnam was a rain goddess. Students read this text in translation along with writings by the 20th-century composer John Cage, who applied Buddhist thought to his practice of composing music and to writing (students also listen to some of Cage's compositions). Students write essays on topics related to the readings and to class discussions of them. There is an emphasis on using the discipline of writing to change rather than to express one's self.

Classics

Greek and Roman Myths

This seminar introduces students to the classical myths and sagas. Using a handbook containing extensive excerpts of the ancient stories, they discuss—and write about—the exploits, personalities, and relations of the Greek gods, heroes, and heroines. The focus is on enhancing writing skills, particularly in the areas of correct argumentation, grammar, and usage.

English 12

Shakespeare

This course develops and sharpens critical reading and writing skills through the study of Shakespearean drama. Students read five plays, such as *Henry IV, Part I*; *A Midsummer Night's Dream*; *The Tempest*; *The Merchant of Venice*; *Othello*; *The Winter's Tale*; or *King Lear*. The seminar requires informed participation of all its members as they improve their habits of writing, reading, and discussion—with the assumption that these three skills are developed fully only by being developed jointly. There are many writing assignments, both formal and informal. Some of the work consists of seriously revising earlier papers. The goal is that students will leave the course knowing how to speak and write about Shakespeare with pleasure and intelligence.

English 141

The Bible and Ancient Authors

In this seminar, students will read, discuss, and write about selected portions of the Bible (which is considered primarily as literature) and works by authors outside the Judeo-Christian tradition, such as the Babylonian epic *Gilgamesh*, **Homer**'s *Odyssey*, the *Oresteia* of **Aeschylus**, **Ovid**'s *Metamorphoses*, and the *Bhagavad-Gita*.

English 176

Portraits of the Self: Images of American Indians: Myths and Realities

Images of American Indians juxtapose myth and reality. Whether real or unreal, they have touched the lives of American Indians in profound ways. What are the origins of American Indian images and why do they continue to proliferate in American culture (for example, the Indian princess)? Were the images designed to justify American colonialism or to facilitate the assimilation of American Indians (for example, the noble savage)? To what extent, and in both negative and positive ways, have popular images affected the culture and identity of American Indians (for example, Indian mascots)? Course texts may include documentary (*In Whose Honor?*), film (*Where the Spirit Lives*), biography (*Lakota Woman*), and fiction (*Love Medicine*). Students write critical essays and responses to material covered in class and give a presentation based on a short research paper.

English 270

The Reading of Fiction

This course examines modern fiction, with an emphasis on the short story and novella. Students write critical essays on authors who flourished between 1870 and the present, such as **James**, **Joyce**, **Woolf**, **Hurston**, **Lawrence**, **Fitzgerald**, **Hemingway**, **Faulkner**, **Rhys**, **Welty**, **Salinger**, and **Morrison**. Reading lists vary from section to section, and some may include a novel, but close, attentive, imaginative reading and writing are central to all.

Philosophy

Socrates: Sophist or Sage?

Socrates professed to know only that he knew nothing. He never wrote anything and founded no school. Nevertheless, he is arguably second only to Jesus in his influence on Western thought. No fewer than five philosophical traditions trace their lineage back to Socrates, and his philosophical predecessors are now known as the pre-Socratics. Socrates appears as a character in Aristophanes's play *The Clouds* and in many of Plato's dialogues, including "The Apology," "Crio," "Gorgias," "Meno," and "Euthyphro." By studying these works, students try to understand and write about why Socrates has been so influential. They also think about Socrates's chief concern: what it is for a human being to live well.

Comparative Literature

Cultural Fiction—Imaging "India": Representations and Narratives of Modern South Asia

An introduction to narratives and representations of India, Pakistan, Bangladesh, and Sri Lanka, this course examines the colonial and postcolonial discourse of South Asia. Students begin by interrogating stereotypes emerging from contemporary popular culture to consider how marketing practices conflate diverse cultures into one exotic India. They then turn to literature of the British Raj and go on to explore the various ways that nations are constructed through narratives focused on the trauma of partitions, nationalisms, and the displacements of individuals and communities. Finally, the course focuses on the diversity of the South Asian diaspora in North America and Great Britain. Students write short responses and longer essays about texts by **Rudyard Kipling**, **Rabindranath Tagore**, **Manto**, **Selvadurai**, **Salman Rushdie**, **Devi**, and films by **Satyajit Ray** and **Mira Nair**.

German Studies

From Fairy Tales to the Uncanny: Exploring the Romantic Consciousness

This seminar explores a variety of themes (doubles, madness, incest, cyborgs, alchemy) expressing a fascination with the paranormal, the supernatural, and the uncanny in the German folktale and its transformations in Romantic fiction and beyond. Reading and writing assignments range from fairy tales of the **Brothers Grimm** and short narratives by Romantic writers (for example, **E.T.A. Hoffman**, **Tieck**, **Kleist**) to other traditions, such as **Mary Shelley**'s *Frankenstein*, tales of **Edgar Allan Poe**, and modern cinematic works by both Disney and Hollywood. No knowledge of German is expected.

Kafka, Hesse, Brecht, and Mann

This seminar is based on complete works (in English translation) by four representative German authors of the first half of the century. Although dealing with works of great popular appeal (*Demian*, *Death in Venice*, *The Metamorphosis*, *Mother Courage*, *Galileo*, and others), the emphasis of the course is on improving writing skills, that is, on perfecting each student's individual style. There are regular private conferences to discuss the papers.

Society for the Humanities

Living on the Edge

This seminar is about non-violent men and women whose ideas, actions, or mere existence put them in mortal danger in Soviet Russia, Nazi Europe, and the American South during the Civil Rights movement. The concern is how they have been portrayed in fiction, nonfiction, and documentary film. Students analyze these portrayals from the rhetorical, moral, and historical perspectives, focussing on trade-offs between factual accuracy and emotive power, and on moral question about heroism and betrayal. Discussion and analytic essays are based on materials that include **Solzhenitsyn**'s *One Day in the Life of Ivan Denisovich*, **Primo Levi**'s *Survival in Auschwitz*, **Juan Williams**'s *Eyes on the Prize*, and videos on the Holocaust and the Civil Rights movement.

Russian Literature

Classics of Russian Thought and Literature

Russian literature has always been closely intertwined with Russian history and culture, and frequently has served as a means of debating the country's future. This course examines the development of Russian literature and culture in the nineteenth and early twentieth centuries. While reading from classics by **Pushkin**, **Gogol**, **Turgenev**, and **Tolstoy**, students discuss and write about the role of the Russian folklore tradition in the development of these authors' works, and transferal of such works to the film medium, which both illuminated the traditional literary canon and broke new ground under the influence of modernism. The overall emphasis is on the ways in which elements of traditional Russian culture are given voice through literature, art, and film. All readings are in English translation.

20th-Century Russian Literary Masterpieces

20th-century Russian literature emerged from some of the most turbulent events in history: two world wars, a civil war, the October Revolution, and Stalin's purges—each of which cost millions of lives, including those of many writers. Finally and most recently, we have seen the collapse of the "great Soviet experiment" and the lifting of censorship. Throughout this course, the focus in discussion and writing assignments is on the manner in which authors create literary works in response to such historical events. The authors read include **Bulgakov**, **Zoshchenko**, **Solzhenitsyn**, **Voinovich**, and **Aitmatov**. All reading is in English translation.

Spanish Literature

Crossing Borders/Rites of Passage

The question this course addresses is "How can we learn about our own lives by reading books that explore the U.S.-Mexico border region?" Through a series of readings on young people and their journeys into foreign territory, students study border crossing as a metaphor for the rites of passage, such as beginning college, that they experience. Students have the opportunity to write autobiographical, critical, and travel essays. Authors may include **Rodolfo Anaya**, **Ana Castillo**, **Sandra Cisneros**, **Richard Rodriguez**, and **Helena Viramontes.**

Latino Autobiography

An increasingly popular trend among contemporary Latino writers is to compose life histories. By recalling and dissecting memories of immigration trauma, childhood adjustments to English speaking schools, and adult forays into the cultural life of the United States, these writers hope to gain a perspective about themselves, their Latino culture, and society. The course considers ways this act of recalling as well as constructing a personal history also creates a Latino public place in the cultural history of the country. Readings may include **Esmeralda Santiago**'s *When I Was Puerto Rican*; selections from **Judity Ortiz Cofer**'s *The Latin Deli*; **Mary Helen Ponce**'s *Hoyt Street: Memories of a Chicano Childhood*; selections from **Richard Rodriguez**'s *Hunger of Memory and Days of Obligation.* Writing assignments consist of a reading journal, a variety of formal/informal assignments, and student autobiographies.

> **Centre College**: Describe a character in fiction, a historical figure, or a creative work (as in art, music, science, etc.) that has had an influence on you, and explain that influence.

Creighton University
2500 California Street
Omaha, NE 68178
(402) 280-2700
http://www.creighton.edu

The following list was developed within Creighton's Department of English and Speech.

List of Books Suggested for Pre-College Reading

	Arthurian Tales
	Bible
	Robin Hood Tales
	Song of Roland
Adams, Henry	*The Education of Henry Adams*
Adler, Mortimer	*How to Read a Book*
Allen, Frederick L.	*Only Yesterday*
Austen, Jane	*Emma; Pride and Prejudice*
Barnett, Lincoln K.	*The Universe and Dr. Einstein*
Bellamy, Edward	*Looking Backward*
Boswell, James	*Life of Johnson*
Brontë, Charlotte	*Jane Eyre*
Brontë, Emily	*Wuthering Heights*
Buck, Pearl	*The Good Earth*
Bulfinch, Thomas	*Mythology*
Bunyan, John	*Pilgrim's Progress*
Butler, Samuel	*The Way of All Flesh*
Carroll, Lewis	*Alice's Adventures in Wonderland*
Carson, Rachel	*The Sea Around Us*
Cather, Willa	*Death Comes for the Archbishop; My Antonia*
Cervantes, Miguel de	*Don Quixote*
Chaucer, Geoffrey	*The Canterbury Tales*

Clark, Walter V.T.	*The Ox-Bow Incident*
Conrad, Joseph	*Lord Jim; Heart of Darkness*
Crane, Stephen	*The Red Badge of Courage*
Defoe, Daniel	*Robinson Crusoe*
Dickens, Charles	*A Tale of Two Cities; David Copperfield; Great Expectations; Oliver Twist*
Dostoevski, Fyodor	*Crime and Punishment; The Brothers Karamazov*
Doyle, Sir Arthur Conan	*Sherlock Holmes*
Dumas, Alexandre	*The Three Musketeers*
Eliot, George	*Adam Bede; The Mill on the Floss*
Faulkner, William	*Intruder in the Dust*
Fielding, Henry	*Tom Jones*
Fitzgerald, F. Scott	*The Great Gatsby*
Flaubert, Gustave	*Madame Bovary*
Forster, E.M.	*A Passage to India*
Franklin, Benjamin	*Autobiography*
Galsworthy, John	*The Forsyte Saga*
Golding, William	*Lord of the Flies*
Goldsmith, Oliver	*She Stoops to Conquer*
Greene, Graham	*The Power and the Glory*
Hamilton, Edith	*The Greek Way*
Hamilton, Alexander, et al.	*The Federalist Papers*
Hardy, Thomas	*Tess of the D'Urbervilles; The Return of the Native*
Hawthorne, Nathaniel	*The House of The Seven Gables; The Scarlet Letter*
Hemingway, Ernest	*For Whom the Bell Tolls; A Farewell To Arms; The Old Man and the Sea*
Hersey, John	*Hiroshima*
Homer	*The Iliad; The Odyssey*
Hudson, W.H.	*Green Mansions*
Hugo, Victor	*Les Misérables*
Huxley, Aldous	*Brave New World*
James, Henry	*The Turn of the Screw*
Joyce, James	*A Portrait of the Artist as a Young Man*
Lewis, Sinclair	*Arrowsmith; Babbitt; Main Street*
London, Jack	*The Call of the Wild*

Maugham, Somerset	*Of Human Bondage*
Melville, Herman	*Moby-Dick*
Miller, Arthur	*Death of a Salesman*
Nordhoff, Charles and James Norman Hall	*Mutiny on the Bounty*
O'Neill, Eugene	*The Emperor Jones*
Orwell, George	*Animal Farm; 1984*
Parkman, Francis	*The Oregon Trail*
Paton, Alan	*Cry, The Beloved Country*
Plutarch	*Lives*
Remarque, Erich Maria	*All Quiet on the Western Front*
Roberts, Kenneth	*Northwest Passage*
Rolvaëag, O.E.	*Giants in the Earth*
Rostand, Edmond	*Cyrano de Bergerac*
Saint Exupery, A. de	*Wind, Sand, and Stars*
Salinger, J.D.	*The Catcher in the Rye*
Scott, Sir Walter	*Ivanhoe*
Shakespeare, William	*Hamlet; Henry IV; MacBeth; Romeo and Juliet*
Shaw, George Bernard	*Pygmalion; Saint Joan*
Sophocles	*Oedipus Rex*
Steinbeck, John	*The Grapes of Wrath*
Stevenson, Robert L.	*Treasure Island*
Swift, Jonathan	*Gulliver's Travels*
Thackeray, William Makepeace	*Vanity Fair*
Thoreau, Henry David	*Walden*
Tolstoy, Leo	*War and Peace*
Turgenev, Ivan	*Fathers and Sons*
Twain, Mark	*The Adventures of Huckleberry Finn; Life on the Mississippi; The Adventures of Tom Sawyer*
Vergil	*The Aeneid*
Warren, Robert Penn	*All the King's Men*
Wharton, Edith	*Ethan Frome*
Wilder, Thornton	*Our Town; The Bridge of San Luis Rey*
Wolfe, Thomas	*Look Homeward, Angel*

Davidson College
PO Box 1719
Davidson, NC 28036
(704) 892-2000
http://www.davidson.edu

The following books are required for Davidson's first-year Humanities program:

For both semesters:

Fowler, H. Ramsey	*The Little, Brown Handbook* 3rd ed.

Fall semester:

Aeschylus	*The Oresteia* (Fagles, tr.)
Apuleius	*The Golden Ass* (Lindsay, tr.)
Aristotle	*Nicomachean Ethics* (Ross, tr.)
Chamber, Mortimer	*Ancient Greece*
Euripides	*Medea & Other Plays* (Vellacott, tr.)
Gruen, Erich	*The Roman Republic*
Homer	*The Iliad* (Lattimore, tr.)
Plato	*Protagoras and Meno* (Guthrie, tr.)
Plato and Aristophanes	*Four Texts on Socrates* (West and West, tr.)
Pollitt, J.J.	*Art and Experience in Classical Greece*
Sophocles	*The Three Theban Plays* (Fagles, tr.)
Tacitus	*The Annals of Imperial Rome* (Grant, tr.)
Thucydides	*History of the Peloponnesian War* (Warner, tr.)
Vergil	*The Aeneid* (Humphries, tr.)

Spring semester:

	Beowulf (Raffel, tr.)
	Bible (The New Oxford Annotated Revised Standard Version with the Apocrypha)
	The Epic of Gilgamesh (Sanders, tr.)
	The Quest of the Holy Grail (Matarasso, tr.)
	The Song of Roland (Harrison, tr.)

Augustine, Saint	*The Confessions of St. Augustine* (Warner, tr.)
Benedict, Saint (Fry and Baker, eds.)	*The Rule of St. Benedict in English*
Chaucer, Geoffrey	*The Canterbury Tales* (Wright, tr.)
Dante	*The Divine Comedy* (Ciardi, tr.)
Eibhard and Notker the Stammerer	*Two Lives of Charlemagne* (Thorpe, tr.)
France, Marie de	*The Lais of Marie De France* (Hanning and Ferrante, tr.)
Hollister, C. Warren	*Medieval Europe: A Short History*, 5th ed.
Kelber, Werner H.	*Mark's Story of Jesus*
O'Brien and Major	*In the Beginning: Creation Myths from Ancient Mesopotamia, Greece, and Israel*
Aquinas, Thomas (Vernon J. Bourke, ed.)	*The Pocket Aquinas*

Optional texts are

Anderson, Bernhard W.	*Understanding the Old Testament*, 4th ed.
Spivey and Smith	*Anatomy of the New Testament*, 4th ed.

I feel the best education is self-education. Because a book isn't assigned does not mean it is not valuable. If you are motivated about a subject, dive in and learn. School should just be an introduction to the many subjects that appear in your life. I hear many of my peers complain that they have no idea what they want to do with their lives. This is because the only thing they read or seek to learn is what is on their syllabus. Break out, find what is interesting to you and go with it. You should always have a book that you are reading, fiction or fact. Feed your brain with the things you are motivated to learn about and retention will be unlike you have ever known it.

As for books that have changed me, I would say when I read *Slaughterhouse 5*, I realized that respected writers may actually write what is on their minds. It seems that everything that had been presented by the school was based on the writing ability or complexity.

> Vonnegut showed me that I could write because I see things differently, everyone does. And that fact alone makes your opinion valuable to the world. Of course, Charles Bukowski said something to the effect of if you don't enjoy your work, no one else will either. Yes, we should all be privy to Twain, Shakespeare, *Moby-Dick*, or whatever the "right" suggests in order to be "educated," but I have never connected to these works because I didn't feel they were talking to me. *The Cider House Rules, A Prayer for Owen Meany, Cat's Cradle, Breakfast of Champions, Tales of Ordinary Madness, My Utmost for his Highest, Elmer Gantry, Screwtape Letters, Demian,* and a host of non-fiction has talked to me. All books I've discovered and enjoyed on my own time away from classroom interpretation.
>
> *Craig Sowder*
> *Sophomore, Indiana University*

University of Delaware
Newark, DE 19716
(302) 831-2000
http://www.udel.edu

The University of Delaware has a recommended reading list for pre-college students. According to Professor Philip Flynn, "students are asked to read three books (of their choice) from this list during the summer before they enter the University and during their freshman year." The lists, which are annotated, vary from year to year. Recently the following works were recommended:

Dubois, W.E.B., *The Souls of Black Folk* A book of essays on the study of the problem of race in America. Written in 1903, it is one of the first scholarly attempts to explain "blackness." When first published, the *Nashville Banner* commented that "this book is dangerous for the Negro to read, for it will only excite discontent and fill his imagination with things that do not exist."

Dubos, René, *Mirage of Health: Utopias, Progress, and Biological Change* From biological adaptation to social evolution, René Dubos presents a panoramic vista of the individual's quest for health and happiness, with some detours along the way. Drawing upon relationships among the fields of biology, geography, history, ecology, mythology, and anthropology, the author reveals humankind's unified trajectory in a universe filled with both predictabilities and surprises. The desire for change for change's sake, the urge for progress and independence, the restless search for freedom are presented as motivators for a dynamic life of adventure and transcendence beyond survival, beyond utopias, and beyond any static concept of health and happiness.

Friedman, Milton and Rose Friedman, *Free to Choose* The Friedmans explore the paradox of intentions involved in the production and distribution of numerous goods and services in today's society and conclude that economic freedom is a requisite for political freedom.

Gilligan, Carol, *In a Different Voice* This book explores the theme of moral development by examining the modes of thought associated with "male and female voices" and, as one reviewer commented, turning "old prejudices against women on their ears."

Marx, Karl and Friedrich Engels, *Manifesto of the Communist Party* The classic analysis by Karl Marx and Friedrich Engels of the modern conditions produced by capitalist economic systems, and the solution to those conditions.

Pirsig, Robert, *Zen and the Art of Motorcycle Maintenance* A spiritual odyssey in the guise of a motorcycle journey. Pirsig's hero finds hope in the pursuit of Quality as a way of combating the shoddy workmanship that so often infects people in every walk of life in our technological world. Though Pirsig's conclusion is ambivalent, the book is a challenging fable about the difficulty of being authentic in the modern age.

Raup, David M., *The Nemesis Affair: A Story of the Death of Dinosaurs and the Ways of Science* A renowned scientist discusses the birth and controversial life of a recent theory. This is a wonderful insider's view of scientists at work.

Shipman, Harry L., *Space 2000: Meeting the Challenge of A New Era* A University of Delaware astronomer and NASA consultant reveals the excitement and the scientific and technical challenges of the American space program. Shipman gives real insight into topics ranging from "Materials Processing in Space" to "Exploration of the Distant Universe."

Tolstoy, Leo, "The Death of Ivan Ilych" The description of an ordinary death of an ordinary man, this is a meditation on the mystery of human life.

Tuchman, Barbara, *The Guns of August* Barbara Tuchman's unforgettable account of how the great powers of Europe stumbled into war in August 1914. It is a cautionary tale about how the momentum of the war took hold of statesmen and began to destroy the very national values they had sought to protect.

Wright, Richard, *Native Son* A grim story of racism in America.

Denison University
100 North Main Street
Granville, OH 43023
(740) 587-0810
http://www.denison.edu

According to Denison's Department of English, this reading list is a carefully selected compilation of "works important to literature in English." Although the list was composed primarily for college students, it is certainly a relevant one for the pre-college student to scan.

Drama

	The Second Shepherd's Play
	Everyman
Beckett, Samuel	*Waiting for Godot*
Chekhov, Anton	*The Cherry Orchard*
Congreve, William	*The Way of the World*

Fuller, Charles	*A Soldier's Play*
Goldsmith, Oliver	*She Stoops to Conquer*
Ibsen, Henrik	*Hedda Gabler*
Miller, Arthur	*Death of a Salesman*
Norman, Marsha	*'Night, Mother*
O'Neill, Eugene	*Long Day's Journey into Night*
Pinter, Harold	"The Dumb Waiter"
Pirandello, Luigi	*Six Characters in Search of an Author*
Shakespeare, William	*Hamlet, Henry IV, Part I, The Tempest, Twelfth Night*
Shaw, George Bernard	*Major Barbara*
Sheridan, Richard B.	*The School for Scandal* or *The Rivals*
Sherman, Martin	*Bent*
Sophocles	*Oedipus Rex*
Webster, John	*The Duchess of Malfi*

Poetry

	Beowulf
	Sir Gawain and the Green Knight
Arnold, Matthew	"Dover Beach"
Auden, W.H.	"Musée de Beaux Arts," "In Memory of W.B. Yeats," "In Praise of Limestone"
Bishop, Elizabeth	"Man-Moth," "The Fish," "The Armadillo" "In the Waiting Room"
Blake, William	Songs of Innocence: "The Lamb," "The Chimney Sweepe." Songs of Experience: "The Tyger," "The Chimney Sweeper," "London"
Bradstreet, Anne	"The Author to Her Book," "In Reference to her Children," "Upon the Burning of Our House"
Brooks, Gwendolyn	"We Real Cool," "Sadie and Maud," "Boy Breaking Glass," "The Lovers of the Poor," "A Bronzeville Mother Loiters in Mississippi …"
Browning, Robert	"My Last Duchess," "Andrea del Sarto," "Fra Lippo Lippi"
Browning, E.B.	Sonnets 21, 22, 32, 43

Chaucer, Geoffrey	*The Canterbury Tales*: the general prologue, The Nun's Priest's Tale, The Wife of Bath's Prologue and Tale, The Pardoner's Introduction, Prologue, and Tale
Coleridge, Samuel Taylor	"The Rime of the Ancient Mariner," "Frost at Midnight," "The Eolian Harp"
Dickinson, Emily	"Because I Could Not Stop for Death—," "There's a Certain Slant of light," "I heard a Fly Buzz—When I Died," "A Narrow Fellow in the Grass," "Safe in Their Alabaster Chambers—," "I Started Early—Took my Dog—," "I Taste a Liquor Never Brewed—," "I Felt a Funeral, in My Brain," "After Great Pain, a Formal Feeling Comes—," "I Died for Beauty—But Was Scarce," "My Life had Stood—a Loaded Gun," "I'm Nobody! Who Are You?"
Donne, John	"The Canonization," "The Sun Rising," "A Valediction: Forbidding Mourning," "A Nocturnal Upon St. Lucy's Day," Holy Sonnet 14, Elegy 19
Dryden, John	"MacFlecknoe"
Eliot, T.S.	"The Love Song of J. Alfred Prufrock," "The Waste Land," "Gerontion"
Frost, Robert	"Home Burial," "After Apple-Picking," "The Death of the Hired Man," "Design"
Ginsberg, Allen	"Howl"
Hayden, Robert	"Those Winter Sundays," "Middle Passage," "Night, Death, Mississippi"
Hopkins, Gerard Manley	"Spring and Fall," "The Windhover," "God's Grandeur," "Pied Beauty"
Keats, John	"Ode to a Nightingale," "Ode on a Grecian Urn"
Lowell, Robert	"Skunk Hour," "For the Union Dead"
Marvell, Andrew	"To His Coy Mistress," "The Garden"
Milton, John	*Paradise Lost*, books I, II, IX; "Lycidas," "When I Consider How My Light Is Spent," "On My Late Espoused Saint," "How Soon Hath Time"
Moore, Marianne	"Poetry," "The Fish," "England," "A Grave," "In Distrust of Merits"

Plath, Sylvia	"Daddy," "Tulips," "Lady Lazarus," "Ariel"
Poe, Edgar Allan	"The City in the Sea"
Pope, Alexander	"The Rape of the Lock"
Rich, Adrienne	"Diving into the Wreck," "Transcendental Etude," "Snapshots of a Daughter-in-Law"
Roethke, Theodore	"My Papa's Waltz," "Four for Sir John Davies," "The Waking," "In a Dark Time"
Shakespeare, William	Sonnets 15, 18, 55, 64, 73, 116, 129, 130
Shelley, P.B.	"Ode to the West Wind," "To a Skylark," "Ozymandias,"
Spenser, Edmund	*The Faerie Queene*, book I, "Epithalamion"
Stevens, Wallace	"The Emperor of Ice Cream," "Thirteen Ways of Looking at a Blackbird," "Sunday Morning," "The Idea of Order at Key West"
Tennyson, Alfred Lord	"Ulysses," "Tithonus," "Song of the Lotos-Eaters"
Whitman, Walt	"Song of Myself," "Crossing Brooklyn Ferry," "When Lilacs Last in the Dooryard Bloom'd"
Williams, W.C.	"Tract," "The Red Wheelbarrow," "The Yachts," "Spring and All," "The Dance"
Wordsworth, William	"Tintern Abbey," "Ode: Intimations of Immortality"
Wright, James	"A Blessing," "Lying in a Hammock at William Duffy's Farm in Pine Island, Minnesota," "This Journey," "The Jewel," "At the Executed Murderer's Grave," "Autumn Begins in Martin's Ferry, Ohio"
Yeats, W.B.	"The Second Coming," "Among School Children," "Sailing to Byzantium," "Easter 1916"

Fiction

Atwood, Margaret	*Surfacing*
Austen, Jane	*Emma* or *Pride and Prejudice*
Baldwin, James	*Go Tell It on the Mountain*
Bellow, Saul	*Seize the Day*
Black Elk	*Black Elk Speaks*
Brontë, Charlotte	*Jane Eyre*

Brontë, Emily	*Wuthering Heights*
Chopin, Kate	*The Awakening*
Douglass, Frederick	*Narrative of the Life of Frederick Douglass*
Ellison, Ralph	*Invisible Man*
Faulkner, William	*The Sound and the Fury* or *Light in August* or *As I Lay Dying* or *Absalom, Absalom!*
Fielding, Henry	*Joseph Andrews* or *Tom Jones*
Fitzgerald, F. Scott	*The Great Gatsby*
Gordimer, Nadine	*Burger's Daughter* or *A Guest of Honour*
Hardy, Thomas	*Jude the Obscure* or *The Mayor of Casterbridge* or *The Return of the Native* or *Tess of the D'Urbervilles*
Hawthorne, Nathaniel	*The Scarlet Letter,* "Young Goodman Brown," "My Kinsman, Major Molineux," "Rappaccini's Daughter"
Hemingway, Ernest	*The Sun Also Rises* or *In Our Time* or *A Farewell to Arms*
Hurston, Zora Neale	*Their Eyes Were Watching God*
James, Henry	*Daisy Miller; The Turn of the Screw*
Joyce, James	*Dubliners* or *A Portrait of the Artist as a Young Man*
Lawrence, D.H.	*Women in Love* or *The Rainbow* or *Sons and Lovers*
Melville, Herman	*Moby-Dick*
Morrison, Toni	*Sula* or *Song of Solomon*
O'Connor, Flannery	"A Good Man is Hard to Find," "Everything That Rises Must Converge," "The Artificial Nigger"
Porter, Katherine Anne	"Flowering Judas," "The Jilting of Granny Weatherall," "Rope"
Swift, Jonathan	*Gulliver's Travels*
Twain, Mark	*The Adventures of Huckleberry Finn*
Walker, Alice	*The Color Purple*
Welty, Eudora	"Why I Live at the P.O.," "A Worn Path," "The Petrified Man"
Wharton, Edith	*The House of Mirth* or *The Age of Innocence*
Woolf, Virginia	*Mrs. Dalloway* or *To the Lighthouse*
Wright, Richard	*Native Son*

Essays and Criticism

Aristotle	*Poetics*
Bentley, Eric	"Plot" from *The Life of the Drama*
Coleridge, Samuel Taylor	*Biographia Literaria*, Chapter 13
Dryden, John	"An Essay of Dramatic Poesy"
Eagleton, Terry	*Literary Theory*
Edwards, Jonathan	"Sinners in the Hands of an Angry God," "Personal Narrative"
Emerson, Ralph Waldo	*Nature*; "The American Scholar"
Keats, John	Letters to Benjamin Bailey, 22/11/1817; to George and Thomas Keats 21, 27/12/1817; to Richard Woodhouse, 27/10/1818
Lawson, John Howard	"Theory and Technique of Playwrighting"
Miller, Arthur	"Tragedy and the Common Man"
Paine, Thomas	"Thoughts on the Present State of American Affairs" from *Common Sense*
Plato	*The Republic*, book X
Poe, Edgar Allan	"The Poetic Principle" and "The Philosophy of Composition"
Rich, Adrienne	"When We Dead Awaken: Writing as Re-Vision"
Sidney, Sir Philip	"The Defence of Poesy"
Thoreau, Henry David	*Walden*
Warren, Robert Penn	"Pure and Impure Poetry"
Whitman, Walt	Preface to 1855 edition of *Leaves of Grass*
Wordsworth, William	Preface to *Lyrical Ballads*

Butler University: You are packing to leave for college. At the top of your suitcase you place three books you want to take with you. Which books? Why? What have you learned from them?

University of Denver
Mary Reed Building #107
Denver, CO 80208-0132
(303) 871-2036
http://www.du.edu

In preparing Denver's list, Dr. Margaret Whitt, Director First Year English, consulted with her colleagues "from a wide assortment of disciplines, asking each of them what books they prefer/assume an entering first-year student would have read. She says, "While some books are pertinent to the discipline, others are simply favorite books of professors who teach in that discipline." And she adds, "Our list is meant to be suggestive, not exhaustive:"

Art History

"At least one visit to an art museum or gallery"

Works of Art

Vermeer, Jan — *Lace Maker; Woman with a Water Jug; Woman Reading a Letter*

Biology

Carson, Rachel — *Silent Spring*
Crichton, Michael — *Andromeda Strain*; *Jurassic Park*
Sun Tzu — The Art of War
Watson, James — *The Double Helix: A Personal Account of the Discovery of the Structure of DNA*
Wilson, Edward O. — *The Diversity of Life*

Business

Flaherty, John — *Peter Drucker: Shaping the Managerial Mind*

Classical Languages

Boccaccio, Giovanni	*The Decameron*
Dante	*The Divine Comedy*
Euripides	*Medea*
Homer	*The Iliad, The Odyssey*
Ibsen, Henrik	*A Doll's House* or *Ghosts* or *Hedda Gabler*
Sophocles	*Oedipus*

Engineering

Toffler, Alvin	*Future Shock*

English

Brontë, Emily	*Wuthering Heights*
Camus, Albert	*Exile and the Kingdom*
Fitzgerald, F. Scott	*The Great Gatsby*
Hawthorne, Nathaniel	*The Scarlet Letter*
Milton, John	*Paradise Lost*
Shakespeare, William	*Hamlet; Romeo and Juliet; King Lear*
Swift, Jonathan	*Gulliver's Travels*
Twain, Mark	*The Adventures of Huckleberry Finn*

French

Beauvoir, Simone de	*Memoires d'une Jeune Fille Rangée*
Corneille, Pierre	*Le Cid*
Flaubert, Gustave	*Madame Bovary*
Hugo, Victor	*Les Misérables*
Voltaire	*Candide*

Hotel, Restaurant, and Tourism

Hailey, Arthur	*Hotel*

Philosophy

	Bible: "Genesis," "Job," one of the Gospels
Camus, Albert	*The Myth of Sysiphus*
Parmenides	"Peri Phuseos"
Plato	*Apology* and *Crito*
Sartre, Jean Paul	*Nausea*

"Any book at all that they really loved."

Political Science

Hamilton, Alexander, et al.	*The Federalist Papers*
Niccolò Machiavelli	*The Prince*
Plato	*The Republic*

Psychology

Albom, Mitch	*Tuesdays with Morrie*
Freud, Sigmund	*Introductory Lectures on Psychoanalysis* and *The Interpretation of Dreams*

Religious Studies

Augustine, Saint	*Confessions* (from books 1–8)

Sociology

Bellah, Robert	*Habits of the Heart*
Hochschild, Arlie	*Ain't No Makin' It*
Riesman, David	*The Lonely Crowd*
Tocqueville, Alexis de	*Democracy in America*
Wilson, William	*The Truly Disadvantaged*

DePaul University
1 East Jackson Boulevard
Chicago, IL 60604-2287
(312) 362-8000
http://www.depaul.edu

Professor Helen Marlborough explains that DePaul freshmen are required to take English 120: Understanding Literature. There are a number of sections of this course. In one section, the text is **Northrop Frye et al.**, *The Practical Imagination: Stories, Poems, Plays.* In addition to numerous shorter works, students in this section read **William Shakespeare**'s *Hamlet* and *The Tempest*, and *Oedipus Rex* by **Sophocles.**

The instructor for another section, Professor Caryn Chaden, states that English 120 "introduces you to the process of reading literature. It invites you to examine a variety of short stories, poems, and plays spanning five centuries and two continents. The course will help you develop a critical vocabulary for discussing these works, both in class and in essays. By giving you the opportunity to read literature and write about it, the course will help you perceive and articulate some of the choices a writer makes when he or she turns blank paper into art." The text for this section is **Robert Scholes, Carl H. Klaus, and Nancy R. Comley**, *Elements of Literature 3: Fiction, Poetry, Drama.* Some of the required readings are

	Everyman
Anderson, Sherwood	"I'm a Fool"
Aristophanes	*Lysistrata*
Auden, W.H.	"As I Walked Out One Evening," "Lullaby," "Musée des Beaux Arts," "The Unknown Citizen"
Baldwin, James	"Sonny's Blues"
Baraka, Imamu Amiri (formerly LeRoi Jones)	Poems
Beckett, Samuel	*Krapp's Last Tape*
Borges, Jorge	"Lottery in Babylon"
Boyle, Kay	"Winter Night"
Brooks, Gwendolyn	Poems

Browning, Robert	"My Last Duchess"
Browning, E.B.	Sonnets
Carter, Angela	"The Snow Child"
Cheever, John	"The Swimmer"
Chekhov, Anton	"Heartache"
Chopin, Kate	"The Story of an Hour"
Coover, Robert	"The Hat Act"
Cortazar, Julio	"Blowup"
Dickinson, Emily	Poems
Donne, John	Poems
Ellison, Ralph	"Battle Royal"
Frost, Robert	Poems
Hughes, Ted	"On the Road," *Mother and Child*
Lessing, Doris	"Sunrise on the Veld"
Maupassant, Guy de	"The Diamond Necklace"
Molière	*The Misanthrope*
O'Conner, Frank	"Guests of the Nation"
O'Connor, Flannery	"Everything that Rises Must Converge"
Olsen, Tillie	"I Stand Here Ironing"
Parker, Dorothy	"You Were Perfectly Fine"
Porter, Katherine Anne	"Rope"
Rich, Adrienne	"Night Pieces: For a Child," "Rape"
Roethke, Theodore	Poems
Stevens, Wallace	"Anecdote of the Jar," "Thirteen Ways of Looking at a Blackbird," "The Snow Man," "A High-Toned Old Christian Woman"
Tennyson, Alfred Lord	"Ulysses," "Tears, Idle Tears"
Wells, H.G.	"The Country of the Blind"
Welty, Eudora	"Why I Live at the P. O."
Whitman, Walt	Poems
Williams, Tennessee	*Cat on a Hot Tin Roof*
Williams, W.C.	Poems

Stanford University: If you were to write a book, on what theme or subject matter would it be based, and why?

DePauw University
South Locust Street
Greencastle, IN 46135
(317) 658-4006
http://www.depauw.edu

While DePauw has no specific official list for pre-college reading, Dr. Martha Rainbolt, Department of English, says, "clearly in this area, more is better. The more a student has read the better will be that individual's reading and writing skills.... I would recommend that students read everything they possibly can, and I would include in my list magazines and newspapers as well as books."

Dr. Rainbolt has two unofficial lists that she gives to students at DePauw who ask what they should read. She recommends their "beginning with the 19th-century British fiction. These works will impress a magnificent syntax and vocabulary on the minds of their readers, so the 'right' way to write sentences will be in the ears of the readers of those books."

On the unofficial list are

19th-Century British Novels

Austen, Jane	*Emma*; *Pride and Prejudice*
Brontë, Charlotte	*Jane Eyre*
Brontë, Emily	*Wuthering Heights*
Butler, Samuel	*The Way of All Flesh*
Dickens, Charles	*Bleak House*; *Great Expectations*
Eliot, George	*Middlemarch*; *The Mill on the Floss*
Hardy, Thomas	*Jude The Obscure*; *Tess of the D'Urbervilles*
Meredith, George	*The Egoist*
Scott, Sir Walter	*The Heart of Midlothian*
Thackeray, William Makepeace	*Vanity Fair*
Trollope, Anthony	*Barchester Towers*

British Novels Other Than 19th-Century

Beerbohm, Max	*Zuleika Dobson*
Bennett, Arnold	*The Old Wives' Tale*
Conrad, Joseph	*Lord Jim; Nostromo*
Defoe, Daniel	*Moll Flanders*
Durrell, Lawrence	*The Alexandria Quartet*
Fielding, Henry	*Joseph Andrews; Tom Jones*
Ford, Ford Madox	*The Good Soldier*
Forster, E.M.	*A Passage to India*
Galsworthy, John	*The Forsyte Saga*
Huxley, Aldous	*Point Counter Point*
Joyce, James	*A Portrait of the Artist as a Young Man; Ulysses*
Lawrence, D.H.	*Sons and Lovers; The Rainbow*
Orwell, George	*1984*
Powell, Anthony	*A Dance to the Music of Time*
Richardson, Samuel	*Clarissa*
Smollett, Tobias	*Humphrey Clinker*
Sterne, Laurence	*Tristram Shandy*
Waugh, Evelyn	*A Handful of Dust*
Wells, H.G.	*Tono-Bungay*
Woolf, Virginia	*Mrs. Dalloway; To the Lighthouse*

American Novels

Cather, Willa	*My Antonia*
Crane, Stephen	*The Red Badge of Courage*
Dos Passos, John	*U.S.A.*
Dreiser, Theodore	*An American Tragedy; Sister Carrie*
Faulkner, William	*Light in August; The Sound and the Fury*
Fitzgerald, F. Scott	*Tender is the Night; The Great Gatsby*
Hawthorne, Nathaniel	*The Scarlet Letter*
Heller, Joseph	*Catch-22*
Hemingway, Ernest	*A Farewell to Arms; The Sun Also Rises*
Howells, William Dean	*The Rise of Silas Lapham*
James, Henry	*The Ambassadors; The Portrait of a Lady*

Kesey, Ken	*One Flew over the Cuckoo's Nest*
Lewis, Sinclair	*Babbitt*
Melville, Herman	*Moby-Dick*
Steinbeck, John	*The Grapes of Wrath*
Twain, Mark	*The Adventures of Huckleberry Finn*
Wharton, Edith	*The Age of Innocence*
Wolfe, Thomas	*Look Homeward, Angel*

Other Novels

Balzac, Honoré de	*Lost Illusions; Père Goriot*
Camus, Albert	*The Plague*
Cervantes, Miguel de	*Don Quixote*
Dostoevski, Fyodor	*Crime and Punishment; The Brothers Karamazov*
Flaubert, Gustave	*Madame Bovary; A Sentimental Education*
Gide, André	*The Counterfeiters*
Goethe, Johann von	*The Sorrows of Young Werther*
Gogol, Nikolai	*Dead Souls*
Goncharov, Ivan	*Oblomov*
Grass, Gunter	*The Tin Drum*
Hugo, Victor	*Les Misérables*
Kafka, Franz	*The Trial*
Laclos, Choderlos de	*Les Liaisons Dangereuses*
Lermontov, Mikhail	*A Hero of Our Time*
Malraux, André	*Man's Fate*
Mann, Thomas	*Buddenbrooks; The Magic Mountain*
Manzoni, Alessandro	*The Betrothed*
Montherlant, Henry de	*The Bachelors*
Murasaki, Lady	*The Tale of Genji*
Musil, Robert	*The Man Without Qualities*
Pasternak, Boris	*Doctor Zhivago*
Proust, Marcel	*Remembrance of Things Past*
Rolvaag, O.E.	*Giants in the Earth*
Silone, Ignazio	*Bread and Wine*
Solzhenitsyn, Alexander	*The First Circle*
Stendhal	*The Charterhouse of Parma; The Red and the Black*

Svevo, Italo	*The Confessions of Zeno*
Tanizaki, Junichiro	*The Makioka Sisters*
Tolstoy, Leo	*Anna Karenina; War and Peace*
Turgenev, Ivan	*Fathers and Sons*
Undsett, Sigrid	*Kristin Lavransdatter*
Voltaire	*Candide*
Zola, Émile	*Germinal*

Great Satires

Austen, Jane	*Northanger Abbey*
Carroll, Lewis	*Alice's Adventures in Wonderland*
Cervantes, Miguel de	*Don Quixote*
Fielding, Henry	*Tom Jones*
Heller, Joseph	*Catch-22*
Kesey, Ken	*One Flew Over the Cuckoo's Nest*
Orwell, George	*Animal Farm* or *1984*
Swift, Jonathan	*Gulliver's Travels*
Updike, John	*Rabbit, Run*
Vonnegut, Kurt	*Player Piano*

Duke University
2138 Campus Drive
Box 90586
Durham, NC 27708
(919) 684-8111
http://www.duke.edu

First-year students at Duke are offered a number of introductory-level seminars. Some examples of the texts required are the following:

In the seminar "Escape to Paris: Expatriate American Women Writers," books have included **Margaret Anderson**, *The Little Review Anthology*; **Djuna Barnes**, *Nightwood, Smoke*; **Janet Flanner**, *Men and Monuments*, Selections of "Letters from Paris"; **Gertrude Stein**, *Melanctha, The Autobiography of Alice B. Toklas*, "Picasso"; **H.D.**, *Hermione.*

Readings in "English Modernism" have included **T.S. Eliot**, "The Waste Land"; **D.H. Lawrence**, *Aaron's Rod*; selections from **John Galsworthy**, *The Forsyte Saga*; **Thomas Hardy**, *Late Lyrics and Earlier*; **James Joyce**, *Ulysses*; **Bronislaw Malinowski**, *The Argonauts of the Western Pacific*; *The Newboldt Report*; **Michael North**, *Reading 1922*; **Ludwig Wittgenstein**, *Tractatus Logico-Philosophicus*; **W.B. Yeats**, *Later Poems*; and **Virginia Woolf**, *Jacob's Room*.

Some texts in "Broken Homes in American Literature" have included **James Baldwin**, *Another Country*; **Charles W. Chesnutt**, *The Marrow of Tradition*; **Kate Chopin**, *The Awakening*; **Edith Wharton**, *Summer*; **William Faulkner**, *Absalom, Absalom!*; **Gayl Jones**, *Corregidora*; **Toni Morrison**, *Sula*; and selections from **Ann Ferguson**, **Robin D.G. Kelley**, **Audre Lorde**, **Wahneema Lubiano**, or **Jana Sawicki**.

"Literature and Decolonization" is a seminar introducing the student to "post-colonial" writing—writing from nations that have been colonized and then have achieved a degree of independence. Texts for the course may include works of the following authors: from Ireland: **Elizabeth Bowen**, **James Joyce**, **Flann O'Brien**, **J.M. Synge**, **W.B. Yeats**; from South Africa: **J.M. Coetzee**, **Nadine Gordimer**, **Bessie Head**, **Alex La Guma**, **Lewis Nkosi**; and from the Caribbean: **Michelle Cliff**, **Wilson Harris**, **George Lamming**, **Mustapha Matura**, and **Derek Walcott**.

The reading list for "Renaissance Theatricalism" includes **Anonymous**, *Hic-Mulier*; **Francis Beaumont**, *The Knight of the Burning Pestle*; **Stephen Gosson**, *Playes Confuted in Five Actions*; **Andrew Gurr**, *The Shakespearean Stage*; **Ben Jonson**, *Bartholomew Fair*; **William Shakespeare**, *Coriolanus*; **Phillip Sidney**, *A Defense of Poesy*.

For "Pleasures of the Text: Sexuality and American Culture," required readings are **Dorothy Allison**, from *Trash*; **James Baldwin**, *Giovanni's Room*; **Ann Bannon**, *Beebo Brinker*; **Emily Dickinson**, selected poetry; **Essex Hemphill**, "Heavy Breathing"; **Henry James**, "Beast in the Jungle"; **Sarah Orne Jewett**, "The Queen's Twin"; **Erica Jong**, *Fear of Flying*; **Audre Lorde**, *Zami*; **Vladimir Nabokov**, *Lolita*; **Andy Warhol**, selections from various medias.

In "The Fairy Tale," readings include selected medieval Robin Hood ballads and plays; **Geoffrey Chaucer**, "The Wife of Bath's Prologue and Tale" and

"The Clerk's Tale"; selections from *The Golden Legend*; the *Lais of Marie de France*; *Sir Gawain and the Green Knight*; *Sir Orfeo*; **Galland**'s translation of the *Arabian Nights Entertainment*; and fairy tales from the collections of **Perrault**, the **Grimm brothers**, and **Hans Christian Anderson.**

"The Pleasures of Genre: Studies in American Popular Fiction" includes some of the following readings: **Louisa Mae Alcott**, *Little Women*; **Horatio Alger**, *Ragged Dick*; **Octavia Butler**, *Kindred*; **Jack Finney**, *Invasion of the Body Snatchers*; **Stephen King**, *Carrie*; **Thomas Harris**, *The Silence of the Lambs*; **Edgar Allan Poe**, *The Murders in the Rue Morgue*, *Ligeia*, and *Berenice*; and selections from **Roland Barthes, Carol Clover, John G. Cawleti, Dashiell Hammett, Fannie Hurst, Jam Radwau**, and **Nora Roberts.**

In "American Women Writers," novels are likely to be selected from Louisa Mae Alcott, *Little Women*; Willa Cather, *My Antonia*; Zora Neale Hurston, *Their Eyes Were Watching God*; Nella Larsen, *Passing*; Gertrude Stein, *Three Lives*; Edith Wharton, *The Age of Innocence*; and short stories by Kate Chopin, Sui-Sin Far, Zitkala-Sa, and Katherine Anne Porter.

Some texts studied in "London Calling: Literature and the Great City" include works by Sir Arthur Conan Doyle, Charles Dickens, T.S. Eliot, Hanif Kureishi, Doris Lessing, Oscar Wilde, Virginia Woolf, and William Wordsworth.

Duquesne University
600 Forbes Avenue
Pittsburgh, PA 15282
(412) 396-6000
http://www.duq.edu

Two introductory classes at Duquesne help freshman learn to think about, write about, and discuss literature. Anthologies are used in these classes rather than single author texts. The required texts are **Blanche Ellsworth**'s *English Simplified* and **Kelly Griffith Jr.**'s *Writing Essays About Literature: A Guide and Style Sheet.* In addition they use two of the following anthologies:

Bain, C.E., Jerome Beaty, and J.P. Hunter	*The Norton Introduction to Literature* (4th ed.)
Behrens, Laurence and Leonard Rosen	*Theme and Variations: The Impact of Great Ideas*
Diyanni, Robert	*Literature: Reading Fiction, Poetry, Drama, and the Essay*
Guerin, Wilfred, et al.	*Lit: Literature and Interpretive Techniques*
Jacobus, Lee A.	*A World of Ideas: Essential Reading for College Writers*
Perrine, Laurence and Thomas Arp	*Literature: Structure, Sound, and Sense*

> **American University**: Imagine you are the editor of a major national news magazine. Write the cover story you would choose for the issue that would be on the newsstands January 1, 2010.

Elizabethtown College
1 Alpha Drive
Elizabethtown, PA 17022
(717) 367-1000
http://www.etown.edu

According to Dr. John A. Campbell, Jr., Department of English, at Elizabethtown all freshmen are required to take the "Introduction to Literature" course, which is "designed to enhance the students' ability to analyze, evaluate, and appreciate literature through the study of several classic and traditional masterworks." The students are introduced to "basic concepts, themes, and world views and trained in the application of literary terms and concepts to enhance reading and writing skills…and sharpen their ability in critical thinking." Required texts for the course include

Hardy, Thomas	*Tess of the D'Urbervilles*
Homer	*The Iliad* (Rouse, tr.)
Perrine, Laurence, ed.	*Sound and Sense*

Shakespeare, William (Cyrus Hoey, ed.)	*Hamlet*
Sophocles	*The Oedipus Cycle* (Fitts and Fitzgerald, tr.)

Emory University
1380 Oxford Road NE
Atlanta, GA 30322
(404) 727-6123
http://www.emory.edu

Throughout its departments, Emory has a number of freshman seminars to help entering students develop their reading, writing, and research skills. The following four seminars have been offered by the English Department:

In "Censorship and Literature, Film, and Art" the texts have included works by **Vladimir Nabokov**, **J.D. Salinger**, **Allen Ginsberg**, **Salman Rushdie**, **Ngugi wa Thiong'o**, **Taslima Nasrin**, **Robert Mapplethorpe**, and the films *Pinky*, *Birth of a Nation*, and *Bonnie and Clyde.*

The focus in "Literature and Politics" is on problems of state that are reflected in literature. The texts include

Achebe, Chinua	*A Man of the People*
Atwood, Margaret	*The Handmaid's Tale*
Barnes, Julian	*The Porcupine*
Coetzee, J.M.	*Waiting for the Barbarians*
Gordimer, Nadine	*July's People*
Orwell, George	*1984*
Shakespeare, William	*Julius Caesar; Antony and Cleopatra*
Shaw, George Bernard	*Caesar and Cleopatra*

"Collecting Cultures" is about the pleasures and dangers as well as the politics and psychology of collecting. Some of the texts have been about **Tippi Hedren**'s role in the Hitchcock film *Marnie* and **John Fowles'** *The Collector.*

Byatt, A.S.	*Angels and Insects*
Chatwin, Bruce	*Utz*
Fowles, John	*The Collector*
Jonson, Ben	*Bartholomew Fair*

Also read are excerpts from **Charles Darwin** and **Captain James Cook**, and course packets with readings from **Sigmund Freud**, **Michel Foucault**, **Jean Baudrillard**, and others.

In "The Novel and The Female Imagination," students examine four novels authored by women controversial in their own time:

Behn, Aphra	*Oroonoko*
Brontë, Emily	*Wuthering Heights*
Shelley, Mary	*Frankenstein*
Stowe, Harriet Beecher	*Uncle Tom's Cabin*

The Philosophy department has several sections of "Introduction to Philosophy" courses, which are for freshmen only. The texts in these courses include

Beauchamp, Blackstone, and Feinberg, eds.	*Philosophy and the Human Condition*
Camus, Albert	*The Plague*

Also read are selections from the works of **René Descartes**, **David Hume**, **Friedrich Nietzsche**, **Plato**, and **Jean-Paul Sartre**.

One of the Psychology department's freshman seminars is "Understanding Human Behavior: Experience and Brain Content." The texts are

Erikson, E.H.	*Young Man Luther* (1958); *Childhood and Society* (1963)
Damasio, A.R.	*Descartes' Error: Emotion, Reason and the Human Brain*

A Classics department seminar is called "Hell, Nowhere and Outer Space: Science Fiction and Fantasy from Homer to *Star Trek: Voyager*." Sample readings are

Dante	*Inferno*
Homer	*The Odyssey*

Herodotus	*The Histories*
Lucian	*A True Story*
Swift, Jonathan	*Gulliver's Travels*

Sample films are *Alien* and *Apollo 13*, the TV series *Star Trek* and and *Star Trek: Voyager* are also studied.

"Sex and Love in Greece and Rome" is the title of another Classics department seminar where the texts include

Aristophanes	*Lysistrata* (Bing and Cohen, tr.)
Ovid	The Erotic Poems
Halperin, Winkler, and Zeitlin eds.	*Before Sexuality*
Petronius	*Satyrica* (Branham and Kinney, tr.)
Plato	*Symposium*

Selections from Homer, Vergil, and others

"Conservation Biology" is the title of the Biology department's freshman seminar. It deals with the preservation and restoration of biological diversity in ecosystems. The text is *Conservation and Biodiversity* by **Andrew P. Dobson.**

"Thinking Mathematically," an Educational Studies seminar, focuses on "the mathematical thinking processes of specializing, generalizing, conjecturing, and justifying, rather than on any particular branch of mathematics." The purpose is to increase students' potential for creative mathematical thinking. Texts include

Mason, J., with L. Burton and K. Stacey	*Thinking Mathematically* (revised edition)
Stevenson, F.W.	*Exploratory Problems in Mathematics*

Another Educational Studies department seminar, "Understanding the Cultural Other," studies the meaning of culture, its influence on the "self" and "the other." For this seminar the text is *Deculturalization and the Struggle for Equality* by **J. Spring.**

"Education and Culture" is a third Educational Studies department seminar. It explores theories of culture and education. Texts include

Grant, C.A., ed.	*Educating for Diversity: An Anthology of Multicultural Voices*
MacLeod, J.	*Ain't No Makin' It: Aspirations and Attainment in a Low-Income Neighborhood*

In the Religion department seminar "Science Fiction as Religion and Irreligion," students explore the point of view Ursula K. LeGuin has expressed that "Science fiction is the mythology of the modern world." Fiction and non-fiction texts assigned are

Asimov, Isaac	*The Foundation Series*
Clarke, A.C.	*Childhood's End*
Keller, E.F. and H.E. Longino, eds.	*Feminism and Science*
Kreuziger, F.A.	*The Religion of Science Fiction*
LeGuin, U.K.	*The Dispossessed*
Reilly, R. ed.	*The Transcendent Adventure: Studies of Religion in Science Fiction/Fantasy*
Shelley, Mary	*Frankenstein*
Snow, C.P.	*The Two Cultures*

The Religion department also offers the seminar "Christianity For and Against Medicine," which takes up different points in Christianity's engagement with medicine. The primary texts include, among others, the *Gospels* of **Mark** and **Luke**; early and modern miracle collections; church laws and Inquisition cases on contraception; **Pope Paul VI**, *Humanae Vitae* (*On the Regulation of Births*); **Richard L. Smith**, *AIDS, Gays, and the Catholic Church*; and **Stanley Hauerwas**, *God, Medicine, and Suffering.*

The Russian department's seminar "War and Peace" examines the concepts of war and peace as reflected in Russian art, music, film, and literature in four periods of Russian history. The texts are *The Lay of Igor's Campaign*, *The Red Calvary*, **Leo Tolstoy**, *War and Peace*, **Boris Pasternak**, *Dr. Zhivago*, and selected short stories from the W.W. II and Afgan/Chechen conflicts.

In the Music Department seminar "We Sing Ourselves," students explore the significance of popular music in the making and expression of consciousness and feeling. Books may include

Allison, Dorothy	*Bastard Out of Carolina*
George, Nelson	*Hip Hop America*
White, Timothy	*The Nearest Faraway Place*
Wright, Richard	*Black Boy*

The texts in the Music department's "Performing Music" seminar include

Dunsby, Jonathan	*Performing Music: Shared Concerns*
Sherman, Bernard D.	*Inside Early Music: Conversations with Performers*
Small, Christopher	*Musicking: The Meanings of Performing and Listening*
Taruskin, Richard	*Text and Act: Essays on Music and Performance*

"Narratives of Asian America," an Interdisciplinary Studies seminar, is concerned with fictional and non-fictional accounts of the experience of Asian immigrants and Asian-descended people in North America. Materials include autobiography, family history, fiction, poetry, journalism, and film by and about Asian Americans such as **Maxine Hong Kingston**, **Carlos Bulosan**, **Ronald Takaki**, **Trinh Minh-ha**, **Arthur Dong**, and others.

Text for an Italian department seminar called "Dante's Divine and Human Comedy" is **The Divine Comedy** by **Dante Alighieri**, a verse translation by Allen Mandelbaum.

The Physics department seminar "Envisioning Light" concerns understanding light and vision from the scientific and the human viewpoints. One of the texts is **Sidney Perkowitz**, *Empire of Light.*

Florida Institute of Technology
150 West University Boulevard
Melbourne, FL 32901-6975
(321) 674-8000
http://www.fit.edu

Beginning students at Florida Institute of Technology take a humanities course called "The Human Imperative." Texts vary according to the theme of the particular class, and in some classes film and texts are combined to stimulate discussion and writing. The following include the books and films that have been used in some of the sections:

I. Texts

Clark, Brian	*Whose Life Is It Anyway?*
Hellman, Lillian	*The Little Foxes*
Ibsen, Henrik	*An Enemy of the People* (Miller adaptation)
Miller, Arthur	*All My Sons*
Rabe, David	*Sticks and Bones*
Shaffer, Peter	*Amadeus; Equus*
Simon, Neil	*Plaza Suite*
Williams, Tennessee	*The Glass Menagerie*

I. Films

All My Sons; Amadeus; Cocoon; Equus; The Glass Menagerie; Hearts and Minds; The Little Foxes; Plaza Suite

II. Texts

Barrett, William	*The Illusion of Technique*
Eliade, Mircea	*The Sacred and the Profane*
Percy, Walker	*The Thanatos Syndrome*

II. Films

The Elephant on the Hill; The Gods Must Be Crazy

III. Texts

Eliot, T.S.	*T.S. Eliot: Selected Poems*
Hesse, Herman	*Magister Ludi: The Glass Bead Game*
West, Nathanael	*Miss Lonelyhearts* and *The Day of the Locust*

IV. Texts

Auel, Jean	*The Clan of the Cave Bear*
Capra, Fritjof	*The Turning Point: Science, Society, and the Rising Culture*
Herr, Michael	*Dispatches*

Florida State University
Tallahassee, FL 32306
(850) 644-2525
http://www.fsu.edu

Florida State has compiled a Suggested Reading List for High School Students, which includes selected poetry from **Robert Browning; George Gordon; Lord Byron; e.e. cummings; Emily Dickinson; John Donne; T.S. Eliot; Robert Frost; John Milton; Alfred, Lord Tennyson; Walt Whitman; William Wordsworth**; and **William Butler Yeats**. In addition the following works are listed:

Austen, Jane	*Pride and Prejudice* or *Sense and Sensibility*
Carroll, Lewis	*Alice's Adventures in Wonderland*
Chaucer, Geoffrey	*The Canterbury Tales*
Dickens, Charles	*Great Expectations* or *Oliver Twist*
Faulkner, William	*The Hamlet* or *Light in August*
Fitzgerald, F. Scott	*The Great Gatsby*
Hardy, Thomas	*Jude the Obscure* or *Tess of the D'Urbervilles*
Hawthorne, Nathaniel	*The Scarlet Letter*
Hemingway, Ernest	*The Old Man and the Sea* or *The Sun Also Rises*
Lee, Harper	*To Kill A Mockingbird*
Lessing, Doris	*Martha Quest*
Olds, Sharon	*The Gold Cell*
Shakespeare, William	*MacBeth*; *Romeo and Juliet*
Thoreau, Henry David	*Walden* ("Economy" or whole book)
Twain, Mark	*The Adventures of Huckleberry Finn*
Vonnegut, Kurt	*Breakfast of Champions*
Walker, Alice	*The Color Purple*
Wright, Richard	*Black Boy*

Fordham University
441 East Fordham Road
Bronx, NY 10458
(718) 817-1000
http://www.fordham.edu

Fordham's freshman core literature course is a survey of English literature from the early 18th century to the 20th century. Professor Philip Sicker of the Department of English lists the following works as being among those frequently taught in the course:

Blake, William	*Songs of Innocence and Experience*
Browning, Robert	Dramatic monologues
Coleridge, Samuel Taylor	"The Rime of the Ancient Mariner"
Conrad, Joseph	*Heart of Darkness*
Eliot, T.S.	"The Love Song of J. Alfred Prufrock"
Swift, Jonathan	*Gulliver's Travels*
Wordsworth, William	Early lyrics

Marquette University: Choose four objects to represent the human experience in today's society. What four objects would you choose and why?

Gallaudet University
800 Florida Ave. NE
Washington, DC 20002
(202) 651-5000
http://www.gallaudet.edu

Professor of English Nancy E. Kensicki, D.A., writes that "since most of our students are not native speakers of English (American sign language is their first language), we adapt English as a Second Language techniques to teach them.... Students [in the English Language Program] must pass our developmental English courses before they are allowed to register for Freshman English." The following reading list was developed for pre-college students at Gailaudet, the only liberal arts institution of higher learning for the deaf and hearing-impaired in the United States.

	Basic Lessons (in-house "grammar" lessons)
	Word Families (in-house series of 25 vocabulary lessons)
American Heritage	*English as a Second Language Dictionary*
Azar, Betty Schrampfer	*Fundamentals of English Grammar*; *Basic English Grammar*
Barnell Loft, LTD	*Specific Skills Series*
Canney, Goldberg, and O'Connor	*Working on Words*
Dixson, Robert J.	*Essential Idioms in English*
Educational Design, Inc.	*Reading Attainment Series*
Elbaum, Sandra	*Grammar in Context*
Globe Publishers	*African-American Biographies*; *American Biographies*; *Hispanic Biographies*; *World Biographies*
Hall, Eugene J.	*Building English Sentences*
Harris, Raymond	*Best Short Stories*
Jamestown Publishers	*Comprehension Skills Series*; *Contemporary Reader* (set); *Surprises, More Surprises, Twists, Sudden Turns*
Longman	*Dictionary of Contemporary English*
Margulies, Stuart and Caleb E. Crowell	*Readings in Cultural Literacy*
New Readers Press	"News for You" (weekly newspaper)
Niemet, Cathy	*Viewpoints*
Reader's Digest	
Smith, R. Kent and Carole Mohr	*Groundwork for a Better Vocabulary*
Wiener, Harvey and Charles Bazerman	*Side by Side*

Georgetown University
37th and O Streets, Northwest
Washington, DC 20057
(202) 687-5055
http://www.georgetown.edu

In Georgetown's Literature and Writing Workshop, a course for freshmen only, students read "different kinds of texts (both literary and non-literary) organized around a particular intellectual and cultural problem. These readings introduce students to various writing strategies and to the different uses to which writing is put—in different eras, perhaps, or in different cultures, or in different generic forms." The course can count as one of the university's two general education requirements in literature. The following are among the works considered in the various sections of the course:

	The Epic of Gilgamesh
Albee, Edward	*Who's Afraid of Virginia Woolf?*
Angelou, Maya	*I Know Why the Caged Bird Sings*
Aristophanes	A play
Atwood, Margaret	*The Handmaid's Tale*
Beckett, Samuel	*Waiting for Godot*
Bellow, Saul	Selections
Berman, Marshall	*All That Is Solid Melts into Air*
Brecht, Bertolt	*The Threepenny Opera*
Brontë, Charlotte	*Jane Eyre*
Burgess, Anthony	*A Clockwork Orange*
Butler, Samuel	*Erewhon*
Cassill, R.V.	*The Norton Anthology of Short Fiction*
Cheever, John	Selected stories
Chekhov, Anton	*The Three Sisters*
Conrad, Joseph	*Heart of Darkness*
Dick, Philip K.	*Do Androids Dream of Electric Sheep?*
Dickens, Charles	Short story

Doyle, Sir Arthur Conan	Short story
Eliot, George	*The Mill on the Floss*
Faulkner, William	*Go Down, Moses; Light in August*
Fitzgerald, F. Scott	*The Great Gatsby*
Forster, E.M.	*The Aspect of the Novel*
Fox and Lears	*The Culture of Consumption*
Fugard, Athol	*Sizwe Bansi Is Dead*
Gardner, John	*Grendel*
Gaskell, Elizabeth	Short stories
Gay, John	*The Beggar's Opera*
Gilman, Charlotte P.	*The Yellow Wallpaper*
Hardy, Thomas	*The Mayor of Casterbridge*
Hawthorne, Nathaniel	*The Scarlet Letter*
Heilbroner, Robert	*The Nature and Logic of Capitalism*
Hemingway, Ernest	*The Old Man and the Sea*
Hongo, Garrett	*Yellow Light*
Hwang, David Henry	*M. Butterfly*
Ibsen, Henrik	*A Doll's House*
Janowitz, Tama	*Slaves of New York*
Johnson, Owen	*Lawrenceville Stories*
Kafka, Franz	Selections
Kennedy, X.J.	*An Introduction to Poetry*
Kingston, Maxine Hong	*The Woman Warrior*
Kipling, Rudyard	Short stories
Kundera, Milan	*The Unbearable Lightness of Being*
Lawrence, D.H.	*Sons and Lovers*
McInerney, Jay	*Bright Lights, Big City*
Malamud, Bernard	Selections
Melville, Herman	*Billy Budd*
Miller, Arthur	*Death of a Salesman*
More, Sir Thomas	*Utopia*
Morrison, Toni	*Beloved; The Bluest Eye*
O'Connor, Flannery	"A Good Man Is Hard to Find"
Paton, Alan	*Cry, The Beloved Country*
Pinter, Harold	*The Homecoming*

Scholes, Robert	*The Nature of Narrative*
Shakespeare, William	*Hamlet*; *Macbeth*; *Othello*; *The Taming of the Shrew*; *Twelfth Night*
Shange, Ntozake	*for colored girls who have considered suicide when the rainbow is enuf*
Shaw, George Bernard	*Pygmalion*
Shelley, Mary	*Frankenstein*
Sophocles	*Antigone*; *Oedipus Rex*
Stoppard, Tom	*Rosencrantz and Guildenstern Are Dead*
Tolstoy, Leo	*What is Art?*
Updike, John	*Rabbit, Run*; *Rabbit Redux*; *Rabbit is Rich*
Vergil	*The Aeneid*
Vonnegut, Kurt	*God Bless You, Mr. Rosewater*
Warren, Robert Penn	*All the King's Men*
Weiss, Samuel	*Drama in the Modern World*
Wells, H.G.	*The Time Machine*
Welty, Eudora	*Collected Stories*
White, E.B.	*The Once and Future King*
Wicomb, Zoe	*You Can't Get Lost in Capetown*
Wiesel, Elie	*Night*
Wilde, Oscar	Short story
Williams, Tennessee	*Cat on a Hot Tin Roof*
Wister, Owen	*The Virginian*
Wright, Richard	*Native Son*

George Washington University
2121 I Street Northwest
Washington, DC 20052
(202) 994-1000
http://www.gwu.edu

Professor Miriam Dow, Director of the Writing Program at George Washington, says that most instructors for the writing classes "design their own courses and choose their own texts, frequently anthologies." One syllabus consistently used, however, is for a Humanities/Composition course for freshmen. The course "does two related things: it is an exploration of texts that have been recognized as formative of our civilization; it is also a composition course, training students in the techniques of expository and argumentative writing." Texts for the course include **Altshuler** et al., *Western Civilization: An Owner's Manual* and the *Random House Handbook.* Although there are "minor variations among the various instructor teams," the following texts are from a syllabus that is "quite representative."

	Bible (Revised Standard Version). Old Testament: "Genesis" 1–11, "II Samuel" 9–20, "I Kings" 1–2, "Deuteronomy," "Job." New Testament: "Mark," "John," "Romans."
Aeschylus (Grene and Lattimore, eds.)	*Prometheus Bound*
Aristophanes	*The Clouds*
Aristotle	*Nicomachean Ethics*; *Poetics* in *Introduction to Aristotle*
Augustine, Saint	*The Confessions,* books I–X
Cicero	"The Dream of Scipio," *On the Good Life*
Euripides (Grene and Lattimore, eds.)	*Hippolytus*
Mishna and Philo (Kee, ed.)	*The Origins of Christianity: Sources and Documents*
Plato	*The Republic*
Sophocles (Grene and Lattimore, eds.)	*Oedipus the King*
Thucydides	*History of the Peloponnesian War*
Vergil	*The Aeneid,* books I–X

Every aspect of life has been repeatedly defined and explained by authors in books.

Hans Gundersen
High School Political Science Teacher

Hamilton College
198 College Hill Road
Clinton, NY 13323
(315) 859-4011
http://www.hamilton.edu

For its first-year English 200, a writing-intensive course, the Hamilton College English Department requires the following literature texts:

Austen, Jane	*Pride and Prejudice*
Chaucer, Geoffrey	*The Canterbury Tales* (the general prologue and any one of the tales)
Donne, John	Some lyrics and some Holy Sonnets
Gottesman, Ronald	*Norton Anthology of English Literature*, Vol. 1
Milton, John	*Paradise Lost*, books I and IX
Pope, Alexander	"An Essay on Criticism," "An Essay on Man," "The Rape of the Lock"
Shakespeare, William	Many sonnets and one play
Swift, Jonathan	*Gulliver's Travels*, book I or II or IV; or "A Modest Proposal"

In the freshman Writing 100 course, the literature texts vary according to the sections. Among the works studied are

	The Harper & Row Reader
Abrams, M.H.	*A Glossary of Literary Terms*
	Bible (King James Edition): "Matthew"
Bielenberg, Christabel	*Right Out of the Dark*
Bulgakov, Mikhail	*The White Guard*
Cassill, R.V.	*Norton Anthology of Short Fiction*
Cather, Willa	*O Pioneers!*
Comley, Nancy M., et al.	*Fields of Writing: Readings Across the Disciplines*
Dickens, Charles	*Great Expectations*
Didion, Joan	*Slouching Towards Bethlehem*

Doig, Ivan	*This House of Sky*
Dreiser, Theodore	*Sister Carrie*
Emerson, Ralph Waldo	"The American Scholar"
Forster, E.M.	*A Passage to India*
Franklin, Benjamin	*Autobiography*
Kingston, Maxine Hong	*The Woman Warrior*
Kureishi, Hanif	*My Beautiful Laundrette*
Plato	*Apology; The Last Days of Socrates*
Rivera, Edward	*Family Installments*
Rushdie, Salman	*Midnight's Children*
Simon, Kate	*Bronx Primitive*
Thomas, Lewis	*The Lives of a Cell*
Thoreau, Henry David	*Walden*
Woolf, Virginia	*A Room of One's Own*

Harvard University
Byerly Hall, 8 Garden Street
Cambridge, MA 02138
(617) 495-1000
http://www.harvard.edu

Principal Reading sections of Harvard's Bibliography for English Undergraduate Concentrators indicate those literary works regarded as most significant by members of the Tutorial Board and of the Department of English and American Literature and Language. Since 1938, the Harvard English Department has provided a bibliography for Harvard undergraduates. The booklet, most recently revised in 1983, was compiled by a committee consisting of Professors Larry Benson (Chairman), W.J. Bate, Marjorie Garber, Alan Heimert, Walter Kaiser, Elizabeth McKinsey, and David Perkins.

The following are portions of the Principal Reading sections from the various literary periods. Except for the medieval period and the section on the Theory and Criticism of Literature, all authors have been included, but not all specific works. The entire booklet may be purchased from the Harvard University Department of English.

I. The Bible and Classical Backgrounds

Bible

Old Testament: "Genesis," "Exodus," "Judges" 13–16 (Samson), "Ruth," "I Samuel," "Job," "Psalms," "Proverbs" 1–9, "Ecclesiastes," "Isaiah," "Lamentations," "Daniel"

New Testament: The four Gospels, "Acts of the Apostles," "Romans," "I Corinthians," "Hebrews," "James," "Revelations"

Classical Epic

Aristotle	*Poetics*
Homer	*The Iliad*; *The Odyssey*
Vergil	*The Aeneid*

Classical Tragedy

Aeschylus	*Agamemnon*; *Choephoroi*; *Eumenides*; *Prometheus Bound*
Aristotle	*Poetics*
Euripides	*Alcestis*; *Hippolytus*; *Ion*; *Medea*; *The Trojan Women*
Seneca	*Hercules Furens*; *Medea*
Sophocles	*Ajax*; *Antigone*; *Oedipus at Colonus*; *Oedipus Tyrannos*; *Philoctetes*

Classical Comedy

Aristophanes	*The Acharneans*; *The Birds*; *The Clouds*; *The Frogs*; *Lysistrata*
Aristotle	*Poetics*
Menander	*Dyskolos*
Plautus	*Amphitruo*; *Menaechmi*; *Miles Gloriosus*; *Mostellaria*; *Rudens*
Terence	*Andria*; *Heauton Timorumenos*; *Phormio*

Classical Mythology

Aeschylus	*Promethus Bound* (Grene and Lattimore, tr.)
Bulfinch, Thomas	*Mythology* (1947), pp. 1–317

Bush, Douglas	*Mythology and the Renaissance Tradition in English Poetry* (2nd. ed., 1963); *Mythology and the Romantic Tradition in English Poetry*
Catullus	Poems 63 and 64 (Quinn, tr.)
Euripides	*Medea* (Grene and Lattimore, tr.)
Harvey, Sir Paul	*The Oxford Companion to Classical Literature* (1937)
Hesiod	*Works and Days*, 11.1–201
Homer	*The Iliad* I–III, XVI–XXIV (Lattimore, tr.)
Lemprière, J.A.	*Classical Dictionary of Proper Names Mentioned in Ancient Authors*, rev. F.A. Wright (1951)
Ovid	*Metamorphoses* I–VIII, X, XII–XIII (Golding or A.E. Watts, tr.)
Seznec, Jean	*The Survival of the Pagan Gods: The Mythological Tradition and Its Place in Renaissance Humanism and Art* (B.F. Sessions, tr.)
Sophocles	*Oedipus Rex* (Grene and Lattimore, tr.)
Vergil	*The Aeneid* I–VI (Fitzgerald, tr.)

II. English Literature from the Beginning to 1500: Major Medieval English Writers

	Beowulf
	Narrative poems: "The Battle of Brunnanburg," "The Battle of Maldon," "The Dream of the Rood," "The Seafarer," "The Wanderer"
Chaucer, Geoffrey	*The Canterbury Tales*; *Troilus and Criseyde*
The "Gawain" Poet	"Pearl," "Sir Gawain and the Green Knight"
Langland, William	*Piers Plowman, Passus* I–VI, XVII–XIX
Malory, Sir Thomas	"Lancelot and Guenevere," "Le Morte D'Arthur," "The Tale of the Sankgreal," "The Tale of Sir Lancelot"

III. English Literature from 1500 to 1660

Drama (Exclusive of Shakespeare)

Baskerville, C.R., et al.	*Elizabethan and Smart Plays* (1934)
Fraser, R.A. and N. Rabkin, eds.	*Drama of the English Renaissance* (2 vols., 1976)

Listed as Principal Reading in the above texts are two plays by anonymous authors: *Everyman* and *Gammer Gurton's Needle* and plays by **Francis Beaumont**, **Francis Beaumont** and **John Fletcher**, **George Chapman**, **Thomas Dekker**, **John Ford**, **Robert Greene**, **John Heywood**, **Ben Jonson**, **Philip Marlowe**, **John Marston**, **Philip Massinger**, **Thomas Middleton**, **Thomas Sackville** and **Thomas Norton**, **Cyril Tourneur**, **Nicholas Udall**, and **John Webster**.

Drama: Shakespeare, William

Evans, G.B., et al., eds.	*The Riverside Shakespeare* (Most of the Shakespeare plays are considered principal reading.)

Prose

Authors listed in this section are **Roger Ascham**, **Sir Francis Bacon**, **Robert Burton**, **Castiglione**, **Thomas Deloney**, **John Donne**, **Sir Thomas Browne**, **Sir Thomas Elyot**, **Thomas Hobbes**, **Richard Hooker**, **John Lyly**, **John Milton**, **Montaigne**, **Sir Thomas More**, **Sir Philip Sidney**, **Jeremy Taylor**, and **Izaak Walton**.

Poetry (Exclusive of Spenser and Milton)

Broadside Ballads and A *Mirror for Magistrates* are the anonymous works listed in this section. The authors are **Thomas Campion**, **Thomas Carew**, **George Chapman**, **Abraham Cowley**, **Richard Crashaw**, **Samuel Daniel**, **Sir John Davies**, **John Donne**, **Michael Drayton**, **George Gascoigne**, **Robert Greene**, **Fulke Greville**, **George Herbert**, **Robert Herrich**, **Ben Jonson**, **Thomas Lodge**, **Richard Lovelace**, **Christopher Marlowe**, **Andrew Marvell**, **John Milton** ("On the Death of a Fair Infant Dying of a Cough"), **Sir Walter Raleigh**, **William Shakespeare** (sonnets and other lyric poetry are in the text mentioned above), **Sir Philip Sidney**, **John Skelton**, **Robert Southwell**, **Edmund Spenser**, **Sir John Suckling**, **Earl of Surrey**, **Thomas Traherne**, **Henry Vaughan**, **Sir Thomas Wyatt**.

Spenser and Milton

Carey, John and Alistair Fowler, eds.	*The Poems of John Milton* (1968)

Hughes, Merritt Y., ed. (1957)	*John Milton: Complete Poems and Major Prose*
Selincourt, Ernest de and J.D. Smith, eds.	*The Poetical Works of Edmund Spenser* (1926)

IV. English Literature from 1660 to 1790

Restoration and 18th-Century Drama

Authors listed are **Sir Joseph Addison, William Congreve, Sir William Davenant, John Dryden, Sir George Etherege, Henry Fielding, George Farquhar, John Gay, Oliver Goldsmith, Thomas Otway, Richard Brinsley Sheridan, Sir Richard Steele, Sir John Vanbrugh, Sir George Villiers,** and **William Wycherley.**

Restoration and Augustan Literature

In this section, the authors are **Joseph Addison, Daniel Defoe, John Dryden, Bernard Mandeville, Alexander Pope, Earl of Shaftsbury,** and **Jonathan Swift.**

The Age of Johnson

Authors include **William Blake, James Boswell, Edmund Burke, Robert Burns, William Collins, William Cowper, Edward Gibbon, Oliver Goldsmith, Thomas Gray, Samuel Johnson,** and **Joshua Reynolds.**

English Fiction Before 1800

In this section the writers are **William Beckford, Aphra Behn, John Bunyan, Fanny Burney, Daniel Defoe, Thomas Deloney, Henry Fielding, William Godwin, Oliver Goldsmith, Samuel Johnson, M.G. Lewis, Thomas Lodge, Henry Mackenzie, Thomas Nashe, Ann Radcliffe, Samuel Richardson, Tobias Smollett, Laurence Sterne,** and **Horace Walpole.**

V. English Literature from 1790 to 1890

Romantic Poetry

The poets listed are **William Blake, George Gordon, Lord Byron, Samuel Taylor Coleridge, John Keats, Percy Bysshe Shelley, William Wordsworth.**

Victorian Poetry

Poets are **Matthew Arnold, Elizabeth Barrett Browning, Robert Browning, Arthur Hugh Clough, Edward Fitzgerald, Thomas Hardy, Gerard Manley Hopkins, George Meredith, Christina Rossetti, Dante Gabriel Rossetti, Algernon Charles Swinburne**, and **Alfred, Lord Tennyson.**

Fiction

The Principal Reading includes two Dickens novels and one novel by each of seven other authors.

Austen, Jane	*Emma; Pride and Prejudice*
Brontë, Charlotte	*Jane Eyre; Villette*
Brontë, Emily	*Wuthering Heights*
Dickens, Charles	*Bleak House; David Copperfield; Great Expectations; Our Mutual Friend*
Eliot, George	*Middlemarch; The Mill on the Floss*
Hardy, Thomas	*Jude the Obscure; The Mayor of Casterbridge; Tess of the D'Urbervilles*
Meredith, George	*The Egoist; The Ordeal of Richard Feverel*
Scott, Sir Walter	*The Heart of Midlothian*
Thackeray, William Makepeace	*Vanity Fair*
Trollope, Anthony	*Barchester Towers*

Prose

Listed are **Matthew Arnold, Thomas Carlyle, Samuel Taylor Coleridge, Thomas DeQuincey, William Hazlitt, T.H. Huxley, Charles Lamb, John Stuart Mill, J.H. Newman, Walter Pater**, and **John Ruskin.**

VI. American Literature to 1890

Principal Reading includes selections from **Bradford, Bradstreet, John Cotton, Hooker, Cotton Mather, Shepard, Sewall, Taylor, Wigglesworth, Winthrop**, and **Wise** in **Alan Heimert** and **Andrew Delbanco**, *The Puritans in America: A Narrative Anthology* (1985) and **J.F. Cooper, Emily Dickinson, Jonathan Edwards, R.W. Emerson, Benjamin Franklin, Nathaniel**

Hawthorne, William Dean Howells, Henry James, Washington Irving, Herman Melville, Edgar Allen Poe, Henry David Thoreau, Mark Twain, and **Walt Whitman.**

VII. English and American Literature from 1890 to the present

Poetry

Ellman, Richard and Robert O'Clair	*The Norton Anthology of Modern Poetry* (1973)

Principal Reading includes the poets **John Ashbery, W.H. Auden, Hart Crane, e.e. cummings, Walter de la Mare, T.S. Eliot, Robert Frost, Allen Ginsberg, Thom Gunn, Thomas Hardy, Seamus Heaney, Langston Hughes, Ted Hughes, Philip Larkin, D.H. Lawrence, Robert Lowell, Archibald MacLeish, Marianne Moore, Wilfred Owen, Sylvia Plath, Ezra Pound, John Crowe Ransom, E.A. Robinson, Wallace Stevens, Dylan Thomas, W.C. Williams,** and **W.B. Yeats.**

English Fiction

Conrad, Joseph	*Heart of Darkness; Lord Jim; Nostromo*
Ford, Ford Madox	*The Good Soldier*
Forster, E.M.	*Howard's End; A Passage to India*
Hardy, Thomas	*The Mayor of Casterbridge; Tess of the D'Urbervilles*
Joyce, James	*Dubliners; A Portrait of the Artist as a Young Man*
Lawrence, D.H.	*The Rainbow; Sons and Lovers; Women in Love*
Woolf, Virginia	*Mrs. Dalloway; To the Lighthouse*

Drama

Baraka, Imamu Amiri (formerly LeRoi Jones)	*Dutchman*
Beckett, Samuel	*Endgame; Waiting for Godot*
Eliot, T.S.	*The Cocktail Party; The Family Reunion; Murder in the Cathedral*
Miller, Arthur	*Death of a Salesman*
O'Casey, Sean	*Juno and the Paycock; The Plough and the Stars*

O'Neill, Eugene	*Desire Under the Elms; The Hairy Ape; Long Day's Journey Into Night*
Pinter, Harold	*The Birthday Party; The Caretaker*
Shaw, George Bernard	*Caesar and Cleopatra; Heartbreak House; Man and Superman; Saint Joan*
Shepard, Sam	*Angel City*
Stoppard, Tom	*Rosencrantz and Guildenstern Are Dead*
Synge, J.M.	*In the Shadow of the Glen; The Playboy of the Western World; Riders to the Sea*
Thomas, Dylan	*Under Milkwood*
Wilde, Oscar	*The Importance of Being Earnest*
Wilder, Thornton	*Our Town*
Williams, Tennessee	*A Streetcar Named Desire*
Yeats, W.B.	*On Baile's Strand; The Death of Cuchulain; At the Hawk's Well; The Only Jealousy of Emer*

American Prose

Adams, Henry	*The Education of Henry Adams*
Anderson, Sherwood	*Winesburg, Ohio*
Bellow, Saul	*Seize the Day*
Cather, Willa	*My Antonia* or *O Pioneers!*
Chopin, Kate	*The Awakening*
Crane, Stephen	*Maggie; The Red Badge of Courage*; short stories
Dreiser, Theodore	*An American Tragedy* or *Sister Carrie*
Ellison, Ralph	*Invisible Man*
Faulkner, William	*Absalom, Absalom!; The Sound and the Fury*
Fitzgerald, F. Scott	*The Great Gatsby*
Hemingway, Ernest	*A Farewell to Arms* or *The Sun Also Rises*; short stories
James, Henry	*Hawthorne; The Portrait of a Lady*
Mailer, Norman	*The Armies of the Night* or *The Naked and the Dead*
Nabokov, Vladimir	*Lolita* or *Pale Fire*
Norris, Frank	*McTeague* or *The Octopus*
O'Connor, Flannery	*Everything that Rises Must Converge* or *Wise Blood*
Stein, Gertrude	*Composition as Explanation; Three Lives*

Toomer, Jean	*Cane*
Wharton, Edith	*The Age of Innocence* or *The House of Mirth*
Welty, Eudora	*The Golden Apples*; short stories
West, Nathanael	*Miss Lonelyhearts*
Wright, Richard	*Native Son*

Marietta College: Respond to the statement, "We do not read great books, they read us."

Hawaii Pacific College
1164 Bishop Street
Honolulu, HI 96813
(808) 544-0200
http://www.hpu.edu

Introduction to Humanities is a required course for all freshmen at Hawaii Pacific. Not all sections have the same specific readings. One section reads **Peter Weiss**, *Marat/Sade* while others teach the *Sermon on the Mount.* The selections for Dr. Deborah Ross' classes, which follow, are indicative of additional works that are studied.

	Bible: Creation and fall, "Job"
Confucius	*Analects*
Dostoevski, Fyodor	*The Grand Inquisitor on the Nature of Man*
Henderson, Harold	*Introduction to Haiku: An Anthology of Poems and Poets from Basho to Shiki*
Murasaki, Shikibu	*The Tale of Genji*
Orwell, George	*Animal Farm*
Plato	*The Last Days of Socrates*
Shakespeare, William	*Romeo and Juliet*
Sophocles	*Antigone*; *Oedipus Rex*
Yohannan, John D., ed.	*A Treasury of Asian Literature*

Hillsdale College
Hillsdale, MI 49242
(517) 437-7341
http://www.hillsdale.edu

Dr. Peter D. Olson, Chairman of the Department of English at Hillsdale, would urge all pre-college students to become familiar with some if not all of the works on the following High School Reading List that was developed by Hillsdale's English Department:

Classical Antiquity

	Bible: Selections from the Old and New Testaments
Homer	*The Odyssey*
Sophocles	*Oedipus Rex*
Vergil	*The Aeneid*

English Literature

	Beowulf
	Everyman
Brontë, Emily	*Wuthering Heights*
Browning, Robert	Selected dramatic monologues
Chaucer, Geoffrey	*The Canterbury Tales* (selections)
Conrad, Joseph	Selected stories
Dickens, Charles	*A Tale of Two Cities*
Donne, John	Selected poems
Joyce, James	*Dubliners*
Keats, John	Selections
Lawrence, D.H.	Selected stories

Milton,John	*Lycidas* and *Paradise Lost* (selected books)
Pope, Alexander	"The Rape of the Lock"
Shakespeare, William	Selected tragedies, comedies, and sonnets
Swift, Jonathan	"A Modest Proposal," *Gulliver's Travels* (selected books)
White, T.H.	*The Once and Future King*
Wordsworth and Coleridge	*Lyrical Ballads* (selections)

19th-Century Russian Literature

Dostoevsky, Fyodor	*Crime and Punishment*

American Literature

Dickinson, Emily	Selected poems
Eliot, T.S.	"Preludes," "The Love Song of J. Alfred Prufrock"
Faulkner, William	*Go Down, Moses*
Fitzgerald, F. Scott	*The Great Gatsby*
Franklin, Benjamin	*Autobiography*
Frost, Robert	Selected poems
Irving, Washington	Selected tales
James, Henry	*The Turn of the Screw*
Hawthorne, Nathaniel	Selected tales and *The Scarlet Letter*
Hemingway, Ernest	*In Our Time* (selected stories)
Melville, Herman	Selected tales
Poe, Edgar Allan	Selected poems and tales
Steinbeck, John	*The Grapes of Wrath*
Thoreau, Henry David	"On Civil Disobedience" and *Walden* (selections)
Twain, Mark	*The Adventures of Huckleberry Finn*
Whitman, Walt	*Leaves of Grass* (selected poems)

Hofstra University
1000 Fulton Ave.
Hempstead, NY 11549
(800) 463-7872
http://www.hofstra.edu

To graduate from Hofstra, students must pass a Proficiency Test, which is designed to ensure that they "achieve at least minimum competence in writing skills, particularly logic, organization, development, sentence structure, and matters of grammar and usage." According to Dr. Robert B. Sargent, former English Department Chairman, two composition/literature courses help freshmen prepare for the test. Although skill in writing "clear expository prose and…a compelling argument" is a goal of the first course, it "should not obscure other important concerns, such as the writer's proper interest in the truth, in aesthetic and moral determinations, and in the identification and refinement of personal values and beliefs."

Readings for the first course are "a mix of classic and contemporary selections" chosen by the individual instructors. In the second course short critical papers and a research paper are required. Some works that have been taught recently in the second course are

Austen, Jane	*Pride and Prejudice*; *Northanger Abbey*
Bellow, Saul	*Seize the Day*
Chaucer, Geoffrey	*The Canterbury Tales* (selections)
Dostoevski, Fyodor	*Notes from the Underground*
Ellison, Ralph	*Invisible Man*
Grubb, Davis	*Night of the Hunter*
Hawthorne, Nathaniel	*The Scarlet Letter*
Ibsen, Henrik	*An Enemy of the People*
James, Henry	*Washington Square*

Lawrence, D.H.	*Sons and Lovers*
Melville, Herman	*Redburn*
Miller, Arthur	*The Crucible*
Poe, Edgar Allan	*Tales*
Shakespeare, William	*Hamlet; King Lear; Henry IV, Part I*
Swift, Jonathan	*Gulliver's Travels*
Walpole, Horace	*The Castle of Otranto*

Hollins College
7916 Williamson Road
Roanoke, VA 24020
(540) 362-6000
http://www.hollins.edu

Textbooks containing a wide selection of poetry and fiction are used in the freshman writing classes at Hollins according to Dr. Eric Trethewey of the Department of English. Two texts commonly used in these classes are Barbara Drake's Writing Poetry and Janet Burroway's Writing Fiction.

In the literature courses open to freshmen the following are among the titles regularly read:

Angelou, Maya	*I Know Why the Caged Bird Sings*
Austen, Jane	*Pride and Prejudice*
Beagle, Peter	*The Last Unicorn*
Brontë, Charlotte	*Jane Eyre*
Brontë, Emily	*Wuthering Heights*
Homer	*The Odyssey*
Shakespeare, William	*Henry IV Part 1; The Taming of the Shrew*
Welty, Eudora	*The Optimist's Daughter; The Robber Bridegroom*

Holy Names College
3500 Mountain Boulevard
Oakland, CA 94619-1699
(510) 436-1000
http://www.hnc.edu

Required courses for freshmen at Holy Names include a Humanities Core and Freshman Composition. According to Sister Francesca Cabrini, Ph.D., Professor of English, some recent selections for those courses have been:

Humanities

	The Epic of Gilgamesh
Goethe, Johann W. von	*Faust*
Greer, Thomas H., ed.	*Classics of Western Thought*
Plato	*The Republic*
Sophocles	Theban Plays
Van Over, Raymond, ed.	*Sun Songs: Creation Myths from Around the World*

Freshman Composition

Generally an essay collection is chosen and other selections have been:

Anaya, Rudolfo A.	*Bless Me, Ultima*
Angelou, Maya	*I Know Why the Caged Bird Sings*
Kingston, Maxine Hong	*Woman Warrior*
Moffett, James and K.R. McElheny, eds.	*Points of View, Anthology of Short Stories*
Morgan, Edmund S.	*Meaning of Independence: John Adams, George Washington, Thomas Jefferson*
Rodriguez, Richard	*Hunger of Memory: The Education of Richard Rodriguez, an Autobiography*

Northwestern University: What character from an existing book, play, or movie best suggests who you are?

Illinois Wesleyan University
PO Box 2900
Bloomington, IL 61702-2900
(309) 556-1000
http://www.iwu.edu

IWU "SELECT 100" OFFERS BROAD-BASED READING LIST

According to Illinois Wesleyan's News Services, "If anyone asks if you've read any good books lately, and your answer is no, then Illinois Wesleyan University has compiled a reading list for you." Ken Browning, Wesleyan's vice president for business and finance, served as the chairman of the advisory committee that initiated the search for IWU's "Select 100" books. IWU English professor James Plath, who served on the advisory committee, suggests that having the list is like a course in itself, a course he said could be called "Great Books 101."

	Bible
	Koran
	Bhagavad-Gita
Angelou, Maya	*I Know Why The Caged Bird Sings*
Aristotle	*Nichomachean Ethics*
Augustine, Saint	*Confessions of St. Augustine*
Austen, Jane	*Pride and Prejudice*
Beckett, Samuel	*Waiting For Godot*
Bergmann, Barbara	*The Economic Emergence of Women*
Bolles, Richard	*The 1991 What Color Is Your Parachute*
Brontë, Charlotte	*Jane Eyre*
Brown, Dee	*Bury My Heart At Wounded Knee*
Camus, Albert	*The Plague; The Stranger*
Cervantes, Miguel de	*Don Quixote*
Chopin, Kate	*The Awakening*
Confucius	*Analects*

Dante	*Divine Comedy*
Darwin, Charles	*The Origin of Species*
Descartes, René	*Meditations on First Philosophy* and selections
Dickens, Charles	*Great Expectations; A Tale of Two Cities*
Dostoyevski, Fyodor	*The Brothers Karamazov; Crime and Punishment*
Eliot, T.S.	*Selected Poems*
Ellison, Ralph	*Invisible Man*
Faulkner, William	*The Sound and the Fury*
Fitzgerald, F. Scott	*The Great Gatsby*
Freud, Sigmund	*An Outline of Psychoanalysis*
Friedman, Milton	*Capitalism and Freedom*
Frost, Robert	*Poems by Robert Frost*
García Márquez, Gabriel	*One Hundred Years of Solitude*
Gilligan, Carol	*In A Different Time*
Goethe, Johann	*Faust*
Golding, William	*Lord of the Flies*
Hamilton, Alexander, et al.	*The Federalist Papers*
Hawking, Stephen	*A Brief History of Time*
Hawthorne, Nathaniel	*The Scarlet Letter*
Heilbroner, Robert	*The Worldly Philosophers*
Heinlein, Robert	*Stranger in a Strange Land*
Heller, Joseph	*Catch-22*
Hemingway, Ernest	*A Farewell to Arms; The Old Man and the Sea; The Sun Also Rises*
Hersey, John	*Hiroshima*
Hesse, Hermann	*Siddhartha*
Hitler, Adolf	*Mein Kampf*
Homer	*The Iliad; The Odyssey*
Hugo, Victor	*Les Misérables*
Hurston, Zora	*Their Eyes Were Watching God*
Huxley, Aldous	*Brave New World*
Joyce, James	*Portrait of an Artist as a Young Man; Ulysses*
Jung, Carl	*Portable Jung*
Kant, Emmanuel	*Perpetual Peace*
Kafka, Franz	*Basic Kafka*
Knowles, John	*A Separate Peace*

Lewis, David L.	*Kind: A Biography*
Lewis, C.S.	*The Screwtape Letters*
Machiavelli, Niccolò	*The Prince*
Malcolm X and Alex Haley	*The Autobiography of Malcolm X*
Marx, Karl	*The Communist Manifesto*
Melville, Herman	*Moby-Dick*
Mill, John Stuart	*On Liberty*
Miller, Arthur	*Death of a Salesman*
Milton, John	*Paradise Lost*
Nietzsche, Friederich	*Thus Spake Zarathustra*
Orwell, George	*Animal Farm; 1984*
Paton, Alan	*Cry, The Beloved Country*
Peters, Thomas	*In Search of Excellence*
Pirsig, Robert	*Zen and the Art of Motorcycle Maintenance*
Plato	*The Republic*
Rand, Ayn	*The Fountainhead*
Rawls, John	*A Theory of Justice*
Rice, Anne	*Interview with the Vampire*
Salinger, J.D.	*Catcher in the Rye*
Shakespeare, William	*Hamlet; Romeo and Juliet*
Sinclair, Upton	*The Jungle*
Solzhenitsyn, Alexander	*The Gulag Archipelago*
Steinbeck, John	*The Grapes of Wrath*
Stowe, Harriet Beecher	*Uncle Tom's Cabin*
Swift, Jonathan	*Gulliver's Travels*
Thoreau, Henry David	*Walden*
Tolkien, J.R.R.	*Fellowship of the Ring*
Tolstoy, Leo	*War and Peace*
Trumbo, Dalton	*Johnny Got His Gun*
Twain, Mark	*The Adventures of Huckleberry Finn*
Tzu, Lao	*The Art of War; Tao Te Ching*
Vonnegut, Kurt	*Slaughterhouse Five*
Walker, Alice	*The Color Purple*
Whitman, Walt	*Leaves of Grass*
Wiesel, Elie	*Night*
Woods, Donald	*Biko: Cry Freedom*

Woolf, Virginia	*A Room of One's Own*
Wright, Richard	*Native Son*

Washington University: What particular creative work (book, poem, play, film, piece of visual art, musical composition, scientific theory, etc.) has been crucial to the way you see the world and see yourself? Discuss its effect on you.

Indiana University
300 N. Jordan Avenue
Bloomington, IN 47405
(812) 855-4848
http://www.indiana.edu

Prefacing Indiana's list for the pre-college student, the compilers have written "Because college itself in some ways *is* the world of books, this list of 114 books for pre-college reading is offered with the hope it will help you get a head start. It is a list selected by a group of Indiana University faculty members and recommended to the high school student who wishes to prepare himself to do well in college.

"The books on the list are extremely varied. Some are fanciful (*Alice's Adventures in Wonderland*); some are informative (*Gods, Graves, and Scholars*); some are great early novels (*Gulliver's Travels*); and some are more recent (*The Sun Also Rises*). We do not intend to imply that these are the only books worth reading or that all are equally valuable. We mean, rather, to suggest that these books, taken together, represent a solid intellectual foundation for a college education. Like any reading list, these books can only point the way."

114 Books for Pre-College Reading

Adams, Henry	*The Education of Henry Adams*
Adler, Irving	*How Life Began*
The American Assembly	*The Population Dilemma*

Anderson, A.R.	*Minds and Machines*
Asimov, Isaac	*The Genetic Code*
Augustine, Saint	*Confessions*
Austen, Jane	*Pride and Prejudice*
Ballou, Robert O., ed.	*The Portable World Bible*
Bellamy, Edward	*Looking Backward*
Benedict, Ruth	*Patterns of Culture*
Benet, Stephen Vincent	*John Brown's Body*
Bowen, Catherine D.	*Yankee from Olympus*
Brinton, Crane	*Ideas and Men: The Story of Western Thought*
Brogan, D.W.	*The American Character*
Brown, Harrison	*The Challenge of Man's Future*
Brown, Robert McAfee	*Observer in Rome*
Buckingham, Walter	*Automation: Its Impact on Business and People*
Bulfinch, Thomas	*Mythology*
Bunyan, John	*The Pilgrim's Progress*
Camus, Albert	*The Stranger*
Carroll, Lewis	*Alice's Adventures in Wonderland*
Carson, Rachel	*The Sea Around Us*
Cather, Willa	*Death Comes for the Archbishop*
Catton, Bruce	*A Stillness at Appomattox*
Ceram, C.W.	*Gods, Graves, and Scholars*
Chase, Stuart	*The Tyranny of Words*
Churchill, Winston	*A History of the English-Speaking Peoples*
Clark, Walter Van T.	*The Ox-Bow Incident*
Commager and Nevins	*Freedom, Loyalty, and Dissent*
Conant, James B.	*Modern Science and Modern Man*
Conrad, Joseph	*Lord Jim*
Courant and Robbins	*What is Mathematics?*
Crane, Stephen	*The Red Badge of Courage*
Curie, Eve	*Madame Curie*
Darwin, Charles	*Autobiography*
Davis, Elmer	*But We Were Born Free*
Dickens, Charles	*David Copperfield*
Dostoevski, Fyodor	*Crime and Punishment*
Dreiser, Theodore	*An American Tragedy*

Durant, Will	*The Story of Philosophy*
Edmonds, Walter D.	*Drums Along the Mohawk*
Faulkner, William	*Three Famous Short Novels*
Franklin, Benjamin	*Autobiography*
Frost, Robert	*Poems*
Galbraith, John K.	*The Affluent Society*
Gardner, Martin, ed.	*Great Essays in Science*
Gilson, Etienne	*God and Philosophy*
Golding, William	*Lord of the Flies*
Goldwater and Treves	*Artists on Art*
Gombrich, Ernst H.	*The Story of Art*
Hamilton, Alexander, et al.	*On the Constitution* (selections from *The Federalist Papers*)
Hardy, Thomas	*The Return of the Native*
Hawthorne, Nathaniel	*The Scarlet Letter*
Heilbronner, Robert	*The Worldly Philosophers*
Hemingway, Ernest	*The Sun Also Rises*
Hersey, John	*Hiroshima*
Highet, Gilbert	*The Art of Teaching*
Hofstadter, Richard	*The American Political Tradition*
Housman, A.E.	*A Shropshire Lad*
Hoyle, Fred	*The Nature of the Universe*
Hugo, Victor	*Les Misérables*
Huxley, Julian	*Man in the Modern World*
James, William	*The Varieties of Religious Experience*
Joyce, James	*A Portrait of the Artist as a Young Man*
Kasuer and Newman	*Mathematics and the Imagination*
Kitto, H.D.F.	*The Greeks*
Koestler, Arthur	*Darkness at Noon*
Ley, Willy	*The Conquest of Space*
Lomax, Louis E.	*The Negro Revolt*
Lucretius	*On the Nature of Things*
Lynd and Lynd	*Middletown, U.S.A.*
McNeill, William	*The Rise of the West*
Maeterlinck, Maurice	*The Life of the Bee*
Mann, Thomas	*The Magic Mountain*; *Buddenbrooks*

Maugham, Somerset	*Of Human Bondage*
Mead, Margaret	*New Lives for Old*
Melville, Herman	*Moby-Dick*
Mill, John Stuart	*On Liberty*
Muller, Herbert J.	*The Uses of the Past*
Orwell, George	*Animal Farm*
Parkman, Francis	*The Oregon Trail*
Paton, Alan	*Cry, The Beloved Country*
Pepys, Samuel	*Diary*
Pevsner, Nikolaus	*An Outline of European Architecture*
Poe, Edgar Allan	*Poems and Selected Tales*
Proust, Marcel	*Swann's Way*
Rawlings, Marjorie K.	*The Yearling*
Reade, Charles	*The Cloister and the Hearth*
Russell, Bertrand	*The ABC of Relativity*
St. Exupéry, Antoine de	*Wind, Sand, and Stars*
Sandburg, Carl	*Harvest Poems*
Schweitzer, Albert	*Out of My Life and Thought*
***Scientific American*, eds.**	*New Chemistry; The Planet Earth; The Physics and Chemistry of Life: The Universe*
Shakespeare, William	*Hamlet; Henry IV, Part I; Julius Caesar; MacBeth; Othello; Romeo and Juliet;* Selections from sonnets
Shaw, Bernard	*Arms and the Man; Caesar and Cleopatra; Candida; Major Barbara; Man and Superman; Pygmalion; Saint Joan*
Snow, C.P.	*The New Men*
Steffens, Lincoln	*Autobiography of Lincoln Steffens*
Steinbeck, John	*The Grapes of Wrath*
Swift, Jonathan	*Gulliver's Travels*
Thackeray, William Makepeace	*Vanity Fair*
Thoreau, Henry David	*Civil Disobedience; Walden*
Tocqueville, Alexis de	*Democracy in America*
Turgenev, Ivan	*Fathers and Sons*
Twain, Mark	*The Adventures of Huckleberry Finn*
Veblen, Thorstein	*The Theory of the Leisure Class*

Ward, Barbara	*The Rich Nations and the Poor Nations*
Wedgwood, C.V.	*Truth and Opinion*
Whitehead, Alfred North	*Science and the Modern World*
Whitman, Walt	*Leaves of Grass*
Wilder, Thornton	*Three Plays*
Williams, Oscar, ed.	*A Pocket Book of Modern Verse*
Wolfe, Thomas	*Look Homeward, Angel*
Yutang, Lin	*The Wisdom of China and India*
Zinsser, Hans	*Rats, Lice, and History*

You should go to a book, any book, without reverence or intimidation. Go for either pleasure or profit. Let it engage you if it can and wherever it can. If you find no hook in it, drop it. That says nothing necessarily one way or the other either about the book or yourself, except that the two were not ready for each other. Later they might be. If so, wait for that time to come whenever it may be. You should come cold, so to speak, and see if there are any attachments to your experience that challenge, interest, or illuminate it. If you are lucky enough to have a teacher who knows the literature well and can in a more or less Socratic fashion tease out by question and discussion more understanding than you thought you were capable of, fine. But even a good teacher cannot be a midwife if there is no pregnancy.

Good literature vastly broadens one's vocabulary and enriches ones language, imagination, and consequently one's ability to think. Words, significant symbols, and the range of them are the chief things which separate humans from animals. Language is like the focusing lens of a camera. The finer the lens, (the more extensive your vocabulary), the more precisely you can focus, get crisper resolution, and both sharper contrasts as well as shades of gradation. The more one can say what one means and have it received as one intends it, the more one can understand someone else. Or analyze the components of a problem to where it might be capable of solution.

Charles W. Phillips
Unitarian Minister, Writer

University of Indianapolis
1400 East Hanna Avenue
Indianapolis, IN 46227-3697
(317) 788-3368
http://www.uindy.edu

To members of the U of I's English Department the following are the "Top 100 Books." The list is offered to students preparing for college and to readers of all ages. It represents a variety of tastes and students are not expected to read every work listed. According to Dr. Charlotte Templin, Department Chair, "In Robert Herrick's words, 'If thou dislik'st the piece thou light'st on first,' select another."

Anderson, Sherwood	*Winesburg, Ohio*
Atwood, Margaret	*The Handmaids's Tale*
Baldwin, James	*Go Tell It on the Mountain*
Barth, John	*The Sot-Weed Factor*
Bellow, Saul	*Henderson the Rain King*
Bowen, Elizabeth	*The Death of the Heart*
Burgess, Anthony	*A Clockwork Orange*
Byatt, A.S.	*Possession*
Capote, Truman	*In Cold Blood*

Cather, Willa	*Death Comes for the Archbishop*
Conrad, Joseph	*Heart of Darkness; Nostromo*
Doctorow, E.L.	*Ragtime*
Dos Passos, John	*USA* (trilogy)
Dreiser, Theodore	*An American Tragedy; Sister Carrie*
Ellison, Ralph	*Invisible Man*
Erdrich, Louise	*Love Medicine*
Faulkner, William	*Alsolom, Absolom!; As I Lay Dying; Light in August; The Sound and the Fury*
Fitzgerald, F. Scott	*The Great Gatsby*
Forster, E.M.	*Howard's End; A Passage to India; A Room With a View*
Fowles, John	*The French Lieutenant's Woman*
Golding, William	*Lord of the Flies*
Gordimer, Nadine	*Burger's Daughter*
Greene, Graham	*The Heart of the Matter*
Hammett, Dashiell	*The Maltese Falcon*
Heller, Joseph	*Catch-22*
Hemingway, Ernest	*A Farewell to Arms; For Whom the Bell Tolls; The Sun Also Rises*
Hurston, Zora Neal	*Their Eyes Were Watching God*
Huxley, Aldous	*Brave New World*
James, Henry	*The Ambassadors; The Wings of the Dove*
Jong, Erica	*Fear of Flying*
Joyce, James	*Ulysses*
Kerouac, Jack	*On the Road*
Kingston, Maxine Hong	*The Woman Warrior*
Kincaid, Jamaica	*The Autobiography of My Mother*
Koestler, Arthur	*Darkness at Noon*
Laurence, Margaret	*The Stone Angel*
Lawrence, D.H.	*Sons and Lovers; Women in Love*
Lessing, Doris	*The Golden Notebook*
Lewis Sinclair	*Main Street*
London, Jack	*The Call of the Wild*

Mailer, Norman	*The Naked and the Dead*
Malamud, Bernard	*The Assistant*
Mason, Bobbie Ann	*In Country*
Maugham, W. Somerset	*Of Human Bondage*
Maxwell, William	*So Long, See You Tomorrow*
McCarthy, Mary	*The Group*
McCullers, Carson	*The Heart is a Lonely Hunter; In Country*
Morrison, Toni	*Beloved; Song of Solomon*
Munro, Alice	*Lives of Girls and Women*
Nabakov, Vladimir	*Lolita*
Naipaul, V.X.	*A Bend in the River*
Naylor, Gloria	*Mama Day*
Oates, Joyce Carol	*Them*
O'Brien, Tim	*Going After Cacciato*
O'Connor, Flannery	*Wise Blood*
Ondaatje, Michael	*The English Patient*
Orwell, George	*Animal Farm; 1984*
Percy, Walker	*The Moviegoer*
Porter, Katherine Anne	*Ship of Fools*
Pynchon, Thomas	*Gravity's Rainbow*
Rhys, Jean	*Wide Sargasso Sea*
Roth, Henry	*Call It Sleep*
Roth, Phillip	*The Counterfeit; Portnoy's Complaint*
Rushdie, Salman	*Midnight's Children*
Salinger, J.D.	*The Catcher in the Rye*
Schaeffer, Susan Fromberg	*Buffalo Afternoon*
Silko, Leslie Marmon	*Ceremony*
Sinclair, Upton	*The Jungle*
Spark, Muriel	*The Prime of Miss Jean Brodie*
Steinbeck, John	*The Grapes of Wrath*
Styron, William	*The Confessions of Nat Turner; Sophie's Choice*
Tan, Amy	*The Joy Luck Club*

Tarkington, Booth	*The Magnificent Ambersons*
Tyler, Anne	*Dinner at the Homesick Restaurant*
Updike, John	*Rabbit Run*
Vonnegut, Kurt	*Slaughterhouse Five*
Walker, Alice	*The Color Purple*
Warren, Robert Penn	*All the King's Men*
Wharton, Edith	*The Age of Innocence*; *House of Mirth*
White, Patrick	*The Eye of the Storm*
Wolfe, Thomas	*Look Homeward, Angel*
Woolf, Virginia	*Mrs. Dalloway*; *To the Lighthouse*
Wright, Richard	*Native Son*

I think my mom first got me interested in books. My family never had much money when I was growing up, but we always had books. Lots of books. *Tons* of books. Every night my mother would tuck me into my bed and open up a copy of *Mike Mulligan and His Steam Shovel* or *Where the Wild Things Are* or *The Giant Jam Sandwich*. I can remember going to sleep dreaming of castles and dragons and monsters and princes and toads that could speak and dogs that could fly.

I was 4 years old when I read my first book, *Ann Likes Red*, all by myself. "Ann likes red," it began. "Red, red, red. Ann has red shoes. Ann has a red hat. Red is the color that Ann likes..." and on and on *ad nauseum*, the way only some children's books can. Ever since that moment I have read everything I could get my hands on.

When I was in kindergarten, I was the only student who could pass out papers because I was the only one who could read each kid's name at the top of his paper. In second grade, I actually went to the third-grade teacher's class for reading because I had read everything my second-grade teacher could offer.

OK, already, you must be saying about now. So you were a good reader. We get that. What's the point? The point, my friends, is simple. Yes, I was a good reader, but I was only a good reader because I had people around me—parents and siblings and teachers—who encouraged me to read each day. I had an insatiable appetite for reading (that I still have to this day) because I learned at an early age that words in books were interesting. There were answers in books. There were new worlds in books. There was an escape from the reality of the world in books. After awhile, books became as important to me as air and water and food and shelter. I needed them to survive.

Today I am a high school teacher, and I still love books. I've certainly moved away from *Ann Likes Red* and *Mike Mulligan*, but I've not forgotten the impact that those books had on me. I read to my students every day. I provide time for reading each week in my classroom. I talk about books with my students. I share my own reading experiences with my students. All because I want my students to appreciate reading even a fraction of the amount that I do. There is nothing more rewarding to me than to see a student of mine get excited about a book, to want to go back to the library and check out another. I think that sometimes students forget that books can be fun. They need to be reminded of that from time to time.

In just a few months I will be a father for the first time. I've been reading everything I can get my hands on (of course) about parenting and childbirth and child safety. Believe me, it's confusing. But despite all of the pressure and confusion of child rearing, there's one thing I *am* sure of. My son will have books. Lots of books. *Tons* of books.

My wife told me recently that no matter how poor we are she will not be able to deny our child a book that he wants. "I just won't have the heart to say no," she said, holding her growing belly in one hand and clutching a copy of *Rainbow Fish* in the other, her brown puppy-dog eyes looking directly into mine.

I smiled as I looked back at her. "Me either," I said as we opened the book together. "Me either."

And that's a promise I know I will keep.

Jim Streisel
High School English Teacher

University of Iowa
107 Calvin Hall
Iowa City, IA 52242-1396
(319) 335-3500
http://www.uiowa.edu

Freshmen at the University of Iowa must take a rhetoric course. After that, they may choose from courses offered in The General Education in Literature program. The following are two courses from a recent publication of "Course Descriptions and Readings" for that program. The first is a prerequisite for the other fourteen courses in the program. Students may test out of it as indicated by the instructions at the end of the Iowa listings.

The Interpretation of Literature

The purpose of this course is "to introduce students to a wide range of literature; we want students to improve their ability to read, to write about, and to discuss literary texts with confidence and enjoyment. The course explores a variety of literary forms, in part to acquaint students with major works in different genres, in part to serve as a background for and anticipation of the more specialized elective courses. The course concentrates on poetry, drama, and prose fiction, although other forms (e.g., film, autobiography, essay) might be included."

Anthologies and books about critical analyses for each section are selected from the following: **C.E. Bain**, et al., *Norton Introduction to Literature*; **David Bergman** and **David Epstein**, *Heath Guide to Poetry*; **R.V. Cassill**, *Norton Anthology of Short Fiction*; **John J. Clayton**, *Heath Introduction to Fiction*; **Joseph DeRoche**, ed., *Heath Introduction to Poetry*; **Daniel F. Howard**, ed., *The Modern Tradition*; **Paul Hunter**, ed., *Norton Introduction to Poetry*; **X.J. Kennedy**, ed., *Introduction to Poetry*; **Alton C. Morris**, ed., *Imaginative Literature*; **Robert Scholes**, et al., *Elements of Literature, 3rd ed.* Other book choices are

Achebe, Chinua	*Things Fall Apart*
Austen, Jane	*Pride and Prejudice*

Beckett, Samuel	*Waiting for Godot*
Brecht, Bertolt	*The Caucasian Chalk Circle*
Camus, Albert	*The Stranger*
Chekhov, Anton	*The Major Plays*
Chopin, Kate	*The Awakening*
Dickens, Charles	*Hard Times*
Fitzgerald, F. Scott	*The Great Gatsby*
Flaubert, Gustave	*Madame Bovary*
García Márquez, Gabriel	*One Hundred Years of Solitude*
Ibsen, Henrik	*Four Major Plays*, vol. 1
Kesey, Ken	*One Flew Over the Cuckoo's Nest*
Miller, Arthur	*Death of a Salesman*
Morrison, Toni	*Sula*
Reinert and Amott, eds.	*Thirteen Plays*
Shaffer, Peter	*Amadeus; Equus*
Shakespeare, William	*Hamlet; King Lear; Macbeth; A Midsummer Night's Dream; Othello*
Shaw, George Bernard	*Pygmalion*
Steinbeck, John	*The Grapes of Wrath*
Stoppard, Tom	*Rosencrantz and Guildentern Are Dead*
Walker, Alice	*The Color Purple*
Wilde, Oscar	*The Importance of Being Earnest*
Williams, Tennessee	*Cat on a Hot Tin Roof*
Woolf, Virginia	*Mrs. Dalloway*

Biblical and Classical Literature

The course description states that "many of the literary, ethical, and intellectual values of Western civilization derive from biblical, Greek, and Roman literature. This course examines the greatness of the literatures, *as literature*, and the richness of its ideas about the human condition. Every class includes, at least, readings from the *Bible*, dialogues of **Plato**, classical drama, lyrical poetry, and an epic or two. Under study will be myth, folk-tale, history, biography, tragedy, epic, oratory, epistle, and lyric. Students have the opportunity to extend their skill in speaking, writing, and literary analysis."

Books for each section are selected from the following list:

	Bible
	Epic of Gilgamesh
Aeschylus	*The Oresteia* (Fagles, tr.)
Aristophanes	*Lysistrata*; *The Complete Plays*
Euripides	*Euripides* (Grene, tr.)
Grene, ed.	*Greek Tragedies*, vol. 1
Homer	*The Iliad*; *The Odyssey*
Ovid	*Metamorphoses*
Plato	*The Last Days of Socrates*; *The Symposium*
Sophocles	*Sophocles*, vol. 1 (Grene, tr.)
Vergil	*The Aeneid*

James Madison University
Harrisonburg, VA 22807
(540) 568-6211
http://www.jmu.edu

The faculty at James Madison lists the following books with which they would like students to be familiar, in addition to a good anthology of poetry:

	Bible: early books
Alexie, Sherman	*The Lone Ranger and Tonto Fistfight in Heaven*
Aurelius, Marcus	*Meditations*
Camus, Albert	*The Stranger* or *The Plague*
Cassill, R.V., ed.	*Norton Anthology of Short Fiction*
Coelho, Paulo	*The Alchemist*
Crane, Stephen	Selected short stories
Dickinson, Emily	A selection of poems
Dostoevski, Fyodor	*Crime and Punishment*
Ellison, Ralph	*Invisible Man*
Faulkner, William	*The Unvanquished*

Fitzgerald, F. Scott	*The Great Gatsby*
Golding, William	*Lord of the Flies*
Halpern, Daniel	Anything edited by him
Hawthorne, Nathaniel	*The Scarlet Letter*
Hemingway, Ernest	*In Our Time*
Homer	*The Odyssey* and *The Iliad*
Hurston, Zora Neale	*Their Eyes Were Watching God*
James, Henry	*Daisy Miller*
Melville, Herman	*Billy Budd*
Morrison, Toni	At least one novel
O'Connor, Flannery	Selected short stories
Plath, Sylvia	A selection of poems
Poe, Edgar Allen	Selected short stories
Salinger, J.D.	*The Catcher in the Rye*
Shakespeare, William	*Hamlet*; one of the comedies; the sonnets
Thomas, Dylan	A selection of poems
Twain, Mark	*The Adventures of Huckleberry Finn*
Whitman, Walt	A selection of poems

Marymount College: All applicants must submit a graded writing sample, such as an English paper, term paper, or book review. Please submit a writing sample that you wrote within the last year.

Kalamazoo College
1200 Academy St.
Kalamazoo, MI 49006-3295
(616) 337-7000
http://www.kzoo.edu

Kalamazoo, according to Professor Gall B. Griffin, Department of English, "has a freshman General Education Program, 'Discovering the Liberal Arts,' which includes self-selected students and offers four courses in different divisions of the college." The literature component, entitled "Literary Questing in the Western World," has used the following works:

	Sir Gawain and the Green Knight
Conrad, Joseph	*Heart of Darkness*
Homer	*The Odyssey*
Mann, Thomas	*Death in Venice*
Shakespeare, William	*King Lear; MacBeth*
Shelley, Mary	*Frankenstein*
Troyes, Chrétien de	*Iwain the Knight of the Lion*
Welty, Eudora	*The Golden Apples*

Kansas State University
Manhattan, KS 66506
(785) 532-6011
http://www.ksu.edu

The Department of English at Kansas State lists eighteen books students should have read before entering college.

	Bible
Brontë, Emily	*Wuthering Heights*
Chaucer, Geoffrey	*The Canterbury Tales* (selections)
Crane, Stephen	*The Red Badge of Courage*
Defoe, Daniel	*Robinson Crusoe*
Dickens, Charles	*A Tale of Two Cities*
Fitzgerald, F. Scott	*The Great Gatsby*
Hamilton, Edith	*Mythology*
Hawthorne, Nathaniel	*The Scarlet Letter*
Hemingway, Ernest	*A Farewell to Arms*
Poe, Edgar Allan	*Selected Tales*
Salinger, J.D.	*The Catcher in the Rye*
Shakespeare, William	*Julius Caesar; MacBeth; Romeo and Juliet*
Steinbeck, John	*The Grapes of Wrath*

Swift, Jonathan	*Gulliver's Travels*
Twain, Mark	*The Adventures of Huckleberry Finn*

> **Saint Lawrence University**: If you could invite any individual from history to dinner, what would you serve, and what would you like to ask him or her?

University of Kansas
Lawrence, KS 66045
(785) 864-2700
http://www.ukans.edu

According to Dr. Albert B. Cook, Coordinator of Undergraduate Studies, University of Kansas, the following list of recommended reading is sent on request to teachers and to their college-preparatory students for some "systematic sampling." Divided into two parts, the list was compiled from suggestions by the Kansas faculty. It is preceded by the following caveats:

RECOMMENDED READING

"There're only three books in the world worth reading, Shakespeare, the *Bible*, and Mike Ahearn's *History of Chicago*."

1. This is not meant to be a magic list that will guarantee success at the University of Kansas, or anywhere else.
2. This is not intended to be a definitive list. We are not saying that a reading of these works and nothing else will make a student an educated person.
3. This list is not meant to have universal appeal. Most students will find at least some of it hard going. They may have to put a book down and come back to it later sometimes much later, and just

possibly not at all! Some of these books may be read several times, and all of them improve with rereading. But the point is, that the list will affect each interested student differently.

4. Nothing will replace the entire, unabridged work. The substitution of *Reader's Digest* abridgements or of outlines like *Cliffs Notes* should be treated as abominations. Still, many paperback editions of entire works are widely available with helpful notes and introductions.
5. Students should be encouraged to pursue reading interests of their own, whether or not these interests are based on this list. This wider reading can include newspapers, magazines, current best-sellers, and "light summer reading." The fact is that almost all young people do not read nearly enough, maybe because outside of English classes it is not encouraged either by precept or example.
6. Our experience is that young people are woefully ignorant of the specific contents of the *Bible*, of classical mythology (both a fertile source of literary allusion), of American history, and even of contemporary culture, broadly interpreted, apart from television shows and popular music lyrics. We don't pretend to know why this is so, or how to reverse this trend, but any efforts you can exert to alter this state of affairs would be much appreciated.

With these qualifications in mind, then, we pass these recommended works on to you.

Works Most Frequently Mentioned

The Bible: The so-called "King James Version" is the traditional "literary" one, but such modern translations as the Revised Standard Version, the New English Bible, or the Jerusalem Bible are certainly acceptable. Specific books of the Bible mentioned are "Genesis," "Exodus," "Judges," "I Samuel," "II Samuel," "Job," "Jonah," selected Psalms, and the Gospels, particularly "Mark."

A Collection or Compendium of Classical Mythology: Edith Hamilton's *Mythology* or **Thomas Keightley's** collections are both good. **Robert Graves'** collection makes exciting reading, but his interpretations have been questioned.

Other works include

Brontë, Charlotte	*Jane Eyre*
Brontë, Emily	*Wuthering Heights*
Dickens, Charles	A novel—probably *David Copperfield* or *Great Expectations*—and again the student is warned away from abridgements
Fitzgerald, F. Scott	*The Great Gatsby* (also short stories)
Hardy, Thomas	A novel, probably *Far from the Madding Crowd*; *Return of the Native*; or *Tess of the D'Urbervilles*
Hawthorne, Nathaniel	*The Scarlet Letter* (also short stories)
Hemingway, Ernest	*A Farewell to Arms*; *The Old Man and the Sea*; *The Sun Also Rises* (also short stories)
Homer	*The Iliad* and *The Odyssey* (Fitzgerald or Lattimore, tr.)
Shakespeare, William	*As You Like It*; *Hamlet*; *Henry IV, PartI*; *Julius Caesar*; *King Lear*; *Macbeth*; *The Merchant of Venice*; *A Midsummer Night's Dream*; *Othello*; *Richard II*; *Romeo and Juliet*; *The Tempest*; *Twelfth Night* (students should note particularly that we recommend here the entire play, in each instance, not a cut version or abridgement)
Sophocles	*Antigone*; *Oedipus Rex*; *Oedipus at Colonus* (Robert Fitzgerald, tr.)
Thoreau, Henry David	*Walden* (also *Civil Disobedience*)
Twain, Mark	*The Adventures of Huckleberry Finn* (also *The Adventures of Tom Sawyer*, if you haven't already read it)

Other Works Mentioned

Pre-History and Classical Antiquity

	The Arabian Nights' Entertainments (especially "Sinbad," "Ali Baba," and "Aladdin")
Aeschylus	Selected plays
Durant, Will	*The Story of Philosophy* or **Zeller's** *Outline of the History of Greek Philosophy*
Euripides	Selected plays

Grimm, Jakob and Wilhelm Grimm	*Fairy Tales* or *Keightley's Fairy Mythology*
Vergil	*The Aeneid* (Fitzgerald or Mandelbaum, tr.)

Middle Ages and Renaissance

Dante	*The Divine Comedy*, especially *The Inferno* (Ciardi or Mandelbaum, tr.)
Cervantes, Miguel de	*Don Quixote* (Putnam, tr.)
Chaucer, Geoffrey	*The Canterbury Tales* (The Middle English text makes for difficult reading, but most college-level editions have handy and helpful glossaries and notes)
Jonson, Ben	*The Alchemist*; *Volpone*
Marlowe, Christopher	*Doctor Faustus*
Milton, John	"Areopagitica"; *Paradise Lost* (Book I for starters); Selected sonnets
Spenser, Edmund	*The Faerie Queene*, book I (inclusion questioned by some)
Webster, John	*The Duchess of Malfi*

17th and 18th Centuries

Blake, William	*Songs of Innocence*; *Songs of Experience*
Bunyan, John	*The Pilgrim's Progress*, book I
Defoe, Daniel	A novel, probably *Moll Flanders* or *Robinson Crusoe*
Fielding, Henry	A novel, probably *Tom Jones*
Franklin, Benjamin	*Autobiography*

Some authentic historical documents, like **Lewis and Clark's** *Journals*, **Francis Parkman**, etc. A close reading of the Declaration of Independence, the Constitution, and the Bill of Rights wouldn't hurt, either.

19th Century

Austen, Jane	A novel, probably *Pride and Prejudice*
Carlyle, Thomas	*Heroes and Hero Worship*
Dickinson, Emily	*The Final Harvest* poems

Dostoevski, Fyodor	*Crime and Punishment* (David Magarshack, tr.) and/or **Leo Tolstoy**, *War and Peace* (Maudes, tr.). The latter, though a "blockbuster," is probably more manageable than the former.
Eliot, George	A novel, probably *Middlemarch* or *Adam Bede* (several professors warned against including *Silas Marner*)
Emerson, Ralph Waldo	*Essays* (especially "The American Scholar" and "Self-Reliance")
Flaubert, Gustave	*Madame Bovary* (Francis Steegmuller, tr.)
Keats, John	Selected poetry, especially "Eve of Saint Agnes," the odes, the sonnets.

One professor suggested that **George Gordon, Lord Byron**, being a perennial adolescent, is particulary good for high school and college students.

Melville, Herman	*Moby-Dick*
Scott, Sir Walter	*Ivanhoe* (or better, one of the Scottish novels, such as *The Heart of Midlothian*)
Stowe, Harriet Beecher	*Uncle Tom's Cabin* (Everyone "remembers" the "Tom Show," but few have read the novel. It is far greater than its reputation.)
Whitman, Walt	*Leaves of Grass*
Wordsworth, William	Selected poetry (especially "Ode: Intimations of Immortality" and such obvious classics)

20th Century and Modern Times

Agee, James	*Let Us Now Praise Famous Men*
Anderson, Kurt	*The Real Thing*
Bierce, Ambrose	*The Devil's Dictionary*; also short stories
Berger, Thomas	*Little Big Man*
Cather, Willa	*My Antonia*; *O Pioneers!*
Conrad, Joseph	*Lord Jim*; *The Nigger of the "Narcissus"*
Cormier, Robert	*The Chocolate War*
Dinesen, Isak	*Out of Africa* (perhaps one should be careful about the influence of the film upon one's understanding of the book)
Faulkner, William	*Intruder in the Dust*; *The Unvanquished*

Frost, Robert	Selected poetry
Gage, Nicholas	*Eleni*
Golding, William	*Lord of the Flies*
Graves, Robert	*I, Claudius*
Grubb, David	*The Night of the Hunter*
Heller, Joseph	*Catch-22*
Hughes, Langston	*Not Without Laughter* or **Gordon Parks**, *The Learning Tree*, two autobiographical novels about growing up black in Kansas
Kafka, Franz	Selected short stories
Joyce, James	*Dubliners*; *A Portrait of the Artist as a Young Man*
McGullers, Carson	*The Member of the Wedding*; short stories
Meltzer, Milton	Any books (This is a good place to mention outstanding books for adolescents by such writers as **S.E. Hinton.**)
Paton, Alan	*Cry, the Beloved Country*
Pirsig, Robert	*Zen and the Art of Motorcycle Maintenance*
Salinger, J.D.	*The Catcher in the Rye*
Wharton, Edith	*The Age of Innocence*; *The House of Mirth*
White, E.B.	*Charlotte's Web*; also selected essays
Wilder, Thornton	*The Bridge of San Luis Rey*; *Heaven's My Destination*; *The Ides of March*
Woolf, Virginia	*A Room of One's Own*; *To the Lighthouse*
Wright, Richard	*Native Son*

High school students don't read nearly enough plays, beyond the mandatory Shakespeare. (Students should likewise make use of every opportunity to see significant dramas performed, either on the stage or on television.) We recommmend in particular such contemporary playwrights as:

Inge, William	*Bus Stop* or *Come Back, Little Sheba*
Miller, Arthur	*Death of a Salesman*
O'Neill, Eugene	*Desire under the Elms*; *The Hairy Ape*; the *S. S. Glencairn* plays
Saroyan, William	*The Time of Your Life*
Williams, Tennessee	*The Glass Menagerie* or *A Streetcar Named Desire*
Wilder, Thornton	*The Skin of Our Teeth*

Miscellaneous

A collection of contemporary short stories: In addition to such authors as **Fitzgerald** or **Hemingway**, already mentioned before, the student should be aware of significant contemporary writers who specialized in this genre—**John Cheever, Frank O'Conner, Flannery O'Connor, Tillie Olsen, John Updike**, to name only a few.

Some good modern essays: Even a regular reading of *Time* or *Newsweek* or the editorial and op-ed columns of a daily newspaper would be useful. Particularly recommended is *The Penguin Book of Contemporary American Essays* (**Maureen Howard**, ed.)

Allen, Woody	*Getting Even*
Edel, Leon	*Writing Lives*
Fischer, Louis	*Life of Mahatma Gandhi*
Hayakawa, S.I.	*Language in Thought and Action*
Potter, Stephen	*The Complete Upmanship*
Strunk and White	*Elements of Style* (but take the usage dicta with a grain of salt)
Wodehouse, P.G.	Any of the Jeeves novels or the Mr. Mulliner stories.

Appalachian State University: Outside of class assignments what are your reading habits? (Please be specific)

University of Kentucky
100 W.D. Funkhouser Building
Lexington, KY 40506
(606) 257-9000
http://www.uky.edu

According to Dr. William R. Campbell, Director of the Writing Program, the Department of English has "no list of readings suggested for entering students. No syllabus here is based on the assumption that certain works are already in the background of entering students, even the *Bible*." The content of the entrance level courses varies, but UK freshmen study a novel in their required writing course. Recently-assigned novels have included

Chopin, Kate	*The Awakening*
Fitzgerald, F. Scott	*The Great Gatsby*
Orwell, George	*Animal Farm*
Steinbeck, John	*Of Mice and Men*
Twain, Mark	*The Adventures of Huckleberry Finn*

> **University of Georgia**: Write an original 250-word essay in response to the following: What time is it? Please explain and defend your response where appropriate.

Kenyon College
Gambier, OH 43022-9623
(740) 427 5000
http://www.kenyon.edu

Students in Kenyon's Freshman English 1 and 2 courses write essays throughout the year, approximately eight during the first semester. Both writing skill and critical ability are evaluated. A sample syllabus from the course includes the anthologies and critical analysis texts *Poetic Meter and Poetic Form*; **Alexander W. Allison,** ed., *The Norton Anthology of Poetry* (shorter ed.); and **R.V. Cassill,** *The Norton Anthology of Short Fiction* (longer ed.). Other books studied are

Brontë, Charlotte	*Jane Eyre*
Dickens, Charles	*Great Expectations*
Homer	*The Odyssey* (Fitzgerald, tr.)
Shakespeare, William	*Henry IV, Part I*; *King Lear*; *Much Ado About Nothing*
Swift, Jonathan	*Travels into Several Remote Nations* (Normally known as *Gulliver's Travels*)

Thoreau, Henry David	*Walden*
Woolf, Virginia	*A Room of One's Own*
Wright, Richard	*Black Boy*

Knox College
Galesburg, IL 61401
(309) 341-7000
http://www.knox.edu

Professor William E. Brady of the Department of English writes that although "you need not have read any particular books before you enter Knox College, it might not be a bad idea to have consumed some of these":

Austen, Jane	*Emma*
Conrad, Joseph	*Heart of Darkness*; *Lord Jim*; "The Secret Sharer"
Dickens, Charles	*Great Expectations*
Fitzgerald, F. Scott	*The Great Gatsby*
Ford, Ford Madox	*The Good Soldier*
Hemingway, Ernest	"The Killers," "The Short Happy Life of Francis Macomber," "The Snows of Kilimanjaro," and other short stories
James, Henry	"The Turn of the Screw"
Joyce, James	*A Portrait of the Artist as a Young Man*
Turgenev, Ivan	*Fathers and Sons*
Woolf, Virginia	*Mrs. Dalloway*

Dr. Brady also recommends "the student get a copy of any anthology of poetry and read the poetry of some of the most famous poets. **Chaucer**, **Shakespeare**, and **Milton** are standard," and others are **W.H. Auden**; **Emily Dickinson**, **Samuel Taylor Coleridge**; **T.S. Eliot**; **Robert Frost**; **Gerard Manley Hopkins**; **Alfred, Lord Tennyson**; **Walt Whitman**; **William Wordsworth**; and **William Butler Yeats**.

He thinks that students should be familiar with the following dramas:

Aeschylus	*Agamemnon*; *Prometheus Bound*
Marlowe, Christopher	*Doctor Faustus*
Miller, Arthur	*Death of a Salesman*
Shakespeare, William	*Hamlet*; *Macbeth*; *Romeo and Juliet*
Sophocles	*Oedipus Rex*

Professor Brady feels the preceding titles "are basic for anyone's education; psychoanalysis, Marxism, deconstructionism, and other studies can be dealt with later in the student's college career."

University of Louisville
2301 South Third Street
Louisville, KY 40292
(502) 852-5555
http://www.louisville.edu

According to Professor Lucy M. Freibert, the English Department advises its undergraduates to "review the *Norton Anthology of English Literature*, and the *Norton Anthology of American Literature*, and to study **Hugh Holman**, *A Handbook to Literature*." In the list that follows, all the authors but not all the specific works have been included from the university's Undergraduate Reading List.

I. Classical Backgrounds

Aeschylus	*Agamemnon*
Aristotle	*The Poetics*
Euripides	*Medea*
Homer	*The Iliad* and *The Odyssey* (Rieu, tr.)
Longinus	"On the Sublime"
Sappho Selected	Poems and fragments
Sophocles	*Oedipus Rex; Antigone*
Vergil	*The Aeneid*

II. English Literature

Old English

	The Battle of Maldon (selections in *Norton Anthology of English Literature*)
	Beowulf
	The Dream of the Rood
	"The Seafarer" (Kennedy, tr.)
	"The Wanderer"

Middle English

	Ballads
	The Cloud of Unknowing (selections)
	Everyman
	Middle English lyrics
	The Second Shepherd's Play
	Sir Gawain and the Green Knight (Rosenberg, tr.)
Chaucer, Geoffrey	*The Canterbury Tales* (except tales of the Cook, the Squire, the Physician, the Shipman, Melibee, the Monk, the Second Nun, and the Manciple)
Julian Of Norwich	*Revelations of Divine Love*
Kempe, Margery	*The Book of Margery Kempe* (Selections in *Norton Anthology of English Literature*)
Langland, William	*Piers Plowman* (Selections in *Norton Anthology of English Literature*)
Malory, Thomas	*Le Morte d'Arthur*, book XXI

Renaissance

Bacon, Francis	*Essays*
Browne, Thomas	*Religion Medici*, first section
Earle, John	*Micro-Cosmographie*; poetry
Hooker, Richard	*Of The Laws of Ecclesiastical Polity*, book I, sections 1–8
Jonson, Ben	*The Alchemist*; *Volpone*; poetry
Lyly, John	*Euphues* (up to mention of Philautus)

Marlowe, Christopher	*Doctor Faustus*; *Tamburlaine the Great*, part I
Milton, John	"Lycidas," *Paradise Lost*, books I–V, IX, X, XIII; *Samson Agonistes.* Sonnets: "Avenge, O Lord, Thy Slaughtered Saints," "Cromwell, Our Chief of Men," "Cyriak, This Three Year's Day," "How Soon Hath Time," "Lady, That in the Prime of Earliest Youth," "On the Morning of Christ's Nativity," "When I Consider How My Light Is Spent"
More, Thomas	*Utopia* (Surtz, tr.)
Shakespeare, William	*Antony and Cleopatra*; *As You Like It*; *Hamlet*; *Henry IV, Part I*; *Henry IV Part II*; *Henry V*; *Julius Caesar*; *Othello*; *Richard II*; *Richard III*; *The Tempest*; *Twelfth Night*; *The Winter's Tale*
Spenser, Edmund	*Amoretti*, selected sonnets; *The Faerie Queene*; "Epithalamion"; Letter to Raleigh; *Shepheardes Calender*: "April," "October," "November"

And the poetry of **Richard Crashaw**, **John Donne**, **George Herbert**, **Robert Herrick**, **Andrew Marvell**, **Philip Sidney**, **Thomas Wyatt**, and **H.H. Surrey**.

Restoration and 18th Century

Addison and Steele	*The Spectator*
Austen, Jane	*Emma* or *Pride and Prejudice*
Blake, William	*Songs of Innocence* and *Songs of Experience* (selections)
Boswell, James	*The Life of Samuel Johnson* (from May 16, 1763)
Congreve, William	*The Way of the World*
Cowper, William	*Retirement*
Crabbe, George	*The Village*
Dryden, John	*Absalom and Achitophel*; *All for Love*; *The Hind and the Panther*; *MacFlecknoe*; "Preface to the Fables"; *Religio Laici*
Goldsmith, Oliver	*The Deserted Village*
Johnson, Samuel	*The Idler* (16, 61); *Life of Addison*; *The Rambler* (4, 25); *Rasselas*; *The Vanity of Human Wishes*
Pope, Alexander	*The Dunciad* (IV); "An Essay on Man"; "The Rape of the Lock"; *Windsor Forest*; and other selections

Sheridan, Richard B.	*The School for Scandal*
Swift, Jonathan	"An Argument Against Abolishing Christianity"; "A Description of the Morning"; *Gulliver's Travels*; "A Modest Proposal"
Walpole, Horace	*The Castle of Otranto*
Wollstonecraft, Mary	*A Vindication of the Rights of Women*
Wycherley, William	*The Plain Dealer*

And the poets **Robert Burns** and **Thomas Gray**.

Early 19th Century

Hazlitt, William	"On Familiar Style"
Lamb, Charles	"Old China"
Peacock, Raymond L.	*Nightmare Abbey*
Scott, Sir Walter	*Quentin Durward* or *Waverley*
Shelley, Mary	*Frankenstein*

And the poets **George Gordon**, **Lord Byron**, **Samuel Taylor Coleridge**, **John Keats**, **Percy Bysshe Shelley**, **William Wordsworth**.

Victorian Period

Arnold, Matthew	*Culture and Anarchy*; *The Function of Criticism at the Present Time*; *poetry*
Brontë, Charlotte	*Jane Eyre*
Brontë, Emily	*Wuthering Heights*
Butler, Samuel	*The Way of All Flesh*
Carlyle, Thomas	*Heroes and Hero-Worship*, I; *Past and Present*, II, III; *Sartor Resartus*, II
Dickens, Charles	*David Copperfield*
Eliot, George	*Adam Bede* or *Middlemarch* or *The Mill on the Floss*
Hardy, Thomas	*The Return of the Native*
Huxley, Thomas	*Science and Culture*
Meredith, George	*The Egoist*
Mill, John Stuart	*On Liberty*
Newman, Cardinal J.H.	*The Idea of a University*
Pater, Walter	*The Renaissance* (conclusion)

Stevenson, Robert L.	*The Master of Ballantrae*
Thackeray, William Makepeace	*Vanity Fair*
Wilde, Oscar	*The Importance of Being Earnest*

And the poets **Robert Browning**; **Gerard Manley Hopkins**; **Alfred, Lord Tennyson**.

The Modern Period, 1890 to the Present

Beckett, Samuel	*Waiting for Godot*
Conrad, Joseph	*Heart of Darkness* or *Lord Jim*
Eliot, T.S.	*Burnt Norton*; "Hamlet and His Problems"; "The Love Song of J. Alfred Prufrock"; "Preludes"; "Tradition and the Individual Talent"; "The Waste Land"
Forster, E.M.	*A Passage to India*
Greene, Graham	*The Power and the Glory*
Joyce, James	*Dubliners*; *A Portrait of the Artist as a Young Man*; *Ulysses*
Lawrence, D.H.	"Bavarian Gentians"; "The Horse Dealer's Daughter"; "Piano"; "Snake"; *Sons and Lovers* or *Women in Love*
Mansfield, Katherine	"The Garden Party," "Her First Ball"
Pinter, Harold	*The Birthday Party* or *Caretaker* or *Homecoming*
Shaw, George Bernard	*Candida;* Preface to *Back to Methuselah*
Synge, J.M.	*The Playboy of the Western World*
Thomas, Dylan	*Fern Hill*
Waugh, Evelyn	*A Handful of Dust*
Woolf, Virginia	*To the Lighthouse*

And selected poetry from **W.H. Auden**, **Philip Larkin**, **John Masefield**, **Wilfred Owen**, **William Butler Yeats.**

III. American Literature

Adams, Henry	*The Education of Henry Adams*, chapters XXV, LIII; *Mont-Saint-Michel and Chartres*, chapter VI
Anderson, Sherwood	*Winesburg, Ohio* (selections)
Ashbery, John	"Self-Portrait on a Convex Mirror"

Baldwin, James	*Go Tell It on the Mountain*
Barth, John	"The Literature of Exhaustion"; selected short stories
Bellow, Saul	*Seize the Day*
Brooks, Gwendolyn	*Maud Martha* (optional); Selected poems
Chopin, Kate	*The Awakening*
Cooper, James Fenimore	*The Pioneers* or *The Last of the Mohicans*
Crane, Hart	*The Bridge*
Crane, Stephen	*Maggie*; "The Open Boat"; *The Red Badge of Courage*
Douglass, Frederick	*Narrative of the Life of Frederick Douglass*
Dreiser, Theodore	*Jennie Gearhardt* or *Sister Carrie*; "Nigger Jeff"
Edwards, Jonathan	*Personal Narrative*; "Sinners in the Hands of an Angry God"
Emerson, Ralph Waldo	Essays ("The American Scholar," "Nature," "Self-Reliance"); selected poems
Faulkner, William	"The Bear"; *Light in August*; *Absalom Absalom* or *As I Lay Dying* or *The Sound and the Fury*
Fitzgerald, F. Scott	*The Great Gatsby*
Franklin, Benjamin	*Autobiography*, first 50 pages
Hawthorne, Nathaniel	Short stories and *The Scarlet Letter*
Hellman, Lillian	*Another Part of the Forest*; *The Little Foxes*
Hemingway, Ernest	*A Farewell to Arms*; *The Nick Adams Stories*; *The Sun Also Rises*
Howells, William Dean	*A Hazard of New Fortunes* or *The Rise of Silas Lapham*
Hurston, Zora Neale	*Their Eyes Were Watching God*
Irving, Washington	"The Legend of Sleepy Hollow"; *Rip Van Winkle*
Jacobs, Harriet A.	*Incidents in the Life of a Slave Girl*
James, Henry	*The American*; "Art of Fiction," "The Beast in the Jungle"; *Daisy Miller*
Lewis, Sinclair	*Main Street*
Mailer, Norman	*Armies of the Night*; *The Naked and the Dead*
Melville, Herman	*Benito Cereno* or *Billy Budd; Moby-Dick;* poems ("Art," "The Maldive Shark")
Miller, Arthur	*Death of a Salesman*

Morrison, Toni	*Beloved*; *The Bluest Eye* or *Sula*
O'Connor, Flannery	"The Artificial Nigger," "Good Country People"
O'Neill, Eugene	*Desire Under the Elms*; *Mourning Becomes Electra*
Paine, Thomas	*Common Sense* (selections); *The Crisis I* (selections in *Norton Anthology of American Literature*)
Poe, Edgar Allan	Critical essay "The Philosophy of Composition"; selected poems and short stories.
Porter, K.A.	"The Jilting of Granny Weatherall"
Rowlandson, Mary	"Narrative of the Captivity of Mary Rowlandson"
Stein, Gertrude	"Melanctha"
Stowe, Harriet Beecher	*Uncle Tom's Cabin*
Thoreau, Henry David	*Civil Disobedience*; *Walden*, chapters I, II, III
Toomer, Jean	*Cane*
Twain, Mark	"The Celebrated Jumping Frog of Calaveras County," *The Adventures of Huckleberry Finn*
Walker, Alice	*The Color Purple*
Wharton, Edith	*Ethan Frome*; *The House of Mirth* (optional); "Roman Fever"
Whitman, Walt	"Crossing Brooklyn Ferry"; 1855 Preface to *Leaves of Grass*; "Out of the Cradle Endlessly Rocking"; *Song of Myself* (1855 ed.); "When Lilacs Last in the Dooryard Bloom'd"
Wilder, Thornton	*Our Town*
Williams, Tennessee	*The Glass Menagerie*
Wright, Richard	*Black Boy* or *Native Son*

And selected poems from **Anne Bradstreet, Emily Dickinson, Robert Frost, H.D. (Hilde Doolittle), Langston Hughes, Robert Lowell, Audrey Lorde, Adrienne Rich, E.A. Robinson, Wallace Stevens, Edward Taylor, William Carlos Williams.**

> **Princeton University**: What book that you've read in the past couple of years left the greatest impression on you? Explain why.

Loyola College
4501 North Charles Street
Baltimore, MD 21210-2699
(410) 617-2000
http://www.loyola.edu

Loyola's reading list is prefaced by the following admonition: "We suggest that you use the list as a guide to the wealth of literature in English that awaits your discovery, not as a checklist of approved works; stray from it freely, explore writers and works that are not listed on it—but keep reading!" While, as Professor Brennan O'Donnell notes, the list is intended primarily for English majors, it offers valuable suggestions for any reader.

British Literature

Old English

	Beowulf

Middle English

	Sir Gawain and the Green Knight
Chaucer, Geoffrey	*The Canterbury Tales* (selections)
Langland, William	*Piers Plowman* (selections)
Malory, Sir Thomas	*Morte D'Arthur* (selections)

16th- and 17th-Century Drama

Jonson, Ben	*Volpone*; *The Alchemist*
Marlowe, Christopher	*Dr. Faustus*
Shakespeare, William	*Romeo and Juliet*, *Hamlet*, or *King Lear*; *Twelfth Night* or *A Midsummer Night's Dream*; *Richard II* or *Henry IV Part I*; and *The Winter's Tale* or *The Tempest*

Restoration and 18th-Century Drama

Congreve, William	*The Way of the World*

Goldsmith, Oliver	*She Stoops to Conquer*
Sheridan, Richard Brinsley	*School for Scandal*
Wycherley, William	*The Country Wife*

Restoration and 18th-Century Prose

Pepys, Samuel	*Diary* (selections)
Swift, Jonathan	*Gulliver's Travels*

18th-Century Novel

Austen, Jane	*Pride and Prejudice*; *Emma*
Defoe, Daniel	*Moll Flanders*; *Robinson Crusoe*
Fielding, Henry	*Joseph Andrews*; *Tom Jones*
Goldsmith, Oliver	*The Vicar of Wakefield*
Richardson, Samuel	*Pamela* or *Clarissa* (abridged)
Smollett, Tobias	*Humphrey Clinker*
Sterne, Laurence	*Tristram Shandy*

19th-Century Novel

Brontë, Charlotte	*Jane Eyre*
Brontë, Emily	*Wuthering Heights*
Dickens, Charles	*Bleak House*; *David Copperfield*; or *Great Expectations*
Eliot, George	*Middlemarch*
Godwin, William	*Caleb Williams*
Hardy, Thomas	*Tess of the D'Urbervilles* or *Jude the Obscure*
Scott, Sir Walter	*Waverly* or *The Heart of Midlothian*
Shelley, Mary	*Frankenstein* or *The Modern Prometheus*
Thackeray, William Makepeace	*Vanity Fair*
Trollope, Anthony	*The Warden*; *Barchester Towers*

20th-Century British Literature

Burgess, Anthony	*A Clockwork Orange* or *Enderby*
Conrad, Joseph	*Heart of Darkness*; *The Secret Sharer*; or *Lord Jim*
Ford, Ford Maddox	*The Good Soldier*

Forster, E.M.	*A Passage to India*
Fowles, John	*The French Lieutenant's Woman*
Greene, Graham	*The Heart of the Matter*
Joyce, James	*Dubliners*; *A Portrait of the Artist as a Young Man*; selections from *Ulysses*
Lawrence, D.H.	*Sons and Lovers*; *The Rainbow*; or *Women in Love*
Murdoch, Iris	*A Severed Head*
Orwell, George	*1984* or *Animal Farm*
Woolf, Virginia	*To the Lighthouse* or *Mrs. Dalloway*

20th-Century British Drama

Beckett, Samuel	*Endgame* or *Waiting for Godot*
Osborne, John	*Look Back in Anger*
Pinter, Harold	*The Homecoming* or *The Birthday Party*
Shaw, G.B.	*Arms and the Man*; *Man and Superman*; *Saint Joan*; or *Major Barbara*
Stoppard, Tom	*Rosencrantz and Guildenstern are Dead* or *Jumpers*
Schaffer, Peter	*Equus* or *Amadeus*

American Literature

17th, 18th, and 19th Centuries Non-Fiction

Edwards, Jonathan	Selected writings
Emerson, Ralph Waldo	Representative essays
Franklin, Benjamin	*Autobiography*
Fuller, Margaret	Selected writings
Irving, Washington	*A History of New York* (selections)
Poe, Edgar Allan	Representative essays
Thoreau, Henry David	*Walden*; *Civil Disobedience*

17th, 18th, and 19th Centuries Novels

Cooper, James Fenimore	One of the *Leatherstocking* novels
Crane, Stephen	*The Red Badge of Courage* or *Maggie, A Girl of the Streets*
Hawthorne, Nathaniel	*The Scarlet Letter*
Howells, W.D.	*The Rise of Silas Lapham*

James, Henry	*The American*; *The Portrait of a Lady*; or *The Ambassadors*
Melville, Herman	*Moby-Dick*
Stowe, Harriet Beecher	*Uncle Tom's Cabin*
Twain, Mark	*The Adventures of Huckleberry Finn*

Poetry selections from **Emily Dickinson, Edgar Allan Poe, Walt Whitman**

20th-Century Fiction

Anderson, Sherwood	*Winesburg, Ohio*
Baldwin, James	*Go Tell It on the Mountain*; "Sonny's Blues"
Barth, John	*The Floating Opera*; selected short fiction
Bellow, Saul	*The Adventures of Augie March*; *Henderson the Rain King*; *Humboldt's Gift*
Cather, Willa	*O Pioneers!* or *My Antonia*
Chopin, Kate	*The Awakening*
Dos Passos, John	One of the *U.S.A.* novels
Dreiser, Theodore	*Sister Carrie* or *An American Tragedy*
Ellison, Ralph	*Invisible Man*
Farrell, James T.	*The Young Manhood of Studs Lonigan*
Faulkner, William	*Absalom! Absalom*; *The Sound and the Fury*; *Light in August*; selected short fiction
Fitzgerald, F. Scott	*The Great Gatsby*
Heller, Joseph	*Catch-22*
Hemingway, Ernest	*The Sun Also Rises* or *A Farewell to Arms*; selected short fiction
Hurston, Zora Neale	*Their Eyes Were Watching God* or selected short stories
Kesey, Ken	*One Flew Over the Cuckoo's Nest*
Lewis, Sinclair	*Babbit*
Malamud, Bernard	*The Natural*
Mailer, Norman	*The Naked and the Dead*
Morrison, Toni	*Song of Solomon*
Norris, Frank	*McTeague* or *The Octopus*
O'Connor, Flannery	Selected short stories
Porter, Katherine Anne	*Pale Horse, Pale Rider*

Pynchon, Thomas	*The Crying of Lot 49*; "Entropy"
Roth, Philip	*Goodbye, Columbus* and selected short stories
Salinger, J.D.	*The Catcher in the Rye*
Sinclair, Upton	*The Jungle*
Stein, Gertrude	*Three Lives*
Steinbeck, John	*The Grapes of Wrath*
Updike, John	*Rabbit, Run*; *The Centaur*; or *Rabbit Redux*; selected stories
Warren, Robert Penn	*All the King's Men*
Welty, Eudora	Selected short stories
West, Nathanael	*Miss Lonelyhearts*
Wharton, Edith	*The House of Mirth* or *The Age of Innocence*
Wright, Richard	*Native Son*

20th-Century Drama

Albee, Edward	*Who's Afraid of Virginia Woolf?* or *Zoo Story*
Miller, Arthur	*Death of a Salesman*
O'Neill, Eugene	*Beyond the Horizon*; *Desire Under the Elms*; *The Iceman Cometh*; or *Long Day's Journey into Night*
Shepard, Sam	*Buried Child*; *The Curse of the Starving Class* or *True West*
Williams, Tennessee	*The Glass Menagerie* or *A Streetcar Named Desire*
Wilson, Lanford	*Fifth of July*

Bookstore browsing has always been one of my favorite pastimes, but I find my focus is a bit different now. I notice how books are displayed, observe employees' interaction with customers, and collect store newsletters, always looking for ways to improve customer service and the ambiance of our store. However, as an avid reader, for me any bookstore always holds out the promise of discovery as I stumble upon a book I just that moment realized I wanted!

Recently we were privileged to have several authors come in to sign their newest books including Catherine Coulter, Norman Mailer, and

Robert Crais. Ms Coulter had just learned her book *The Maze* had claimed a spot on *The New York Times* bestseller list. Her delight was infectious as she enthusiastically chatted with customers as she signed copies of the book. Mr. Mailer came in just before his lecture appearance at University of Cincinnati and we admit to being a bit apprehensive in conversing with an author of such repute. Our concerns were unfounded, as he signed copies of *The Gospel According to the Son*, he was charming and very easy to talk with. It was pure coincidence that Robert Crais' latest paperback *Sunset Express* was our staff's favorite book of the month when he unexpectedly stopped by. We could tell he was pleased with our selection and we were thrilled to meet one of our favorite authors!

Visit books stores frequently and browse as long as you can—you never know what wonderful book you may discover or whom you will meet!!!

Lesley Kleiser
Cincinnati Bookstore Owner

Lyon College
PO Box 2317
2300 Highland Rd.
Batesville, AR 72503
(800) 423-2542
http://www.lyon.edu

Freshmen at Lyon College take Masterpieces of the Western World, two world literature courses that are required in the core curriculum. The first course covers:

	The Song of Roland
Dante	*Inferno*
Euripides	*Medea*
Homer	*The Iliad* and *The Odyssey*

Shakespeare, William	*Hamlet*
Sophocles	*Oedipus Rex*

Studied in the second course are the following works (the brief defining comments are those Dr. Terrell Tebbetts includes in the syllabus):

Blake, William	Poems
Camus, Albert	"The Guest" (a story on the existential self)
Chekhov, Anton	*The Cherry Orchard* (realism triumphant)
Coleridge, Samuel Taylor	"Kubla Khan"
Eliot, T.S.	"The Love Song of J. Alfred Prufrock" (a poem on self-destruction)
Ellison, Ralph	"King of the Bingo Game" (a story on identity and power)
Faulkner, William	"Barn Burning" (a story on self-assertion)
Flaubert, Gustave	*Madame Bovary* (the death of a romanticist)
Goethe, Johann W. von	*Faust* (romantic desire)
Ibsen, Henrik	*Hedda Gabler* (modern woman)
Kafka, Franz	*The Metamorphosis* (a fable on imposed identity)
Keats, John	Poems
Lawrence, D.H.	"Odour of Chrysanthemums"
Mann, Thomas	"Mario and the Magician" (a story on the individual and society)
Molière	*Tartuffe* (a satire on a religious hypocrite)
Racine, Jean	*Phaedra* (a tragedy on passion)
Shelley, Percy Bysshe	"Ode to the West Wind"
Stevens, Wallace	Poems (poetry on individualism)
Swift, Jonathan	*Gulliver's Travels* (a satire on passions)
Tolstoy, Leo	*The Death of Ivan Ilych* (the death of a realist)
Voltaire	*Candide* (a fable on the limits of reason)
Wordsworth, William	Poems (man and nature)
Yeats, W.B.	Poems (poetry on the individual and society)

University of Maine
Orono, ME 04469
(207) 581-1110
http://www.umaine.edu

Although the University of Maine at Orono has no specific reading list for the pre-college student, its pamphlet "What to Study in High School" makes several comments about reading and reading skills.

In their recommendations for specific course work in English the authors of the pamphlet state that they expect that "all entering freshmen will be active and critical readers as well as fluent and flexible writers." With regard to reading they stress that the student should have (1) "learned how to participate in literature: how to follow textual clues to genre, tone, and context in reliving poetic, narrative, and dramatic texts," (2) "learned how to read critically both literary and non-literary texts by knowing how to recognize their constituents, and by knowing how to discover a text's assumption and implications," and (3) "studied some classic literary texts in depth and have come to understand those texts as embodying beliefs and values central to human experience."

The pamphlet makes specific recommendations for "a more rigorous college preparatory curriculum," also noting that "the quality of high school course work is more important than its quantity." It stresses "the importance of the senior year in the transition to college-level work saying students who choose undemanding courses in the senior year will find difficulty adjusting to work at UMO."

Anyone interested in learning more about Maine's recommendations for pre-college high school study in the fields of english, history, science, mathematics, and the arts may obtain the pamphlet from the Office of the Vice President for Academic Affairs, 201 Alumni Hall, University of Maine at Orono, Orono, Maine 04469, telephone (207) 581-1547.

Marietta College
215 5th Street
Marietta, OH 45750
(740) 376-4643
http://www.marietta.edu

For several years Marietta has required its new students to read a particular book as part of an integrated program of lectures, discussions, and other presentations. According to Dr. Gerald L. Evans of the Department of English, "The book is also used as a basis for at least one essay in English 101, and one oral presentation in Speech 101. A copy of the book selected is sent to each entering freshman in the summer before matriculation."

Some of the books in recent years have been:

Eiseley, Loren	*All the Strange Hours*
Frankel, Victor	*Man's Search for Meaning*
Hersey, John	*Hiroshima*
Niess, Judith	*Seven Women*
O'Neill, William L.	*Coming Apart: An Informal History of America in the 60's*

Duke University: Consider the books you have read in the last year or two either for school or for leisure. Please discuss the way in which one of them changed your understanding of the world, other people, or yourself.

Marquette University
Milwaukee, WI 53201-1881
(414) 288 7302
http://www.marquette.edu

Marquette's booklet "An Incomplete Reading List" is addressed to students entering or already in the university. It is a long list that makes frequently annotated recommendations across the disciplines. All the authors on the list have been included below as well as representative samples of the annotations in the various sections. Students interested in Marquette may obtain the entire pamphlet from the Department of English.

In his preface to the booklet, the Dean of the College of Arts and Sciences, the Rev. John P. Schlegel, SJ, writes that the list is "an invitation to join the ranks of educated people who passionately enjoy reading and firmly believe, along with John Milton, that books 'do contain a potency of life in them to be as active as that soul was whose progeny they are.'"

An Incomplete Reading List

Anthropology

Gould, Stephen Jay, *Ontogeny and Phylogeny* A very important critique of the social use of biology with clear implications for evaluating the use of science to support social policies.

Marriott, Alice, *The Ten Grandmothers* A beautifully told biography showing what it is to be human in another cultural tradition. Looks at American history from the viewpoint of America's native people.

Other books include

Beauvoir, Simone de	*The Second Sex*
Douglas, Mary	*Purity and Danger*
Hudson, Liam	*The Cult of the Fact*
Schneider, David	*American Kinship*

Biology

Attenborough, David, *Life on Earth, The Living Planet* Explores the survival strategies of various species. Illustrated with photographs.

Darwin, Charles, *The Origin of Species by Means of Natural Selection* or *The Preservation of Favored Races in The Struggle for Life* Presents the major evidence for evolution known in 1872.

The Voyage of the Beagle Darwin's own chronicle of the expedition that produced the discoveries and observations that eventually led him to a theory of evolution.

Sagan, Carl, *Broca's Brain: Reflections on the Romance of Science* Explores a wide range of topics about the universe and ourselves.

The Dragons of Eden: Speculations on the Evolution of Human Intelligence A speculative explanation of the evolution of our central nervous system. Winner of the Pulitzer Prize.

Other works include

Bronowski, Jacob	*Insight; On Being an Intellectual; Science and Human Values; The Ascent of Man; A Sense of the Future: Essays in Natural Philosophy; Magic, Science, and Civilization; The Origins of Knowledge and Imagination; The Visionary Eye; Essays in the Arts, Literature, and Science*
Burnet, F. MacFarlane	*Immunology, Aging, and Cancer*
Carson, Rachel	*The Sea Around Us; Silent Spring; The Sense of Wonder; The Edge of the Sea*
Drlica, Karl	*Understanding DNA and Gene Cloning*
Ehrlich, Paul and Anne Ehrlich	*Extinction*
Gould, Stephen Jay	*The Panda's Thumb*
Heyerdahl, Thor	*Kon Tiki*
Leopold, Aldo	*A Sand County Almanac*
Lewin, Roger	*Thread of Life: The Smithsonian Looks at Evolution*
Lorenz, Konrad	*King Solomon's Ring*
Miller, Jonathan	*The Body in Question; Darwin for Beginners*

Restak, Richard	*The Brain*
Romer, Alfred	*The Procession of Life*
Schaller, George	*The Serengeti Lion: A Study of Predator-Prey Relations*
Stableford, Brian	*Future Man*
Stebbins, G. Ledyard	*Darwin to DNA: Molecules to Humanity*
Storer, John H.	*The Web of Life*
Thomas, Lewis	*The Lives of a Cell: Notes of a Biology Watcher; The Medusa and the Snail: More Notes of a Biology Watcher*
Watson, James D.	*The Double Helix*
Zinsser, Hans	*Rats, Lice, and History*

Chemistry

Schrodinger, Erin C., *Science, Theory, and Man* Essays written by a Nobel Laureate in physics on man and the changing world of science.

Other works include

Glasstone, Samuel	*Sourcebook on Atomic Energy*
MacDonald, Malcolm M. and Robert E. Davis	*Chemistry and Society*
Pauling, Linus	*The Architecture of Molecules; The Nature of the Chemical Bond*
Weinberg, Alvin M.	*Reflections on Big Science*

Criminology and Law Studies

Abbot, Jack H.	*In the Belly of the Beast*
Cullen, Francis T.	*Reaffirming Rehabilitation*
Krisberg, Barry, and James Austin	*The Children of Ishmael: Critical Perspectives on Juvenile Justice*
Silberman, Charles E.	*Criminal Violence, Criminal Justice*
Walker, Samuel	*The Police in America*

Essays and Letters

Lewis, C.S., *The Screwtape Letters* An exchange of letters between two devils on how to undermine human hopes, efforts, and desires. Acutely understanding of human beings and of why and how they go wrong.

White, E.B., *Essays of E. B. White*; *Letters of E. B. White* White has been described as a "civilized human being an order of man that has always been distinguished for its rarity." His essays and letters are urbane, witty, and graceful. Arguably the best American prose stylist of this century, White is not to be missed.

Other works include

Brown, John Mason, ed.	*The Portable Charles Lamb*
Chesterton, G.K.	*Orthodoxy*
Davies, Robertson	*A Voice from the Attic*
Howarth, William L., ed.	*The John McPhee Reader*
O'Connor, Flannery	*The Habit of Being: Letters of Flannery O'Connor*
Percy, Walker	*The Message in the Bottle*; *Lost in the Cosmos: The Last Self-Help Book*
Weaver, Richard	*The Ethics of Rhetoric*

Fine Arts

Belloli, Andrea, *A Day in the Country: Impressionism and the French Landscape* Over 130 color plates each accompanied by a descriptive and interpretive statement. Excellent, thought-provoking text on the nature of impressionist painting. Monet, Pissaro, and Sisley are featured primarily.

Other works include

Arnheim, Rudolf	*Art and Visual Perception*
Berenson, Bernard	*The Italian Painters of the Renaissance*
Bodkin, Maud	*Archetypal Patterns in Poetry*
Bowness, Alan	*Forty Years of Modern Art, 1945–1985*
Brooks, Cleanth and Robert Penn Warren, eds.	*Understanding Poetry*

Byron, Robert	*The Appreciation of Architecture*
Clark, Kenneth	*Looking at Pictures*; *The Nude: A Study of Ideal Form*
Cooke, Deryck	*The Language of Music*
Copland, Aaron	*What to Listen for in Music*
Cross, Milton	*The Story of the Opera*
Frye, Northrop	*The Anatomy of Criticism*
Gordey, Beverly	*The World of Marc Chagall*
Haviland, Jenny	*A Picture History of Art*
Hitchcock, H.R.	*Architecture*
Langer, Susanne K.	*Feeling and Form*; *Philosophy in a New Key*
Machlis, Joseph	*The Enjoyment of Music: An Introduction to Perceptive Listening*
Maritain, Jacques	*Creative Intuition in Art and Poetry*
Panofsky, Erwin	*Meaning in the Visual Arts*
Pratt, Carroll C.	*The Meaning of Music*
Read, Sir Herbert	*The Art of Sculpture*
Sessions, Roger	*The Musical Experience of Composer, Performer, Listener*
Sullivan, J.W.N.	*Beethoven: His Spiritual Development*
Weitz, Morris	*Philosophy of the Arts*
Zevi, Bruno	*Architecture as Space*

History

Fraser, Antonia, *Mary Queen of Scots* The story of the romantic, adventurous, and bloody career of Mary Stuart.

Moorhead, Alan, *Gallipoli* An account of the disastrous landing in the Dardanelles by the British and their allies during World War I. The studies the Marine Corps made of this operation formed the basis of U.S. amphibious doctrine in World War II.

Tuchman, Barbara, *The Guns of August* Retells the events of the opening months of World War I. The best work of one of America's most widely-read historians.

Wiesel, Elie, *Night* A spellbinding account of the author's experiences as a young boy in a Nazi death camp.

Other works include

Aries, Phillippe	*Centuries of Childhood: A Social History of Family Life*
Auerbach, Jerold	*Unequal Justice: Lawyers and Social Change in Modern America*
Bartlett, Merrill L.	*Assault from the Sea*
Blake, Robert	*Disraeli*
Castillo, Bernal D. del	*The Conquest of New Spain*
Fieldhouse, David	*The Colonial Empires: A Comparative Survey from the 18th Century*
Freeman, Douglas S.	*Lee's Lieutenants: A Study of Command*
Gross, Robert A.	*The Minutemen and Their World*
Guevara, Ernesto "Che" (Brian Loveman and Thomas Davies, eds.)	*Guerrilla Warfare*
Keegan, John	*The Face of Battle: A Study of Agincourt, Waterloo, and the Somme*
Lafeber, Walter	*Inevitable Revolutions: The United States and Central America*
Laslett, Peter	*The World We Have Lost: England Before the Industrial Age*
Lukacs, John	*The Last European War: September 1939–December 1941*
Mallon, Floencia	*The Defense of Community in Peru's Highlands: Peasant Struggle and Capitalist Tradition*
Mandrou, Robert	*Introduction to Modern France: An Essay in Historical Psychology*
Mattingly, Garrett	*The Armada*
Morgan, Edmund	*American Slavery, American Freedom: The Ordeal of Colonial Virginia*
Nash, Gary B.	*Red, White, and Black: The Peoples of Early America*
Pluvier, J.M.	*South-East Asia from Colonialism to Independence*
Preston, Robert and Sydney Wise	*Men in Arms*

Ruiz, Ramon	*The Great Rebellion: Mexico, 1905–1924*
Schlesinger, Jr., Arthur	*The Imperial Presidency*
Singer, Peter	*Marx*
Smith, Tony	*The Pattern of Imperialism: The U.S., Great Britain, and the Late-Industrializing World Since 1815*
Solzhenitsyn, Alexander	*Cancer Ward*
Soustelle, Jacques	*Daily Life of the Aztecs on the Eve of the Spanish Conquest*
Toynbee, Arnold	*The Study of History*
Weber, Eugen	*Peasants and Frenchmen: The Modernization of Rural France*
Wiebe, Robert	*A Search For Order*

World Literature

Classical

Aeschylus	*Oresteia*
Augustine, Saint	*Confessions*
Herodotus	*History*
Homer	*The Iliad; The Odyssey*
Horace	*Carmina*
Vergil	*The Aeneid*

American

Ellison, Ralph	*Invisible Man*
Faulkner, William	*The Sound and the Fury*
Fitzgerald, F. Scott	*The Great Gatsby*
Hawthorne, Nathaniel	*The Scarlet Letter*
Hemingway, Ernest	*The Sun Also Rises*
James, Henry	*The Portrait of a Lady*
Melville, Herman	*Moby-Dick*
Miller, Arthur	*Death of a Salesman*
Thoreau, Henry David	*Walden*
Twain, Mark	*The Adventures of Huckleberry Finn*

Poems of **Emily Dickinson, Robert Frost, Edgar Allan Poe, Ezra Pound, Wallace Stevens, William Carlos Williams,** and **Walt Whitman.**

English

Austen, Jane	*Pride and Prejudice*
Chaucer, Geoffrey	*The Canterbury Tales*
Conrad, Joseph	*Heart of Darkness*
Dickens, Charles	*Great Expectations*
Eliot, George	*Middlemarch*
Fielding, Henry	*Tom Jones*
Joyce, James	*Ulysses*
Milton, John	*Paradise Lost*
Shakespeare, William	*Hamlet; King Lear; The Tempest*
Shaw, George Bernard	*Major Barbara*
Swift, Jonathan	*Gulliver's Travels*

Poems of **Robert Browning; Samuel Taylor Coleridge; T.S. Eliot; John Keats; Alfred, Lord Tennyson; William Wordsworth; W.B. Yeats.**

French

Balzac, Honoré de	*Eugenie Grandet (The Human Comedy)*
Flaubert, Gustave	*Madame Bovary*
Molière	*The Misanthrope*
Montaigne, Michel de	*Essays*
Pascal, Blaise	*Thoughts*
Proust, Marcel	*Swann's Way (Remembrance of Things Past)*
Rabelais, François	*Gargantua*
Racine, Jean	*Phaedra*
Rousseau, Jean-Jacques	*Emile (On Education)*
Voltaire	*Candide*

German

	The Song of the Nibelungs
Böll, Heinrich	*The Lost Honor of Katharina Blum*
Brecht, Bertolt	*Mother Courage and Her Children*

Eschenbach, Wolfram yon	*Parzifal*
Fontane, Teodor	*Effie Briest*
Goethe, Johann W. von	*Faust*
Grass, Günter	*The Tin Drum*
Kafka, Franz	*The Trial*
Kleist, Henrich von	*Michael Kohlhaas*
Lessing, Gotthold E.	*Nathan the Wise*
Mann, Thomas	*The Magic Mountain*
Rilke, Rainer Maria	*New Poems*
Schiller, Friedrich	*Wilhelm Tell*
Wolf, Christa	*Divided Heaven*

Italian

Calvino, Italo	*The Cosmicomics*
Dante	*The Divine Comedy*
Eco, Umberto	*The Name of the Rose*
Fallaci, Oriana	*Interview with History*
Ginzberg, Natalia	*Valentine; Le Voci Della Sera*
Goldini, Carlo	*Autobiography; The Fan*
Machiavelli, Niccolò	*The Prince*
Manzoni, Alessandro	*The Betrothed*
Morante, Elsa	*History*
Pirandello, Luigi	*The Late Mattia Pascal; Henry IV*
Pomilio	*Natale 1848*
Sciascia, Leonardo	*Gli Zii D'America*
Silone, Ignazio	*Bread and Wine*
Svevo, Italo	*The Confessions of Zeno*
Verga, Giovanni	*The House by the Medlar Tree*

Russian

Aksyonov, Vasilii	*Crimea Island; A Starry Ticket*
Dostoevski, Fyodor	*The Brothers Karamazov; Crime and Punishment*
Fadeyev, Alexander	*Young Guard*

Gogol, Nikolae	*Dead Souls*
Gorky, Maxim	*The Lower Depths; The Mother*
Pasternak, Boris	*Dr. Zhivago*
Pushkin, Alexander	*Captain's Daughter; Eugene Onegin*
Rasputin, Valentin	*Live and Remember*
Sholokov, Mikhail	*The Silent Don*
Shukshin, Vasilii	*Snowball Berry Red*
Solzhenitsyn, Alexander	*Cancer Ward; First Circle*
Tolstoy, Leo	*Anna Karenina; War and Peace*
Turgenev, Ivan	*Fathers and Sons*

Spanish

Cervantes, Miguel de	*Don Quixote*
García Márquez, Gabriel	*One Hundred Years of Solitude*
Lorca, Federico Garcia	*Three Tragedies* (including *House of Bernarda Alba, Yerma, Blood Wedding*)
Paz, Octavio	*The Labryinth of Solitude*
Unamuno, Miguel de	*Abel Sanchez and Other Stories*

Mathematics

Davis, Phillip and Reuben Hersh	*The Mathematical Experience*
Hardy, G.H.	*A Mathematician's Apology*
Hofstadter, Douglas	*Gödel, Escher, Bach*
Kidder, Tracy	*The Soul of a New Machine*
Klein, Felix	*Famous Problems of Elementary Geometry*
Kline, Morris	*Mathematical Thought from Ancient to Modern Times*
Newman, James R.	*The World of Mathematics*
Poincare, Henri	*Science and Hypotheses*
Polya, George	*Mathematics and Plausible Reasoning*
Reid, Constance	*Hilbert*
Weizenbaum, Joseph	*Computer Power and Human Reason*

Mysteries

A good mystery is ideal for whiling away a quiet evening or staving off the tedium of travel. But mysteries can also be delicate probes into the nature of justice, the conflict of good and evil, and the perplexities of human motivation. There is no shortage of writers in this genre: **Agatha Christie**, **Michael Innes**, **P.D. James**, **Ngaio Marsh**, **Dorothy Sayers** in the "classic" school; **Raymond Chandler**, **Dashiell Hammett**, and **Robert B. Parker** in the "hard-boiled" one. You will find your favorites; however, the ones below are especially recommended.

Buchan, John	*The Thirty-Nine Steps*
Collins, Wilkie	*The Moonstone*
Sayers, Dorothy L.	*Gaudy Night*; *The Nine Tailors*

Philosophy

Ancient Period

Plato, *Dialogues* (especially *Apology*, *Phaedo*, and *The Republic*) Plato raises basic questions about the nature of man, the origin of knowledge, the immortality of the soul, and the nature of justice.

Other works include

Aristotle	*Nicomachean Ethics*

Medieval Period

Saint Augustine, *City of God*; *Confessions* A mixture of autobiography, philosophy, and theology containing some unusual reflections on memory and time.

Other titles include

Anselm, Saint	*Proslogion*
Aquinas, Saint Thomas	*Summa Theologia*, I. q.2
Boethius	*The Consolation of Philosophy*
Bonaventure, Saint	*Journey of the Mind to God*

Classical Modern Period

Descartes, René, *Meditations on First Philosophy* Written with verve and style, this work opened the new way of philosophizing of the classic modern period.

Other works include

Berkeley, George	*Three Dialogues Between Mylas and Philonous*
Hume, David	*Enquiry Concerning Human Understanding*
Kant, Immanuel	*Grounding for the Metaphysics of Morals*
Locke, John	*An Essay Concerning Human Understanding*
Pascal, Blaise	*Les Pensées*

Modern Period

Nietzsche, Friedrich, *Thus Spake Zarathustra* A manifesto of creative individualism, breaking with mass movements and culture and arguing for a transformation of the pivotal values that shape human life.

Other works include

Bergson, Henri	*Introduction to Metaphysics*
Hegel, Georg	*The Philosophy of History*
Kierkegaard, Søren	*Fear and Trembling*
Marx, Karl	*The Communist Manifesto*

Contemporary Period

Heidegger, Martin, *Being and Time* Issues a call to contemporary persons to rediscover the temporal and historical foundations of their lives, and, in the process, to recover their proper truth as participants in the global community. One of the most influential works of the 20th century.

Other works include

Buber, Martin	*I and Thou*
Moore, G.E.	*Principia Ethica*
Sartre, Jean-Paul	*Existentialism and Humanism*

American Philosophy

Dewey, John, *Reconstruction in Philosophy* Presents the view that philosophy at once is influenced by and is the necessary critic of history and changing social conditions.

Other works include

James, William	*Pragmatism*
Whitehead, Alfred North	*Adventures in Ideas*

Contemporary Catholic Philosophy

Marcel, Gabriel, *Man Against Mass Society* A critique of contemporary techniques of degradation and depersonalization.

Other works include

Gilson, Étienne	"The Middle Ages and Philosophy," *The Spirit of Medieval Philosophy*
Maritain, Jacques	"The Tragedy of Humanism," *True Humanism*

Physics

Bohr, Niels, *Atomic Physics and Human Knowledge* Essays on the impact of atomic physics on human thought and culture.

Other works include

Bronowski, Jacob	*Science and Human Values*
Cohen, I. Bernard	*The Birth of a New Physics*
Duhem, Pierre	*To Save the Phenomena: An Essay on the Idea of Physical Theory from Plato to Galileo*
Dyson, Freeman	*Disturbing the Universe*
Feynman, Richard	*The Character of Physical Law*
Heisenberg, Werner	*Physics and Philosophy*; *Across the Frontier*; *Physics and Beyond*
Langford, Jerome J.	*Galileo, Science, and the Church*
Weinber, Stephen	*The First Three Minutes*
Ziman, John	*Public Knowledge: The Social Dimension of Science*

Political Science

Aristotle	*Ethics; Politics*
Art, Robert and Robert Jervice	*International Politics*
Bagehot, Walter	*The English Constitution*
Baradat, Leon P.	*Political Ideologies*
Barber, James David	*Presidential Character*, 2nd ed.
Ebenstein, William	*Today's "Isms"*
Hamilton, Alexander, et al.	*The Federalist Papers*
Lowi, Theodore	*The End of Liberalism*
Neustadt, Richard	*Presidential Power: The Politics of Leadership from Roosevelt to Carter*
O'Connor, James	*The Fiscal Crisis of the State*
Plato	*The Republic*
Reich, Robert	*The Next American Frontier*
Simon, Yves	*Philosophy of Democratic Government*
Sola Pool, Ithiel de	*Technologies of Freedom*
Tocqueville, Alexis de	*Democracy in America*
Waltz, Kenneth	*Man, the State, and War*
Wolfer, Arnold	*Discord and Collaboration*
White, Theodore	*The Making of the President: 1960*

Psychology

Allport, Gordon	*Becoming*
Arieti, Silvano	*Creativity: The Magic Synthesis*
Coleman, J.C., J.N. Butcher, and R.C. Carson	*Abnormal Psychology & Modern Life*
Cronbach, Lee J.	*Essentials of Psychological Testing*
Erikson, Erik	*Childhood & Society*
Flavell, John H.	*The Developmental Psychology of Jean Piaget*
Freud, Sigmund	*The Interpretation of Dreams*
Hall, C. and G. Lindzey	*Theories of Personality*, 3rd ed.
James, William	*Principles of Psychology*
Loehlin, J.C. and J.N. Spuhler	*Race Differences in Intelligence*
MacCoby, Eleanor E.	*Social Development: Psychological Growth and the Parent-Child Relationship*

Maslow, Abraham	*Toward a Psychology of Being*
May, Rollo	*Existence*
Neisser, Ulric	*Memory Observed*
Penfield, Wilder	*The Mystery of the Mind*
Skinner, B.F.	*Beyond Freedom and Dignity*

Science and Liberal Education

Conant, James Bryant, *On Understanding Science* Emphasizes the importance of an understanding of science for all citizens and the advantage of a historical approach to teaching science. Lectures by a chemist and former president of Harvard.

Other works include

Dubos, René	*Reason Awake: Science for Man*
Harrington, J.W.	*Discovering Science*
Whitehead, Alfred North	*The Aims of Education*

Social Work

Addams, Jane, *Hull House* The story of the settlement-house movement in Chicago by one of its greatest leaders.

Other works include

Napier, Augustus	*The Family Crucible*
Satir, Virginia	*Conjoint Family Therapy*
Tratner, William	*From Poor Law to Welfare State*

Sociology

Berger, Peter L. and Thomas Luckmann, *The Social Construction of Reality* One of the most influential books in modern sociology, especially in the movement toward a sociology of knowledge perspective.

Other works include

Bellah, Madsen, Sullivan, Swidler, and Tipton	*Habits of the Heart: Individualism and Commitment in American Life*

Braverman, Harry	*Labor and Monopoly Capital*
Cloward, Richard and Francis Fox Piven	*Regulating the Poor*
Durkheim, Emile	*The Division of Labor in Society*
Erickson, Kai T.	*Wayward Puritans: A Study in the Sociology of Deviance*
Garfinkle, Harold	*Studies in Ethnomethodology*
Goffman, Erving	*The Presentation of Self in Everyday Life*
Mead, George Herbert	*Mind, Self, and Society*
Mills, C. Wright	*The Sociological Imagination; The Power Elite*
Weber, Max	*Economy and Society; The Protestant Ethic and the Spirit of Capitalism*
Whyte, William Foote	*Street Corner Society*

Theology

Edwards, Jonathan, *Freedom of the Will* Classic argument against freedom by one of the greatest American Protestant preachers and theologians.

Schweitzer, Albert, *The Quest for the Historical Jesus* Classic example of historical-critical research.

Other works include

	Bible
Ahlstrom, Sydney	*A Religious History of the American People*
Anderson, Bernhard	*Understanding the Old Testament*
Aquinas, Saint Thomas	*Summa Contra Gentiles*
Augustine, Saint of Hippo	*The Confessions*
Bornkamm, Gunther	*Jesus of Nazareth*
Brown, Robert M.	*The Spirit of Protestantism*
Charpentier, Étienne	*How to Read the Old Testament*
Childs, Brevard	*The New Testament as Scripture*
Day, Dorothy	*The Long Loneliness*
De Vaux, Roland	*Ancient Israel*
Dulles, Avery	*A Church to Believe In*
Erickson, Erik	*Gandhi's Truth*

Hellwig, Monika	*Understanding Catholicism*
Heschel, Abraham	*God in Search of Man*
Johnson, Paul	*History of Christianity*
Jerimias, J.	*The Parable of Jesus*
Kasper, Walter	*Jesus the Christ*
Kelly, J.N.D.	*Early Christian Doctrines*

Bennington College: Respond to A or B.

A. "No method nor discipline can supersede the necessity of being forever on the alert. What is a course of history, or philosophy, or poetry, or the most admirable routine of life compared with the discipline of looking always at what is to be seen?"

—Henry David Thoreau

Choose a person, object, or site located within one-quarter mile of your home, and interpret it from three different perspectives.

B. "The greatest thing by far is to be a master of metaphor. It is the one thing that cannot be learned from others; and it is also a sign of genius, since a good metaphor implies an intuitive perception of the similarity in dissimilars."

—Aristotle

At Bennington, teachers and students are continually making metaphors—creating connections between ideas, media, disciplines, and all the other elements of experience. We invite you to prove yourself a "master of metaphor" by demonstrating your ability to make compelling connections between things that might appear to be unrelated.

Kierkegaard, Søren	*Fear and Trembling*
Kung, Hans	*On Being a Christian*
Latourelle	*Theology of Revelation*
Luther, Martin	*Christian Liberty*
Merton, Thomas	*Seeds of Contemplation*
Murray, John Courtney	*We Hold These Truths: Catholic Reflections on the American Proposition*
Niebuhr, H. Richard	*Christ and Culture*; *The Responsible Self*
Niebuhr, Reinhold	*The Nature and Destiny of Man*
Rahner, Karl	*Foundations of Christian Faith*
Ratzinger, Josef	*Introduction to Christianity*
Smith, John	*Experience and God*
Sobrino, Jon	*Christology at the Crossroads*
Teresa of Avila	*The Autobiography of Saint Teresa*
Chardin, P. Teilhard de	*The Divine Milieu*
Tillich, Paul	*Love, Power, and Justice*
Trevor, Meriol	*Newman* (2 vols.)
Yoder, John Howard	*The Politics of Jesus*

University of Maryland
College Park, MD 20742
(301) 405-1000
http://www.umd.edu

Maryland's English Department offers students a number of introductory literature courses. The following is a general description and examples of the reading in some of those courses.

Western World Literature, Homer to the Renaissance

This course is an introduction to European or "Western" literature. Among the considerations the class is concerned with are the ethical values implicit in the works, the literary conventions of each era, and the influences on works in later Western societies. Principal works from Greek, Hebrew, and Medieval Christian civilization are studied. Some texts read are **Homer**'s *Iliad* and *Odyssey*, a Greek play, the *Bible* (studied as literature), **Vergil**'s *Aeneid*, **Dante**'s *Inferno, The Song of Roland, Beowulf,* and *Sir Gawain and the Green Knight.*

Western World Literature, Renaissance to the Present

In this course students read from such authors as **Shakespeare**, **Goethe**, **Molière**, **Swift**, **Voltaire, Dostoevski, Cervantes, Camus**, **Lorca**, and **Paz**. The ethical values implicit in the works, literary conventions of the era, and the influences of these works on later Western societies are among the considerations for discussion.

Western World Literature Renaissance to the Present (Honors English)

Through a number of European writers, the course explores two principal ways of looking at the world and the tensions between those two ways: one asserting the primacy of the human being and the other, traditional until the Renaissance, conceiving the human being as subordinate to "a range of other beings and ultimately to God." Some of the writers considered are **Dante Alighieri**, **Niccolò Machiavelli**, **Michel Eyquem de Montaigne**, **William Shakespeare**, **Johann Wolfgang von Goethe**, **Pierre Charles Baudelaire, Leo Tolstoy**, **Franz Kafka**, **Thomas Mann**, and **William Butler Yeats**.

Introduction to Shakespeare

Considerations in this course concern human psychology, the differences between theater and other forms of story telling, and the differences between "tragic and comic outlook."

English Literature from the Beginning to 1800

Students read texts from each of the major periods—Medieval (Anglo-Saxon and Middle English), Renaissance, Restoration, and 18th century. Texts usually included are *Beowulf* and works by **Geoffrey Chaucer**, **Edmund Spenser**, **John Milton**, **Jonathan Swift**, **and Alexander Pope**.

English Literature from 1800 to the Present

This course offers students a survey of English literature from the Romantic, Victorian, and Early Modern traditions. Students study works by such authors as **William Wordsworth**; **Percy Bysshe Shelley**; **Mary Shelley**; **John Keats**; **Jane Austen**; **Charles Dickens**; **George Eliot**; **Alfred, Lord Tennyson**; **Robert Browning**; **William Butler Yeats**; **T.S. Eliot**; **D.H. Lawrence**; and **Virginia Woolf**.

American Literature, 1865–Present

Authors read include **Walt Whitman**, **Emily Dickinson**, **Mark Twain**, **Henry James**, **Stephen Crane**, **F. Scott Fitzgerald**, **William Faulkner**, **Ernest Hemingway**, **Eugene O'Neill**, and **T.S. Eliot**.

Introduction to Drama

In a broad survey of many types of drama such as classical comedy and tragedy, melodrama, romance, and black comedy, students read works from such playwrights as **Sophocles**, **Aristophanes**, **Aeschylus**, **William Shakespeare**, **Molière**, **Eugene O'Neill**, **Harold Pinter**, **Samuel Beckett**, and **Edward Albee**.

Special Topics in Literature: Love, Adventure, and Identity in Early English Literature

Students read narratives written from the early English period through the 18th century. Authors and their works may include *Beowulf*; *Sir Gawain and the Green Knight*; **William Shakespeare**, *Othello*; **Elizabeth Cary**, *The Tragedy of Mariam*; **John Donne**, poems; **John Milton**, *Samson Agonistes*; **Aphra Behn**, *Oroonoko*; and **Daniel Defoe**, *Robinson Crusoe*.

Introduction to Latino Literature in the U.S.

In this course students read **Alvar Nuñez Cabeza de Vaca**'s 16th-century narrative and selected essays by **Jose Marti**. The majority of texts, however, are contemporary, and include **Oscar Hijuelos**, *The Mambo Kings Play Songs of Love*, and **Sandra Cisneros**, *The House on Mango Street*.

Terrapin Reading Society

Undergraduate students at the University of Maryland may join the Terrapin Reading Society where they may share their reading experiences with faculty and staff. The society selects a book of the year, and each year, Undergraduate Studies sponsors activities and events related to that book. Some instructors may choose to include the current year's society book on their lists of required or suggested reading. Free copies of Terrapin Reading Society books are distributed during summer orientation to all new first year students and new transfer students taking a required English 101, Introduction to Writing.

Messiah College
College Avenue
Grantham, PA 17027-8000
(717) 766-2511
http://www.messiah.edu

Professor William Jolliff has listed several books that are used in Messiah's freshman Integrated Studies course Skill and Perceptions. "It is a one-semester course that integrates elements of traditional literature, composition, social psychology, and life skills courses." In it, students read a number of essays, short stories, and poems from **Carolyn Shrodes, et al., eds.**, *The Conscious Reader*, and the following complete works:

Angelou, Maya	*I Know Why the Caged Bird Sings*
Conrad, Joseph	*Heart of Darkness*
Mauriac, François	*Vipers' Tangle*
O'Neill, Eugene	*Long Day's Journey Into Night*
Potok, Chaim	*The Chosen*

Johns Hopkins: At Hopkins, a political science professor uses contemporary fiction by African authors to teach about the politics of southern Africa. If you were to design a course around the music, art, film, or literature that you like, what would that course be about? What would you hope to teach your students? Please include a listening/viewing/reading list with your essay.

Miami University
Oxford, OH 45056
(513) 529-1809
http://www.muohio.edu

Miami has the following suggested reading list for high school students:

Adams, Henry	*The Education of Henry Adams*
Adler, Irving	*How Life Began*
Aesop	*Fables*
Asimov, Isaac	*The Genetic Code*
Augustine, Saint	*Confessions*
Aurelius, Marcus	*Meditations*
Austen, Jane	*Pride and Prejudice*
Ballou, Robert O., ed.	*The Portable World Bible*
Barnett, Lincoln	*The Universe and Dr. Einstein*
Beard, Charles A.	*The Rise of American Civilization*
Bellamy, Edward	*Looking Backward*
Benedict, Ruth	*Patterns of Culture*
Benet, Stephen Vincent	*John Brown's Body*
Boehm, G.A.W.	*The New World of Math*
Bowen, Catherine D.	*Yankee from Olympus*
Brogan, D.W.	*The American Character*
Brown, Harrison	*The Challenge of Man's Future*
Bulfinch, Thomas	*Mythology*

Bunyan, John	*The Pilgrim's Progress*
Carroll, Lewis	*Alice's Adventures in Wonderland*
Carson, Rachel	*The Sea Around Us*
Catton, Bruce	*A Stillness at Appomattox*
Ceram, C.W.	*Gods, Graves, and Scholars*
Cerf, Bennett, ed.	*Great Modern Short Stories*
Chase, Stuart	*Proper Study of Mankind*
Churchill, Winston	*A History of the English-Speaking Peoples*
Coleman, James A.	*Relativity for the Layman*
Commager and Nevins	*Freedom, Loyalty, and Dissent*
Conant, James B.	*Modern Science and Modern Man*
Conrad, Joseph	*Lord Jim*
Crane, Stephen	*The Red Badge of Courage*
Creekmore, Hubert, ed.	*A Little Treasury of World Poetry*
Curie, Eve	*Madame Curie*
Darwin, Charles	*Autobiography*
Davis, Elmer	*But We Were Born Free*
Day, Clarence	*Life with Father*
Dean, Vera M.	*The Culture of the Non-Western World*
Defoe, Daniel	*Moll Flanders*
Dickens, Charles	*David Copperfield*
Dostoevski, Fyodor	*Crime and Punishment*
Doyle, Sir Arthur Conan	*The Adventures of Sherlock Holmes*
Dreiser, Theodore	*An American Tragedy*
Durant, Will	*The Story of Philosophy*
Epictetus	*Enchiridion*
Faulkner, William	*Three Famous Short Novels*
Franklin, Benjamin	*Autobiography*
Frazer, James George	*The Golden Bough*
Frost, Robert	*Poems*
Gamow, George	*The Creation of the Universe*
Gardner, Martin, ed.	*Great Essays on Science*
Hamilton, Alexander, et al.	*On the Constitution* (Selections from *The Federalist Papers*)
Hamilton, Edith	*The Greek Way*

Hardy, Thomas	*The Return of the Native*
Hawthorne, Nathaniel	*The Scarlet Letter*
Heilbroner, Robert	*The Worldly Philosophers*
Hemingway, Ernest	*For Whom the Bell Tolls*
Hofstadter, Richard	*The American Political Tradition*
Homer	*The Iliad; The Odyssey*
Housman, A.E.	*A Shropshire Lad*
Huxley, Aldous	*Brave New World*
Huxley, Julian	*Man in the Modern World*
James, William	*The Varieties of Religious Experience*
Jean, James	*The Mysterious Universe*
Joyce, James	*A Portrait of the Artist as a Young Man*
Kasuer and Newman	*Mathematics and the Imagination*
Kennedy, John F.	*Profiles in Courage*
Kluckhohn, Clyde	*Mirror for Man*
Koestler, Arthur	*Darkness at Noon*
Loesser, Arthur	*Men, Women, and Pianos*
Lucretius	*On the Nature of Things*
Lynd and Lynd	*Middletown, U.S.A.*
Maeterlinck, Maurice	*The Life of the Bee*
Maugham, Somerset	*Of Human Bondage*
Mead, Margaret	*New Lives for Old*
Melville, Herman	*Moby-Dick*
Mill, John Stuart	*On Liberty*
Moore, Ruth	*Man, Time, and Fossils*
Muller, Herbert J.	*The Uses of the Past*
Orwell, George	*1984*
Parkman, Francis	*The Oregon Trail*
Poe, Edgar Allan	*Poems and Selected Tales*
St. Exupéry, Antoine de	*The Little Prince*
Sandburg, Carl	*Harvest Poems*
Schweitzer, Albert	*Out of My Life and Thought*
***Scientific American*, eds.**	*New Chemistry; The Planet Earth; The Physics and Chemistry of Life: The Universe*
Shakespeare, William	*Hamlet; Henry IV, Part I; Julius Caesar; MacBeth; Othello; Romeo and Juliet;* selections from sonnets

Shaw, George Bernard	*Arms and the Man; Caesar and Cleopatra; Candida; Major Barbara; Man and Superman; Pygmalion; Saint Joan*
Steffens, Lincoln	*Autobiography*
Steinbeck, John	*The Grapes of Wrath*
Swift, Jonathan	*Gulliver's Travels*
Thackeray, William Makepeace	*Vanity Fair*
Thoreau, Henry David	*Civil Disobedience; Walden*
Tocqueville, Alexis de	*Democracy in America*
Twain, Mark	*The Adventures of Huckleberry Finn*
Van Loon, Hendrik	*The Story of Mankind*
Wells, H.G.	*An Outline of History*
Whitehead, Alfred North	*Science and the Modern World*
Whitman, Walt	*Leaves of Grass*
Wilder, Thornton	*Three Plays*
Williams, Oscar, ed.	*A Pocket Book of Modern Verse*
Yutang, Lin	*The Wisdom of China and India*
Zinsser, Hans	*Rats, Lice, and History*

The novel list for Miami's English 112 (freshman English) includes:

Amis, Kingsley	*Lucky Jim*
Anderson, Sherwood	*Winesburg, Ohio*
Angelou, Maya	*I Know Why the Caged Bird Sings*
Atwood, Margaret	*Surfacing*
Austen, Jane	*Pride and Prejudice*
Baldwin, James	*Go Tell It on the Mountain*
Barth, John	*The End of the Road*
Bellow, Saul	*Henderson the Rain King; Seize the Day*
Bradbury, Ray	*Dandelion Wine*
Brontë, Charlotte	*Jane Eyre*
Camus, Albert	*The Stranger*
Cather, Willa	*O Pioneers!*
Chopin, Kate	*The Awakening*
Conrad, Joseph	*Heart of Darkness* and *The Secret Sharer*
Ellison, Ralph	*Invisible Man*

Fitzgerald, F. Scott	*The Great Gatsby*
Fowles, John	*The Collector*
Greene, Graham	*Brighton Rock*
Hardy, Thomas	*Far from the Madding Crowd*
Hawkes, John	*Second Skin*
Hawthorne, Nathaniel	*The House of the Seven Gables*
Hemingway, Ernest	*A Farewell to Arms; The Sun Also Rises*
James, Henry	*The American*
Joyce, James	*A Portrait of the Artist as a Young Man; Dubliners*
Kesey, Ken	*One Flew over the Cuckoo's Nest*
Koestler, Arthur	*Darkness at Noon*
Lawrence, D.H.	*Sons and Lovers*
Malamud, Bernard	*The Assistant; The Fixer*
McCullers, Carson	*The Heart is a Lonely Hunter*
Melville, Herman	*Billy Budd*
O'Connor, Flannery	*Three by Flannery O'Connor* (*Wise Blood; The Violent Bear It Away; A Good Man is Hard to Find*)
Orwell, George	*Animal Farm*
Pynchon, Thomas	*The Crying of Lot 49*
Salinger, J.D.	*The Catcher in the Rye*
Steinbeck, John	*Of Mice and Men*
Wallant, Edward Louis	*The Tenants of Moonbloom*
Wiesel, Elie	*Night*
West, Nathanael	*Day of the Locust; Miss Lonelyhearts*
Wilde, Oscar	*The Picture of Dorian Gray*
Wright, Richard	*Native Son*

Titles studied in English 112, a freshman drama class, are

Albee, Edward	*Who's Afraid of Virginia Woolf?; The Zoo Story*
Anouilh, Jean	*Becket*
Aristophanes	*Lysistrata*
Baraka, Imamu Amiri (formerly LeRoi Jones)	*Dutchman*
Beckett, Samuel	*Waiting for Godot*
Dryden, John	*All for Love*

Eliot, T.S.	*Murder in the Cathedral*
Ibsen, Henrik	*A Doll's House; An Enemy of the People; Hedda Gabler*
Ionesco, Eugene	*MacBett; Rhinoceros*
Kopit, Arthur	*Indians*
MacLeish, Archibald	*J.D.*
Miller, Arthur	*Death of a Salesman; The Crucible*
Molière	*The Misanthrope; Tartuffe*
O'Neill, Eugene	*Desire under the Elms; The Emperor Jones; The Hairy Ape*
Shakespeare, William	Any play
Shaw, George Bernard	*Arms and the Man; Candida; Pygmalion; Saint Joan*
Sophocles	*Antigone; Oedipus Rex*
Stoppard, Tom	*Rosencrantz and Guildenstern Are Dead*
Synge, John	*The Playboy of the Western World*
Wilde, Oscar	*The Importance of Being Earnest*
Williams, Tennessee	*A Streetcar Named Desire*

University of Michigan
1220 Student Activities Building
Ann Arbor, MI 48109
(734) 764-1817
http://www.umich.edu

Students in the University of Michigan's Undergraduate English Association advise pre-college students, especially those planning a concentration in English, to have a knowledge of the *Bible* and of Greek mythology, "for many concepts and plots throughout literature are drawn from these sources." They add, "exposure to some works by **Shakespeare** and a **Dickens** novel would be helpful in developing the necessary skill of analyzing and comparing different authors' styles." And they also suggest high school students "expand their reading beyond the traditional English and American works to include writers from various parts of the world." The English faculty of the university have compiled an "unofficial reading list," which suggests some of the works they consider important.

DEPARTMENT OF ENGLISH LANGUAGE AND LITERATURE UNOFFICIAL READING LIST

	Sir Gawain and the Green Knight
Anderson, Sherwood	*Winesburg, Ohio*
Austen, Jane	*Emma*; *Northanger Abbey*; *Pride and Prejudice*
Baldwin, James	*Notes of a Native Son*
Barth, John	Selections
Beckett, Samuel	*Waiting for Godot*
Behn, Aphra	*Oroonoko* or *The Royal Slave*
Brontë, Charlotte	*Jane Eyre*
Chaucer, Geoffrey	*The Canterbury Tales*
Congreve, William	*Plays*
Conrad, Joseph	*Heart of Darkness*
Defoe, Daniel	*The Fortunate Mistress* or *Roxanna*
Dickens, Charles	*Great Expectations*; *Hard Times*
Dickinson, Emily	Poems and letters
Dryden, John	*All for Love*
Eliot, T.S.	*The Waste Land and Other Poems*
Faulkner, William	*As I Lay Dying*; "The Bear"; *Go Down Moses*
Fielding, Henry	*Joseph Andrews*; *Tom Jones*
Fitzgerald, F. Scott	*The Last Tycoon*
Greene, Graham	*The Quiet American*
Hardy, Thomas	*Jude the Obscure*; *Tess of the D'Urbervilles*
Hawthorne, Nathaniel	*The Scarlet Letter*
Hemingway, Ernest	*African Stories*; *In Our Time*; *The Snows of Kilamanjaro and Other Stories*
James, Henry	*The Turn of the Screw*; *The Wings of the Dove*
Jonson, Ben	*Bartholomew Fayre*; *Volpone*; selected poetry
Joyce, James	*Dubliners*
Kafka, Franz	*In the Penal Colony*
Kyd, Thomas	*The Spanish Tragedy*
Lawrence, D.H.	*Lady Chatterley's Lover*

Mann, Thomas	*Mario the Magician*
Marlowe, Christopher	*Dr. Faustus*; *Jew of Malta*
Miller, Arthur	Plays
Milton, John	*Paradise Lost*
More, Thomas	*Utopia*
Orwell, George	*Keep the Aspidistra Flying*
Pinter, Harold	Plays
Pynchon, Thomas	*The Crying of Lot 49*
Shakespeare, William	*Richard III*
Shaw, George Bernard	*Pygmalion*
Shelley, Mary	*Frankenstein*
Shepard, Sam	*Seven Plays*
Spenser, Edmund	*The Faerie Queene*
Sterne, Laurence	Selections
Stowe, Harriet Beecher	*Uncle Tom's Cabin*
Swift, Jonathan	*Gulliver's Travels* and other writings
Thoreau, Henry David	*Civil Disobedience*; *Walden*
Trollope, Anthony	*The Warden*
Twain, Mark	*A Connecticut Yankee in King Arthur's Court*; *The Adventures of Huckleberry Finn*
Updike, John	*Rabbit, Run*
Walker, Alice	*The Color Purple*
Webster, John	*The Duchess of Malfi*
West, Nathanael	*Day of the Locust*
Wilde, Oscar	Plays
Wollstonecraft, Mary	Selections
Woolf, Virginia	*A Room of One's Own*; *To the Lighthouse*
Wordsworth, Dorothy	Selections
Wycherly, William	*The Country Wife*
Yearsley, MacLeod	Selections

And selected poetry from **Matthew Arnold**; **William Blake**; **Samuel Taylor Coleridge**; **John Donne**; **Ralph Waldo Emerson**; **Peter Finch**; **Robert Frost**; **George Herbert**; **John Keats**; **Andrew Marvell**; **Alexander Pope**; **Sir Walter Raleigh**; **Percy Bysshe Shelley**; **Philip Sidney**; **Alfred, Lord Tennyson**; **Walt Whitman**; **William Wordsworth**; **Thomas Wyatt**; and **William Butler Yeats**.

Mount Holyoke College: Culture and identity are closely linked. Describe how your experience of cultures has influenced your sense of self. 2. Imagine that you're a philanthropist, able to donate considerable financial resources to any institution, charity, or cause. What would you support? Why?

University of Minnesota
230 Williamson Hall,
231 Pillsbury Drive S.E.
Minneapolis, MN 55455
(612) 625-5880
http://www.umnu.edu

University of Minnesota Professor Beverley M. Atkinson suggests a list of "fifteen works of literature most important to incoming freshmen" with the following reservations: that it is "by no means the one and only list," because "the content would continue to change according to the point of view of the compiler."

She said the following list is based on the assumptions "one, that the work of literature should be widely representative of both the form in which it is written and the culture; two, that any anthology included should teach the reader methods and techniques for understanding the literature."

	Bible (King James Version)
Brontë, Charlotte	*Jane Eyre*
Dickens, Charles	*Great Expectations*
Dickinson, Emily	Poems
Dostoevski, Fyodor	A novel (or one by **Tolstoy**)
Drew, Elizabeth	*Understanding Poetry*
Ellmann, Richard and Robert O'Clair, eds.	*The Norton Anthology of Modern Poetry*
Ellison, Ralph	*Invisible Man*

Homer	*The Iliad; The Odyssey*
Ibsen, Henrik	*A Doll's House*
Melville, Herman	*Moby-Dick*
Milton, John	"L'Allegro" and "Il Penseroso"
Scholes, Robert, ed.	*Elements of Fiction* (1981)
Shakespeare, William	*As You Like It; Hamlet; King Lear; Richard III*
Synge, John	*Riders to the Sea*
Tolstoy, Leo	A novel (or one by **Dostoevski**)
Whitman, Walt	*Leaves of Grass*

Dr. Atkinson adds that "unrepresented on this list are many, many authors and many other forms of literature notably, the essay (**Ralph Waldo Emerson**, **Henry Thoreau**, **Virginia Woolf**, **Joan Didion**, **E.B. White**, **James Thurber**, **Adrienne Rich**, etc.) and the journal or memoir (**Anaïs Nin**, **Anne Frank**, **Dorothy Wordsworth**, **Patricia Hampl**, **James Boswell**, etc.). Women authors are noticeably few on the list but are more represented in the anthologies."

Dr. Atkinson also has recommended the following two reading lists of American fiction and nonfiction:

American Fiction

Baldwin, James	*Go Tell It on the Mountain*
Cather, Willa	*My Antonia*
Faulkner, William	*The Hamlet*
Hawthorne, Nathaniel	*The Scarlet Letter*
Hemingway, Ernest	*In Our Time; The Sun Also Rises*
Kingston, Maxine Hong	*The Woman Warrior*
Melville, Herman	*Moby-Dick*
Petry, Ann	*The Street*
Stowe, Harriet Beecher	*Uncle Tom's Cabin*
Twain, Mark	*The Adventures of Huckleberry Finn*
Wolfe, Thomas	*Look Homeward, Angel*

American Non-Fiction

Didion, Joan	Essays
Emerson, Ralph Waldo	Essays

Franklin, Benjamin	*Autobiography*
Goodman, Ellen	Essays
James, Henry	*The Art of Fiction*
Thoreau, Henry David	*Walden*
Wheatley, Phillis	Essays

In addition to **J.J. Clayton,** *The Heath Introduction to Fiction* (2nd ed., 1984), the following is a sample of the texts that have been required for University of Minnesota's English 1018, Introduction to Modern Fiction:

Conrad, Joseph	*Heart of Darkness*
Erdrich, Louise	*Love Medicine*
Fitzgerald, F. Scott	*The Great Gatsby*
Hemingway, Ernest	*The Sun Also Rises*
Olsen, Tillie	*Tell Me a Riddle*
Roth, Philip	*Goodbye, Columbus*

University of Montana
Missoula, MT 59812
(406) 243-4636
http://www.umt.edu

Montana offers beginning students a number of introductory courses. Explorations in Literature, for example, is designed to help the student develop "critical thinking about, and strong responses to: the signs, signals, political messages, news stories, essays, poems, fiction, film, TV, and popular song." The texts used in this class are

McCormick, Waller, and Flower	*Reading, Writing, Responding*
Scholes, Robert, et al.	*An Introduction to Literary Language*
Waller, Gary F., et al.	*The Lexington Introduction to Literature*
Scholes, R., et al.	*An Introduction to Literary Language*

In other introductory courses, the following texts are used: **R.V. Cassill,** *Norton Anthology of Short Fiction*; *Heath Introduction to Drama*; **J.H. Picketing,** *Fiction 100: An Anthology of Short Stories* and *Sir Gawain and the Green Knight*

Donne, John	*John Donne's Poetry*
Dostoevski, Fyodor	*The Brothers Karamazov*
Erdrich, Louise	*Love Medicine*
Ferlinghetti, Lawrence	*A Coney Island of the Mind*
Keats, John	Selected poems
Lawrence, D.H.	Selected poems
Leslie, Craig	*Winterkill*
Milton, John	*Paradise Lost*
Nims, John	*Western Wind*
Olds, Sharon	*The Dead and the Living*
Oliver, Mary	*American Primitive*
Ransom, J.C. ed.	*Selected Poems of Thomas Hardy*
Robinson, Marilynne	*Housekeeping*
Shakespeare, William	*Julius Caesar*; sonnets
Stevenson, R.L.	*Dr. Jekyll and Mr. Hyde*

University of Chicago: Describe a few of your favorite books, poems, authors, films, plays, music, paintings, artists, magazines, or newspapers. Feel free to touch on one, some, or all of the categories listed or add a category of your own.

Montana State University
Bozeman, MT 59717
(406) 994-0211
http://www.montana.edu

This list of 100 books all educated people should read was compiled by the students in English 300 Literary Criticism Spring 1999 under the guidance of

Professor Michael Sexson of the Department of English. The list reflects the interests of these students and does not necessarily reflect the views of either the Department of English or of Montana State University.

	Beowulf
	Bhagavat Gita
	Bible
	Epic of Gilgamesh
	One Thousand and One Nights or *Arabian Nights*
	Tristan and Iseult
Aeschylus	*Oresteia*
Austen, Jane	*Pride and Prejudice*
Beckett, Samuel	*Three novels: Molloy, Malone Dies, The Unnamable; Endgame/Waiting for Godot*
Blake, William	Collected poems
Borges, Jorge	Collected fictions
Brontë, Charlotte	*Jane Eyre*
Brontë, Emily	*Wuthering Heights*
Calasso, Robert	*The Marriage of Cadmus and Harmony*
Calvino, Italo	*If On a Winter's Night A Traveler*
Carroll, Lewis	*Alice's Adventures in Wonderland*
Cather, Willa	*My Antonia*
Cervantes, Miguel de	*Don Quixote*
Chaucer, Geoffrey	*The Canterbury Tales*
Chekhov, Anton	Short stories
Conrad, Joseph	*Heart of Darkness*
Dante	*The Divine Comedy*
Dickens, Charles	*Great Expectations*
Dickenson, Emily	Collected poems
Dinesen, Isak	*Anecdotes of Destiny*
Dostoevski, Fyodor	*The Brothers Karamazov*; *The Idiot*
Eliot, George	*Middlemarch*
Eliot, T.S.	*The Four Quartets*
Ellison, Ralph	*Invisible Man*
Emerson, Ralph Waldo	"Nature"

Euripides	*The Bacchae*
Faulkner, William	*Absalom, Absalom!*
Fielding, Henry	*Tom Jones*
Fitzgerald, F. Scott	*The Great Gatsby*
Flaubert, Gustave	*Madame Bovary*
Forster, E.M.	*Passage to India*
Fowles, John	*The Magus*
Frazer, James G.	*The Golden Bough*
Freud, Sigmund	*The Interpretation of Dreams*
García Márquez, Gabriel	*One Hundred Years of Solitude*
Grahame, Kenneth	*Wind in the Willows*
Grass, Günter	*The Tin Drum*
Grimm, Jacob and Wilhelm Grimm	*Grimms' Fairy Tales*
Hardy, Thomas	*Tess of the D'Urbervilles*
Heller, Joseph	*Catch-22*
Hemingway, Ernest	*A Farewell to Arms*
Homer	*The Odyssey*
Hurston, Zora Neale	*Their Eyes Were Watching God*
Ibsen, Henrik	*A Doll's House*
Joyce, James	*Finnegan's Wake; Ulysses*
Kafka, Franz	*The Metamorphosis*
Lao Tzu	*Tao te Ching*
Lawrence, D.H.	*Women in Love*
Lee, Harper	*To Kill a Mockingbird*
Levi-Straus, Claude	*Tristes Tropiques*
Marlowe, Christopher	*Dr. Faustus*
Matthissen, Peter	*At Play in the Fields of the Lord*
McCarthy, Cormac	*All the Pretty Horses*
Melville, Herman	*Moby-Dick*
Milton, John	*Paradise Lost*
Molière	*The Miser*
Morrison, Toni	*Beloved*

Murdoch, Iris	*The Black Prince; The Sea, The Sea*
Nabokov, Vladimir	*Pale Fire; Lolita; Speak Memory*
Nietzsche, Frederich	*Genealogy of Morals*
Plato	*Dialogues*
Potocki, Jan	*The Manuscript Found in Saragossa* (MacLean tr.)
Proust, Marcel	*Remembrance of Things Past*
Ovid	*Metamorphoses*
Pushkin, Alexander	*Eugene Onegin*
Rabelais	*Gargantua and Pantagruel*
Rushdie, Salman	*Midnight's Children*
Salinger, J.D.	*The Catcher in the Rye*
Shakespeare, William	Collected works
Silko, Leslie Marmon	*Ceremony*
Somadeva	*Kathasaritsagara*
Sophocles	*Theban Trilogy*
Sterne, Lawrence	*Tristram Shandy*
Stevens, Wallace	*Collected Poems*
Thackery, William Makepeace	*Vanity Fair*
Thomas, Lewis	*Lives of the Cell: Notes of a Biology Watcher*
Thoreau, Henry David	*Walden*
Tolstoy, Leo	*War and Peace*
Turgenev, Ivan	*Fathers and Sons*
Twain, Mark	*The Adventures of Huckleberry Finn*
Vargas Llosa, Mario	*The Storyteller*
Vergil	*The Aeneid*
White, E.B.	*Charlotte's Web*
Whitman, Walt	*Leaves of Grass*
Wilde, Oscar	*The Importance of Being Earnest*
Woolf, Virginia	*To the Lighthouse*
Wright, Richard	*Native Son*
Yates, Frances A.	*The Art of Memory*
Yeats, William B.	*Collected Poems*

Mount Holyoke College
College Street
South Hadley, MA 01075-1488
(413) 538-2000
http://www.mtholyoke.edu

Elizabeth A. Green, Professor Emeritus of English at Mount Holyoke College, has written for the college a pamphlet of reading suggestions for college-bound high school students. More than a quarter of a million copies of the pamphlet have been distributed since it was first published in 1967. Although it is now in the process of another revision, the suggestions in the present issue are still relevant.

The list below is of the specific books mentioned in the pamphlet, but it should be viewed with reservations, its author states. She says the list "has grown out of the conversations of a number of Mount Holyoke students and faculty about what they read or wished they had read before college. It reflects a variety of individual enthusiasms, is offered as an aid to further personal discovery, and, by intention, is incomplete and unsystematic."

"Some of the best stories of love and separation come from the great age of the novel in the 19th century:

Austen, Jane	*Pride and Prejudice*
Brontë, Charlotte	*Jane Eyre*
Brontë, Emily	*Wuthering Heights*

"20th-century love stories range just as widely:

Bowen, Elizabeth	*The House in Paris*
Hemingway, Ernest	*A Farewell to Arms*

"The relations between men and women that run counter to the standards of society have fascinated storytellers ever since the days of Helen of Troy. Three fine 19th-century instances are:

Eliot, George	*Adam Bede*
Hardy, Thomas	*Tess of the D'Urbervilles*
Hawthorne, Nathaniel	*The Scarlet Letter*

"The beginnings of a real feeling for the past can often be traced to the early reading of novels such as:

Dickens, Charles	*Bleak House; David Copperfield; Great Expectations; The Pickwick Papers; A Tale of Two Cities*
Dostoevski, Fyodor	*The Brothers Karamazov; Crime and Punishment*
Scott, Sir Walter	*Ivanhoe; Kenilworth; The Heart of Midlothian*
Tennyson, Alfred Lord	*Idylls of the King*
Thackeray, William Makepeace	*Vanity Fair*
Tolstoy, Leo	*War and Peace*

"Among recent historical novelists worth knowing are:

Bryher, Winifred	*The Fourteenth of October*
Renault, Mary	*The Last of the Wine*
White, T.H.	*The Once and Future King*

"The problems of the sensitive young person growing up in an alien world have concerned many contemporary writers:

Faulkner, William	"The Bear"
Joyce, James	*A Portrait of the Artist as a Young Man*
Salinger, J.D.	*The Catcher in the Rye*

"From desegregation to atom bombs, the unsolved problems of society continue to rouse novelists and their readers." Examples can be found in:

Conrad, Joseph	*Heart of Darkness; Lord Jim*
Faulkner, William	*Intruder in the Dust*
Fitzgerald, F. Scott	*The Great Gatsby*
Golding, William	*Lord of the Flies*
Huxley, Aldous	*Brave New World*
Lewis, Sinclair	*Main Street*

Orwell, George	*Animal Farm*
Steinbeck, John	*The Grapes of Wrath*

"Some of the most stirring novels of the 20th century deal with race relations:

Baldwin, James	*Go Tell It on the Mountain*
Forster, E.M.	*A Passage to India*
Lee, Harper	*To Kill a Mockingbird*
Paton, Alan	*Cry, The Beloved Country*
Wright, Richard	*Native Son*

"The best of English poetry is both unique and priceless, and high school readers are strongly urged to make special efforts to discover the poems that will give them immediate pleasure and those that will stay with them all their lives:

Arnold, Matthew	"Dover Beach"
Blake, William	Selections
Browning, Robert	Dramatic monologues
Byron, George Gordon	Selections
Coleridge, Samuel Taylor	Selections
Gray, Thomas	"Elegy Written in a Country Churchyard"
Keats, John	Selections
Milton, John	"L'Allegro" and "Il Penseroso"
Shakespeare, William	Songs and sonnets
Shelley, Percy Bysshe	Selections
Tennyson, Alfred Lord	"The Lotos-Eaters"
Wordsworth, William	Selections

"Among the later 19th- and 20th-century poets for whom many Mount Holyoke students and faculty developed enthusiasm before college are **T.S. Eliot**, "The Love Song of J. Alfred Prufrock," and selections from **W.H. Auden**, **Emily Dickinson**, **e.e. cummings**, **Robert Frost**, **Gerard Manley Hopkins**, **A.E. Houseman**, **Theodore Roethke**, **Dylan Thomas**, **W.B. Yeats**.

"One of the treasures of the English-speaking world, which is in some danger of being lost to coming generations, is the *Bible* (King James edition).

"The plays of Shakespeare ought to be a part of everyone's education:

Shakespeare, William	*As You Like It*; *Hamlet*; *Julius Caesar*; *MacBeth*; *The Merchant of Venice*; *A Midsummer Night's Dream*; *Othello*; *Romeo and Juliet*

"The heritage of ancient Greece is increasingly accessible to high school students as good translations multiply:

Homer	*The Iliad* (Lattimore, tr.); *The Odyssey* (Fitzgerald, tr.)

"Acquaintance with classical mythology is strongly urged:

Hamilton, Edith	*Mythology*

"Those ready to explore the great plays of the golden age of Greece frequently start with:

Sophocles	*Oedipus Rex*

Among more recent plays, Professor Green mentions

Hansberry, Lorraine	*A Raisin in the Sun*
Ibsen, Henrik	*A Doll's House*
Miller, Arthur	*Death of a Salesman*
O'Neill, Eugene	*Ah, Wilderness*
Shaw, George Bernard	*Androcles and the Lion*; *Major Barbara*; *Pygmalion*; *Saint Joan*
Wilder, Thornton	*Our Town*; *The Skin of Our Teeth*

Among other favorites that should be mentioned are

Carroll, Lewis	*Alice's Adventures in Wonderland*
Doyle, Sir Arthur Conan	*The Hound of the Baskervilles*
Sayers, Dorothy	*The Nine Tailors*

In a postscript Professor Green commented on

Hemingway, Ernest his "chilling dialogue"

Malamud, Bernard his "ironic studies of urban Jewish life"

O'Connor, Flannery her "grim but fascinating pictures of the rural South"
Tolkien, J.R.R. *The Lord of the Rings*
Updike, John his "observations of high school mores"

She also wrote that "the omission of the large category called 'non-fiction' has left out older favorites as well as recent volumes, for instance:

Herriot, James	*All Creatures Great and Small*
Maxwell, Gavin	*Ring of Bright Water*
Thurber, James	Selected essays
Watson, James	*The Double Helix*
White, E.B.	Essays and letters

Dr. Green reminds students that the pamphlet is "far from comprehensive, indeed, that entire categories have been omitted: short stories, biographies, essays, philosophy, history, interpretations of the contemporary scene." And she adds that "it is assumed that high school readers, like their elders before them, will also be exploring the ephemeral. From sampling best sellers, magazine fiction, and assorted trivia can come entertainment, a range of useful information, and a growing power to distinguish between what is short-lived and what is lasting. The important thing for every high school reader to remember is that reading is fun. A Catholic taste in books may produce all sorts of benefits, including an excellent background for college, but the fundamental advantage is to broaden and deepen one of the enduring pleasures of civilized men and women. Observing that the attitude that 'reading is work' seems to be held by numbers of students in both high school and college, one Mount Holyoke junior says, 'If I were preparing for college today, I would form two regular habits. Every morning I would take time to scan a newspaper and every night before I went to bed I would relax for a while with a book that I was reading for pure enjoyment.'

"Whatever a student's destination after high school, the habit of reading good books can enhance experience and open new possibilities for enjoyment throughout his or her lifetime."

Students contemplating applying to Mount Holyoke may obtain the revised pamphlet by writing The Office of Admissions, Mount Holyoke College, College Street, South Hadley, MA 01075-1488.

Oregon State University: Suppose a visitor from another planet has offered to change places with you, live in your body, and take your place in life. What instructions will you give this visitor about living a meaningful life as a human being? (required for Scholars Application) 2. Imagine it is fifty years in the future and you have been asked to provide a draft copy of your obituary. How would you like to be able to summarize your life, your education, and/or your contributions?

Mount Union College
1972 Clark Avenue
Alliance, OH 44601
(800) 992-6682
http://www.muc.edu

According to Dr. Gloria S. Malone of the Department of English, the recommended reading list for Mount Union's freshman English courses includes the following works:

Albee, Edward	*Who's Afraid of Virginia Woolf?*
Austen, Jane	*Pride and Prejudice*
Baldwin, James	*Go Tell It on the Mountain; Nobody Knows My Name*
Brontë, Charlotte	*Jane Eyre*
Brontë, Emily	*Wuthering Heights*
Camus, Albert	*The Stranger*
Chaucer, Geoffrey	*The Canterbury Tales*
Chopin, Kate	*The Awakening*
Crane, Stephen	*The Red Badge of Courage*
Dickens, Charles	*Great Expectations; A Tale of Two Cities*
Ellison, Ralph	*Invisible Man*
Faulkner, William	*The Sound and the Fury*
Fitzgerald, F. Scott	*The Great Gatsby*

Haley, Arthur	*Roots*
Hawthorne, Nathaniel	*The Scarlet Letter*
Hemingway, Ernest	*A Farewell to Arms*; *The Sun Also Rises*
Hesse, Herman	*Siddhartha*
Hurston, Zora Neale	*Their Eyes Were Watching God*
Huxley, Aldous	*Brave New World*
Ibsen, Henrik	*A Doll's House*
Irving, Washington	*The Legend of Sleepy Hollow*
Joyce, James	*A Portrait of the Artist as a Young Man*
Kafka, Franz	*The Metamorphosis*
Marlowe, Christopher	*Dr. Faustus*
Miller, Arthur	*Death of a Salesman*
Morrison, Toni	*Song of Solomon*
Paton, Alan	*Cry, The Beloved Country*
Salinger, J.D.	*The Catcher in the Rye*
Shakespeare, William	*Hamlet*; *King Lear*; *Macbeth*; *The Merchant of Venice*; *Othello*; *Romeo and Juliet*; *The Taming of the Shrew*
Twain, Mark	*The Adventures of Huckleberry Finn*; *The Adventures of Tom Sawyer*
Walker, Alice	*The Color Purple*
Wilder, Thornton	*Our Town*
Wright, Richard	*Native Son*

University of Nebraska
14th and Q Streets
Lincoln, NE 68588
(402) 472-7211
http://www.unl.edu

University of Nebraska's Introduction to Literature course for beginning college students is designed to meet the university's general education humanities requirements. The core list comprises "about 50% of the minimum reading for each section, the rest of the reading being chosen by the individual instructors." The required list is planned to ensure "some reasonable balance among the genres, with attention paid to literature from various times and places, including literature that addressed issues of special concern to women and minorities."

In accordance with "the college standards for general education courses, approximately ten pages of formal writing, upon which the instructor comments in writing, is expected from each student, in addition to any in-class writing, examinations, journals, and the like that the instructor might assign." Dr. R.V. Stock of the Department of English says this is the only course Nebraska has at any level that has a core reading list.

The anthology used in the course is **Bain, Carl E., et al., eds.**, *The Norton Introduction to Literature.* Other readings are

Fiction

Baldwin, Richard	"Sonny's Blues"
Chopin, Kate	*The Awakening*
Conrad, Joseph	*The Secret Sharer*
Fitzgerald, F. Scott	"Babylon Revisited"
Faulkner, William	"Barn Burning"
Hawthorne, Nathaniel	"Young Goodman Brown"
Hemingway, Ernest	"The Short Happy Life of Francis Macomber"
Lawrence, D.H.	"Odour of Chrysanthemums"
Munro, Alice	"Boys and Girls"
Walker, Alice	"The Revenge of Hannah Kemhuff"

Poetry

Arnold, Matthew	"Dover Beach"
Browning, Robert	"My Last Duchess"
cummings, e.e.	"anyone lived in a pretty how town"
Dickinson, Emily	"Because I could Not Stop for Death"
Donne, John	"The Flea"
Eliot, T.S.	"The Love Song of J. Alfred Prufrock"
Frost, Robert	"Range-Finding"
Hughes, Ted	"Theme for English B"
Keats, John	"Ode on a Grecian Urn"
Knight, Etheridge	"Hard Rock Returns to Prison from the Hospital for the Criminal Insane"
Lorde, Audrey	"Recreation"
Marvell, Andrew	"To His Coy Mistress"
McKay, Claude	"America"
Milton, John	(Before the Fall)
Okara, Gabriel	"Piano and Drums"
Piercy, Marge	"Barbie Doll"
Rich, Adrienne	"Orion"
Roethke, Theodore	"I Knew a Woman"
Shakespeare, William	"Sonnet X"
Shelley, Percy Bysshe	"Ozymandias"
Stevens, Wallace	"Sunday Morning"
Thomas, Dylan	"Fern Hill"
Tennyson, Alfred Lord	"Ulysses"
Wakoski, Diane	"Uneasy Rider"
Whitman, Walt	"When Lilacs Last in the Dooryard Bloom'd"
Yeats, William Butler	"Leda and the Swan"

Drama

Ibsen, Henrik	*Hedda Gabler*
Sophocles	*Oedipus Rex*

Northeastern University
360 Huntington Avenue
Boston, MA 02115
(617) 373-2000
http://www.neu.edu

Professor Kathleen Kelly, Director of Assessment and Placement and of the Basic Writing Program in the Department of English, states that Northeastern does not have a required reading list. Dr. Kelly says that, when she receives calls from parents and prospective students asking about a recommended list, she encourages students to use their summer before college to explore their own reading interests. She also suggests that students begin to think about the genres of their disciplines, and to read examples: What does a lab report look like? A literary analysis? What is expected in research papers in sociology or geology?

Background knowledge is a key factor not only in increasing reading comprehension, but in a student's understanding of any subject matter. To understand the meaning of a text, readers not only decode words but also use their prior knowledge about the topic. Reading related texts is an effective method of generating background knowledge on an unfamiliar topic. Conceptually related materials, such as a novel that addresses a field of study, is an enjoyable way to introduce oneself to an area of potential interest. A student who has read *Jurassic Park* is bound to demonstrate a more significant degree of understanding than the average student when reading a biology chapter on genetics. And, as always, reading will make anyone a better reader.

Sherri Pankratz
High School Reading/English Teacher

University of Notre Dame
Notre Dame, IN 46556
(219) 631-5000
http://www.nd.edu

Notre Dame has two Reading Lists For College-Bound Students: I, compiled by the undergraduate director aided by some of the graduate students, and II, compiled from a questionnaire sent to college and university teachers.

I.

	Everyman
	Selections from Romantic poetry
Brontë, Emily	*Wuthering Heights*
Dante	*Inferno*
Dickens, Charles	*Great Expectations*
Dickinson, Emily	Poetry
Faulkner, William	"The Bear"
Fitzgerald, F. Scott	*The Great Gatsby*
Hawthorne, Nathaniel	*The Scarlet Letter*
Homer	*The Odyssey*
Miller, Arthur	*Death of a Salesman*
Shakespeare, William	*Hamlet*; *King Lear*
Twain, Mark	*The Adventures of Huckleberry Finn*

II.

The authors of this second list asked the teachers "to consider what books they would most like their students to have read before coming to college." They ask that you notice "that this is a very limited list. It is taken for granted, for example, that students would read several plays of Shakespeare, certain selections from major English poets, etc."

Very Highly Recommended

	Arthurian Tales ("Important as background for college reading.")

	Bible ("A student without knowledge of the *Bible* is lost.")
	Robin Hood tales
Cervantes, Miguel de	*Don Quixote*
Defoe, Daniel	*Robinson Crusoe*
Dickens, Charles	*David Copperfield* ("An enjoyable acquaintance with Dickens is a 'must.'")
Homer	*The Iliad* and *The Odyssey* ("Necessary background for understanding much of English and American literature.")
Melville, Herman	*Moby-Dick*
Twain, Mark	*The Adventures of Huckleberry Finn*
Swift, Jonathan	*Gulliver's Travels* ("The best introduction to satire.")
Vergil	*The Aeneid* ("Not sufficient to read only what you have in Latin class!")

Highly Recommended

Brontë, Charlotte	*Jane Eyre*
Brontë, Emily	*Wuthering Heights*
Buck, Pearl	*The Good Earth*
Cather, Willa	*My Antonia*
Conrad, Joseph	*Lord Jim*
Cooper, James Fenimore	*Leatherstocking Tales*
Crane, Stephen	*The Red Badge of Courage*
Dickens, Charles	*Great Expectations; Oliver Twist; A Tale of Two Cities*
Dostoevski, Fyodor	*Crime and Punishment*
Doyle, Sir Arthur Conan	*Sherlock Holmes*
Eliot, George	*The Mill on the Floss*
Emerson, Ralph Waldo	*Essays*
Fitzgerald, F. Scott	*The Great Gatsby*
Hawthorne, Nathaniel	*The House of the Seven Gables*
Hemingway, Ernest	*For Whom the Bell Tolls; The Old Man and the Sea*
Huxley, Aldous	*Brave New World*
Lewis, Sinclair	*Main Street; Babbit*
London, Jack	*The Call of the Wild*

Miller, Arthur	*Death of a Salesman*
Nordhoff and Hall	*Mutiny on the Bounty*
O'Neill, Eugene	*The Emperor Jones*
Parkman, Francis	*Oregon Trail*
Paton, Alan	*Cry, The Beloved Country*
Poe, Edgar Allan	*Tales*
Remarque, Erich Maria	*All Quiet on the Western Front*
Roberts, Kenneth	*Northwest Passage*
Rostand, Edmond	*Cyrano de Bergerac*
Scott, Sir Walter	*Quentin Durward*
Shaw, George Bernard	*Pygmalion; Saint Joan*
Sheridan, Richard	*The Rivals*
Sienkiewicz, Henryk	*Quo Vadis*
Steinbeck, John	*The Grapes of Wrath*
Thackeray, William Makepeace	*Vanity Fair*
Tolstoy, Leo	*War and Peace*
Verne, Jules	*Around the World in Eighty Days*
Wilder, Thornton	*Our Town*

Recommended

Adler, Mortimer	*How to Read a Book*
Alien, Frederich L.	*Only Yesterday*
Austen, Jane	*Mansfield Park*
Carroll, Lewis	*Alice's Adventures in Wonderland*
Cather, Willa	*Death Comes for the Archbishop*
Chesterton, G.K.	*Father Brown Stories*
Clark, Walter V.	*The Ox-Bow Incident*
Dante	*Inferno*
Dumas, Alexandre	*The Three Musketeers; The Count of Monte Cristo*
Fermi, Laura	*Atoms in the Family: My Life With Enrico Fermi*
Galsworthy, John	*Man of Property*
Greene, Graham	*The Power and the Glory*
Hudson, W.H.	*Green Mansions*
Kipling, Rudyard	*Jungle Books*
Lewis, C.S.	*Out of the Silent Planet*

Plato	*Dialogues*
Sandburg, Carl	*Lincoln*
Scott, Sir Walter	*Ivanhoe*
Stevenson, R.L.	*Treasure Island*
Twain, Mark	*Life on the Mississippi*
White, E.B.	*One Man's Meat*

The privilege and pleasure of reading is a way of relaxing, learning, and enjoying the tiny fragments of life the author records. We cannot change their comments or conclusions, nor they ours, because we all share the experience differently. We start, stop, pause, reflect, review and reread at our choice, at our speed anytime and anywhere we choose. Such freedom, such convenience, for the author's words only go as far as our eyes. The reader is not passive in this process either, for we each bring our own imagination into the effort, and in so doing give a unique enrichment to the work.

James F. Shaffer
Retired Executive

Occidental College
1600 Campus Road
Los Angeles, CA 90041
(213) 259-2500
http://www.oxy.edu

The lists below are some of the required readings in several of Occidental's introductory and survey courses.

Introduction to Literary Analysis

Abrams, M.H., ed.	*A Glossary of Literary Terms*
Bain, C.E., et al., eds.	*The Norton Introduction to Literature*

Bambara, Toni Cade	"My Man Bovanne"
Beaty, Jerome, ed.	*The Norton Introduction to Short Fiction*
Bierce, Ambrose	"Occurrence at Owl Creek Bridge"
Conrad, Joseph	*The Secret Sharer*
Hemingway, Ernest	"The Short Happy Life of Francis Macomber"
Jackson, Shirley	"The Lottery"
Joyce, James	"Araby"
Lawrence, D.H.	"Odour of Chrysanthemums"; "The Fox"
Lessing, Doris	"Our Friend Judith"
Morrison, Toni	*Sula*
Paley, Grace	"A Conversation with My Father"

American Literature from the Puritans to the Moderns

Bradstreet, Anne	Selected poems
Cather, Willa	"Neighbor Rosicky"
Chopin, Kate	*The Awakening*
Crane, Stephen	"The Open Boat"
cummings, e.e.	Selected poems
Dickinson, Emily	Selected poems (including "Because I Could Not Stop for Death," " I Like to See It Lap the Miles")
Dreiser, Theodore	*Sister Carrie* (recommended)
Dubois, W.E.B.	"Of Mr. Booker T. Washington and Others"
Edwards, Jonathan	"Personal Narrative," "Sinners in the Hands of an Angry God"
Eliot, T.S.	"The Love Song of J. Alfred Prufrock," "Tradition and the Individual Talent," *The Waste Land*
Ellison, Ralph	*Invisible Man*
Emerson, Ralph Waldo	*Nature*; "The American Scholar," "Experience," "Self-Reliance"
Faulkner, William	"The Bear," "Delta Autumn," *Go Down Moses*
Fitzgerald, F. Scott	*The Great Gatsby*
Franklin, Benjamin	*Autobiography*
Frost, Robert	"Design," "The Oven Bird"
Gottesman, Ronald, et al.	*The Norton Anthology of American Literature*, vols. 1 and 2, 2nd ed.
Hawthorne, Nathaniel	Selected stories

Hemingway, Ernest	*In Our Time*
Melville, Herman	*Billy Budd*
Stevens, Wallace	"Anecdote of the Jar," "The Emperor of Ice-Cream," "The Idea of Order at Key West," "Sunday Morning," "A Study of Two Pears"
Taylor, Edward	Selected poems
Thoreau, Henry David	"Resistance to Civil Government," selections from *Walden*
Washington, Booker T.	*Up from Slavery* (selections)
Whitman, Walt	"Out of a Cradle Endlessly Rocking," Preface to the 1855 edition of *Leaves of Grass*; "Song of Myself," "When Lilacs Last in the Dooryard Bloom'd"

18th- and 19th-Century English Literature

Selected poetry from **Matthew Arnold**; **William Blake**; **Robert Browning**; **Lewis Carroll**; **Samuel Taylor Coleridge**; **William Collins**; **William Cowper**; **Thomas Gray**; **John Keats**; **Christina Rossetti**; **Alfred, Lord Tennyson**; **James Thomson**; and **William Wordsworth**.

Abrams, M.L., et al.	*The Norton Anthology of English Literature*, 5th ed., vols. 1 and 2
Astell, Mary	"Some Reflections upon Marriage"
Brontë, Charlotte	*Jane Eyre*
Carlyle, Thomas	"Characteristics," and sections of "Industrialism," "The Woman Question"
Congreve, William	*The Way of the World*
Dickens, Charles	*Great Expectations*
Dryden, John	"Absalom and Achitophel"
Fielding, Henry	*Joseph Andrews*
Johnson, Samuel	*The History of Rasselas, Prince of Abyssinia*
Montague, Lady Mary W.	"The Lover: A Ballad," "Epistle from Mrs. Yonge to Her Husband"
Pope, Alexander	"An Essay on Man," "The Rape of the Lock," "Epistle to Dr. Arbuthnot"
Swift, Jonathan	*Gulliver's Travels*

Ohio State University
190 North Oval Mall
Columbus, OH 43210
(614) 292-6446
http://www.osu.edu

Ohio State has the following suggested reading list for english majors. Since this is literature the department deems important, pre-college students considering this university may want to consult it as a guide for their own reading.

Medieval

Choose four works; your list must include *Beowulf* and two *Canterbury Tales.*

	Beowulf
	The Dream of the Rood
	Sir Gawain and the Green Knight
Chaucer, Geoffrey	from *The Canterbury Tales*: General Prologue, Miller's Tale, Wife of Bath's Prologue and Tale; Pardoner's Tale, Nun's Priest's Prologue and Tale
Kempe, Margery	*Book of Margery Kempe*, chapters 1–22
Malory, Sir Thomas	*Morte D'Arthur*, books 1–4, 13–21

Renaissance

Choose four works; two of the works must be Shakespeare plays.

Donne, John	"The Sun Rising," "The Canonization," "A Valediction: Forbidding Mourning," "Batter My Heart, Three-Personed God" (Holy Sonnet 14)
Milton, John	*Paradise Lost*
Shakespeare, William	*Hamlet*; *King Lear*; *As You Like It*; *The Tempest*; Sonnets 12, 18, 29, 30, 55, 73, 116, 129, 130
Sidney, Sir Philip	"The Defense of Poesy"
Spenser, Edmund	*The Fairie Queene*, books I and VI

Romanticism

Choose five works, selecting works by both American and British writers, and both prose and poetry.

Austen, Jane	*Pride and Prejudice*
Brontë, Emily	*Wuthering Heights*
Brontë, Charlotte	*Jane Eyre*
Coleridge, Samuel Taylor	*The Rime of the Ancient Mariner*
Shelley, Mary	*Frankenstein*
Shelley, Percy Bysshe	"Ode to the West Wind," "Ozymandias,"
Keats, John	"Ode to a Nightingale," "Ode on a Grecian Urn"
Douglass, Frederick	*Narrative of the Life of Frederick Douglass*
Emerson, Ralph Waldo	"Nature" or "The Poet"
Hawthorne, Nathaniel	*The Scarlet Letter*
Melville, Herman	*Moby-Dick*
Thoreau, Henry David	*Walden* or *Civil Disobedience*
Wordsworth, William	"Tintern Abbey," "Ode on Intimations of Immortality," preface to *Lyrical Ballads*

Later 19th Century

Choose five works, selecting works by both American and British writers, and both prose and poetry.

Arnold, Matthew	"The Function of Criticism at the Present Time"
Conrad, Joseph	*Heart of Darkness* or *Lord Jim*
Dickens, Charles	*Great Expectations* or *Bleak House*
Eliot, George	*Middlemarch*
Browning, Robert	"My Last Duchess"
Chesnutt, Charles W.	*The Conjure Woman*
Chopin, Kate	*The Awakening*
Dickinson, Emily	"I Heard a Fly Buzz," "Because I Could Not Stop for Death," "A Narrow Fellow in the Grass," "Much Madness Is Divinest Sense"
Jacobs, Harriet	*Incidents in the Life of a Slave Girl*
James, Henry	*The Portrait of a Lady*

Tennyson, Alfred Lord	"Ulysses"
Twain, Mark	*The Adventures of Huckleberry Finn*
Whitman, Walt	"Song of Myself" 1–8, 30–31, 51–52

Modern Period

Choose eight works, selecting works by both American and British writers, and drama, prose, and poetry.

Beckett, Samuel	*Waiting for Godot*
Eliot, T.S.	"The Love Song of J. Alfred Prufrock"
Ellison, Ralph	*Invisible Man*
Erdrich, Louise	*Love Medicine*
Faulkner, William	*The Sound and the Fury* or *Light in August*
Fitzgerald, F. Scott	*The Great Gatsby*
Frost, Robert	"Design," "Birches"
Ginsberg, Allen	"Howl"
Hemingway, Ernest	*In Our Time; The Sun Also Rises; A Farewell to Arms*
Hurston, Zora Neale	*Their Eyes Were Watching God*
Joyce, James	*A Portrait of the Artist as a Young Man* or *Ulysses*
Lawrence, D.H.	*Sons and Lovers* or *Women in Love*
Miller, Arthur	*Death of a Salesman*
Moore, Marianne	Poetry
Morrison, Toni	*Sula* or *Beloved*
O'Neill, Eugene	*The Iceman Cometh* or *Long Days Journey into Night*
Plath, Sylvia	"Lady Lazarus"
Pynchon, Thomas	*The Crying of Lot 49*
Rich, Adrienne	"Diving into the Wreck"
Sexton, Anne	"For My Lover, Returning to His Wife"
Stevens, Wallace	"Sunday Morning"
Woolf, Virginia	*To the Lighthouse* or *Mrs. Dalloway*
Yeats, William Butler	"The Second Coming," "Sailing to Byzantium," "Leda and the Swan"

Oral Roberts University
7777 South Lewis Avenue
Tulsa, OK 74171
(918) 495-6518
http://www.oru.edu

Oral Roberts provides two reading lists for students. The first is for anyone who wishes to become a well-educated person. The second is for entering freshmen. Dr. William R. Epperson, English Department chairman, precedes the first list with the following comments:

TO BE WELL READ

"The fundamental values men have traditionally espoused and lived by have been passed from one generation to another through the history of our race. One mode of this passage has been literature, in which, by conceptual and mimetic images, the relationship of values to life has been powerfully illustrated."

"These values transcend national, religious, cultural confines in their broad outline. They are included in the world's major religions; they are not 'Western,' 'Eastern,' or even 'Christian,' although the Christian world view incorporates the values and centers them upon a unique vision of the relation between man and the universe, man and God."

"The books on this reading list form a literary core representing the orthodox values, called the *Tao* in **C.S. Lewis**'s excellent book, *The Abolition of Man.* The task of the educated person is to know the values, the *Tao,* the dimensions of humanness as traditionally conceived and imaged. You will find yourself becoming educated only as you choose to engage in the perennial, yet personal, formulation, clarification, actualization of the values that make you fully human.

"I hope this guide to selected readings will help you in this task. It is not a 'summer's reading list,' although I urge you to begin on it this summer. It is rather an essential foundation for your living, education, becoming process as a human person."

Ancient Literature: Greek, Roman, Hebrew, Oriental

	Bible (read in approximately 10 months)
Aeschylus	*Oresteia*
Aesop	*Fables*
Aristotle	*The Poetics* and *The Ethics*, books I and X
Confucius	*The Analects* (selections)
Euripides	*Medea*
Hamilton, Edith	*Mythology*
Homer	*The Iliad*; *The Odyssey*
Lao Tse	*The Wisdom of Lao Tse* (or A. Waley, tr. *The Way*)
Marcus Aurelius	*Meditations* (selections)
Plato	*Phaedrus*; *The Republic*
Plutarch	*The Makers of Rome*
Sophocles	*Antigone*; *Oedipus Rex*
Vergil	*The Aeneid*

Medieval Literature

	Beowulf
	Sir Gawain and the Green Knight
Aquinas, Saint Thomas (Anton C. Pegis, ed.)	*Introduction to Saint Thomas Aquinas*
Augustine, Saint	*The City of God* (abridged by Vernon Bourke); *Confessions*
Boccaccio, Giovanni	*The Decameron*
Chaucer, Geoffrey	*The Canterbury Tales*
Dante	*The Divine Comedy* (Sayers or Carlyle, Okey, Wicksteed, trs.)
Francis, Saint	*The Little Flowers*

Renaissance Literature

Bunyan, John	*The Pilgrim's Progress*; *Grace Abounding unto the Chief of Sinners*
Cervantes, Miguel de	*Don Quixote*

Donne, John	Poems
Jonson, Ben	*Volpone*
Machiavelli, Niccolò	*The Prince*
Milton, John	*Paradise Lost*; *Paradise Regained*
Montaigne, Michel de	Essays (selected)
Shakespeare, William	Plays

Modern Literature

18th Century

Austen, Jane	*Emma*; *Pride and Prejudice*; *Sense and Sensibility*
Boswell, James	*Life of Johnson*
Fielding, Henry	*Tom Jones*
Grimm, Jacob and Wilhelm Grimm	*Grimm's Fairy Tales*
Johnson, Samuel	"Preface" to *Shakespeare*
Pope, Alexander	"Essay on Man"
Swift, Jonathan	*Gulliver's Travels*
Voltaire	*Candide*

19th Century

Brontë, Charlotte	*Jane Eyre*
Brontë, Emily	*Wuthering Heights*
Browning, Robert	Selected poetry
Chopin, Kate	*The Awakening*
Coleridge, Samuel Taylor	Selected poetry
Dickens, Charles	*David Copperfield*; *Hard Times*
Dostoevski, Fyodor	*The Brothers Karamazov*; *Crime and Punishment*
Emerson, Ralph Waldo	"Nature" and "The Poet"
Hardy, Thomas	*Tess of the D'Urbervilles*
Hawthorne, Nathaniel	*The Scarlet Letter*
Keats, John	Selected poetry
Melville, Herman	*Billy Budd*; *Moby-Dick*
Tennyson, Alfred Lord	Selected poetry

Thoreau, Henry David	*Walden*
Tolstoy, Leo	*The Death of Ivan Illych*; *War and Peace*
Whitman, Walt	*Song of Myself*
Wordsworth, William	Selections

20th Century

Achebe, Chinua	*Things Fall Apart*
Baldwin, James	"Sonny's Blues"
Beckett, Samuel	*Waiting for Godot*
Bellow, Saul	*Mr. Sammler's Planet*; *Herzog*
Böll, Heinrich	*The Clown*
Bonhoeffer, Dietrich	*The Cost of Discipleship*
Borges, Jorge Luis	*Ficciones*
Buber, Martin	*I and Thou*
Camus, Albert	*The Fall*; *The Plague*; *The Stranger*
Cela, Camillo José	*The Family of Pascual Duarte*
Chardin, P. Teilhard de	*The Phenomenon of Man*
Chekhov, Anton	*Three Sisters*; *The Cherry Orchard*
Conrad, Joseph	*Lord Jim*; *The Heart of Darkness*; *Nostromo*
Eliot, T.S.	*Four Quartets*; *The Waste Land*
Ellison Ralph	*Invisible Man*
Faulkner, William	*The Sound and the Fury*; *Light in August*; "The Bear"
Frankel, Victor	*Man's Search for Meaning*
Freud, Sigmund	*General Introduction to Psychoanalysis*
García Márquez, Gabriel	*One Hundred Years of Solitude*
Gide, André	*The Counterfeiters*
Heller, Joseph	*Catch-22*
Hemingway, Ernest	*For Whom the Bell Tolls*; *The Old Man and the Sea*
Hesse, Herman	*Siddhartha*
James, Henry	*The Ambassadors*
Joyce, James	*A Portrait of the Artist as a Young Man*; *Ulysses*
Jung, Carl	*Modern Man in Search of a Soul*
Kafka, Franz	"The Metamorphosis"
Lawrence, D.H.	*Sons and Lovers*; "The Blind Man"

Lewis, C.S.	*That Hideous Strength; Till We Have Faces*
Mann, Thomas	*Death in Venice*
Morrison, Toni	*Song of Soloman; Beloved*
Neruda, Pablo	Selected poetry
Orwell, George	*Animal Farm; 1984*
Sartre, Jean-Paul	*Nausea; No Exit*
Silone, Ignazio	*Bread and Wine*
Solzhenitsyn, Alexander	*One Day in the Life of Ivan Denisovich*
Stevens, Wallace	*The Palm at the End of the Mind*
Synge, J. Millington	*Riders to the Sea*
Unamuno, Miguel de	*Abel Sanchez*
Woolf, Virginia	*To the Lighthouse*

This second ORU list is for entering freshmen.

American Literature

Baldwin, James	*Go Tell It on the Mountain*
Chopin, Kate	*The Awakening*
Faulkner, William	*Intruder in the Dust*
Hawthorne, Nathaniel	*The Scarlet Letter*
Hemingway, Ernest	*For Whom the Bell Tolls; The Sun Also Rises*
Melville, Herman	*Moby-Dick*
Poe, Edgar Allan	Short stories
Thoreau, Henry David	*Walden*
Twain, Mark	*The Adventures of Huckleberry Finn*
Wright, Richard	*Black Boy*

English Literature

Austen, Jane	*Emma; Pride and Prejudice*
Brontë, Charlotte	*Jane Eyre*
Brontë, Emily	*Wuthering Heights*
Conrad, Joseph	*Lord Jim*
Fielding, Henry	*Joseph Andrews*
Hardy, Thomas	*The Return of the Native; Tess of the D'Urbervilles*
Huxley, Aldous	*Brave New World*

Joyce, James	*A Portrait of the Artist As a Young Man*
Milton, John	*Paradise Lost*
Orwell, George	*Animal Farm*
Shakespeare, William	*Hamlet; Julius Caesar; King Lear; MacBeth; Romeo and Juliet*

World Literature

Camus, Albert	*The Plague; The Fall*
Dostoevski, Fyodor	*Crime and Punishment*
Gide, André	*The Pastoral Symphony*
Hesse, Herman	*Siddhartha*
Homer	*The Iliad; The Odyssey*
Mann, Thomas	*Death in Venice*
Sophocles	*Antigone; Oedipus Rex*
Tolstoy, Leo	*The Death of Ivan Illych*
Vergil	*The Aeneid*

Non-Fiction Literature

Emerson, Ralph Waldo	*The Essays of R.W. Emerson*
Franklin, Benjamin	*Autobiography*

Cornell University: "The great aim of education is not knowledge, but action." (Herbert Spencer, English philosopher, 1820–1903) Discuss a situation in your life outside of school in which you put into action what you learned in the classroom. How did you benefit from this experience? What has the situation led you to believe about what education should or should not do?

Oregon State University
Corvallis, OR 97331-4501
(541) 737-1000
http://www.orst.edu

Oregon State precedes its Readers' Guide for the Pre-college Student with the following statement:

> *What is a great book?*
>
> *Obviously, some books are more significant and influential than others. Although many people have attempted to decide which are the truly great ones, our purpose here is more modest. This guide offers you some suggestions of widely appreciated books, arranged in eight subject categories. Within each category, we have subdivided the readings into two groups. First, listed with a brief description, are books that you, as an interested high school student, can read with both pleasure and profit. Second are those that help mark one as a member of the community of educated men and women.*
>
> *There are few better ways to prepare yourself for college than by gaining a familiarity with at least two or three of the works in each of the categories presented here. Indeed, your college experience would be enhanced significantly by continued reading of the books on this list—in addition to the texts required in your classes. We hope this guide will be useful both to those of you who are beginning your higher education and to all who realize that education is a lifelong process.*

I. Adventure

Bradbury, Ray, *Fahrenheit 451* This work is a distinctive contribution to the speculative science fiction of our time. Ultimately, the author probes, through symbolic terms, the nature of man as a creative and yet destructive creature.

Brown, Dee, *Bury My Heart at Wounded Knee* The Indian perspective on the history of the relationship between Native Americans and the U.S. government. Historically shaky at times, it nevertheless is a highly charged and emotional discussion, certain to prompt more thought.

Nordhoff, Charles and James Normal Hall, *Mutiny on the Bounty* A gripping novel about life at sea, based on the 1787 mutiny against Captain William Bligh, commander of the British warship *H.M.S. Bounty*. The book is part of a trilogy that also includes *Men Against the Sea* and *Pitcairn's Island.*

Other books include

Dana, Richard Henry	*Two Years Before the Mast*
Defoe, Daniel	*Robinson Crusoe*
Hemming, John	*The Conquest of Peru*
Heyerdahl, Thor	*Kon Tiki*
Hilton, James	*Lost Horizon*
London, Jack	*The Call of the Wild*
Prescott, William	*The Conquest of Mexico*
Roberts, Kenneth	*Northwest Passage*
Stevenson, Robert Louis	*Treasure Island*
St. Exupéry, Antoine de	*Night Flight*

II. Biography and Autobiography

Franklin, Benjamin, *Autobiography* Scientist, statesman, inventor, and pragmatic philosopher, Franklin was a colonial intellectual and leader whose ideas helped shape American thought.

Keller, Helen, *The Story of My Life* An inspiring account of the author's struggle against incredible odds. A moving testimony of the grandeur of the human spirit that bears rereading whenever one feels that one has been treated unfairly by an unjust fate.

Malcolm X and Alex Haley, *The Autobiography of Malcolm X* An absorbing story of a man who rose from hoodlum, thief, dope peddler, and pimp to become a dynamic leader of the black revolution. It is filled with the power and passion of an entire people in their agonizing search for identity.

Sandoz, Mari, *Crazy Horse: The Strange Man of the Oglalas* The best biography of a Native American, this book deals with the life and achievements of the man who crushed Custer at Little Bighorn.

Washington, Booker T., *Up From Slavery* Born on a Virginia plantation, the author records his own phenomenal rise from the inhuman institution of slavery. Simply and absorbingly written, the book is a significant document of how perseverance brings success even in the face of overwhelming odds.

Other books include

Adams, Henry	*The Education of Henry Adams: An Autobiography*
Bainton, Roland	*Here I Stand: A Biography of Martin Luther*
Boswell, James	*Life of Johnson*
Bullock, Alan	*Hitler: A Study in Tyranny*
Clark, Robert	*Einstein: His Life and Times*
Erikson, Erik	*Gandhi's Truth on the Origins of Militant Nonviolence*
Lutz, Alma	*Susan B. Anthony: Rebel, Crusader, Humanitarian*
Sandburg, Carl	*Abraham Lincoln: The Prairie Years and the War Years*
Womack, John	*Zapata and the Mexican Revolution*
Wolfe, Thomas	*Look Homeward, Angel*

III. Classical, Medieval, and Renaissance Writings

Bible The basic sacred literature of Judaism and Christianity, thc *Bible* is a treasure of religious ideas fundamental to an understanding of Western thought. *Ecclesiastes*: A philosopher reflects on man's fate, the vanity of human striving, and the search for a good life. *Job*: A profound literary analysis of the relationship between faith and suffering, this Old Testament book deals with such questions as "Why does a good man suffer?" and "If God is good, why does he permit suffering?" *Matthew*: A biography of Jesus emphasizing his teachings, including the Sermon on the Mount, and relating the idea of the Messiah to a Jewish audience. It reveals the view of the early church about Jesus as the Christ. *Romans*: A letter written by Saint Paul to the Christian church at Rome explaining his understanding of the life and work of Christ and developing key concepts such as law, faith, grace, and salvation.

Chaucer, Geoffrey, *The Canterbury Tales* (Coghill, tr.) Sometimes moral, sometimes ribald, always entertaining tales told by a fascinating variety of characters, presenting a panorama of medieval mind and culture.

Plato, *Apology* Plato, perhaps the greatest of the Greek thinkers, pays tribute to his teacher Socrates, whose trial and death he here describes.

Crito An excellent example of Plato's method of teaching through the use of dialogues.

The Republic Plato's vision of the ideal state and how to perpetuate it. Especially important is the allegory of the cave in book VII.

Shakespeare, William, *Julius Caesar* Political intrigue and assassination in ancient Rome containing some of the most quoted lines in world literature.

Other works include

Aeschylus	*Prometheus Bound*
Aesop	*Fables*
Aristotle	*The Ethics; The Politics*
Cervantes, Miguel de	*Don Quixote*
Cicero	*On Friendship; On Old Age*
Herodotus	*The Persian Wars*
Homer	*The Iliad; The Odyssey*
Shakespeare, William	*Hamlet*
Sophocles	*Antigone; Oedipus Rex*

IV. Cross-Cultural Writings

Achebe, Chinua, *Things Fall Apart* Set in Africa, this sensitive book deals with the trauma that occurs when traditional cultures come into conflict with the modern world.

Lao Tzu, *The Tao Te Ching* A Chinese religious classic that describes the sacred in terms of the Tao (pronounced *dow*) and inculcates passivity and a reverence for nature.

Leon-Portilla, Miguel, *The Broken Spears: The Aztec Account of the Conquest of Mexico* The chronicle of an event comparable to an invasion from outer space by a superior alien race, this translation of writings by eyewitnesses of the Spaniards' destruction of a civilization is as exciting as it is unique.

Sembène, Ousmane, *God's Bits of Wood* A classic novel about the independence struggle in Africa by one of Africa's leading novelists and the continent's foremost filmmaker. It reveals all the different levels of struggle for national independence: Africans versus Europeans; elders versus youth; males versus females; tradition versus modernity.

Other works include

Benedict, Ruth	*The Chrysanthemum and the Sword: Patterns of Japanese Culture*
Boulding, Elise	*The Fifth World*
Confucius	*The Analects (The LunYu)*
Fanon, Franz	*The Wretched of the Earth*
Fitzgerald, Edward tr.	*The Rubaiyat of Omar Khayyam*
García Márquez, Gabriel	*One Hundred Years of Solitude*
Lappé, Frances Moore and Joseph Collins	*Food First: Beyond the Myth of Scarcity*
Lin Yutang	*The Importance of Understanding*
Muhammad	The Koran
Myrdal, Gunnar	*The Challenge of World Poverty: A World Anti-Poverty Program in Outline*
Snow, Edgar	*Red Star Over China*

V. Ideas in the Humanities

Frankl, Viktor, *Man's Search for Meaning* After three grim years in a Nazi concentration camp, this psychiatrist writes of his life-affirming search for a higher meaning in human existence.

Huxley, Aldous, *Brave New World* An imaginative vision of an assembly-line future where the state has learned that easy pleasure and comfort can more effectively control creativity and dissent than can torture and repression.

Josephson, Matthew, *The Robber Barons: The Great American Capitalists 1861–1901* History that reads like a novel, *The Robber Barons* brings alive a pivotal epoch of the American past by describing the origins of the nation's great fortunes.

Mill, John Stuart, *On Liberty* One of the finest and most eloquent essays on liberty in English, perhaps in any language, this slim volume was exceptionally farsighted in recognizing that social pressures toward conformity could constitute a tyranny more formidable than many kinds of political oppression.

Schumacher, E.F., *Small is Beautiful: Economics As If People Mattered* One of the more important treatises of our times, this small book has planted seeds that may yet crack the foundations of modern economics. A wise, compassionate, and highly rewarding book.

Other works include

Adams, Henry	*Mont-Saint-Michel and Chartres*
Beauvoir, Simone de	*The Second Sex*
Clark, Sir Kenneth	*Civilization*
Hamilton, Alexander, et al.	*The Federalist Papers*
Machiavelli, Niccolò	*The Prince*
Marx, Karl and Friedrich Engels	*The Communist Manifesto*
Pirsig, Robert	*Zen and the Art of Motorcycle Maintenance*
Snow, C.P.	*The Two Cultures and the Scientific Revolution*
Toqueville, Alexis de	*Democracy in America*
Tuchman, Barbara	*A Distant Mirror: The Calamitous 14th Century*

VI. Ideas in the Sciences

Asimov, Isaac, *Asimov on Astronomy* From the moon's effects on tides through an exploration of the planets and onward to interstellar space, supernovas, and exploding galaxies, astronomy with the sense of wonder preserved intact, engagingly presented by a master of both science fact and science fiction.

Bronowski, Jacob, *Science and Human Values* Three short essays on the creative mind, the habit of truth, and the sense of human dignity by one of the great scientist-humanists of our day.

Eiseley, Loren, *The Immense Journey* In an unusual blend of scientific knowledge and poetic vision, a famous naturalist explores the mysteries of nature and mankind.

Mead, Margaret, *Coming of Age in Samoa* The rites of passage in the South Seas and what they tell us about young adults not only there but the world over. A seminal work by a world-rcnowned anthropologist.

Other works include

Benedict, Ruth	*Patterns of Culture*
Bronowski, Jacob	*The Ascent of Man*
Carson, Rachel	*Silent Spring*
Darwin, Charles	*The Descent of Man*
Dubos, René	*So Human an Animal*
Freud, Sigmund	*The Psychopathology of Everyday Life*
Hall, Edward	*The Hidden Dimension*
Kuhn, Thomas	*The Structure of Scientific Revolutions*
Thomas, Lewis	*Lives of a Cell: Notes of a Biology Watcher*
Whitehead, Alfred N.	*Science and the Modem World*

VII. Modern Literature: American

Hemingway, Ernest, *The Old Man and the Sea* Stubborn courage, rugged strength, and marvelous skill sustain an aura of suspense in this story until the tragic end. In many ways the book represents the struggle between man and nature and mankind's compulsion to destroy those things of beauty—a human failure for which both the human race and nature suffer.

Melville, Herman, *Billy Budd* A short work by one of America's greatest writers, *Billy Budd* is on the one hand the suspenseful story of a young man's unjust fate and at the same time a powerfully moving and insightful statement about the relationships between good and evil, law and justice, and individuals and institutions.

Miller, Arthur, *Death of a Salesman* A modern tragedy of a failing, two-martini salesman, his family, his loves, his end.

Twain, Mark, *The Adventures of Huckleberry Finn* Termed a "joy forever and an American masterpiece," this story deals with the reconciliation of piety with human decency. Through wit and humor it considers human hypocrisies, dishonesties, and cruelties and one character's decision to follow moral impulse rather than "village morality."

Other works include

Crane, Stephen	*The Red Badge of Courage*
Faulkner, William	*Collected Stories*
Fitzgerald, F. Scott	*The Great Gatsby*
Hawthorne, Nathaniel	*The Scarlet Letter*
Melville, Herman	*Moby-Dick*
Poe, Edgar Allan	*Selected Poetry and Prose*
Steinbeck, John	*The Grapes of Wrath*
Thoreau, Henry David	*Walden*
Warren, Robert Penn	*All the King's Men*
Whitman, Walt	*Leaves of Grass*
Wilder, Thorton	*Our Town*

VIII. Modern Literature: European

Dickens, Charles, *David Copperfield* As he progresses from boyhood and extremely hard times through school years to adulthood, love, marriage, and success, Dicken's most nearly autobiographical hero meets some of the most extraordinary characters in English literature.

Hugo, Victor, *Les Misérables* In this epic of the masses Hugo paints a vast fresco of French society. His hero, Jean Valjean, spends twenty years in prison for stealing bread, and the rest of his life trying to become a member of "respectable" society.

Orwell, George, *1984* Here is a vision of the future that portrays a nightmare rather than a paradise. The book is both a prophecy and a warning of what life might be if individuals allow themselves to be coerced into conformity by the state.

Remarque, Erich Maria, *All Quiet on the Western Front* A searing indictment of war built around the experiences of a young German soldier in World War I.

Swift, Jonathan, *Gulliver's Travels* A savage attack on human pride, ignorance, and perversity that has delighted readers of all ages for over 250 years.

Voltaire, *Candide* A scathingly satirical attack on the fallacies of blind optimism and on human foibles in general.

Austen, Jane	*Pride and Prejudice*
Camus, Albert	*The Plague*
Carroll, Lewis	*Through the Looking Glass*
Conrad, Joseph	*Heart of Darkness*
Dostoevski, Fyodor	*Crime and Punishment*
Flaubert, Gustave	*Madame Bovary*
Forster, E.M.	*A Passage to India*
Golding, William	*Lord of the Flies*
Kafka, Franz	*The Trial*
Tolstoy, Leo	*War and Peace*
White, T.H.	*The Once and Future King*

IX. Social Commentary

Barnet, Richard	*The Lean Years: Politics in the Age of Scarcity*
Boulding, Kenneth	*The Meaning of the 20th Century*
Braverman, Harry	*Labor and Monopoly Capital: The Degradation of Work in the 20th Century*
Commoner, Barry	*The Poverty of Power: Energy and the Economic Crisis*
Daly, Herman	*Steady-State Economics: The Economics of Biophysical Equilibrium and Moral Growth*
Fromm, Erich	*The Sane Society*
Galbraith, J.K.	*The Affluent Society*

Hayek, F.A.	*The Constitution of Liberty*
Heilbroner, Robert	*An Inquiry Into the Human Prospect*
Kahn, Herman	*Thinking About the Unthinkable*
Mumford, Lewis	*The Myth of the Machine*
Roszak, Theodore	*Where the Wasteland Ends: Politics and Transcendence in Post-Industrial Society*
Thompson, William Irwin	*The Edge of History: Speculations on the Transformation of Culture*
Thurow, Lester	*The Zero-Sum Society*

University of Pennsylvania
3452 Walnut
Philadelphia, PA 19104
(215) 898-5000
http://www.upenn.edu

The Department of English at Pennsylvania has compiled the following pre-college reading list:

Austen, Jane	*Pride and Prejudice*
Brontë, Charlotte	*Jane Eyre*
Brontë, Emily	*Wuthering Heights*
Browning, Robert	Selections: "My Last Duchess," "The Bishop Orders his Tomb…," "Fra Lippo Lippi"
Cervantes, Miguel de	*Don Quixote*
Chaucer, Geoffrey	A taste of Chaucer, some in Middle English, if possible (say, the prologue to *The Canterbury Tales* and the Wife of Bath's Prologue and Tale)
Chopin, Kate	*The Awakening*
Conrad, Joseph	*Heart of Darkness*
Dante	Selections
Defoe, Daniel	One novel (or one by **Fielding**)
Dickens, Charles	One novel (perhaps *A Tale of Two Cities*)

Dickinson, Emily	Selections
Donne, John	Selections
Eliot, T.S.	"The Love Song of J. Alfred Prufrock"
Ellison, Ralph	*Invisible Man*
Faulkner, William	"The Bear"
Fielding, Henry	One novel (or one by **Defoe**)
Fitzgerald, F. Scott	*The Great Gatsby*
Flaubert, Gustave	*Madame Bovary*
Golding, William	*Lord of the Flies*
Hawthorne, Nathaniel	*The Scarlet Letter*
Hemingway, Ernest	*A Farewell to Arms* or *The Sun Also Rises*
Homer	*The Iliad* or *The Odyssey*
James, Henry	*Daisy Miller*
Joyce, James	*Dubliners*
Keats, John	"Ode on a Grecian Urn"
Lawrence, D.H.	*Sons and Lovers*
Melville, Herman	*Billy Budd*
Milton, John	Selections from *Paradise Lost* and "L'Allegro and Il Penserosa," "Lycidas"
Poe, Edgar Allan	Selections
Pope, Alexander	"The Rape of the Lock"
Shakespeare, William	*As You Like It*; *Hamlet*; *Macbeth*; *A Midsummer Night's Dream*; *Romeo and Juliet*; sonnets, selections
Spenser, Edmund	Perhaps "Epithalamion"
Stevens, Wallace	Selections: "Sunday Morning" or "The Idea of Order at Key West" or "Thirteen Ways of Looking at a Blackbird"
Swift, Jonathan	"A Modest Proposal"; *Gulliver's Travels*
Tennyson, Alfred Lord	Selections from *Idylls of the King*, and "Ulysses," "Tithonas," "The Lotos-Eaters"
Twain, Mark	*The Adventures of Huckleberry Finn*
Whitman, Walt	Selections from *Leaves of Grass*
Wordsworth, William	Selections from *Lyrical Ballads* and "Tintern Abbey"
Yeats, William Butler	"Sailing to Byzantium" or other selections

Pennsylvania State University
201 Old Main
University Park, PA 16802
(814) 865-8700
http://www.psu.edu

All students at Penn State must take some General Education courses. In one such course offered by the English Department, Understanding Literature, some of the readings include

Ballads	"Thomas Rymer," "Lord Randall,""Binnorie"
Bishop, Elizabeth	"The Fish"
Blake, William	"The Mental Traveller"
Brontë, Charlotte	*Jane Eyre*
Browning, Elizabeth Barrett	"How Do I Love Thee?" and "A Musical Instrument"
Coleridge, Samuel Taylor	"Christabel," "Kubla Khan," "Frost at Midnight"
Chaucer, Geoffrey	*The Canterbury Tales*: prologue, The Miller's Tale, The Wife of Bath
Donne, John	"The Good Morrow," "Go and Catch a Falling Star," "A Valediction: Of Weeping," "Love's Alchemy," "A Valediction: Forbidding Mourning," Elegy XIX "To His Mistress, Going to Bed," Holy Sonnet XIV "Batter My Heart..."
Emerson, Ralph Waldo	"Hamatreya"
Hawthorne, Nathaniel	"Rappacini's Daughter"
Hayden, Robert	"On Lookout Mountain"
Homer,	*The Odyssey*, selections
Hopkins, Gerard Manley	"God's Grandeur," "The Starlight Night," "The Windhover," "Pied Beauty," "Spring and Fall," "As Kingfishers Catch Fire"
Keats, John	"Eve of Saint Agnes," "Ode to a Nightingale"
Morrison, Toni	*Beloved*
Owen, Wilfred	"Dulce et Decorum Est"
Poe, Edgar Allan	"Ligeia"

Rossetti, Christina	"Goblin Market"
Shakespeare, William	*The Tempest*
Shaw, George Bernard	*Pygmalion*
Shelley, Percy Bysshe	"Ozymandias"
Tennyson, Alfred Lord	"Mariana," "The Lady of Shalott," "Ulysses,"
Whitman, Walt	"When Lilacs Last in the Dooryard Bloom'd.
Wilbur, Richard	"Advice to a Prophet"
Wilder, Thornton	*The Bridge of San Luis Rey*
Wordsworth, William	"Ode: Intimations of Immortality from Recollections of Early Childhood"
Yeats, William Butler	"The Lake Isle of Innisfree"

Pomona College
333 College Way
Claremont, CA 91711-6312
(909) 621-8000
http://www.pomona.edu

All freshmen at Pomona take a writing-intensive course their first semester. As is true in many colleges and universities, the course combines writing with learning across the curriculum. The topics for writing vary from section to section according to the interests of the particular professors. In a section taught recently by Dr. Richard Barnes, for example, the students read and wrote about **Dante** and his world.

In their second semester, students may begin the first of a two-semester course, Major British Authors. For the second half of that course, instructors choose works from the 18th, 19th, and 20th centuries. Some of the works in the first semester are

Chaucer, Geoffrey	*The Canterbury Tales*, and the medieval lyric
Spenser, Edmund	*The Faerie Queen*, and the Elizabethan lyric
Milton, John	*Paradise Lost*, and the 17th-century lyric

Presbyterian College
503 South Broad Street
Clinton, SC 29325
(800) 476-7272
http://www.presby.edu

Presbyterian College's required freshman class in composition and literature focuses on a survey of world masterpieces. Dr. Neal Prater of the Department of English says the major emphasis is on the following authors and types of literature:

A Greek Epic

Homer	*The Iliad*; *The Odyssey*

A Greek Tragedy

Aeschylus	Any play
Euripides	Any play
Sophocles	Any play

A Roman Epic

Vergil	*The Aeneid*

Medieval Poetry

Chaucer, Geoffrey	The Canterbury Tales
Dante	*Inferno*

Elizabethan Drama

Shakespeare, William	Any play

18th-Century Satire

Molière	*Tartuffe*
Voltaire	*Candide*

19th-Century Poetry and Drama

A collection of English Romantic poems

Goethe, Johann W. von *Faust*

19th-Century Novel

Turgenev, Ivan *Fathers and Sons*

20th-Century Novel

Faulkner, William A novel

Golding, William *Lord of the Flies*

> **Dartmouth College**: You have been asked many questions on this application, all asked by someone else. If you yourself were in a position to ask a thought-provoking and revealing question of college applicants, what would that question be?

Princeton University
Princeton, NJ 08544
(609) 258-3000
http://www.princeton.edu

Freshmen at Princeton are offered extra incentives in their pursuit of academic excellence. Two prizes are given each year to freshmen who excel in English:

The Class of 1883 English Prize for Academic Freshmen: This prize, the yearly income of $2,300, is given to that freshman, a candidate for the degree of Bachelor of Arts, who has done the best work in the English studies of the year, and has submitted the best essay on a subject approved by the Department of English.

The Class of 1883 English Prize for Freshmen in the School of Engineering: This prize, the yearly income of $2,300, is given to that freshman, a candidate for the degree of Bachelor of Engineering, who has done the best work in the English studies of the year, and has submitted the best essay on a subject approved by the Department of English.

The following list is of works recently studied in two of the freshman literature courses:

I. Shakespeare

Shakespeare, William	*A Midsummer Night's Dream*; *Henry IV, Part I*; *Twelfth Night*; *Hamlet*; *Coriolanus*; *King Lear*; *The Tempest*

II. Major American Writers

Cather, Willa	*A Lost Lady*
Chopin, Kate	*The Awakening*
Crane, Stephen	*The Red Badge of Courage*; "The Open Boat," "The Blue Hotel"
Faulkner, William	"Red Leaves," "Wash," "The Bear," "Old Man"
Hemingway, Ernest	"Indian Camp," "The End of Something," "Three-Day Blow," "Big Two-Hearted River," "Fathers and Sons"
Melville, Herman	*Bartleby the Scrivener*; *Benito Cereno*; *Billy Budd*
O'Neill, Eugene	*Long Day's Journey into Night*
Poe, Edgar Allan	"The Fall of the House of Usher," "The Tell-Tale Heart," "The Raven," "The Philosophy of Composition," "The Purloined Letter"
Shepard, Sam	*True West*
Twain, Mark	*The Adventures of Huckleberry Finn*
Walker, Alice	*The Color Purple*

Also the poets:

Dickinson, Emily	"Success is Counted Sweetest," "I'm 'Wife' I've Finished That," "I Taste a Liquor Never Brewed," "Safe in Their Alabaster Chambers," "There's a Certain Slant of Light," "The Soul Selects Her Own

	Society," "He Fumbles at Your Soul," "A Bird Came Down the Walk," "What Soft Cherubic Creatures," "This Is My Letter to the World," "I Heard a Fly Buzz When I Died," "This World Is Not Conclusion," "I Cannot Live with You," "I Dwell in Possibility," "Because I Could Not Stop for Death," "My Life Had Stood a Loaded Gun," "A Narrow Fellow in the Grass," "Tell All the Truth But Tell It Slant," "A Route of Evanescence," "There Is a Solitude of Space," "Elysium Is as Far as to"
Frost, Robert	"Mending Wall," "After Apple-Picking," "The Wood-Pile," "The Road Not Taken," "The Oven Bird," "Birches," "Out, Out" "Stopping by the Woods on a Snowy Evening," "For Once, Then, Something," "Spring Pools," "Once by the Pacific," "West-Running Brook," "Two Tramps in Mud Time," "Desert Places," "Design," "The Silken Tent"

Purdue University
West Lafayette, IN 47907
(765) 494-1776
http://www.purdue.edu

In a course introducing students to an important group of American literary texts, the seven to eight books required have been from the following:

Alcott, Louisa May	*Little Women*
Auster, Paul	*Leviathan*
Cather, Willa	*The Song of the Lark*
Chopin, Kate	*The Awakening*
DeLillo, Don	*Libra*
Dickinson, Emily	Selected poetry
Ellison, Ralph	*Invisible Man*
Erdrich, Louise	*Love Medicine*
Faulkner, William	*Absalom, Absalom!*

Hawthorne, Nathaniel	*The Scarlet Letter*
Hemingway, Ernest	*In Our Time*
Hurston, Zora Neale	*Their Eyes Were Watching God*
Kingston, Maxine Hong	*Tripmaster Monkey*
Jewett, Sarah Orne	*The Country of the Pointed Firs*
Malamud, Bernard	*The Assistant*
Melville, Herman	*Moby-Dick*
Morrison, Toni	*Beloved*
Roth, Philip	*Operation Shylock*
Stowe, Harriet Beecher	*Uncle Tom's Cabin*
Twain, Mark	*The Adventures of Huckleberry Finn*
Welty, Eudora	*Delta Wedding*
Wharton, Edith	*The House of Mirth*
Whitman, Walt	Selected poetry

The Purdue Student Union Board and the university's Department of English several times a year sponsor a thirty minute book review for a "general audience of intelligent readers." Called Books and Coffee, it is held in the South Ballroom, Purdue Memorial Union.

Following, according to the year, are some of the books which have been reviewed.

2000

Bayley, John	*Elegy for Iris*
Chang-rae Lee	*A Gesture Life*
Harris, Thomas	*Hannibal*

1999

Axtell, James	*The Pleasure of Academe: A Celebration & Defence of Higher Education*
Cunningham, Michael	*The Hours*
Downes, Larry and Chunka Mui	*Unleashing the Killer App: Digital Strategies for Market Dominance*
Klemperer, Victor	*I Will Bear Witness*

1998

Jourdain, Robert	*Music, The Brain, and Ecstacy*
Joyce, James	*Twilight, A Symphony*
Morrison, Toni	*Paradise*
Rice, Anne	*Violin*

1997

Barker, Pat	*The Ghost Road*
Delaney, Elizabeth and Sarah Delaney	*Having Our Say*
Negroponte, Nicholas	*Being Digital*
Parker, Hershel	*Herman Melville*
Salzman, Mark	*Lost in Place: Growing Up Absurd in Suburbia*

1996

Behn, Aphra	*The Rover*
Boiardo, Matteo and C.S. Ross	*Orlando Innamorato*
Ishiguro, Kazuo	*The Unconsoled*
Kaplan, Robert D.	*Balkan Ghosts*
Norris, Kathleen	*Dakota: A Spiritual Autobiography*
Smiley, Jane	*Moo*

1995

Butler, Octavia	*Mind of My Mind*
Calasso, Roberto	*The Marriage of Cadmus and Harmony*
McCarthy, Cormac	*The Crossing*
Munro, Alice	*Open Secrets*
Nuland, Sherwin B.	*How We Die: Reflections on Life's Final Chapter*

1994

Alexie, Sherman	*The Lone Ranger and Tonto Fistfight in Heaven*
Auster, Paul	*Leviathan*
LeCarré, John	*The Night Manager*

Miller, James	*The Passion of Michel Foucault*
Nicholl, Charles	*The Reckoning: The Murder of Christopher Marlowe*
Sperber, Murray	*Shake Down the Thunder:The Creation of Notre Dame Football*

1993

Byatt, A.S.	*Possession: A Romance*
Grafton, Sue	*"I" is for Innocent*
Henley, Patricia	*The Secret of Cartwheels*
Palazzeschi, Aldo	*Man of Smoke*
Stone, Robert	*Outerbridge Reach*
Vollman, William T.	*Fathers and Crows*

1992

Bache, William B.	*Design and Closure in Shakespeare's Major Plays*
Kozol, Jonathan	*Savage Inequalities: Children in American Schools*
Lax, Eric	*Woody Allen: A Biography*
Middlebrook, Diane W.	*Anne Sexton: A Biography*
Ripley, Alexandra	*Scarlett*
Rutherford, Edward	*Russka: A Novel of Russia*

1991

Harrison, Sue	*Mother Earth, Father Sky*
Lyotard, Jean-François	*The Postmodern Condition*
Rich, Adrienne	*Your Native Land, Your Life*
Rushdie, Salman	*The Satanic Verses*
Tannen, Deborah	*You Just Don't Understand: Women and Men in Conversation*
Turow, Scott	*Burden of Proof*

1990

Booth, Wayne C.	*The Company We Keep: An Ethics of Fiction*
Brady, Frank	*Citizen Welles*
Eco, Umberto	*Foucault's Pendulum*

Fraser, Antonia	*The Warrior Queens*
Mayer, Arno J.	*Why Did The Heavens Not Darken?*
Walker, Alice	*The Temple of My Familiar*

1989

Attenborough, David	*The First Eden*
Bishop, Elizabeth	*The Complete Poems: 1927–1979*
Bradbury, Ray	*My Strange Quest for Mensonge*
Fuentes, Carlos	*Christopher Unborn*
Kennedy, Paul M.	*The Rise and Fall of the Great Powers*
Stone, I.F.	*The Trial of Socrates*

Randolph-Macon Woman's College
2500 Rivermont Avenue
Lynchburg, VA 24503-1526
(804) 947-8100
http://www.rmwc.edu

First-year students at Randolph-Macon take a one-semester writing course, which is a pre-requisite for Introduction to Literary Studies. Reading assignments for the writing course vary from section to section. Some recent examples of topics include "Logical Reasoning and Argumentation," "Growing Up Female," "A Community of Writers," "Family Values," "Pearl S. Buck Online," "Americans and the Environment," and "Youth Culture."

Texts included in the first semester of Introduction to Literary Studies include readings from the English Romantics and the Imagist poets and the following authors: **Vergil**, **Theocritus**, **Shakespeare**, **Milton**, **Pope**, **George Eliot, Chekhov**, **Emerson**, **Thoreau**, **Melville, Welty**, and **O'Connor**. The second semester considers the reasons for the continued popularity of **Jane Austen**'s novels. Books read are *Northanger Abbey, Sense and Sensibility, Pride and Prejudice, Mansfield Park, Emma, and Persuasion.*

University of Rochester
Wilson Boulevard
Rochester, NY 14627
(716) 275-6111
http://www.rochester.edu

According to Dr. Morris Eaves of the Department of English, "all freshmen at Rochester are required to take one basic writing course and two upper-level writing courses. The basic course is taught in the English department, and the upper-level courses in almost all departments; therefore, students may receive instruction geared specifically to their discipline." In all of these courses, the writing is based on reading and subsequent discussion. Almost all freshmen take one of the three following courses:

I. Ventures

Approximately half of the freshman course work is included in each segment of this program. Each venture "organizes popular freshman courses around an important question so that you can examine this question from the perspectives of different disciplines." Freshmen interested in ventures must apply for admission. Texts vary greatly depending on the theme of the particular course. The themes are Foundations of Western Culture; Ourselves and Others; The Organizing Mind: Science, Music, and Writing; Social and Biological Determinants of Behavior; Resources, Environment, and Political Choice; and Personality and Human Development.

II. Fictions and Realities

This course analyzes some of the fictions that have been offered to explain reality. Instructors choose from these books:

Berger, John	*Ways of Seeing*
Freud, Sigmund	*Three Case Histories*
Goffman, Erving	*Presentation of Self*
Gould, Stephen Jay	*The Mismeasure of Man*

Horney, Karen	*Our Inner Conflicts*
Kingston, Maxine Hong	*The Woman Warrior*
Mailer, Norman	*The Armies of the Night*
Underhill, Ruther	*Papago Woman*
Watson, James	*The Double Helix*

III. Writing and Thinking

This course combines the analysis of fiction, poetry, and non-fiction prose with instruction in expository and persuasive writing. Instructors most frequently use one of the following anthologies of readings:

Booth and Marshall, eds.	*The Harper & Row Reader*
Shrodes, Carolyn, et al.	*The Conscious Reader*

They also have included the following novels or long prose works in their courses:

Barth, John	*Lost in the Funhouse*
Brontë, Charlotte	*Jane Eyre*
Brontë, Emily	*Wuthering Heights*
Camus, Albert	*The Plague*
Hardy, Thomas	*Jude the Obscure*
Hawthorne, Nathaniel	*The Scarlet Letter*
Hurston, Zora Neale	*Their Eyes Were Watching God*
Kafka, Franz	*The Trial*
Lewis, C.S.	*Till We Have Faces*
Melville, Herman	*Billy Budd* and other stories
Morrison, Toni	*Song of Solomon*
Naylor, Gloria	*The Women of Brewster Place*
Roth, Philip	*The Ghost Writer*
Sayers, Dorothy	*Murder Must Advertise*
Shelley, Mary	*Frankenstein*
Sontag, Susan	*Illness as Metaphor*
Warren, Robert Penn	*All the King's Men*
Waugh, Evelyn	*A Handful of Dust*
Wharton, Edith	*The Age of Innocence; The House of Mirth*

> **Transylvania University**: What person (real or fictional), place, or event in your life has had the most profound effect on you and why?

Rutgers-Newark University
University Heights
Newark, NJ 07102
(973) 353-1766
http://www.rutgers.edu

Dr. William C. Dowling, Professor of English at Rutgers, writes concerning the following list:

> *English majors in my generation had to take a comprehensive examination in the spring term of our senior year, and we studied from a list of 'standard' works and authors. I have reconstructed this as 'A Reading List for English Majors' for my students at Rutgers...The list has been passed along by Rutgers undergraduates to friends at other schools, and has subsequently been circulated among students at a number of colleges and universities as 'the Rutgers reading list.'...*
>
> *Since no copy of the original comprehensives list was able to be located in departmental files at Dartmouth, the list below is an attempt to reconstruct from memory the version given to English majors in 1962. That list, one now realizes, reflected what must have been an agreement within the department to cut things off at the end of the 1930s, probably because the English faculty thought it too difficult to say which post–World War II writers and works would turn out to have lasting importance.*
>
> *Those using the list now should therefore be aware that much important writing—e.g.,* ***Nabokov****'s* Pale Fire, ***Jarrell****'s*

Pictures from an Institution, ***Williams'*** *Stoner, poetry by* ***Bishop, Berryman, Merrill, Hill, Larkin,*** *etc.—lies on this side of the WWII divide.*

The list below also contains several items meant to reflect more recent attitudes about cultural diversity, etc. (Such works as ***Equiano****'s Narrative had been lost or forgotten at the time the original list was issued, and have now, as is appropriate, been restored to the English curriculum.)*

English Literature

Anglo Saxon

Beowulf
The Dream of the Rood
The Battle of Maldon

These texts should be read in the original language or dialect. Note: in the case of *Beowulf* and other Anglo-Saxon items, this will mean taking a course in Anglo Saxon. This is, however, one of the most intellectually rewarding experiences you can have as an English major—great literature, a totally fascinating period of cultural history, and linguistic training that immeasurably increases your understanding of Shakespeare and other later English authors. In some departments, undergraduates can't get an Anglo Saxon course even if they want one; there's nobody on the faculty competent to teach it. So you are supremely fortunate at Rutgers not only to have the course offered on a regular basis, but taught by faculty renowned in Anglo Saxon studies.

Middle Ages

	Sir Gawain and the Green Knight
	"Patience"
	"Purity"
Chaucer, Geoffrey	*The Canterbury Tales*: General Prologue, Knight's Prologue and Tale, Miller's Prologue and Tale, Wife of Bath's Prologue, The Nun's Priest's Tale
Langland, William	*Piers Plowman*: Prologue

Drama

	Everyman
	The Second Shepherd's Play
Malory, Sir Thomas	*Morte D'Arthur: the Passing of Arthur*

Renaissance

Campion, Thomas	"When Thou Goest Home to Shades of Underground"
Dyer, Sir Edward	"My Mind to Me a Kingdom Is"
Foxe, John	*Acts and Monuments*: Death of Ridley and Latimer
Hooker, Richard	*Laws of Ecclesiastical Polity*: preface and book I
Howard, Henry, Earl of Surrey	"My Friend, the Things that Do Attain Love, That Doth Reign and Live Within My Thought"
Marlowe, Christopher	"The Passionate Shepherd to His Love," *Doctor Faustus*
More, Sir Thomas	*Utopia*
Nashe, Thomas	"Litany in Time of Plague"
Shakespeare, William	Sonnets: 12, 18, 29, 55, 71, 73, 104, 106, 116, 129, 130, 144; *Hamlet*; *King Lear*; *Othello*; *Macbeth*; *Richard II*; *Richard III*; *Henry IV, Part I*; *Love's Labour's Lost*; *Much Ado About Nothing*; *The Tempest*
Sidney, Sir Phillip	"Astrophel and Stella," "An Apology for Poetry"
Skelton, John	"Upon a Dead Man's Head Mannerly Margery"
Spenser, Sir Edmund	*The Fairie Queene*: Books I and II , "Epithalamion"
Wyatt, Sir Thomas	"They Flee From Me Mine Own"

The 17th Century

Andrewes, Lancelot	*Whitehall Sermon* ("A Cold Coming They Had Of It")
Bacon, Francis	Essays: "Of Marriage and Single Life," "Of Friendship," "Of Travel," "Of Studies," "Of Truth," *The Advancement of Learning*, book 1
Browne, Sir Thomas	*Hydriotaphia*: chapters 1–5

Burton, Robert (Democritus Junior)	*The Anatomy of Melancholy*; *The Causes of Melancholy*, section 2, part I ("Love of Learning," or "Overmuch Study")
Carew, Thomas	"Elegy on the Death of Donne"
Cowley, Abraham	*Discourses*: "Of Solitude," "Of Obscurity," "Of Myself"
Denham, Sir John	"Coopers Hill"
Donne, John	"The Good-Morrow," "The Canonization," "A Valediction: Forbidding Mourning," "The Sunne Rising," "Aire and Angels," "The Relique," Elegy XIX (To His Mistress Going to Bed), "Good Friday, 1613," "Riding Westward," "Hymn to God My God, in My Sickness" Sermon XV ("The Last Enemy That Shall Be Destroyed Is Death")
Earle, John	*Microcosmography*: "An Antiquary," "A Gallant," "An Upstart Knight"
Herbert, George	*The Temple*: "The Church Porch," "The Altar," "Easter Wings," "The Agony," "Jordan" (1), "The Collar," "The Pulley," "Discipline," "Love" (3)
Herrick, Robert	"Prayer to Ben Jonson," "His Grange, or Private Wealth," "Upon Julia's Clothes," "The Country Life"
Jonson, Ben	"To Penshurst," "To the Memory of My Beloved Master William Shakespeare," "To the Memory of Sir Lucius Cary and Sir H. Morison" ("Cary-Morison Ode"), *Volpone*; *Bartholomew Fair*
Lovelace, Richard	"To Althea, from Prison," "To Lucasta, Going to the Wars"
Marvell, Andrew	"To His Coy Mistress," "Upon Appleton House," "The Garden," "The Mower Against Gardens"
Milton, John	*Paradise Lost*, "Lycidas," *Samson Agonistes*, " L'Allegro," "Il Penseroso," Sonnet XV (Piedmont Massacre), Sonnet XVI (On His Blindness), "Areopagetica," "Of Education"
Overbury, Sir Thomas	*Characters*: A Courtier, A Fine Gentleman, A Pedant, A Puritan, A Jesuit, An Excellent Actor
Taylor, Jeremy	*Holy Dying*: sections 1–3
Walton, Izaak	"Life of John Donne"

Victorian

Arnold, Matthew	"Dover Beach," "The Buried Life," "Stanzas on the Grande Chartreuse," *Culture and Anarchy*: chapters 1–5
Browning, Robert	"Childe Roland to the Dark Tower Came," "Caliban Upon Setebos," "The Bishop Orders His Tomb," "My Last Duchess," " Fra Lippo Lippi," "Andrea del Sarto"
Carlyle, Thomas	*Past and Present*
Dickens, Charles	*Our Mutual Friend*; *Little Dorrit*; *Bleak House*
Eliot, George	*Adam Bede*; *Middlemarch*
Gissing, George	*New Grub Street*
Hardy,Thomas	*Jude the Obscure*; "Channel Firing New Year's Eve"
Mill, John Stuart	*On Liberty*; *Autobiography*
Newman, John Henry	*Apologia Pro Sua Vita*: chapters 2–5
Pater, Walter	*The Renaissance*: Winckelmann and Conclusion
Rossetti, Christina	"Goblin Market"
Rossetti, Dante Gabriel	"The Blessed Damozel," *The House of Life*: Sonnets 4, 49, 71–73
Ruskin, John	*The Stones of Venice* vol. 2, chapter 6 ("The Nature of Gothic"); *The Storm-Cloud of the Nineteenth Century*
Swinburne, Algernon	"In the Orchard," "Hymn to Proserpine," "Dolores"
Tennyson, Alfred Lord	"Ulysses," "In Memoriam," "Maud," "The Charge of the Light Brigade," *Idylls of the King*: the Passing of Arthur
Thackeray, William Makepeace	*Vanity Fair*
Trollope, Anthony	*The Way We Live Now*
Wilde, Oscar	*The Importance of Being Earnest*; *The Picture of Dorian Gray*

20th Century

Auden, W.H.	"Letter to Lord Byron," "Musée des Beaux Arts," "In Praise of Limestone," "In Memory of W.B. Yeats"
Beckett, Samuel	*Endgame*; *Waiting for Godot*

Conrad, Joseph	*Nostromo*
Eliot, T.S.	"The Love Song of J. Alfred Prufrock," "The Waste Land," " Journey of the Magi," *Four Quartets*: "Little Gidding,"; *Tradition and the Individual Talent*
Ford, Ford Madox	*The Good Soldier*
Forster, E.M.	*Howards End*
Hopkins, Gerard Manley	"The Windhover," "Duns Scotus' Oxford ," "Spring and Fall"
Joyce, James	*Dubliners*: "Araby," "Clay," "Ivy Day in the Committee Room," "The Dead"; *Ulysses*
Lawrence, D.H.	*Women in Love*
Shaw, George Bernard	*Major Barbara*; *Saint Joan*
Waugh, Evelyn	*Decline and Fall*
Woolf, Virginia	*To the Lighthouse*; *A Room of One's Own*
Yeats, Willam Butler	"The Rose of the World," "The Fascination of What's Difficult," "The Wild Swans at Coole," "Easter 1916," "The Second Coming," "Sailing to Byzantium," "Leda and the Swan," "Among School Children," "Crazy Jane Talks to the Bishop," "Lapis Lazuli," "The Circus Animals' Desertion"

American Literature

Colonial

Adams, John and Abigail Adams	Letters: 16 Sept 1774; 9 October 1774; 16 October 1775; 23 July 1775; 3 July 1776; 21 July 1776; 3 August 1776
Barlow, Joel	*Advice to a Raven in Russia*; *The Conspiracy of Kings*
Bradford, William	*History of Plymouth Plantation* books 1–2
Bradstreet, Anne	"The Flesh and the Spirit," "To Her Husband, Absent Upon Public Employment," "Upon the Burning of Our House," "Before the Birth of One of Her Children"
Crevecoeur, Michel Guillaume St. Jean de	*Letters from an American Farmer*: Letters 3, 4, 7, 9, 12; "Revolution and Early Republic"
Dwight, Timothy	*The Triumph of Infidelity*
Edwards, Jonathan	"Sinners in the Hands of an Angry God," Letter to Dr. Benjamin Colman

Equiano	Narrative
Franklin, Benjamin	*Autobiography*; "The Way to Wealth"
Irving, Washington	"Rip Van Winkle," "The Legend of Sleepy Hollow"
Jefferson, Thomas	*Notes on the State of Virginia*: queries 5, 14, 19
Mather, Cotton	*Magnalia Christi Americana* chapter IV, *Nehemias Americanus* (The Life of John Winthrop)
Paine, Thomas	*Common Sense*
Taylor, Edward	"Meditations": 16, 22, 38, "Upon a Wasp Child with Cold," "Huswifery"
Tyler, Royall	*The Contrast*

American Renaissance to Modern

Adams, Henry	*The Education of Henry Adams*
Dickinson, Emily	"I Never Lost As Much But Twice," "How Many Times These Low Feet Staggered," "The Soul Selects Her Own Society," "This Is My Letter to the World," "It Was Not Death, for I Stood Up," "Pain—Has an Element of Blank," "A Narrow Fellow in the Grass" "A Word Made Flesh Is Seldom," "My Life Closed Twice Before Its Close"
Douglass, Frederick	*Narrative of the Life of Frederick Douglass*
Emerson, Ralph Waldo	"Nature," "Divinity School Address," "Self-Reliance"
Hawthorne, Nathaniel	*The Scarlet Letter*; "Young Goodman Brown," "The Minister's Black Veil"
Holmes, Oliver Wendell	*The Autocrat of the Breakfast Table*
Howells, William Dean	*A Modern Instance*
James, Henry	*The Ambassadors*
Melville, Herman	*Moby-Dick*; *Bartleby*; *The Scrivener*; *Benito Cereno*
Norris, Frank	*Vandover and the Brute*
Poe, Edgar Allan	"The Purloined Letter," "The Cask of Amontillado," "The Fall of the House of Usher"
Thoreau, Henry David	*Walden*; "Thomas Carlyle and His Works"
Twain, Mark	*The Adventures of Huckleberry Finn*
Wharton, Edith	*The House of Mirth*

Whitman, Walt	"Song of Myself ," "Out of the Cradle Endlessly Rocking," "Whoever You Are Holding Me Now in Hand," "When Lilacs Last in the Dooryard Bloom'd"

Modern

Cather, Willa	*The Professor's House*
cummings, e.e.	"Buffalo Bill's," "the Cambridge ladies," "i sing of Olaf glad and big," "anyone lived in a pretty how town"
Faulkner, William	"A Rose for Emily," *Light in August*
Fitzgerald, F. Scott	*The Great Gatsby*
Frost, Robert	"Mending Wall," "After Apple-Picking," "The Road Not Taken," "Stopping by Woods on a Snowy Evening," "Once by the Pacific," "Design," "Provide, Provide," "The Gift Outright"
Hemingway, Ernest	*The Sun Also Rises*
Pound, Ezra	"In a Station of the Metro," *Cantos*: 1, 9, 17, 45
Stevens, Wallace	"The Snow Man," "Sunday Morning," "Anecdote of the Jar," "Thirteen Ways of Looking at a Blackbird," "The Idea of Order at Key West"

> **Georgetown College**: In your own handwriting, please write a 250–400 word essay on an issue of ethical/moral significance.

St. John's College

PO Box 2800	1160 Camino Cruz Blanca
Annapolis, MD 21404	Sante Fe, NM 87501
(800) 727-9238	(800) 331-5232
http://www.sjca.edu	http://www.sjcsf.edu

St. John's, one college on two campuses, is known for its distinctive "great books" curriculum. In the "1987 Statement of Educational Policy," Dr. Thomas J. Slakey, former dean, explains the uniqueness of the college. First, all students "follow a common curriculum throughout four years, embracing to the greatest extent possible the most important subject matters and methods of inquiry."

Second, the faculty, "to the greatest extent possible teach throughout the curriculum, not confining themselves to any one subject matter or method."

Third, study centers around "the so-called 'great books,' those texts that over time have proved best at forcing their readers to rethink fundamental questions, and at helping them understand themselves and the world around them. The books [are] arranged roughly in chronological order so as to take beginning students completely out of their own familiar world, and so as to place them in the world of **Homer**, of **Plato**, of **Ptolemy**, and so on, so that when they arrive after four years at 20th-century authors, they can read them with open eyes. The chronological order also profits from the remarkable degree to which the truly important authors draw upon their few truly important fellows from the past, as **Vergil** goes back to **Homer**, **Dante** to **Vergil**, **Kant** to **Artistotle**, **Einstein** to **Newton**, and so on. Thus occurs what Buchanan called 'the great conversation' among the authors, shared by the readers, shared especially in the discussion and questioning that follow careful reading."

The college believes that "students who develop habits of shared inquiry, turning to the best authors for help, but relying ultimately on their own imaginations and judgments, will grow as men and women and as responsible citizens." The St. John's program is symbolized by the fourfold Latin pun on its seal: *Facio liberos ex liberis, libris libraque*, "I make free men out of children by means of books and a balance."

The St. John's List of Great Books

Following is the most recent list of books on which the St. John's program is based. The list is subject to constant review and revision. Some books are read only in part.

Freshman Seminar Reading List

Aeschylus	*Agamemnon; Eumenides; Libation Bearers; Prometheus Bound*
Aristophanes	*Clouds*

Aristotle	*Metaphysics; Nicomachean Ethics; Physics; Poetics; Politics*
Euripides	*Bacchae; Hippolytus*
Herodotus	*Histories*
Homer	*The Iliad; The Odyssey*
Lucretius	*Nature of Things*
Plato	*Apology; Crito; Gorgias; Meno; Phaedo; Phaedrus; The Republic; Sophist; Symposium; Timaeus*
Sophocles	*Ajax; Antigone; Oedipus Rex; Oedipus at Colonus; Philocretes*
Thucydides	*Peloponnesian War*

Sophomore Seminar Reading List

	Bible: Links to the *Bible* in Latin Vulgate, French, and German
Anselm	*Proslogium; Response to Gaunilon's Reply*
Aquinas, Saint Thomas	*Summa Theologica*
Aristotle	*Metaphysics; On The Soul; On Interpretation; Categories*
Augustine, Saint	*Confessions*
Bacon, Sir Francis	*Novum Organum*
Chaucer, Geoffrey	*The Canterbury Tales*
Cicero	*De Republica*
Dante	*The Divine Comedy*
Decartes, René	*Discourse on Method; Geometry*
Epictetus	*Discourses*
Livy	*The Early History of Rome*
Luther, Martin	*A Commentary of Saint Paul's Epistle to the Galatians*
Machiavelli, Niccoló	*Discourses; The Prince*
Montaigne, Michel de	*Essays*
Plotinus	*The Enneads*
Plutarch	*Lives: Antony, Brutus, Caesar, Cato the Younger*
Polybius	*The Histories*

Shakespeare, William	*Hamlet; Henry IV Part I; Henry IV Part II; King Lear; Macbeth; A Midsummer Night's Dream; Richard II; The Tempest; Twelfth Night*
Tacitus	*Annals*
Vergil	*The Aeneid*

Junior Seminar Reading List

Austen, Jane	*Emma*
Berkeley, George	*Treatise Concerning the Principles of Human Knowledge*
Cervantes, Miguel de	*Don Quixote*
Descartes, René	*Meditations*
Faraday, Michael	*On the Various Forces in Nature*
Fielding, Henry	*Tom Jones*
Galileo	*Two New Sciences*
Hawthorne, Nathaniel	*Scarlet Letter*
Hobbes, Thomas	*Leviathan*
Hume, David	*Second Inquiry, Treatise of Human Nature*
Kant, Immanuel	*Critique of Pure Reason; Foundation of the Metaphysics of Morals*
Leibniz, Gottfried Wilhelm	Philosophical essays
Locke, John	*Second Essay on Civil Government*
Maxwell, James Clerk	Selected essays on electromagnetism
Melville, Herman	*Benito Cereno*
Milton, John	*Paradise Lost*
Molière	*Le Misanthrope*
Mozart, Wolfgang Amadeus	*Don Giovanni*
Newton, Sir Isaac	*The Principia*
Pascal, Blaise	*Pensées*
Rousseau, Jean-Jacques	*Social Contract*
Racine, Jean	*Phaedra*
Smith, Adam	*The Wealth of Nations*

Swift, Jonathan	*Gulliver's Travels*
Tocqueville, Alexis de	*Democracy in America*

Selected Essays: *American Revolution Documents*; *Anti-Federalist Papers*; *Federalist Papers*; *Notes of Debate in the Federal Convention*

Senior Seminar Reading List

Arendt, Hannah	*Men in Dark Times*
Darwin, Charles	*The Origin of Species*
Dostoevski, Fyodor	*Brothers Karamazov*
Einstein, Albert	*The Principle of Relativity*
Douglass, Frederick	*Narrative of the Life of Fredrick Douglass*
Faulkner, William	"The Bear"
Freud, Sigmund	*Dora*; *Introductory Lectures on Psychoanalysis*
Goethe, Johann W. Von	*Faust*
Hegel, Georg	*Phenomenology of Spirit*
Heidegger, Martin	*Basic Writings*
Husserl, Edmund	*The Origin of Geometry*
James, William	*Psychology, The Briefer Course*
Joyce, James	*The Dead*
Kafka, Franz	*The Burrow, A Hunger Artist*
Kierkegaard, Søren	*Fear and Tremblng*; *Philosophical Fragments*
Marx, Karl	*Capital*; *A Contribution to the Critique of Political Economy, Economic and Philosophic Manuscripts of 1844*
Nietzsche, Friedrich	*Beyond Good and Evil*
Twain, Mark	*The Adventures of Huckleberry Finn*
Tolstoy, Leo	*War and Peace*
U.S. Supreme Court Cases	*Dred Scott vs. Sanford*; *Plessy vs. Ferguson*; *Brown vs. Board of Education*; *Regents of the University of California vs. Bakke*
Wagner, Wilhelm Riachard	*Tristan and Isolde*
Woolf, Virginia	*Mrs. Dalloway*

The notion of a suggested reading list sits well with the ideology of a liberal education, wherein experts guide novitiates through wide ranging topics of learning, inscribing the blank slates of their minds to form fully developed, educated human beings. The humanities, the human arts, we are told build character by broadening horizons, engendering compassion, and instilling the value of reflection and deliberation. Though as a staunch defender of the institution of the university, I often find myself reciting such homilies, I fear something is lost in these antiseptic, indexical schemes. We don't come to reading, to books, with a blank slate. Nor do many have the leisure to follow orchestrated plans. Reading, the pursuit of knowledge, strikes me as a restless activity. Something is needed. Something is to be done. Reading is insurgent and rebellious. With Caliban we are able to say, "You taught me language and my profit on't is I know how to curse!" Like Fredrick Douglass, whose master tried to prevent him from learning to read, we understand that our ability to learn makes us forever unfit to be slaves.

Michael Drexler, Ph.D. Candidate
Brown University

Siena College
515 Loudon Road
Loudonville, NY 12211-1462
(518) 783-2300
http://www.siena.edu

The Siena Research Institute surveyed 126 faculty members from 126 colleges and universities to determine what books they felt entering college students should have read. The faculty members thought that on the average students should have read at least 15 of the following books. Siena's list of the most frequently mentioned works follows and includes the percentage of those faculty surveyed who recommended each book. The percentages in parentheses represent the share of 1,138 entering freshmen at 37 colleges in 25 states who said they had read each book. The average number was 10 books per student.

	Declaration of Independence—91% (58%)
	Bible—80% (55%)
Aristotle	*Politics*—10% (4%)
Austen, Jane	*Pride and Prejudice*—49% (14%)
Chaucer, Geoffrey	*The Canterbury Tales*—48% (52%)
Dickens, Charles	*Great Expectations* and *A Tale of Two Cities*—83% (55%)
Dickinson, Emily	Poems—68% (53%)
Dostoevski, Fyodor	*Crime and Punishment*—21% (10%)
Emerson, Ralph Waldo	Essays and poems—44% (42%)
Faulkner, William	Novels—29% (23%)
Fitzgerald, F. Scott	*The Great Gatsby*—65% (41%)
Frost, Robert	Poems—87% (55%)
Hawthorne, Nathaniel	*The Scarlet Letter*—81% (59%)
Homer	*The Iliad* or *The Odyssey*—72% (43%)
Machiavelli, Niccolò	*The Prince*—14% (8%)
Marx, Karl and Friedrich Engels	*Communist Manifesto*—31% (11%)
Melville, Herman	*Moby-Dick*—29% (30%)
Milton, John	*Paradise Lost*—20% (21%)
Orwell, George	*1984*—59% (38%)
Plato	*The Republic*—30% (7%)
Salinger, J.D.	*The Catcher in the Rye*—62% (32%)
Shakespeare, William	Works—91% (68%)
Sophocles	*Oedipus Rex*—60% (29%)
Steinbeck, John	*The Grapes of Wrath*—62% (37%)
Thoreau, Henry David	*Walden*—64% (28%)
Tocqueville, Alexis de	*Democracy in America*—26% (3%)
Tolstoy, Leo	*War and Peace*—6% (6%)
Twain, Mark	*The Adventures of Huckleberry Finn*—96% (68%)
Vergil	*The Aeneid*—25% (8%)
Whitman, Walt	*Leaves of Grass*—45% (9%)

Smith College
Northampton, MA 01063
(413) 584-2700
http://www.smith.edu

Among the works in Smith's list of "Suggested Reading For Students Planning To Enter Smith College" are

	Bible (King James Version: "the best preparation for literary studies")
Aeschylus	*Prometheus Bound*
Euripides	*The Trojan Women*
Homer	*The Odyssey*
Sophocles	*Antigone*; *Oedipus Rex* (these two works "invite study of Greek mythology")
Shakespeare, William	*Julius Caesar*; *Macbeth*; *Richard II* (or perhaps *Henry V* in connection with Olivier's film); *Twelfth Night*

Novels

Austen, Jane	*Pride and Prejudice*; *Emma*
Brontë, Charlotte	*Jane Eyre*
Brontë, Emily	*Wuthering Heights*
Conrad, Joseph	*Heart of Darkness*; *The Secret Sharer*
Dickens, Charles	*Great Expectations*
Dreiser, Theodore	*Sister Carrie*
Eliot, George	*The Mill on the Floss*
Ellison, Ralph	*Invisible Man*
Faulkner, William	*As I Lay Dying*; *Light in August*
Hardy, Thomas	*The Mayor of Casterbridge*; *Tess of the D'Urbervilles*
Hawthorne, Nathaniel	*The Scarlet Letter* or some of the tales
Hemingway, Ernest	*A Farewell to Arms*
James, Henry	*The Turn of the Screw* or *Washington Square*
Joyce, James	*A Portrait of the Artist as a Young Man*; *Dubliners*

Lawrence, D.H.	*The Fox* or *Sons and Lovers* or any collection of short stories
Melville, Herman	*Billy Budd*
Poe, Edgar Allan	Selected tales
Waugh, Evelyn	*Decline and Fall* or *A Handful of Dust*
Wharton, Edith	*Ethan Frome* or *The House of Mirth*

The author of the list also would include "a couple of novels by contemporary writers currently esteemed (twenty years ago I would have said **Salinger**, ten years ago **Vonnegut**): **Ann Beattie, Bobbie Ann Mason, Alice Munro**."

The author also feels that pre-college reading should include "poetry in a good anthology" with "substantial samples of the major British and American poets. Students would do well to study two or three poets, one of them 20th century, 'in depth.'" Plays by **Anton Chekov**, **Henrik Ibsen**, **Arthur Miller, Harold Pinter**, **George Bernard Shaw** are also highly recommended.

South Dakota State University
PO Box 504
Brookings, SD 57007
(605) 688-5195
http://www.sdstate.edu

Dr. George West of the Department of English at South Dakota State suggests the following "to high school teachers or to anyone who writes in for a list of recommended readings."

A Very Selective Reading List

Classics

	Bible
Hamilton, Edith	*Mythology*
Homer	*The Iliad; The Odyssey*
Sophocles	*Oedipus Rex*
Vergil	*The Aeneid*

English

Middle Ages

Chaucer, Geoffrey	Prologue to *The Canterbury Tales* and a tale or two

Renaissance

Shakespeare, William	*Julius Caesar*; *Macbeth*; *The Merchant of Venice*; *Romeo and Juliet*

17th Century

Milton, John	*Paradise Lost* (selections)

18th Century

Pope, Alexander	*The Rape of the Lock*

Romantics

Poetry: **Samuel Taylor Coleridge**, **John Keats**, **William Wordsworth**

Victorians

Austen, Jane	*Pride and Prejudice*
Brontë, Charlotte	*Jane Eyre*
Brontë, Emily	*Wuthering Heights*
Dickens, Charles	Anything
Tennyson, Alfred Lord	Poems

20th Century

Conrad, Joseph	A short story or novel
Golding, William	*Lord of the Flies*
Hardy, Thomas	Poems or a novel
Housman, A.E.	Poems

American

Cather, Willa	*My Antonia*
Crane, Stephen	*The Red Badge of Courage*
Ellison, Ralph	*Invisible Man*
Emerson, Ralph Waldo	Selections
Faulkner, William	*As I Lay Dying*
Fitzgerald, F. Scott	*The Great Gatsby*
Franklin, Benjamin	Selections
Hawthorne, Nathaniel	*The Scarlet Letter*
Hemingway, Ernest	*The Sun Also Rises*
Lewis, Sinclair	*Main Street*
London, Jack	*The Call of the Wild*
Melville, Herman	*Moby-Dick*
Neihardt, John G.	*Black Elk Speaks*
Salinger, J.D.	*The Catcher in the Rye*
Steinbeck, John	*The Grapes of Wrath*
Thoreau, Henry David	Selections
Twain, Mark	*The Adventures of Huckleberry Finn*
Wright, Richard	*Native Son*

Poetry: **Emily Dickinson, T.S. Eliot, Robert Frost, Edgar Allan Poe, E.A. Robinson, Carl Sandburg, Wallace Stevens, Walt Whitman, William Carlos Williams**

Drama: **Edward Albee, Arthur Miller, Tennessee Williams**

Short Stories: **Sherwood Anderson, Willa Cather, Stephen Crane, William Faulkner, F. Scott Fitzgerald, Nathaniel Hawthorne, Ernest Hemingway, Washington Irving, Jack London, Sinclair Lewis, Herman Melville, Flannery O'Connor, Edgar Allan Poe, Katherine Ann Porter, John Steinbeck**

Some highly regarded contemporary fiction writers: **Ann Beattie, E.L. Doctorow, Louise Erdrich, John Gardner, Gail Godwin, John Irving, Ursula Le Guin, Toni Morrison, Joyce Carol Oates, Thomas Pynchon, Philip Roth, Leslie Marmon Silko, Anne Tyler, John Updike, Alice Walker, James Welch**

Truman State University: The media like to talk about some people—Maya Angelou, Stephen Jay Gould, Andrew Wyeth, Magic Johnson, Jimmy Carter, Steven Spielberg, Bruce Springsteen—as "National Living Treasures" because their work adds to American traditions in the arts and sciences, helps other citizens, or enhances the quality of contemporary life. What living person(s) would you nominate as a "national living treasure" and why?

Spelman College
350 Spelman Lane SW
Atlanta, GA 30314-4399
(404) 681- 3643
http://www.spelman.edu

According to Dr. J.M. Aldridge of the Department of English at Spelman, the following list was developed by a faculty committee to send to incoming freshmen. One custom has been for the books to be discussed in group sessions in dormitories as a part of freshman orientation.

Freshman Reading List

Theme: The Significance of Black Culture

Baldwin, James	*The Fire Next Time* (1963)
Baraka, Imamu Amiri (LeRoi Jones)	*Blues People* (1965)
Cole, Johnnetta B., ed.	*All American Women* (1986)
Dubois, W.E.B.	*The Souls of Black Folk* (1903)

Franklin, John Hope	*From Slavery to Freedom* (6th ed.)
Giddings, Paula J.	*When and Where I Enter: The Impact of Black Women on Race and Sex in America* (1984)
Hughes, Langston	*The Best of Simple* (1961)
Hurston, Zora Neale	*Their Eyes Were Watching God* (1937)
King, Martin Luther, Jr.	*Why We Can't Wait* (1964)
Maynard, Olga	*Judith Jamison: Aspects of a Dancer* (1982)
Shange, Ntosake	*for colored girls who have considered suicide when the rainbow is enuf: a choreopoem* (1971)
Walker, Alice	*Meridian* (1976)
Washington, Mary Helen	*Invented Lives: Narratives of Black Women 1860–1960* (1987)
Woodson, Carter G.	*The Mis-Education of the Negro* (1933)

State University of New York at Albany
1400 Washington Avenue
Albany, NY 12222
(518) 442-3300
http://www.albany.edu

Professor David C. Redding of the English Department states that the University at Albany has no reading lists for pre-college students, but "if anyone asks me what I recommend, I say the *Bible*: it's basic to literature and culture." He also says that there are no fixed lists of readings for freshman courses. "For the last several years incoming students have been asked to read two books and discuss them when they come, but the books are simply ones of current interest and change each year."

Stetson University
421 N. Woodland Boulevard
DeLand, FL 32720-3771
(800) 688-0101
http://www.stetson.edu

Freshmen at Stetson take three required courses: two in English and one in religion. The required text for the English course is **J.W. Corder** and **John Jay Ruszkiewicz**, *Handbook of Current English*, 8th edition. For the religion course, students read **J. Benton White**'s *From Adam to Armageddon* and **Olive A. Burns**' *Cold Sassy Tree.*

Swarthmore College
500 College Avenue
Swarthmore, PA 19081-1397
(610) 328-8000
http://www.swarthmore.edu

The following is a partial list of works included in the Freshman English syllabi at Swarthmore:

	Arabian Nights (Muhsin Mahdi, ed.)
Alcott, Louisa May	*Behind a Mask*
Alexie, Sherman	*Reservation Blues*
Allison, Dorothy	*Bastard out of Carolina*
Arnold, Matthew	Selections from *Culture and Anarchy*
Blake, William	*Songs of Innocence; Songs of Experience; Marriage of Heaven and Hell: In Full Color*
Brecht, Bertolt	*Galileo*
Browning, Elizabeth Barrett	*Aurora Leigh*
Campbell, Maria	*Halfbreed*
Chang-rae Lee	*Native Speaker*

Chaucer, Geoffrey	*The Canterbury Tales*
Dangarembga, Tsitsi	*Nervous Conditions*
Dante	*Inferno* (Robert Pinsky, tr.)
Dash, Julie	*Daughters of the Dust*
Dickens, Charles	*Great Expectations*
Douglas, Ellen	*Can't Quit You, Baby*
Dove, Rita	*Thomas and Beulah; Darker Face of the Earth*
Eaglcton, Tcrry	*Literary Theory*
Elaw, Zilpha	*Memoirs*
Ellison, Ralph	*Invisible Man*
Fanon, Frantz	*Wretched of the Earth*
Gish Jen	*Typical American*
Hale, Janet Campbell	*Bloodlines: Odyssey of a Native Daughter*
Haien, Jeannette	*The All of It*
Harjo, Joy	*The Woman Who Fell from the Sky*
Hemingway, Ernest	*The Garden of Eden*
Hwang, David Henry	*M. Butterfly*
Jacobs, Harriet	*Incidents in the Life of a Slavegirl*
Kafka, Franz	*Metamorphosis*
Kincaid, Jamaica	*A Small Place*
Kushner, Tony	*Angels in America*
Lang, Andrew	*Beauty and the Beast*
Larsen, Nella	*Passing*
LeGuin, Ursula	*Left Hand of Darkness*
Lippard, Lucy, ed.	*Partial Recall: Essays on Photographs of Native North Americans*
Marlowe, Christopher	*Dr. Faustus*
Melville, Herman	*Benito Cereno*
Louis, Adrian	*Wild Indians and Other Creatures*
Meredith, George	*Modern Love*
Morrison, Toni	*Playing in the Dark*
Pinter, Harold	*The Collection*
Rodriquez, Richard	*Hunger of Memory*
Rushdie, Salmon	*Haroun and the Sea of Stories*
Seth, Virran	*The Golden Gate*

Shakespeare, William	*King Lear; Measure for Measure; Othello; The Tempest; Twelfth Night*
Shelley, Mary	*Frankenstein*
Silko, Leslie Marmon	*Storyteller*
Sirk, Douglas	*Imitation of Life*
Sophocles	*Oedipus* (Hughes, tr.)
Stein, Gertrude	*Four Saints in Three Acts; Lifting Belly*
Sterne, Laurence	*Tristram Shandy*
Swift, Jonathan	*Gulliver's Travels*
Taylor, Drew Hayden	*Funny, You Don't Look Like One: Observations of a Blue-eyed Ojibway*
Tahimik, Kidlat	*Perfumed Nightmare*
Vizenor, Gerald	*The Heirs of Columbus*
Vizenor, Gerald, ed.	*Native American Literature*
Wells, H.G.	*The Island of Dr. Moreau*
Wharton, Edith	*The House of Mirth*
Wilde, Oscar	*The Importance of Being Earnest*
Yamanaka, Lois Ann	*Wild Meat & the Bully Burgers*

Carleton College: If you could have lunch with any one person (living, dead, or fictional), who would it be and what would you discuss?

Temple University
1801 N. Broad Street
Philadelphia, PA 19122-6096
(215) 204-7000
http://www.temple.edu

The Undergraduate Division of the English Department at Temple lists in its pamphlet "The Green Bag II" the works read in its various courses. In their first year, students usually take a composition course and "Introduction to Literature." The following lists include the works often read in other courses open to underclassmen.

American/Afro-American Literature

Brooks, Gwendolyn	Poetry
Brown, William Wells	*Clotel*
Chesnutt, Charles W.	*The Marrow of Tradition*
Chopin, Kate	*The Awakening*
Crane, Stephen	*The Red Badge of Courage*
Delany, Martin	*Blake*
Dickinson, Emily	Various poems
Douglass, Frederick	*Narrative of the Life of Frederick Douglass*
Dreiser, Theodore	*Sister Carrie*
Dubois, W.E.B.	*The Souls of Black Folk*
Eliot, T.S.	*The Waste Land*
Ellison, Ralph	*Invisible Man*
Emerson, Ralph Waldo	*Essays*
Equiano, Olaudah	Slave narrative
Faulkner, William	*The Sound and the Fury*
Fitzgerald, F. Scott	*The Great Gatsby*
Franklin, Benjamin	*Autobiography*
H.D. (Hilde Doolittle)	Poems
Hawthorne, Nathaniel	*The Scarlet Letter*
Hemingway, Ernest	*The Sun Also Rises*
Hughes and Bontemps	*The Book of Negro Folklore*
Hughes, Langston	Poetry
Hurston, Zora Neale	*Their Eyes Were Watching God*
Jacobs, Harriet	"Linda Brent"
James, Henry	*The Portrait of a Lady*
Johnson, James Weldon	*Autobiography of an Ex-Colored Man*
Larsen, Nella	*Passing*
Lorde, Audrey	Poetry
Melville, Herman	*Moby-Dick*
Morrison, Toni	*Beloved; Sula*
Nabokov, Vladimir	*Lolita*
O'Neill, Eugene	*Desire Under the Elms*
Poe, Edgar Allan	"The Fall of the House of Usher"

Pound, Ezra	*Hugh Selwyn Mauberley*
Sanchez, Sonia	Poetry
Toomer, Jean	*Cane*
Twain, Mark	*The Adventures of Huckleberry Finn*
Walker, Alice	*Meridan; The Color Purple*
Walker, Margaret	*Jubilee*
Wharton, Edith	*The House of Mirth*
Whitman, Walt	*Song of Myself*
Wilson, Harriet	*Our Nig*
Wright, Richard	*Native Son*

Drama

Beckett, Samuel	*Waiting for Godot*
Brecht, Bertolt	*Mother Courage and Her Children*
Buchner, Georg	*Woyzeck*
Calderon, Pedro	*Life Is a Dream*
Congreve, William	*The Way of the World*
Ibsen, Henrik	*A Doll's House*
Miller, Arthur	*Death of a Salesman*
Molière	*The Misanthrope*
Pirandello, Luigi	*Six Characters in Search of an Author*
Shakespeare, William	Tragedies, comedies, romances, and historical plays
Shaw, George Bernard	*Major Barbara*

English Literature

	Beowulf
	Everyman
	Sir Gawain and the Green Knight
	"The Seafarer"
	"The Wanderer"
Auden, W.H.	*Selected Poems, 1930–1955*
Austen, Jane	*Emma; Sense and Sensibility*
Beckett, Samuel	*Happy Days; Murphy*
Blake, William	*Songs of Innocence; Songs of Experience*
Boswell, James	*The Life of Johnson*

Burns, Robert	*The Poetry of Bums*
Byron, George Gordon	"Childe Harold's Pilgrimage"
Chaucer, Geoffrey	*Troilus and Criseyde*; *The Canterbury Tales*
Coleridge, Samuel Taylor	"Kubla Khan"
Congreve, William	*The Way of the World*
Conrad, Joseph	*Heart of Darkness*; *Lord Jim*
De Quincey, Thomas	*Confessions of an English Opium-Eater*
Eliot, T.S.	*Prufrock and Other Observations*; *The Waste Land*
Fielding, Henry	*Joseph Andrews*
Ford, Ford Maddox	*The Good Soldier*
Forster, E.M.	*A Passage to India*
Gay, John	*The Beggar's Opera*
Johnson, Samuel	*Rasselas*
Joyce, James	*A Portrait of the Artist as a Young Man*; *Ulysses*
Keats, John	"Ode on a Grecian Urn"
Langland, William	*Piers Plowman*
Lawrence, D.H.	*Lady Chatterley's Lover*; *Women in Love*
Lewis, Matthew	*The Monk*
Malory, Sir Thomas	*Morte D'Arthur*
Pope, Alexander	"The Rape of the Lock"
Shaw, George Bernard	*Heartbreak House*; *Man and Superman*
Shelley, Mary	*Frankenstein*
Shelley, Percy Bysshe	"Mont Blanc"
Swift, Jonathan	*Gulliver's Travels*
Wollstonecraft, Mary	*A Vindication of the Rights of Women*
Woolf, Virginia	*To the Lighthouse*
Wordsworth, William	"Tintern Abbey"
Yeats, W.B.	*The Tower* and *The Winding Stair*

Contemporary Literature

Achebe, Chinua	*Things Fall Apart*
Barth, John	*Lost in the Funhouse*
Barthelme, Donald	*City Life*
Calvino, Italo	*T Zero*
Fuentos, Carlos	*The Death of Artemio Cruz*

García Márquez, Gabriel	*One Hundred Years of Solitude*
Grass, Günter	*The Tin Drum*
Pinter, Harold	*The Homecoming*
Pynchon, Thomas	*Gravity's Rainbow*
Simon, Claude	*The Flanders Road*

Bellarmine College: If you could have a conversation with any person in history, whom would you choose and why?

The University of Texas at Austin
Austin, TX 78712-1111
(512) 471- 3434
http://www.utexas.edu

The Texas List of Unrequired Reading

The University of Texas has compiled lists of 12 books and 12 alternates for each of the four college undergraduate years. The Unrequired Reading List Committee includes in its brochure the following note: "This is not a list of the books we think every student should read. Rather, its purpose is to encourage reading and to provide a good starting point and plan for future reading. Alternate titles are provided, because we recognize the vast differences among individuals in reading experience and taste. We encourage you to start by following your own inclinations.

"The topics covered in these volumes are a good sampling of the most important ideas and events responsible for intellectual life and struggle in Western civilization. A serious effort to examine at least selected topics in history, literature, philosophy, and science is an essential beginning in your education beyond secondary school. And this effort does not have to constitute a great burden. Only one book per month completes the reading program."

Freshman

Philosophy and Other Topics

Heilbroner, Robert	*The Worldly Philosophers*
Russell, Bertrand	*The Problems of Philosophy*
Smith, Huston	*The Religions of Man*

Alternates:

Plato	*The Republic*
Rousseau, Jean-Jacques	*The Social Contract*
Russell, Bertrand	*A History of Western Philosophy*

Science

Sacks, Oliver	*Awakenings*
Thomas, Lewis	*The Lives of a Cell*
Watson, James	*The Double Helix*

Alternates:

Boorstin, D.J.	*The Discoverers*
Gould, Stephen Jay	*The Panda's Thumb*
Lorenz, Konrad	*King Solomon's Ring*

Literature

Hemingway, Ernest	*The Sun Also Rises*
Homer	*The Odyssey* (Lawrence, tr.)
Twain, Mark	*The Adventures of Huckleberry Finn*

Alternates:

Austen, Jane	*Pride and Prejudice*
Conrad, Joseph	*Heart of Darkness*
Sophocles	*Antigone; Oedipus Rex*

History

Bloch, Marc	*The Historian's Craft*
Erikson, Erik H.	*Young Man Luther*
Hofstadter, Richard	*The American Political Tradition*

Alternates:

Franklin, Benjamin	*Autobiography*
Southern, R.W.	*The Making of the Middle Ages*
Wain, John, ed.	*Samuel Johnson*

Sophomore

Philosophy and Other Topics

Aristotle	*The Nicomachean Ethics*
	Bible. Old Testament: "Genesis," "Exodus," "Job," "Proverbs," "Ecclesiastes," "Isaiah," "Amos." New Testament: "Luke," "John," "Acts," "Galatians," "Ephesians."
Tocqueville, Alexia de	*Democracy in America*

Alternates:

Hallie, Phillip P.	*Lest Innocent Blood Be Shed*
Machiavelli, Niccolò	*The Prince*
Weber, Max	*The Theory of Social and Economic Organization*

Science

De Kruif, Paul	*Microbe Hunters*
Weinberg, Steven	*The First Three Minutes*
Whitehead, Alfred North	*Science and the Modern World*

Alternates:

Bernstein, Jeremy	*Einstein*
Pfeiffer, John E.	*The Creative Explosion*
Weisskopf, Victor F.	*Knowledge and Wonder*

Literature

Carroll, Lewis	*Alice's Adventures in Wonderland* and *Through the Looking Glass*
Melville, Herman	*Moby-Dick*
Shakespeare, William	*Richard II*

Alternates:

Fielding, Henry	*Tom Jones*
Milton, John	*Paradise Lost*
Waugh, Evelyn	*Brideshead Revisited*

History

Catton, Bruce	*This Hallowed Ground*
Cecil, David	*Melbourne*
Mattingly, Garrett	*The Defeat of the Spanish Armada*

Alternates:

Adams, Henry	*The Education of Henry Adams*
Prescott, William H.	*History of the Conquest of Mexico*
Woodward, C. Vann	*Origins of the New South*

Junior

Philosophy and Other Topics

Elsen, A.E.	*Purposes of Art*, 2nd ed.
James, William	*The Varieties of Religious Experience*
Mill, J.S.	*Utilitarianism; On Liberty*

Alternates:

Chambers, Whitaker	*Witness*
James, William	*Pragmatism*
Norberg-Schulz, C.	*Meaning in Western Architecture*

Science

Hardy, G.H.	*A Mathematician's Apology*
Pagels, Heinz	*The Cosmic Code*
Reichenbach, Hans	*The Rise of Scientific Philosophy*

Alternates:

Ravetz, Jerome R.	*Scientific Knowledge and Its Social Problems*

Snow, C.P.	*The Two Cultures and the Scientific Revolution*
Wilson, E.O.	*On Human Nature*

Literature

Allison, Alexander W., ed.	*The Norton Anthology of Poetry*, 3rd ed.
Shakespeare, William	*Hamlet*
Voltaire	*Candide*

Alternates:

Cervantes, Miguel de	*Don Quixote*
Dickens, Charles	*Hard Times*
Woolf, Virginia	*To the Lighthouse*

History

Bullock, Alan	*Hitler: A Study in Tyranny*
Moorehead, Alan	*The White Nile*
Schlesinger, Arthur	*The Crisis of the Old Order*

Alternates:

Tocqueville, Alexis de	*The Old Regime and the French Revolution*
James, Marquis	*The Raven*
Williams, T.H.	*Huey Long*

Senior

Philosophy and Other Topics

Hamilton, Alexander, et al. (B.F. Wright, ed.)	*The Federalist Papers*
Kant, Immanuel	*Groundwork of the Metaphysic of Morals*
Lewis, C.S.	*The Screwtape Letters*

Alternates:

Hayek, Friedrich A.	*The Road to Serfdom*
Marx, Karl	*A Contribution to the Critique of Political Economy*
Orwell, George	*The Road to Wigan Pier*

Science

Dobzhansky, Theodosius	*Mankind Evolving*
Gardner, Martin	*Science: Good, Bad, and Bogus*
Kuhn, Thomas S.	*The Structure of Scientific Revolutions*

Alternates:

Mayr, Ernst	*The Growth of Biological Thought*
Minnaert, M.	*The Nature of Light and Color in the Open Air*
Monod, Jacques	*Chance and Necessity*

Literature

Dostoevski, Fyodor	The Brothers Karamazov
Shakespeare, William	*A Midsummer Night's Dream*
Silone, Italo	*Bread and Wine*

Alternates:

Faulkner, William	*Light in August*
Mann, Thomas	*The Magic Mountain*
Tolstoy, Leo	*War and Peace*

History

Donovan, Robert J.	*The Tumultuous Years*
Kennan, George F.	*Russia and the West Under Lenin and Stalin*
Tuchman, Barbara	*Stillwell and the American Experience in China*

Alternates:

Camus, Albert	*The Rebel*
Malcolm X and Alex Haley	*The Autobiography of Malcolm X*
Tucker, Robert C.	*Stalin as Revolutionary*

Trinity College
300 Summit Street
Hartford, CT 06106-3100
(860) 297-2000
http://www.trincoll.edu

Trinity has a number of freshman seminars. Among these courses are the following:

In the seminar "What is Reality?" students examine a few of the great crises in knowledge in the Western tradition. Authors include **Thucydides**, **Plato**, **Michel de Montaigne**, **René Descartes**, **Jean-Paul Sartre**, and others.

The seminar titled "The Legal History of Race Relations" is concerned with the interrelationship between the American legal system and American race relations. Students read Supreme Court civil rights cases in the areas of education and public accommodations and background material on the historical and political climates in which the decisions were rendered.

In "Curiosity and Madness in English Literature" readings include **William Shakespeare** *Hamlet* and *King Lear*; **Mary Shelley** *Frankenstein*; **Henry James** *The Turn of the Screw*; **Charlotte Perkins Gilman** *The Yellow Wallpaper*; and works by **Jonathan Swift**, **Sir Arthur Conan Doyle**, **Edgar Allan Poe**, **Lewis Carroll**, and **John Fowles**.

The seminar "Dante's Divine Comedy" studies **Dante**'s epic poem in its historical context and its relationship to our own culture. A variety of works of literature and art that develop important themes from *The Divine Comedy* are considered.

In "The Myth of Faust: Goethe's Cosmic Drama" students study poems and passages from **Johann Wolfgang von Goethe**'s *Faust* and, with help of experiments and demonstrations led by faculty, explore Goethe's scientific concepts. A trip to the Faust collection of Yale University is often included.

Readings in the seminar "Athens at the Dawn of Democracy" include selections from **Thucydides**, **Plutarch**, **Aeschylus**, **Sophocles**, **Euripides**, **Aristophanes**, **Aristotle**, and **Xenophon**.

Students in the seminar "The Things We Carry" read 19th- and 20th-century American fiction and non-fiction and view films to discover how "the weight of the things the characters carry—their relationships, values, prejudices, and knowledge—define them and forge their experiences." Texts used include such works as **Harriet Jacobs** *Incidents in the Life of a Slave Girl*; **Rebecca H. Davis** *Life in the Iron Mills*; **Tim O'Brien** *The Things They Carried*; **Gwendolyn Parker** *Trespassing: My Sojourn in the Hall of Privilege*; **Pete Hamill** *A Drinking Life*; **Orson Scott Card** *Ender's Game*; and selections from *Best American Short Stories of the Century* edited by **John Updike.** Possible films include *The Fountainhead*, *Grease*, *Bastard out of Carolina* and an episode from HBO's "The Sopranos."

Another Trinity freshman seminar is titled "Highlanders: Peoples and Cultures." **Heinrich Harrer**'s *Seven Years in Tibet*, **Martin Scorese**'s *Kundun*, and **David Breashear**'s film on the ill-fated Everest expeditions of 1996 are among the works considered in relation to the experiences of Western adventurers, amateur religious investigators, and mountain climbers in Tibet and Nepal. A trek in Nepal is sometimes offered students.

Saint Norbert College: If you could travel back in time and only take one item from today's society with you, what item would you select and why?

University of Tulsa
600 South College Avenue
Tulsa, OK 74104
(918) 631-2000
http://www.utulsa.edu

In the Tulsa curriculum, students study primary works in six general areas: "Artistic Imagination, study of the products and creative processes of art and literature; Social Inquiry, the laws and practices that shape social, economic, and political life; Cultural Interpretation, the historical record and evolution of a variety of cultures; Scientific Investigation, modern science and technology; Contemporary Experience, issues and ideas of contemporary importance; and Methods of Inquiry, formal and informal logic, reasoning, and theories of learning."

According to the pamphlet that contains the Tulsa reading list for the curriculum, "whatever their prospective colleges and majors, however specialized their professional interest, students who complete the Tulsa curriculum carry the hallmark of educated men and women."

Following is the reading list. Twenty-five professors at the University of Tulsa chose "works that have been of special significance to them and that have helped shape and challenge human life." Each book is annotated by the professor who selected it. The date after the author and title is the first date of the book's publication.

Abbott, Edwin A., *Flatland: A Romance of Many Dimensions* (1884) "Abbott's social satire, *Flatland,* is about intelligent beings who live in a world of two dimensions...reminding us that the world may only appear to be what science and society teach, and that discovery of the true world is left to the inquisitive mind." (Janet A. Haggerty, Geosciences)

Arrow, Kenneth J., *Social Choice and Individual Values* (1951) "Arrow's book considers the problem of identifying, from a set of alternatives, that which best serves the interests of society. It not only provides one of several important perspectives from which to consider the choice of financial accounting alternatives, but has many additional applications." (Don Vickrey, Accounting)

Beckmann, Petr, *A History of Pi* (1971) "This delightful book offers astute commentary on the development of mathematics, focusing on the contributions of a handful of great mathematicians over the past 2000 years. There is quite a bit of commentary about history, politics, sociology, and science, produced by an author who, although highly opinionated, has a lot to say that won't be found in the standard textbooks." (John R. Hendrickson, Physics)

Burney, Charles, *Dr. Charles Burney's Continental Travels* (written 1770) "A compilation of journals kept by Charles Burney on his extended tours of Europe's leading musical centers, this book contains Burney's comments not only on music, but on a wide range of artistic and social issues." (Frank Ryan, Music)

Darwin, Charles, *The Voyage of the Beagle: Journal of Researches into the Geology and Natural History of the Various Countries Visited by H.M.S. Beagle* (1839) "The lands Darwin saw, extending millions of years into the past, provided one of the most exciting discoveries in the brief history of the human species." (James R. Stewart, Zoology)

Eliot, T.S., *Four Quartets* (1943) "When I first read them, the *Four Quartets* said something to me about the present and my senses…As I became acquainted with Augustine, San Juan de la Cruz, and the *Bhagavad-Gita*, the writers Eliot loves began to echo in the poems for me. The *Quartets* will say something terribly important to you about how to live in time." (Jane Ackerman, Foreign Languages and Comparative Literature)

Feynman, Richard P., *The Character of Physical Law* (1967) "Pulled out of school to work on the Manhattan Project that built the atom bomb, Feynman went on to win the Nobel Prize in 1965. *The Character of Physical Law* contains seven lectures delivered to undergraduates at Cornell University in 1964." (Roger N. Blais, Physics)

Freud, Sigmund, *A General Introduction to Psychoanalysis* (1920, Riviere, tr.) "A series of lively, engaging lectures for a nonacademic audience, the book contains most of the key insights of psychoanalysis." (Robert Hogan, Psychology)

Frost, Robert, *The Poems of Robert Frost* (1946) "Frost's is a poetry that represents the range of literature: nature, lyric, drama, wisdom, and invective in native terms." (Manly Johnson, English Language and Literature)

Grosser, Maurice, *The Painter's Eye* (*c* 1951) "This little book is filled with fresh insights and perceptions, revealing the delightful connections between the mundane technical problems of the painter and the elusive nature of the aesthetic experience." (Glenn Godsey, Art)

Hardy, G.H., *A Mathematician's Apology* (1967) "In this essay, a major figure of 20th-century mathematics explains what mathematicians do and why it is worth doing. For example, number theory, Hardy's specialty, is now essential for national security." (Kevin O'Neil, Mathematical and Computer Sciences)

Hofstadter, Douglas, *Gödel, Escher, Bach: An Eternal Golden Braid* (1979) Professor Clark pretending to speak from the 22nd century writes "Hofstadter's book transmitted with amazing accuracy the fundamental theorems in mathematical logic, philosophy, and computer science that provided the foundation for subsequent breakthroughs." (Austen G. Clark, Philosophy)

Homer, *The Iliad* (9th century B.C.; Lattimore or Fitzgerald, tr.) "Of all the literary works that helped shape Western civilization as we know it, Homer's *Iliad* is second in importance only to the Jewish Bible and the Christian New Testament." (Paul A. Rahe, History)

Jefferson, Thomas, *Notes on the State of Virginia* (1787) "Probably no other contemporary document captures so well both the brilliance and limitations of the world Jefferson knew." (Lawrence D. Cress, History)

Kuhn, Thomas S., *The Structure of Scientific Revolutions* (1962) "Kuhn's book altered the way many scientists think about their work. It is among the ten most often-cited science books of this century." (Robert E. Howard, Chemistry)

Lévi-Strauss, Claude, *Tristes Tropiques* (1955; Russell, tr.) An account of the author's experiences in Brazil's hinterland searching for untouched native tribes, "...this book is a foundational statement of structuralism, the widely influential theory that the vast particularity of life's surface can be reduced to a finite set of deep, universal, mental structures." (Lamont Lindstrom, Anthropology)

Meyrowitz, Joshua, *No Sense of Place* (1985) "How have electronic media changed the situations in which we interact with other people? Meyrowitz answers this important question. To discover the available means of persuasion in this electronic age, this book is essential reading." (Robert J. Doolittle, Communication)

Montaigne, Michel de, *Essays* (1580–92, Frame, tr.) "Montaigne...in the critical spirit of the French Renaissance, delights in challenging the reader in his reflections on the human condition—on problems in epistemology, morals, and politics." (Elaine Ancekewicz, Foreign Languages and Comparative Literature)

Orwell, George, *Homage to Catalonia* (1938) In a book about the Spanish Civil War, Orwell's "insights on the nature of totalitarianism, whether of the right or the left, are a monument to a man who advocated clear thinking as well as clear writing." (Mary Lee Townsend, History)

Paton, Alan, *Ah, But Your Land Is Beautiful* (1981) A novel about South Africa and apartheid, "it treats all the main parties to the struggle—Afrikaners, English, Blacks, Coloreds, Marxists—and shows how the religious moralities involved have wrought both demonic hypocrisy and true saintliness." (Denise Lardner Carmody, Religion)

Plato, *Republic* (4th century BC; Bloom, tr.) "Almost any issue (philosophical, literary, scientific, historical, economic, psychological, sociological, etc.) can be discussed within the context of Plato's *Republic*, which treats the broader possibilities of human knowledge and social relationships in a discussion of the ideal political state." (D. Thomas Benediktson, Foreign Languages and Comparative Literature)

Smith, Adam, *An Inquiry into the Nature and Causes of Wealth of Nations* (1776) "Smith's seminal work, written at the beginning of the Industrial Revolution, provided a conduit through which 18th-century thought about human nature and the system of 'natural liberty' influenced the study of economies." (R. Lynn Rittenoure, Economics)

Smith, Adam, *The Theory of Moral Sentiments* (1759) The work "considers the place wealth, and the desire for it, should occupy in our lives. Smith had no great respect for wealth, greatness, or driving ambition. Instead, he recommended "humanity, justice, generosity, and public spirit."" (Thomas A. Horne, Political Science)

Swift, Jonathan, *Gulliver's Travels* (1726) This book about "the imaginary voyages of an Englishman, Lemuel Gulliver, carries us away with its story while making us think—and laugh—about our own vanities, offering the painful pleasure of self-recognition." (Darcy O'Brien, English Language and Literature)

Whitman, Walt, *Leaves of Grass* (1855, 1891–92) "Written in innovative free verse, Whitman's book celebrates both community and individual, projecting a 'cosmic hero' into an idealized 'America,' where greed, intolerance, and corruption are defeated by transcendental thinking and energetic art." (Winston Weathers, English Language and Literature)

University of the Pacific
Stockton, CA 95211
(209) 946-2285
http://www.uop.edu

The following list is "quite unofficial and chatty," according to Professor Arlen J. Hansen of the University of the Pacific's Department of English. It is what the department sends out when high school students, teachers, or counselors ask for their recommendations for pre-college reading.

The list is entitled:

SOMETHING TO READ

Serious Stuff

Brontë, Emily, *Wuthering Heights* The whole cycle: affection, love, and heartbreak. Almost as good as the 1939 movie.

Crane, Stephen, *The Red Badge of Courage* A young soldier rationalizes that he's not a coward, war's not bloody, and nature's not cruel.

Defoe, Daniel, *Robinson Crusoe* Desert island tale about having to reinvent civilization, not to mention the wheel.

Dickens, Charles, *Great Expectations* Don't let the title fool you. The 19th-century English disillusionment novel.

A Tale of Two Cities Opens with one of the all-time greatest lines and keeps the beat to the very end.

Faulkner, William, *Intruder in the Dust* About racism and resistance to change; probably the most accessible of Faulkner's novels.

Fitzgerald, F. Scott, *The Great Gatsby* The American dream fails to deliver the goods and yet ennobles the dreamer.

Hawthorne, Nathaniel, *The Scarlet Letter* Good old American subjects: sex, guilt, sin, love, hypocrisy, and self-torture.

Hemingway, Ernest, *The Nick Adams Stories* Covers all kinds of "initiation"—a boy gets burned in just about every way possible.

Lewis, Sinclair, *Arrowsmith* Implicates the ambitious doctors and the phonies around them.

Poe, Edgar Allan, "The Tell-Tale Heart" (a guy's guilt-ridden imagination gives him away), "The Black Cat" (a guy hates his cat and kills his wife, or is it the other way around?), "The Cask of Amontillado" (a guy buries his rival alive), and "The Pit and the Pendulum" (a guy trapped by time, the pendulum, and by space, the pit).

Scott, Sir Walter, *Ivanhoe* A sentimental romance filled with historical inaccuracies makes a lively adventure.

Shakespeare, William, *Hamlet* What would you do if your uncle killed your father and married your mother?

Julius Caesar Maybe the easiest play by Shakespeare but has some great lines. Your basic betrayal story.

MacBeth A wife gets carried away in her ambition for her husband. Don't miss the "sound and fury" speech.

Stevenson, Robert Louis, *Dr. Jekyll and Mr. Hyde* Assumes we're all evil underneath but lack the chemistry to release that side of us.

Twain, Mark, *The Adventures of Huckleberry Finn* Don't let *Tom Sawyer* fool you, this is an angry book. Hilarious too, of course.

Innocents Abroad This'll be one of the funniest books you'll ever get to read.

Just for the Fun of It

Beckett, Samuel, *Waiting for Godot* A play in which nothing much happens but it makes a lot of sense anyway. Like life that way.

Didion, Joan, *Slouching Towards Bethlehem* Some absolutely unforgettable examples of "the new journalism" or whatever you call it.

Ellison, Ralph, *Invisible Man* A reflective, intelligent novel loaded with poignant incidents from the life of a black man.

Heller, Joseph, *Catch-22* Out-M.A.S.H.es *M.A.S.H.* in hilarity and contempt for war.

Mailer, Norman, *The Armies of the Night* This "history as a novel" is about a 1967 anti-war march. But mostly, of course, about Mailer.

Malamud, Bernhard, *The Magic Barrel* Curious but rich stories about urban life and man's tendency to deceive himself and others.

Salinger, J.D., *The Catcher in the Rye* Lays into phoniness.

Vonnegut, Kurt Jr., *The Slaughterhouse Five* Billy Pilgrim, the Dresden bombing, and a time-warp loop.

Williams, Tennessee, *The Glass Menagerie* You can't help loving—and even, at times, admiring—these pathetic, dear dreamers.

Wolfe, Tom, *The Right Stuff* Unabashed hero-worship, but loaded with solid cultural analysis and insights into human nature.

University of the South
735 University Ave.
Sewanee, TN 37375
(931) 598-1000
http://www.sewanee.edu

According to Dr. Edwin Stirling, Department of English, no reading list per se is sent out to prospective students, but a list is provided for those interested in majoring in English to "help them begin their reading in a particular period or author."

General texts include *The Norton Anthology of English Literature* (2 vols.) and the *Macmillan Anthology of American Literature.* Also suggested are **Albert C. Baugh**'s *A Literary History of England*, and a "useful popular history," *The Land and Literature of England* by **Robert M. Adams**. Other recommendations are **Robert E. Spiller**, et al., *Literary History of the United States* and **Marcus Cunliffe**'s *Literature of the United States* "short, perceptive, and readable." **C. Hugh Holman**'s *A Handbook to Literature* is also mentioned. Authors and some of the fides on the reading list follow:

Background

	Bible: Especially "Genesis," "Job," "Psalms," and the Gospels (King James Authorized Version)
Aeschylus	*The Oresteia*
Aristotle	*Poetics*
Boethius	*The Consolation of Philosophy*
Dante	*The Divine Comedy*
Homer	*The Iliad*; *The Odyssey*
Sophocles	*Antigone*; *Oedipus Rex*
Vergil	*The Aeneid*

Medieval

	Beowulf
	The Battle of Maldon
	The Dream of the Rood
	Everyman
	Pearl
	"The Seafarer"
	Sir Gawain and the Green Knight
	"The Wanderer"
	The Wakefield Second Shepherd's Play
Chaucer, Geoffrey	*The Canterbury Tales*; *Troilus and Criseyde*
Malory, Sir Thomas	*Morte d'Arthur* (I, VII, VIII)

Renaissance

Lyric poets: **Thomas Campion**; **Samuel Daniel**; **John Donne**; **Michael Drayton**; **George Herbert**; **Robert Herrick**; **Henry Howard, Earl of Surrey**; **Andrew Marvell**; **John Milton**; **Sir Philip Sidney**; **Edmund Spenser**; and **Sir Thomas Wyatt**.

Jonson, Ben	*The Alchemist*; *Volpone*; poetry
Kyd, Thomas	*The Spanish Tragedy*

Marlowe, Christopher	*Doctor Faustus*
Milton, John	*Paradise Lost*; *Samson Agonistes*; other poetry
More, Sir Thomas	*Utopia*
Shakespeare, William	Plays and sonnets
Spenser, Edmund	*The Faerie Queene*; *The Shepheardes Calendar* ("October"); "Epithalamion"
Webster, John	*The Duchess of Malfi*

Restoration and 18th Century

Bunyan, John	*The Pilgrim's Progress*
Boswell, James	*Life of Johnson*
Congreve, William	*The Way of the World*
Defoe, Daniel	*Moll Flanders*
Dryden, John	*Absalom and Achitophel* and other works
Fielding, Henry	*Joseph Andrews*; *Tom Jones*
Goldsmith, Oliver	*She Stoops to Conquer*; "The Deserted Village"
Gray, Thomas	"Elegy Written in a Country Churchyard," and other poetry
Johnson, Samuel	Preface to *Dictionary* and other works
Pope, Alexander	*An Essay on Criticism* and other works
Richardson, Samuel	*Pamela*
Sheridan, R.B.	*The Rivals*
Sterne, Laurence	*A Sentimental Journey*
Swift, Jonathan	*Gulliver's Travels* and other works
Wycherley, William	*The Country Wife*

19th Century

Lyric poets: **Matthew Arnold; William Blake; Robert Browning; Robert Burns; George Cordon; Lord Byron; Samuel Taylor Coleridge; Gerard Manley Hopkins; John Keats; Percy Bysshe Shelley; Alfred, Lord Tennyson;** and **William Wordsworth.**

Austen, Jane	*Pride and Prejudice*
Brontë, Charlotte	*Jane Eyre*
Brontë, Emily	*Wuthering Heights*
Dickens, Charles	*Bleak House*; *Hard Times*

Eliot, George	*Middlemarch*
Hardy, Thomas	*Tess of the D'Urbervilles*
Pater, Walter	Conclusion to *The Renaissance*
Scott, Sir Walter	*The Heart of Midlothian*
Trollope, Anthony	*Barchester Towers*
Wilde, Oscar	*The Picture of Dorian Gray*

American Literature

Crane, Stephen	*The Red Badge of Courage*; "The Open Boat"
Dickinson, Emily	Selected poems
Edwards, Jonathan	*Personal Narrative*; "Sinners in the Hands of an Angry God"
Emerson, Ralph Waldo	"Nature," "The Poet," "Self-Reliance"
Franklin, Benjamin	*Autobiography*
Hawthorne, Nathaniel	*The Scarlet Letter* and short stories
James, Henry	*The Portrait of a Lady* and short stories
Melville, Herman	*Benito Cereno*; *Moby-Dick*
Poe, Edgar Allan	Tales
Thoreau, Henry David	*Civil Disobedience*; *Walden*
Twain, Mark	*The Adventures of Huckleberry Finn*
Whitman, Walt	Selected poetry

20th Century

Lyric poets: **W.H. Auden**, **T.S. Eliot**, **Robert Frost**, **Thomas Hardy**, **Robert Lowell**, **Ezra Pound**, **John Crowe Ransom**, **Wallace Stevens**, **Allen Tate**, **Dylan Thomas**, **William Carlos Williams**, and **William Butler Yeats**.

Conrad, Joseph	*Heart of Darkness*; *Lord Jim*
Faulkner, William	*Absalom, Absalom!*; *Go Down Moses*; *The Sound and the Fury*
Fitzgerald, F. Scott	*The Great Gatsby*
Hemingway, Ernest	*For Whom the Bell Tolls*
Joyce, James	*Dubliners*; *A Portrait of the Artist as a Young Man*; *Ulysses*
Lawrence, D.H.	*Women in Love*
O'Neill, Eugene	*Long Day's Journey Into Night*

O'Connor, Flannery	"Good Country People," "A Good Man Is Hard To Find"
Shaw, George Bernard	*Heartbreak House*; *Major Barbara*
Welty, Eudora	"The Petrified Man," "A Worn Path," "Why I Live at the P.O."
Woolf, Virginia	*To the Lighthouse*

> **University of Miami**: If you could be another person, real or fictional, for one day, who would you be, and why? 2. What book, poem, musical, or other cultural artifact is important to you, and why?

Vassar College
124 Raymond Avenue
Poughkeepsie, NY 12604
(914) 437-7000
http://www.vassar.edu

According to Dr. Robert DeMaria, Department of English at Vassar, freshman courses are "individually designed and change every year." The following is a representative sampling of literature commonly taught in some of the courses:

American Dreams

Alger, Horatio	*Ragged Dick*
Fitzgerald, F. Scott	*The Great Gatsby*
Hellman, Lillian	*Little Foxes*
Lewis, Sinclair	*Babbitt*
Miller, Arthur	*Death of a Salesman*
Tyler, Anne	*Dinner at the Homesick Restaurant*
Williams, Tennessee	*The Glass Menagerie*

And short fiction by **James Baldwin**, **Ambrose Bierce**, **Roy Blount**, **Willa Cather**, **John Cheever**, **Stephen Crane**, **William Faulkner**, **Ernest Hemingway**, **Langston Hughes**, **Ring Lardner**, **Jane Martin**, **Louis Nordan**,

Flannery O'Connor, **William Sydney Porter**, **Philip Roth**, **Irwin Shaw**, **James Thurber**, **Mark Twain**, **John Updike**, and **Richard Wright**.

Autobiography and Fiction

Barthelme, Frederick	"Monster Deal" (*Granta* #8)
Carter, Angela	"Sugar Daddy"
Carver, Raymond	"The Bath," "A Small, Good Thing," "Where I'm Calling From," the Carver interview from *Paris Review*
Didion, Joan	*Slouching Towards Bethlehem*
Ephron, Nora	"A Few Words About Breasts," "On Never Having Been a Prom Queen"
Ford, Richard	"Rock Springs"
Ignatieff, Michael	Essay in *Granta* #14
Joyce, James	*Dubliners*
Kingston, Maxine Hong	*The Woman Warrior*
Lessing, Doris	Essay in *Granta* #14
McEwen, Christian	Essay in *Granta* #14
Mason, Bobble Ann	"Still Life with Watermelon" (*Granta* #8)
Nabokov, Vladimir	*Lolita*
O'Connor, Flannery	"Everything That Rises Must Converge," "Greenleaf"
Olsen, Tillie	"I Stand Here Ironing," *Tell Me A Riddle*
Paley, Grace	"Enormous Changes at the Last Minute"
Phillips, Jayne Anne	"Rayme—A Memoir of the Seventies" (*Granta* #8)
Roth, Philip	*The Ghost Writer*
Wolff, Geoffrey	*Duke of Deception*
Wolff, Tobias	"Barracks Thief" (*Grants* #8)

The Development of English Literature

	Sir Gawain and the Green Knight
Chaucer, Geoffrey	*The Canterbury Tales* (the general prologue; tales: the Franklin's, the Wife of Bath's, the Merchant's, the Nun's Priest's, the Miller's)
Gardner, Helen, ed.	*The Metaphysical Poets*

Lewis, Matthew	*The Monk*
Milton, John	*Paradise Lost*
Pope, Alexander	"The Rape of the Lock," selected poetry
Shakespeare, William	*Antony and Cleopatra*; *Hamlet*; *A Midsummer Night's Dream*; *Romeo and Juliet*; *The Winter's Tale*
Spenser, Edmund	*Selected Poetry* (book I, III)
Walpole, Horace	*The Castle of Otranto*

Forms of Drama

Baraka, Imamu Amiri (LeRoi Jones)	*Bloodrites*
Jonson, Ben	*Volpone*
Marlowe, Christopher	*Dr. Faustus*
Shakespeare, William	*The Tempest*
Sophocles	*Antigone*
Van Itallie, Jean-Claude	*America Hurrah*
Wycherley, William	*The Country Wife*

And scenes or plays by **Samuel Beckett**, **Bertolt Brecht**, **Ed Bullins**, **Erskine Caldwell**, **Churchill**, **Martha Clarke**, **Hughes**, **Jackson**, **Harold Pinter**, **Oscar Wilde**, and **Robert Wilson**.

Forms of the Essay

Barthes, Roland	"The Brain of Einstein," "The Face of Garbo," "Strip Tease"
Horkheimer and Adorno	"The Culture Industry: Enlightenment as Mass Deception"
Marcus, Greil	Essay on Elvis Presley
Orwell, George	"Shooting an Elephant," "The Art of Donald McGill"
Smart, William	*Eight Modern Essayists*
White, E.B.	"The Essayist"
Woolf, Virginia	"Death of the Moth"

And essays by **Ralph Waldo Emerson**, **Samuel Johnson**, **Michel de Montaigne**, **Adrienne Rich**, **Lewis Thomas**, and **Alice Walker**.

Forms of Narrative

Austen, Jane	*Pride and Prejudice*
Brontë, Charlotte	*Jane Eyre*
Charters, ed.	*The Story and Its Writer*
Dickens, Charles	*Great Expectations*
Eliot, George	*The Mill on the Floss*
Fielding, Henry	*Joseph Andrews*
Hardy, Thomas	*The Return of the Native*
Joyce, James	*A Portrait of the Artist as a Young Man*
Lawn, ed.	*The Short Story: 30 Masterpieces*
Lessing, Doris	*Martha Quest*; *A Proper Marriage*

Literary Kinds: Narrative

Austen, Jane	*Pride and Prejudice*
Beckett, Samuel	*The Lost Ones*
Hawthorne, Nathaniel	*Hawthorne's Short Stories*
Homer	*The Odyssey* (Fitzgerald, tr.)
James, Henry	*Eight Tales from the Major Phase*; *The Portrait of a Lady*; *The Turn of the Screw*
Joyce, James	*Dubliners*; *A Portrait of the Artist as a Young Man*
Scott, Walter	*Waverley*
Vergil	*The Aeneid* (Fitzgerald, tr.)

Literary Kinds: Poetry

Allison, Alexander W., ed.	*The Norton Anthology of Poetry*, 3rd ed.
Agoos, Julie	*Above the Land*
Joyce, James	"The Dead" (compared with the John Huston movie)
Welty, Eudora	"Place in Fiction"
Wright, James	*Two Citizens*

And among others, poems by **Elizabeth Bishop**, **Robert Browning**, **John Donne**, **Langston Hughes**, **Ted Hughes**, **Robert Lowell**, **Ishmael Reed**, and **Walt Whitman**.

Major British and American Writers from Pope to Eliot

Austen, Jane	*Emma*
Chopin, Kate	*The Awakening*
Dickens, Charles	*Hard Times*
Dickinson, Emily	*Final Harvest: Emily Dickinson's Poems*
Eliot, T.S.	Selected poems
Fielding, Henry	*Joseph Andrews*
Hawthorne, Nathaniel	Selected tales and sketches
James, Henry	*The Turn of the Screw*
Keats, John	Selected poems and letters
Lamb, Charles	Selected essays
Owen, Wilfred	*Collected Poems*
Pope, Alexander	*Poetry and Prose of Alexander Pope*
Rose, Phyllis	*Parallel Lives*
Tennyson, Alfred Lord	Selected poems
Whitman, Walt	*Leaves of Grass*
Wilde, Oscar	*The Importance of Being Earnest*

Personal Narratives and Political Identity

Atwood, Margaret	*The Handmaid's Tale*; *Journals of Susanna Moodie*
Davies, Robertson	*Fifth Business*
Forster, E.M.	*A Passage to India*
Gallant, Mavis	*Home Truths*
Gordimer, Nadine	*July's People*
Jhabvala, Ruth Prawer	*Heat and Dust*
Jolley, Elizabeth	*Woman in a Lampshade*
Joyce, James	*A Portrait of the Artist as a Young Man*
Keneally, Thomas	*The Chant of Jimmy Blacksmith*
MacPherson, Jay	*The Boatman*
Munro, Alice	*The Beggar Main*
Naipaul, V.S.	*A Bend in the River*
Ondaatje, Michael	*Billy the Kid*
Rushdie, Salman	*Shame*

Shakespeare, William	*The Tempest*
Shelley, Mary	*Frankenstein*
Soyinka, Wole	*Ake; The Years of Childhood*
Walcott, Derek	Selections
White, Patrick	*The Aunt's Story*
Yeats, William Butler	Poetry

Self-Discovery: Visions and Revisions

O'Neill, Eugene	*The Iceman Cometh*
Shepard, Sam	*A Lie of the Mind*
Tyler, Anne	*The Accidental Tourist*
Woolf, Virginia	*The Waves*

The Vassar English Department recommends to its students the following magazines and newspapers:

Daedalus
Encounter
London Magazine
New American Review
New York Review of Books
Partisan Review
Poetry
Scientific American
The Manchester Guardian
The New Statesman and The Nation
The New Yorker
The New York Times
Times Literary Supplement (London)

Pomona College: Identify a real or fictional person or character who is a personal hero or heroine and describe the influence this person or character has had on you.

University of Vermont
194 South Prospect Street
Burlington, VT 05401
(802) 656-3480
http://www.uvm.edu

According to Professor Huck Gutman, this is "a personal and thus idiosyncratic list of books, and occasionally movies, paintings, and music, which you might want to encounter. Every work is a marvel of human creation, and a rich resource for human self-exploration and self-development. Besides, I loved everything listed below! And, as Wordsworth wrote, "What we have loved others will love, And we will teach them how…"

I hope you enjoy, and find benefit in, what follows."

Novels

19th Century: The Golden Age of Fiction

One way to enter the 19th century is to read novels about it, not written in it. In this vein, I highly recommend Gore Vidal (stepbrother to Jackie Kennedy, by the way) whose *Lincoln* and *Empire* are marvelous—especially if you like history.

But turning to the 19th-century writers themselves, if you haven't tried her, and if you can stomach a novel about courtship and love, read **Jane Austen**. There never was a better novelist in English. *Pride and Prejudice* is so good, and so enticing, that I have read it eight or ten times. I like all her other novels, too, but especially *Mansfield Park* and yes, the books are much better than the movies.

The most captivating novel I ever read was a romance by the great French 19th-century novelist **Stendhal** *The Charterhouse of Parma.*

Another romantic novel of the period is **Goethe**'s *The Sorrows of Young Werther.* But I don't recommend it nearly as highly as a strange novel (not reputed to be his best) by **Thomas Mann**, the towering figure of German fiction in the 20th century. His *The Beloved Returns* is a gem. It is about Goethe's love affair with Charlotte (the basis of Goethe's novel) and how years later this lover comes to visit him. If you read this and like it and are ready to take on the BIG classics, you could also try **Mann**'s great novella *Death in Venice* or his huge novel *The Magic Mountain.*

The wonderful "humane" or "humanist" novel of the 19th century is **George Eliot**'s *Middlemarch.*

No doubt about it, the greatest to write in English was believe it or not, **Charles Dickens**. Really? Really!!! His best novels are *Great Expectations*, *David Copperfield*, and especially *Bleak House*...no one foresaw the life of the city and the tensions of class better than Dickens. No one ever—save Tolstoy and Balzac—had a broader canvas.

The greatest novel, ever, is by someone who admired Dickens (as did all the Russian novelists): *War and Peace* by **Leo Tolstoy**. And if you haven't had enough of Tolstoy with that work, after you take a deep breath, plunge into his *Anna Karenina*, which to many readers, including me, is just as good—or almost.

No American novel is as big and good as Tolstoy's, though two "greatest American novels" come close. One is—you guessed it—*Moby-Dick* by **Herman Melville** (19th century) and the other **William Faulkner**'s *Absalom, Absalom* (20th century).

20th Century

Absalom, Absalom is also **Faulkner**'s toughest. But it says more about race, class, history, stubbornness, pride, and family, than any single book ever written in America. If you are new to Faulkner, who is always experimental, you might start with his novella "The Bear" and move on to *The Sound and the Fury*. None are easy; all are wonderfully rich and wise.

E.M. Forster is another fine modernist writer. He has no need to dazzle, though his novels reverberate on the deepest levels of the heart. The best is *Howard's End*, the most enjoyable *A Room With a View.*

While I'm on the modernists, one of the triumphs of American literature is *The Sun Also Rises* by **Ernest Hemingway**, a pared-down but scintillant prose style, characters, vision.

And another good but LONG work is **John Dos Passos'** trilogy of nobles in the 20s and 30s called *U.S.A.*

I am a great admirer of **Saul Bellow's** earlier fiction, especially the novella "Seize the Day" (an extraordinary enquiry in what it is to be human) and the comic novel *Henderson the Rain King*. Another favorite novella is **Tillie Olsen**'s extraordinarily moving story of an older woman facing illness, "Tell Me A Riddle."

The novel I have read which is most resonant with life experience, be it politics or searching for identity or the American city, is **Ralph Ellison**'s *Invisible Man*. It is the best novel of the post-war period in America.

Joseph Heller's *Catch-22* is hilarious, and also deep.

Oh, want a comic and happy novel that is also a good novel? My favorite is the British (truly uproarious) *Lucky Jim* by **Kingsley Amis**. And I also found **Michael Malone**'s *Handling Sin* hilarious. A flawed novel, but happy and even slapstick.

Spellbinding on the 1960s and the Civil Rights movement is **Taylor Branch**'s *Parting the Waters*, the first volume of his biography of Martin Luther King. It truly reads like a novel—the second volume has appeared recently to fine reviews.

Short Fiction

I have two recommendations for short stories. **Anton Chekhov** is astonishing. My favorite of his hundreds is "Gooseberries." No one I have ever read can so seamlessly move from life to words on a page. And no one ever wrote more dense and suggestive stories than **Franz Kafka**: Read "The Metamorphosis," "The Judgement," "In the Penal Colony," and his claustrophobic and overpowering novel *The Trial*.

Poetry

I only teach poetry nowadays. Perhaps it is the intensity of the words in poems, perhaps it is that the words themselves of the poems remain, or perhaps it is just my own idiosyncracies, but poems last, stay with me, longer than novels.

I will start with some of my favorite poets. Read some poems of **Emily Dickinson** and **Walt Whitman**. They are right up there with **Wordsworth** and **Williams**.

William Wordsworth, *The Prelude*...The first modern autobiography, the story of the growth of the poet's consciousness, the best long poem in English of the past two centuries. At 250+ pages, this may not be something you want to read unless you have a spare four or five days and are hiking through the wilderness, but I have been known to teach it in freshman poetry courses!

William Butler Yeats, the greatest Irish poet, died in 1939. Try "Sailing to Byzantium," "The Second Coming," and "In Memory of Eva Gore-Booth and Con Markiewicz." Try some of the late poems, when he is tired of conventional wisdom, and embraces the body and the heart: "Politics," the last stanza of "Circus Animals' Desertion," "Why Should Not Old Men Be Mad," "Speech After Long Silence," and "Lapis Lazuli." No English poet, not even **Keats** and **Shakespeare** ever sang as well as Yeats.

Seamus Heaney, Nobel Prize winner. I particularly recommend a series of poems, "Station Island, " but they are tough; start with his early poems, like "Digging" and "Mid-Term Break." I like Heaney because he confronts politics in his poetry.The greatest political poet of our century, I think, is the German leftist **Bertholt Brecht**.

At the opposite end of the spectrum, the greatest German poet of our century is so esthetic I sometimes don't think I can stand him. He is **Rainer Maria Rilke**. Try the sonnets "The Panther" and the strongest poem I know, "Archaic Torso of Apollo," which is about how art can have more of life than our own lives. Try also the longer and more difficult "Requiem" and if you are a real glutton for punishment, the difficult but exceptionally rich series "Duino Elegies." The translation by Stephen Mitchell is by far the best.

This year I finally made my way into **Paul Celan**. Profoundly influenced by Emily Dickinson, he is a Romanian who writes in German even though he as a Jew was imprisoned by the Nazis and saw his family exterminated. His "Death Fugue" is the most widely known poem on the concentration camps, a remarkable tour de force; but I like his late short lyrics, which owe much to Dickinson, even better. He, like Rilke, is tough and lyrical; unlike Rilke, he faces into history instead of away from it.

If Emily Dickinson has a rival for the finest woman poet of all time, it is surely **Anna Akhmatova**. Russian, she is intensely lyrical after a brilliant beginning life closed down about her: Her husband was killed, then her lover; then her only son was jailed for twenty years. She has many wonderful poems, but the most moving is a sequence dedicated to the Russian mothers who stood alongside Akhmatova waiting for news of the imprisoned children and spouses. Entitled "Requiem," the sequence of eleven poems may be the greatest work of poetry of our century. The translations by Thomas and Hayward/Kunitz are excellent.

My choice for the poet most likely to win a Nobel Prize is **Zbigniew Herbert**, a seemingly simple, ironic, engaged, brilliant poet with an unerring ear for non-rhetorical statement and a profound wisdom about our modern human condition. Polish, he is well translated by both Milsoz and Carpenter.

Now that the movie *The Postman* has been widely shown, many people in the U.S. have heard of the Chilean poet **Pablo Neruda**. Perhaps most accessible, and to me most wonderful, are his late poems, especially the three volumes of *Elemental Odes.* On simple everyday subjects, they are written in a language even common people and children can understand—but are luminescent and lyrical nevertheless.

If one single poet can be said to have imagined and created our modernity, it was **Charles Baudelaire**. A good place to start is his series of four poems entitled "Spleen," which gives remarkable sense of what depression/boredom/self-loathing feel like. He is best in French.

American poets? **William Carlos Williams** is the height, for me, of 20th-century poetry. Try the short lyrics in his selected poems, especially "This Is Just to Say," "Between Walls," "To a Poor Old Woman," and the slightly longer "By the Road to the Contagious Hospital." The best love poem, as well as the best poem on aging, of the 20th century is, in my view, "Asphodel, that Greeny Flower." Another long poem of his about a walk over the Mexican border at El Paso is one of my favorites, "The Desert Music." Both these long poems are in his last book *Pictures from Brueghel.*

Williams' contemporary and sort of friend, **Wallace Stevens**, is a different sort of aesthete than Rilke, but like Rilke, is always concerned with the workings of the imagination. In fact, it is likely that no poet, ever, has charted the workings of the imagination more thoroughly than Stevens. He is a very great, and nowadays, a very influential, poet. I recommend almost anything, but you might start with "Of Modern Poetry," "The Idea of Order at Key West," and "Poems of Our Climate." In my view his single most successful poem is the four page "Sunday Morning," the meditation of an old woman who dreamily wonders what death means and whether life might not be better than heaven. If you are really a glutton for reading, among the many confusions of his long poem "Poetry as a Supreme Fiction," there are stanzas which are incandescent in their lyrical beauty and their seeming wisdom.

My great recent discovery is a poet who came a bit after Williams and Stevens. **Elizabeth Bishop** wrote in the '30s, '40s, and '50s. Wonderful and accessible are "At the Filling Station" and "In the Waiting Room." My favorite is the superb meditation on truth and time, "At the Fishhouses."

Read **Allen Ginsberg**'s "Howl" (on his own madness in crazy America) or his less-known "Kaddish" (on the death of his insane mother) for a sense of what the best of beat poetry could be.

I love **A.R. Ammons**' meditative poem about taking a walk at the beach, "Corson's Inlet."

If you prefer walking around cities, try some of **Frank O'Hara**'s poems about walking around New York, like "The Day Lady Died" or "A Step Away from Them."

Of poets writing right now, I love **Robert Hass** (try "The Privilege of Being" and "Meditation at Lagunitas"); **Rita Dove** (try her most recent book, a sequence of sonnets called *Mother Love*); **C.K.Williams** (try "The Gas Station"); **Louise Gluck** (try the flower poems of her recent *The Wild Iris*); and **Maxine Kumin** (try "Morning Swing" and "Family Reunion").

Music

When our souls speak their own language, it seems to me they sing in Italian to the melodies of **Mozart**. His best is the comic *The Marriage of Figaro*. Get a videotape—opera has to be seen performed and the words do matter, so don't just listen to a record. The best movie of an opera I have ever seen is **Ingmar Bergman**'s *The Magic Flute*. It even blew the mind of my 10 year old when I dragged him to it (we had nothing else to do that day).

Listen to **Beethoven**'s *Ninth Symphony*. It's gigantic, but the second time you hear it you will be bowled over—and even more so if you read a translation of the "Ode to Joy" which is sung in the last movement. The most powerful and moving piece of classical music is, I think, the "Heilege Gedanksang," the slow movement of Beethoven's *Fourteenth String Quartet*.

In it he gives thanks for his blessings, a remarkable situation since he, a composer, had turned deaf. It captures the aspiration to the heavenly.

If you can bear symphonies of even longer duration, it is worth trying **Gustav Mahler**. What I use on the CD player for endless replays for hours to blot out the world is **Johannes Brahms** *Variations on a Theme by Handel.*

There is so much wonderful music to listen to; I can't really give you a list. Only don't be satisfied with what the hype tells you is the music of the moment. Try to extend the range of what you try, especially into classical music, jazz and blues, and music of other cultures.

Art

Go to art museums. My most depressing experience of the past two years has been teaching **Robert Lowell**'s wonderful "last" poem, "Epilogue" in which he compares what he does with words to what Vermeer did with paints. In two years, two classes, 60 students, no student knew who Vermeer was!

You are missing much of what the world has to offer if your visual understanding ranges only from Michael Jordan's leaps to sunsets over Lake Champlain to Homer Simpson's outbursts with maybe a rock video or Seinfeld thrown in for variety. Unlike literature, art can be directly perceived by the senses. So standing in front of a painting is, at its most fundamental level, a physical experience even before it is an intellectual one. You don't have to KNOW what you are expected to look for. That's worth remembering so that you can revel in delight instead of feeling unworthy because you do not understand.

The Italian Renaissance was really a golden age, so here is a list of my favorite Renaissance artists: **Duccio**, **Giotto**, **Piero della Francesca**, **Giovanni Bellini**, **Fra Angelico**, **Michelangelo**, **Raphael**, **Massaccio**, **Bennozzo**, **Kambrogio Lorenzetti**, **Bennozzo Gozzoli**, and **Luca Della Robbia**.

But not all great art is of the Renaissance. Believe it or not, the period of modernism, and the period following—the age of abstract expressionism—are among the golden ages of painting. In the mid and late 19th century there is **Vincent van Gogh**, with his fabulous colors and brushstrokes and immediacy, and **Edouard Manet**, whose committed realism is more powerful than any of the impressionists who painted in the same era.

A great fascinating figure (whom I go up and down on) is the endlessly inventive **Pablo Picasso;** the most wonderful and satisfying painter is **Henri Matisse.** And for abstract expressionists, there are lots who can blow you away from **Jackson Pollack** to **Willem de Kooning** to **Mark Rothko.**

I could go on longer, but I have temporarily run out of ideas, and my fingers are tired of pounding the keyboard.

Happy reading!

When I was a child, I read almost anything I could get my hands on, the more fantastical, the better. Madeleine L'Engle's mystical science fiction, among others, made me think life for all grown ups (a category that then included anyone over age 12) must be filled with both stunning adventure and deep relationships, and I bided my time until, I imagined, I would be old enough to enter the thrilling almost-adult world she described. Of course, by the time I became a teen-ager, I recognized the difference between fantasy and non-fiction; and I kept thinking in my much more practical inner world that I should be reading non-fiction. I was concluding that it would take me places in real life that mere fantasy never could—that knowing more facts about the world would make it more certain that I would succeed.

It wasn't until I got to college that I began to understand why books—all books—are valuable. Reading books was teaching me not just what to think, but HOW to think. Accounts of history made me think I knew what happened in World War II and before; the writings of Gertrude Stein and Doris Lessing made me think about seeing those facts through a wholly different lens, and made me skeptical that any one account of history could tell the whole true story. The writings of James Joyce, Virginia Woolf, Sylvia Plath, and so many others made me realize the infinite depth of language, the manifold possible meanings of every word, and the ways one's words can carry multiple messages to different listeners—and that meaning can depend as much on the reader as on the writer.

The minute I left school and started off on my own, I realized that these lessons would have value in whatever I pursued, in history and world affairs, of course in writing and in art, and even (perhaps especially) in science and law. The skill of skepticism and the willingness to recognize multiple meanings have been invaluable to me. And I gained them every bit as much from *A Wrinkle in Time* as from *Farnsworth on Contracts*. Read whatever inspires you.

Deborah Pearlstein
U.S. Supreme Court Law Clerk

University of Virginia
PO Box 9017
Charlottesville, VA 22903
(804) 924-0311
http://www.virginia.edu

The University of Virginia Department of English offers students a basic or introductory list of works "generally considered most important for acquiring an educated perspective on Western literature." The department notes that "for works not originally in English, the translation is of real importance. Translation invariably alters an author's creation; bad translation can wholly destroy the quality of a work. Most modern translations are acceptable, particularly those published by Penguin and Signet. When a distinguished translation exists, the translator's name is in parenthesis."

SUGGESTED READINGS

I. Classical

Aeschylus	*Oresteia* (Fagles, tr.)
Aristophanes	*Lysistrata*
Aristotle	*Poetics* (Butcher or Else, tr.)
Euripides	*Bacchae*
Homer	*The Iliad* (Lattimore, tr.); *The Odyssey* (Fitzgerald, tr.)

Ovid	*Metamorphoses* (Gregory, tr.)
Plato	*Republic* (Cornford, tr.)
Sophocles	*Antigone* (Lattimore, tr.); *Oedipus Rex* (Grene, tr.)
Vergil	*The Aeneid* (Mandelbaum, tr.)

II. Medieval

	Bible (Authorized Version, 1611): "Genesis"; "II Samuel"; "Psalms" 23, 53, 103, 104, 107, 121, 130, 137; "Job"; "Isaiah" 40, 55; "I Corinthians"; "Revelations"
	Beowulf
	Everyman
	Sir Gawain and the Green Knight (Boroff, tr.)
	The Song of Roland
Augustine, Saint	*Confessions*
Boccaccio, Giovanni	*The Decameron*
Chaucer, Geoffrey	*The Canterbury Tales*
Dante	*The Divine Comedy* (Singleton, tr.)
Petrarch, Francesco	Poems

III. Renaissance and 17th Century

Cervantes, Miguel de	*Don Quixote*
Donne, John	*Songs and Sonnets*
Dryden, John	*Absalom and Achitophel*
Jonson, Ben	*Volpone*
Marlowe, Christopher	*Dr. Faustus*
Marvell, Andrew	*Selected Poems* (especially "To His Coy Mistress," "The Garden")
Milton, John	"Lycidas"; *Paradise Lost*
Molière	*The Misanthrope* (Wilbur, tr.)
Montaigne, Michel de	*Essays*
Pascal, Blaise	*Thoughts*
Rabelais, François	*Gargantua and Pantagruel*
Racine, Jean	*Phaedra* (Lowell, tr.)
Sidney, Philip	*Astrophel and Stella*

Spenser, Edmund	*The Faerie Queene*
Shakespeare, William	*Hamlet*; *Henry IV Part I*; *King Lear*; *A Midsummer Night's Dream*; *The Tempest*; sonnets

IV. 18th Century

Congreve, William	*The Way of the World*
Defoe, Daniel	*Moll Flanders*
Fielding, Henry	*Tom Jones*
Gay, John	*The Beggar's Opera*
Goethe, Johann W. von	*Faust* (Passage, tr.); *The Sorrows of Young Werther*
Goldsmith, Oliver	*She Stoops to Conquer*
Johnson, Samuel	*Rasselas*
Pope, Alexander	*Selected Poems* (especially "An Essay on Man," "The Rape of the Lock")
Richardson, Samuel	*Clarissa*
Sheridan, Richard B.	*The School for Scandal*
Sterne, Laurence	*Tristram Shandy*
Swift, Jonathan	*Gulliver's Travels*
Voltaire	*Candide*

V. 19th Century

Austen, Jane	*Emma*
Baudelaire, Charles P.	*Flowers of Evil*
Blake, William	*The Marriage of Heaven and Hell*; *Songs of Innocence and Experience*
Brontë, Charlotte	*Jane Eyre*
Brontë, Emily	*Wuthering Heights*
Browning, Robert	*Selected Poems* (especially "Fra Lippo Lippi," "My Last Duchess")
Byron, George Gordon	*Don Juan*
Coleridge, Samuel T.	"Dejection: An Ode," "Frost at Midnight," *The Rime of the Ancient Mariner*
Crane, Stephen	*The Red Badge of Courage*
Dickens, Charles	*Bleak House*; *Great Expectations*
Dickinson, Emily	Poems

Dostoevski, Fyodor	*The Brothers Karamazov*; *Crime and Punishment*
Eliot, George	*Middlemarch*
Emerson, Ralph Waldo	*Essays*
Flaubert, Gustave	*Madame Bovary*
Hardy, Thomas	*Tess of the D'Urbervilles*
Hawthorne, Nathaniel	*The Scarlet Letter*
Ibsen, Henrik	*A Doll's House*
Keats, John	Selected poems (especially "The Eve of Saint Agnes," "Ode on a Grecian Urn," "Ode to a Nightingale," "To Autumn")
Marx, Karl and Friedrich Engels	*Communist Manifesto*
Melville, Herman	*Moby-Dick*
Pushkin, Alexander	*Eugene Onegin*
Rossetti, Christina	Selected poems (especially "Goblin Market")
Stendahl	*The Red and the Black* (Moncrieff, tr.)
Shelley, Percy Bysshe	Selected poems (especially "Adonais," "Mont Blanc," "Ode to the West Wind," "Prometheus Unbound")
Tennyson, Alfred Lord	*Idylls of the King*; *In Memoriam*
Thackeray, William Makepeace	*Vanity Fair*
Thoreau, Henry David	*Walden*
Tolstoy, Leo	*Anna Karenina* (Maude, tr.); *War and Peace* (Maude, tr.)
Trollope, Anthony	*The Warden*
Turgenev, Ivan	*Fathers and Sons*; *First Love*
Twain, Mark	*The Adventures of Huckleberry Finn*
Whitman, Walt	*Song of Myself*
Wordsworth, William	Selected poems (especially "Ode: Intimations of Mortality," "Tintern Abbey"); *The Prelude*

VI. 20th Century

Akhmatova, Anna	Selected poems
Auden, W.H.	Selected poems (especially "In Memory of W.B. Yeats," "Musée des Beaux Arts," "The Sea and the Mirror," "September 1, 1939," "The Shield of Achilles")
Beckett, Samuel	*Waiting for Godot*

Borges, Jorge	*Ficciones*
Brecht, Bertolt	*Mother Courage and Her Children*
Brodsky, Joseph	*A Part of Speech*
Camus, Albert	*The Stranger*
Chopin, Kate	*The Awakening*
Conrad, Joseph	*Heart of Darkness*
Ellison, Ralph	*Invisible Man*
Eliot, T.S.	*Four Quartets*; "The Love Song of J. Alfred Prufrock"; "The Waste Land"
Faulkner, William	*Absalom, Absalom*; *The Sound and the Fury*
Ford, Ford Madox	*The Good Soldier*
Forster, E.M.	*A Passage to India*
Freud, Sigmund	*Civilization and Its Discontents*
García Márquez, Gabriel	*One Hundred Years of Solitude*
Hemingway, Ernest	*The Snows of Kilimanjaro*
James, Henry	*The Portrait of a Lady*
Joyce, James	*Dubliners*; *A Portrait of the Artist as a Young Man*
Kafka, Franz	*The Metamorphosis*; *The Trial*
Kundera, Milan	*The Book of Laughter and Forgetting*
Lawrence, D.H.	*The Rainbow*; *Women in Love*
Lorca, F.G.	*Three Tragedies*
Mandelstam, Osip	Selected poems
Mann, Thomas	*Death in Venice*; *The Magic Mountain*
Milosz, Czeslaw	Selected poems
Montale, Eugenio	Selected poems
Morrison, Toni	*Sula*
Nabokov, Vladimir	*Lolita*
Pasternak, Boris	*Doctor Zhivago*
Proust, Marcel	*Swann's Way*
Rilke, Rainer Maria	*Letters to a Young Poet*; *Sonnets to Orpheus*
Sartre, Jean-Paul	*No Exit*
Stevens, Wallace	*Collected Poems* (especially "The Idea of Order at Key West," "Sunday Morning")
Walker, Alice	*The Color Purple*
Williams, W.C.	"Asphodel, That Greeny Flower," *Paterson*
Woolf, Virginia	*A Room of One's Own*; *To the Lighthouse*

Wright, Richard	*Native Son*
Yeats, William Butler	Selected Poems (especially "Among School Children," "The Circus Animals' Desertion," "Easter 1916," "Sailing to Byzantium," "The Second Coming")

Eckerd College: What book or author has made an important impact on you? How? (You could also use a film, play, piece of music or art.)

Washington State University
Pullman, WA 99164-2630
(509) 335-4581
http://www.wstu.edu

REQUIRED READING SUGGESTIONS

Fiction/Literature

Alexie, Sherman	*The Lone Ranger and Tonto Fistfight in Heaven*
Camus, Albert	*The Plague*
Crane, Stephen	*The Red Badge of Courage*
Doctorow, E.L.	*Ragtime*
Dostoevski, Fyodor	*The Brothers Karamazov*; *Crime and Punishment*
Ellison, Ralph	*Invisible Man*
García Márquez, Gabriel	*100 Years of Solitude*
Golding, William	*Lord of the Flies*
Heller, Joseph	*Catch-22*
Hurston, Zora Neal	*Their Eyes Were Watching God*
Huxley, Aldous	*Brave New World*
Jacobs, Harriet	*Incidents in the Life of a Slave Girl*
Miller, Walter M.	*A Canticle for Leibowitz*
Morrison, Toni	*The Bluest Eye*
Orwell, George	*1984*

Rostand, Edmond	*Cyrano de Bergerac*
Salinger, J.D.	*Catcher in the Rye*
Silko, Leslie Marmon	*Ceremony*
Twain, Mark	*The Adventures of Tom Sawyer*
Voltaire	*Candide*
Wibberley, Leonard	*The Mouse that Roared*

Philosophy/Social/Political

Achebe, Chinua	*Things Fall Apart* (fiction)
Anzaldua, Gloria	*Borderlands/La Frontera*
Ayer, A.J.	*Language, Truth, and Logic*
Gaarder, Jostein	*Sophie's World* fiction
Harris, Marvin	*Cows, Pigs, Wars and Witches: The Riddles of Culture*
Leopold, Aldo	*A Sand County Almanac*
Lipsitz, George	*The Possessive Investment in Whiteness*
Malcolm X	*The Autobiography of Malcolm X*
Marx, Karl and Friedrich Engels	*The Communist Manifesto*
Mill, John Stuart	*On Liberty*
Pirsig, Robert	*Zen and the Art of Motorcycle Maintenance*
Plato	*Apology; Republic*
Russell, Bertrand	*The Problems of Philosophy*
Said, Edward W.	*Orientalism*

Historical

Anderson, Benedict	*Imagined Communities*
Berlin, Ira	*Many Thousands Gone: The First Two Centuries of Slavery in North America*
Crosby, Alfred W. Jr.	*Ecological Imperialism: The Biological Expansion of Europe, 900–1900*
Diamond, Jared	*Guns, Germs and Steel: The Fates of Human Societies*
Fussell, Paul	*The Great War and Modern Memory*
Kerber, Linda, et al.	*U.S. History as Women's History*
Keegan, John	*The Face of Battle: A Study of Agincourt, Waterloo, and the Somme*
Ladurie, Emmanuel LeRoy	*Montaillou: The Promised Land of Error*

Landes, David	*The Wealth and Poverty of Nations*
Limerick, Patricia	*The Legacy of Conquest*
Lockridge, Kenneth	*A New England Town: The First Hundred Years*
Thompson, E.P.	*The Making of the English Working Class*
Zinn, Howard	*A People's History of the United States*

Other

Goodall, Jane	*In the Shadow of Man*
Hesse, Herman	*Siddhartha*
Owens, Kelly and Mary-Clair King	"Genomic Views of Human History," *Science*, October 15, 1999, pages 451–453
King, Martin Luther Jr.	Selected speeches
Sagan, Carl	*The Dragons of Eden: Speculations on the Evolution of Human Intelligence*
Wolfe, Tom	*The Right Stuff*

Spelman College: What cultural work (literature, art, music, or dance) has had a significant effect on your life.

Washington University in St. Louis
One Brookings Drive
St. Louis, MO 63130
(314) 935-5000
http://www.wustl.edu

According to Dr. Robert Wiltenburg, the English Department has "no reading lists, either required or recommended, either pre-college or year-by-year." Book selections for Washington University's English Composition 100/199 courses change from year to year, and no particular item is ever required. Each year, however, a few books are suggested. Recent lists for these courses have included the following:

Autobiography

Adams, Henry	*The Education of Henry Adams*
Dinesen, Isak	*Out of Africa*
Graves, Robert	*Goodbye to All That*
Nabokov, Vladimir	*Speak, Memory*
Welty, Eudora	*One Writer's Beginnings*
Wolff, Geoffrey	*The Duke of Deception*

History and Society

Lawrence, D.H.	*D.H. Lawrence and Italy*
Narayan, R.K.	*The Vendor of Sweets*
Twain, Mark	*Life on the Mississippi*
Williams, William Carlos	*In the American Grain*
Wylie, L.	*Village in the Vaucluse*

Nature and Science

Gould, Stephen Jay	*The Flamingo's Smile*
Leopold, Aldo	*A Sand County Almanac*
Sacks, Oliver	*The Man Who Mistook His Wife for a Hat*
Thomas, Lewis	*Late Night Thoughts on Listening to Mahler's Ninth Symphony*
Thoreau, Henry David	*The Maine Woods*

Humanities

Malamud, Bernard	*The Assistant*
O'Connor, Flannery	*The Complete Stories*
Orwell, George	*Essays*
Paley, Grace	*Enormous Changes at the Last Minute*
Smart, William	*Eight Modern Essayists*
Woolf, Virginia	*Death of the Moth and Other Essays*

Handbooks

Baker, Sheridan	*The Practical Stylist*
Leggett, Glenn H., et al.	*The Prentice-Hall Handbook*

Wheaton College
Norton, MA 02766
(508) 285-8200
http://www.wheatonma.edu

Wheaton's First-Year Seminar, according to Dr. Richard Pearce, is "divided into five clusters, which share a set of common meetings and readings." Some of the subjects to be considered in the cluster meetings are environment and the threat of nuclear arms; Freedom Summer and the Democratic Party Convention in 1964 (including the significance of songs and spirituals to the Black Freedom Movement); intelligence testing; Marxism and the Industrial Revolution; and optical illusions. The following are books and films considered for tentative cluster assignments:

Books

Atwood, Margaret	*The Handmaid's Tale*
Orwell, George	*Animal Farm*
Watson, James	*The Double Helix*

Films

PBS Video	*Human Mind*
	Danton
	Eyes on the Prize
	Powers of Ten
	The Return of Martin Guerre (film reflecting medieval family)
Father, Rainer W.	*The Marriage of Maria Braun*
Eisenstein, Sergei	*Potemkin*

Williams College
Hopkins Hall
Williamstown, MA 01267
(413) 597-3131
http://www.williams.edu

Although Williams College does not have a reading list as such, the following are among the authors and works considered in some of its freshman English classes:

Allison, Alexander W., et al.	*Norton Anthology of Poetry* (shorter edition)
Arnold, Matthew	"Dover Beach"
Auden, W.H.	"The Unknown Citizen," "In Memory of W.B. Yeats"
Bain, C.E., et al., eds.	*The Norton Introduction to Literature*
Baldwin, James	"Sonny's Blues"
Baraka, Imamu Amiri (LeRoi Jones)	"In Memory of Radio"
Beckett, Samuel	*Waiting for Godot*
Bishop, Elizabeth	"The Fish"
Blake, William	"The Sick Rose"
Brecht, Bertolt	*The Good Woman of Setzuan*
Brooks, Gwendolyn	"We Real Cool"
Browning, Robert	"My Last Duchess"
Carver, Raymond	*Cathedral*
Cassill, R.V., ed.	*The Norton Anthology of Short Fiction*
Chekhov, Anton	"The Bishop," "The Lady with the Pet Dog"
Coleridge, Samuel T.	*The Rime of the Ancient Mariner*
Conrad, Joseph	*Heart of Darkness*
Coover, Robert	"The Babysitter"
Crane, Stephen	"The Blue Hotel"
cummings, e.e.	"in just spring"
Couto, Nancy	"1958"
DeMott, Benjamine	*Close Imaginings*

Dickey, James	"Cherrylog Road"
Dickinson, Emily	"After Great Pain," "I Heard a Fly Buzz," "Because I Could Not Stop for Death"
Digges, Deborah	"The New World"
Donne, John	"Batter My Heart…"
Doyle, Sir Arthur Conan	"A Scandal in Bohemia"
Dunn, Stephen	*Local Time*
Eliot, T.S.	"The Love Song of J. Alfred Prufrock," "The Journey of the Magi"
Ellison, Ralph	"King of the Bingo Game"
Faulkner, William	"Barn Burning," "A Rose for Emily," "Spotted Horses"
Ferlinghetti, Lawrence	"Dog"
Fitzgerald, F. Scott	"Babylon Revisited"
Frost, Robert	"The Silken Tent," "Design," "In White," "Mending Wall," "Home Burial"
Gaines, Ernest	*Of Love and Dust*
Gilman, Charlotte P.	"The Yellow Wallpaper"
Gluck, Louise	"The Triumph of Achilles"
Hardy, Thomas	"The Convergence of the Twain"
Hemingway, Ernest	"Hills Like White Elephants"
Hempel, Amy	"In the Cemetery Where Al Jolson Is Buried"
Hopkins, Gerard M.	"God's Grandeur," "Spring and Fall"
Hughes, Ted	"The Thought-Fox"
Ibsen, Henrik	*A Doll's House*
Jarrell, Randall	"The Death of the Ball Turret Gunner"
Joyce, James	"Araby," "A Little Cloud," "The Dead"
Kafka, Franz	*The Metamorphosis,* "The Hunger Artist"
Kauffman, Janet	"My Mother Has Me Surrounded"
Keats, John	"Ode on a Grecian Urn," "To Autumn," "Bright Star"
Kennedy, X.J.	*An Introduction to Poetry* (6th ed)
Kinnell, Galway	"Blackberry Eating," "To Christ Our Lord"
Lawrence, D.H.	"Odour of Chrysanthemums"
Levine, Philip	"You Can Have It"
Lowell, Robert	"Skunk Hour"

MacLeish, Archibald	"Ars Poetica"
Malamud, Bernard	*The Magic Barrel*
Mann, Thomas	*Death in Venice*
Marvell, Andrew	"To His Coy Mistress"
Mason, Bobbie A.	*Shiloh* and other stories
Meredith, William	"Parents"
Moore, Marianne	"Poetry"
Morrison, Toni	*The Bluest Eye*; *Song of Solomon*
Nabokov, Vladimir	*Pnin*; *Lolita*; *Nabokov's Dozen*; "Signs and Symbols"
Nemerov, Howard	"Boom!"
O'Connor, Flannery	"Everything That Rises Must Converge," "Revelation," "A Good Man Is Hard to Find," "Guests of the Nation"
Oliver, Mary	"The Black Snake"
Paley, Grace	"A Conversation with My Father"
Pinter, Harold	*Betrayal*
Plath, Sylvia	"Daddy," "Metaphors," "Morning Song"
Poe, Edgar Allan	"The Cask of Amontillado"
Porter, Katherine Anne	"Flowering Judas"
Pound, Ezra	"In a Station of the Metro"
Pynchon, Thomas	*The Crying of Lot 49*
Reed, Ishmael	"'beware' do not read this poem"
Rich, Adrienne	*The Facts of a Door Frame: Selected Poems*
Robinson, Marilynn	*Housekeeping*
Roethke, Theodore	"My Papa's Waltz," "Elegy for Jane"
Schnackenberg, Gjertrud	"Signs"
Shakespeare, William	Sonnets 65, 71, 73, 116
Shelley, Percy Bysshe	"Ozymandias"
Shepard, Sam	*Seven Plays*; *True West*
Singer, Isaac	"Gimpel the Fool"
Snyder, Richard	"A Mongoloid Child Handling Shells on the Beach"
Stafford, William	"Traveling through the Dark"
Stevens, Wallace	"Anecdote of the Jar"
Strunk and White	*The Elements of Style*
Thomas, Dylan	"In My Craft or Sullen Art," "Do Not Go Gentle into That Good Night"

Trimmer and Jennings	*Fictions*
Wakoski, Diane	"Uneasy Rider," "The Photos"
Walcott, Derek	"The Camps Hold Their Distance—Brown Chestnut and Grey Smoke," "There Was One Syrian, With His Bicycle, in Our Town"
Waller, Edmund	"Go Lovely Rose"
Welty, Eudora	"Petrified Man"
Wilbur, Richard	"The Writer," "Merlin Enthralled"
Williams, Tennessee	*The Glass Menagerie*
Williams, William Carlos	"The Use of Force," "Spring and All," "The Red Wheelbarrow," "This Is Just to Say"
Wolff, Tobias	"In the Garden of the North American Martyrs"
Yeats, William Butler	"A Dream of Death," "Crazy Jane Talks with the Bishop," "Leda and the Swan," "Sailing to Byzantium," "A Second Coming"
Zagajewski, Adam	"A Polish Dictionary," "Without End," "Song of an Emigre"

New York University: Select a creative work—a novel, a film, a poem, a musical piece, a painting, or other work of art—that has influenced the way you view the world and the way you view yourself. Discuss the work and its effect on you.

Wittenberg University

PO Box 720
Springfield, OH 45501
(937) 327-6231
http://www.wittenberg.edu

The English program at Wittenberg has three comprehensive objectives for its students. First, the program "helps the student to be receptive to all literature, to be sensitive to new ideas and feelings, to acquire a sense of cultural identity, to develop a sense of human values pertaining to literature, and lastly, to gain pleasure in reading and rereading." Second, the "program helps the student to share personal responses and perceptions, to participate in new forms of imaginative thinking and expression, to communicate with clarity and style, to gain experience in writing fiction, poetry, and drama, to study avant-garde literature, and to explore the relationship between literature and fine arts." Third, the "program helps the student to know major authors/works in English, American, and world literature, to know Biblical, mythic, and contemporary works, to know how the language of a certain culture reflects a perception of reality, and to know the nuances of the English language, the methodology of literary research, and the development and use of an organizing thesis."

Wittenberg's English majors are expected to be familiar with the following works:

	Bible: "Genesis," "Exodus," "Job," "Psalms," "Matthew"
Aeschylus	One play
Aristophanes	One play
Austen, Jane	*Emma* or *Pride and Prejudice*
Bacon, Francis	*Essays* or **More**'s *Utopia*
Blake, William	*Songs of Innocence*; *Songs of Experience*
Browning, Robert	Selections
Bunyan, John	*The Pilgrim's Progress*
Cervantes, Miguel de	*Don Quixote* (selections)
Chaucer, Geoffrey	*The Canterbury Tales* (prologue and selected tales)
Conrad, Joseph	A representative novel
Dante	*Inferno*
Dickens, Charles	One novel, plus one additional novel from a Victorian author
Donne, John	Selected lyrics
Dostoevski, Fyodor	A major work
Eliot, T.S.	*The Waste Land*
Ellison, Ralph	*Invisible Man*
Euripides	One play
Faulkner, William	A representative novel
Fielding, Henry	*Tom Jones*
Goethe, Johann W. von	*Faust*, part 1

Hemingway, Ernest	A representative novel or group of short stories
Homer	*The Iliad* or *The Odyssey*
James, Henry	A representative novel
Jonson, Ben	*The Alchemist* or *Volpone*
Joyce, James	*A Portrait of the Artist as a Young Man* or a major novel by **Virginia Woolf**
Kafka, Franz	Selected stories
Keats, John	Selected poems and letters
Melville, Herman	*Moby-Dick*
Miller, Arthur	*Death of a Salesman*
Milton, John	*Paradise Lost*
More, Thomas	*Utopia* or selected essays by **Bacon**
O'Neill, Eugene	*Long Day's Journey into Night* or a play by **Miller** or **Williams**
Ovid	*Metamorphoses* or **Vergil**'s *The Aeneid*, books 1, 6
Pope, Alexander	"Essay on Criticism" or "Essay on Man" or "The Rape of the Lock"
Shakespeare, William	Four plays (tragedy, history, comedy, and romance)
Sophocles	*Oedipus the King*
Spencer, Edmund	Selections from *The Faerie Queene*
Swift, Jonathan	*Gulliver's Travels*
Tennyson, Alfred Lord	Selections
Thoreau, Henry David	*Walden*
Tolstoy, Leo	A major work
Twain, Mark	*The Adventures of Huckleberry Finn*
Vergil	*The Aeneid*, books 1, 6 or selections from **Ovid**
Whitman, Walt	Selections
Williams, Tennessee	*The Glass Menagerie* or a play by **Miller** or **O'Neill**
Woolf, Virginia	A major novel or **Joyce**'s *A Portrait of the Artist as a Young Man*
Wordsworth and Coleridge	Selections from *Lyrical Ballads*
Yeats, William Butler	Selected lyrics

McGill University: List up to a maximum of six books or major articles read during the past year (exclude selections which were required for school or CEGEP courses). Choose one of them and explain in a maximum of 200 words why you read it and why it was significant.

Wright State University
Dayton, OH 45435-0001
(937) 775-3333
http://www.wright.edu

The English Department faculty at Wright State compiled the following lists: Classical Fiction, Contemporary Fiction, and World Drama. (They also have a reading list for children's fiction that is available on their Web site.) The department states that the purpose of these lists is to guide those seeking recommendations of quality fiction and drama. "The lists do not claim to be exhaustive. Thus they include only one title for each author (with one exception: **William Shakespeare**) and they omit works of substantial reputation considered too esoteric to be of general interest."

The parentheses beside the books contain the nationality of the author and the first date of publication.

A Reading List for the General Public

Classical Fiction

Acevedo Diaz, Eduardo	*The Cry of Glory* (Uruguayan 1894)
Alegria, Ciro	*Broad and Alien Is the World* (Peruvian 1941)
Anderson, Sherwood	*Winesburg, Ohio* (American 1919)
Austen, Jane	*Pride and Prejudice* (British 1813)
Austin, Mary	*Land of Little Rain* (American 1903)
Balzac, Honoré de	*Père Goriot* (French 1834)
Baroja, Pio	*The Restlessness of Shanti Andia* (Spanish 1911)
Bennett, Arnold	*The Old Wives' Tale* (British *1908*)

Bernanos, Georges	*The Diary of a Country Priest* (French 1936)
Bierce, Ambrose	*In the Midst of Life* (American 1891)
Bowen, Elizabeth	*The Death of the Heart* (Anglo-Irish 1939)
Bromfield, Louis	*The Rains Came* (American 1937)
Brontë, Charlotte	*Jane Eyre* (British 1847)
Brontë, Emily	*Wuthering Heights* (British 1848)
Buck, Pearl	*The Good Earth* (American 1931)
Bulgakov, Mikhail	*The Master and Margarita* (Russian 1940)
Bunyan, John	*The Pilgrim's Progress* (British 1678)
Burney, Fanny	*Evelina* (British 1778)
Butler, Samuel	*The Way of All Flesh* (British 1903)
Cable, George Washington	*The Grandissimes* (American 1880)
Caldwell, Erskine	*God's Little Acre* (American 1933)
Camus, Albert	*The Stranger* (French 1942)
Canetti, Elias	*Auto-da-fe* (Bulgarian 1935)
Carroll, Lewis	*Alice's Adventures in Wonderland* (British 1865)
Cary, Joyce	*The Horse's Mouth* (Anglo-Irish 1944)
Cather, Willa	*Death Comes for the Archbishop* (American 1927)
Cela, Camilo Joséó	*The Family of Pascual Duarte* (Spanish 1942)
Céline, Louis-Ferdinand	*Journey to the End of the Night* (French 1932)
Cervantes, Miguel de	*Don Quixote* (Spanish 1606)
Chandler, Raymond	*The Big Sleep* (American 1939)
Chekhov, Anton	*Short Stories* (Russian 1880s and 90s)
Chopin, Kate	*The Awakening* (American 1899)
Clark, Walter Van Tilburg	*The Ox-Bow Incident* (American 1940)
Collins, Wilkie	*The Moonstone* (British 1868)
Conan Doyle, Sir Arthur	*The Adventures of Sherlock Holmes* (British 1891)
Conrad, Joseph	*Heart of Darkness* (British 1902)
Cooper, James Fenimore	*The Prairie* (American 1827)
Crane, Stephen	*The Red Badge of Courage* (American 1895)
cummings, e.e.	*The Enormous Room* (American 1922)
Defoe, Daniel	*Robinson Crusoe* (British 1719)
Dickens, Charles	*Great Expectations* (British 1860–61)
Dinesen, Isak	*Seven Gothic Tales* (Danish 1934)
Dos Passo, John	*U.S.A.* (American 1919–36)

Dostoevsky, Fyodor	*Crime and Punishment* (Russian 1866)
Dreiser, Theodore	*Sister Carrie* (American 1900)
Dunbar, P.C.	*Sport of the Gods* (American 1902)
Eliot, George	*Middlemarch* (British 1872)
Farrell, James T.	*Studs Lonigan* (American 1932–34)
Faulkner, William	*The Sound and the Fury* (American 1932)
Fielding, Henry	*Tom Jones* (British 1872)
Fitzgerald, F. Scott	*The Great Gatsby* (American 1925)
Flaubert, Gustave	*Madame Bovary* (French 1857)
Ford, Ford Madox	*The Good Soldier* (British 1915)
Forster, E.M.	*Howards End* (British 1910)
Frederic, Harold	*The Damnation of Theron Ware* (American 1896)
Gallegós, Romulo	*Doñna Bárbara* (Venezuelan 1939)
Galsworthy, John	*A Man of Property* (British 1906)
Garland, Hamlin	*Main-Travelled Roads* (American 1891)
Gaskell, Elizabeth	*Cranford* (British 1853)
Gide, André	*The Immoralist* (French 1902)
Goethe, Johann W. von	*The Sorrows of Young Werther* (German 1774)
Gògol, Nicolai	*Dead Souls* (Russian 1842)
Gold, Michael	*Jews Without Money* (American 1930)
Goldsmith, Oliver	*The Vicar of Wakefield* (British 1766)
Goncharov, Ivan	*Oblomov* (Russian 1855)
Gorky, Maxim	*Mother* (Russian 1907)
Graves, Robert	*I, Claudius* (British 1934)
Güiraldes, Ricardo	*Don Segundo Sombra* (Argentinian 1926)
Hammett, Dashiell	*The Maltese Falcon* (American 1930)
Hardy, Thomas	*The Return of the Native* (British 1878)
Hawthorne, Nathaniel	*The Scarlet Letter* (American 1850)
Hemingway, Ernest	*A Farewell to Arms* (American 1929)
Hémon, Louis	*Maria Chapdelaine* (Canadian 1914)
Hesse, Herman	*Demian* (German 1919)
Howells, William Dean	*The Rise of Silas Lapham* (American 1885)
Hughes, Richard	*The High Wind in Jamaica* (British 1929)
Hugo, Victor	*Les Misérables* (French 1862)
Hurston, Zora Neal	*Their Eyes Were Watching God* (American 1937)

Huxley, Aldous	*Brave New World* (British 1932)
Irving, Washington	*Short Stories* (American 1820s, 30s)
James, Henry	*The Portrait of a Lady* (American 1881)
Johnson, Samuel	*Rasselas, Prince of Abyssinia* (British 1759)
Joyce, James	*Dubliners* (Irish 1914)
Kafka, Franz	*The Trial* (German-Canadian 1925)
Kleist, Heinrich von	*Michael Kohlhass* (German 1810)
Koestler, Arthur	*Darkness at Noon* (Hungarian 1940)
Lawrence, D.H.	*Sons and Lovers* (British 1913)
LaSueur, Meridel	*The Girl* (American 1939)
Lewis, Sinclair	*Babbitt* (American 1922)
London, Jack	*The Call of the Wild* (American 1903)
Malraux, André	*Man's Fate* (French 1934)
Mann, Thomas	*Death in Venice* (German 1913)
Mansfield, Katherine	*Collected Stories* (New Zealand 1945)
Marquand, John P.	*The Late George Apley* (American 1937)
Maugham, Somerset	*Of Human Bondage* (British 1915)
Maupassant, Guy de	*Short Stories* (French 1880s)
Mauriac, François	*The Nest of Vipers* (French 1932)
McCullers, Carson	*The Heart Is a Lonely Hunter* (American 1940)
Melville, Herman	*Moby-Dick* (American 1851)
Meredith, George	*The Egoist* (British 1879)
Moore, George	*Esther Waters* (British 1894)
Murasaki, Shikibu	*The Tale of Genji-One* (Japanese about 1000)
Norris, Frank	*The Octopus* (American 1901)
O'Hara, John B.	*Appointment in Samarra* (American 1934)
Poe, Edgar Allan	*Short Stories* (American 1820s and '30s)
Proust, Marcel	*Swann's Way* (French 1913–17)
Pushkin, Alexander	*Short Stories* (Russian 1820s and '30s)
Rabelais, François	*Gargantua and Pantagruel* (French 1532–64)
Remarque, Erich Maria	*All Quiet on the Western Front* (German 1928)
Richardson, Samuel	*Clarissa* (British 1747–48)
Rivera, José Eustasio	*The Vortex* (Colombian 1924)
Röolvaag, O.E.	*Giants of the Earth* (Norwegian-American 1927)
Roth, Henry	*Call It Sleep* (American 1934)

Scott, Sir Walter	*Ivanhoe* (British 1819)
Shelley, Mary	*Frankenstein* (British 1818)
Silone, Ignazio	*Bread and Wine* (Italian 1937)
Sinclair, Upton	*The Jungle* (American 1901)
Smollett, Tobias	*Humphry Clinker* (British 1771)
Steinbeck, John	*The Grapes of Wrath* (American 1938)
Stegner, Wallace	*The Big Rock Candy Mountain* (American 1938)
Stendhal	*The Red and the Black* (French 1830)
Sterne, Laurence	*Tristram Shandy* (British 1760–67)
Stevenson, Robert Louis	*Dr. Jekyll and Mr. Hyde* (British 1886)
Stowe, Harriet Beecher	*Uncle Tom's Cabin* (American 1852)
Swift, Jonathan	*Gulliver's Travels* (Irish 1726)
Tate, Allen	*The Fathers* (American 1938)
Thackeray, William Makepeace	*Vanity Fair* (British 1847–48)
Tolstoy, Leo	*Anna Karenina* (Russian 1873–76)
Toomer, Jean	*Cane* (American 1923)
Trollope, Anthony	*Barchester Towers* (British 1857)
Turgenev, Ivan	*Fathers and Sons* (Russian 1892)
Twain, Mark	*The Adventures of Huckleberry Finn* (American 1885)
Unamuno, Miquel de	*Abel Sanchez and Other Stories* (Spanish 1931)
Undset, Sigrid	*Kristin Lavransdatter* (Norwegian 1920–22)
Voltaire	*Candide* (French 1759)
Walpole, Horace	*The Castle of Otranto* (British 1764)
Waugh, Evelyn	*Brideshead Revisited* (British 1944)
Webb, Mary	*Precious Bane* (British 1924)
Wells, H.G.	*The Time Machine* (British 1895)
West, Nathanael	*The Day of the Locust* (American 1939)
Wharton, Edith	*The Age of Innocence* (American 1920)
Wilde, Oscar	*The Picture of Dorian Gray* (British 1891)
Wilder, Thornton	*The Bridge of San Luis Rey* (American 1927)
Wister, Owen	*The Virginian* (American 1902)
Wolfe, Thomas	*Look Homeward, Angel* (American 1929)
Woolf, Virginia	*To the Lighthouse* (British 1927)
Wright, Richard	*Native Son* (American 1940)
Zola, Émile	*Germinal* (French 1885)

Contemporary Fiction

Abe, Kobo	*The Woman in the Dunes* (Japanese 1964)
Achebe, Chinua	*Things Fall Apart* (Nigerian 1958)
Agee, James	*A Death in the Family* (American 1957)
Amis, Kingsley	*Lucky Jim* (British 1954)
Amis, Martin	*A Suicide Note* (British 1984)
Anand, Mulk Raj	*Untouchable* (Indian 1935)
Anthony, Patricia	*The Happy Policeman* (American 1994)
Atwood, Margaret	*Surfacing* (Canadian 1972)
Auster, Paul	*City of Glass* (American 1985)
Babel, Isaac	*The Collected Stories* (Russian 1955)
Baldwin, James	*Another Country* (American 1960)
Barker, Pat	*Regeneration* (British 1991)
Barth, John	*The Sot-Weed Factor* (American 1960)
Beattie, Ann	*Falling in Place* (American 1980)
Bellow, Saul	*Sammler's Planet* (American 1969)
Böll, Heinrich	*Billiards at Half-Past Nine* (German 1962)
Borges, Jorge	*Ficciones* (Argentinian 1965)
Bowles, Paul	*The Sheltering Sky* (American 1949)
Boyle, T. Coraghessan	*World's End* (American 1987)
Brink, André	*A Dry White Season* (South African 1979)
Brown, Claude	*Manchild in the Promised land* (American 1965)
Burgess, Anthony	*A Clockwork Orange* (British 1962)
Burke, Phyllis	*Atomic Candy* (American 1989)
Burroughs, William S.	*The Naked Lunch* (American 1959)
Butler, Octavia	*Xenogenesis* (*trilogy*) (American 1987–9)
Butler, Robert Olen	*The Alleys of Eden* (American 1981)
Byatt, A.S.	*Possession* (British 1989)
Calvino, Italo	*If on a Winter's Night a Traveller* (Italian 1981)
Carey, Peter	*Oscar and Lucinda* (Australian 1988)
Carter, Angela	*Nights at the Circus* (British 1984)
Carver, Raymond	*Cathedral* (American 1983)
Cheever, John	*Collected Short Stories* (American 1963)
Chin, Frank	*Donald Duk* (Chinese-American 1991)
Coetzee, J.M.	*From the Heart of the Country* (South African 1977)

Connell, Evan	*Mrs. Bridge* (American 1958)
Coover, Robert	*The Public Burning* (American 1977)
Cortázar, Julio	*Hopscotch* (Argentinian 1963)
Crews, Harry	*Car* (American 1972)
Davies, Robertson	*Fifth Business* (Canadian 1970)
DeLillo, Don	*White Noise* (American 1985)
Desai, Anita	*Clear Light of Day* (Indian 1980)
Dick, Philip K.	*The Man in the High Castle* (American 1962)
Dickey, James	*Deliverance* (American 1970)
Didion, Joan	*Play It As It Lays* (American 1970)
Doctorow, E.L.	*Ragtime* (American 1975)
Donleavy, J.P.	*The Ginger Man* (American-Irish 1955)
Drabble, Margaret	*The Garrick Year* (British 1964)
Duncan, David James	*The Brothers K* (American 1992)
Duong, Thu Huong	*Novel Without a Name* (Vietnamese 1995)
Duras, Marguerite	*The Lover* (French 1985)
Durrell, Lawrence	*Justine* (British 1957)
Ellison, Ralph	*Invisible Man* (American 1947)
Emedheta, Buchi	*The Joys of Motherhood* (Nigerian 1979)
Endo, Shusaku	*Silence* (Japanese 1969)
Erdrich, Louise	*Love Medicine* (American 1984)
Exley, Frederick	*A Fan's Notes* (American 1968)
Farah, Nuruddin	*Naked Needle* (Somalian 1976)
Findley, Timothy	*Famous Last Words* (Canadian 1981)
Ford, Richard	*Independence Day* (American 1995)
Fowles, John	*The French Lieutenant's Woman* (British 1969)
Frame, Janmet	*Owls Do Cry* (New Zealand 1960)
Friedman, Bruce Jay	*Stern* (American 1962)
Fuentes, Carlos	*The Death of Artemio Cruz* (Mexican 1962)
Gaddis, William	*J.R.* (American 1975)
García Márquez, Gabriel	*One Hundred Years of Solitude* (Colombian 1967)
Gardner, John	*Grendel* (American 1971)
Gibson, William	*Neuromancer* (American 1984)
Gironella, José	*The Cypresses Believe in God* (Spanish 1953)
Godwin, Gail	*A Mother and Two Daughters* (American 1982)

Golding, William	*Lord of the Flies* (French 1954)
Gordimer, Nadine	*Burger's Daughter* (South African 1979)
Gordon, Mary	*Final Payments* (American 1978)
Grace, Patricia	*Mutuwhenua or the Moon Sleeps* (New Zealand 1978)
Grass, Günter	*The Tin Drum* (German 1959)
Greene, Graham	*The Heart of the Matter* (British 1948)
Hanna, Barry	*Hey Jack!* (American 1987)
Harris, Mark	*Bang the Drum Slowly* (American 1956)
Harris, Wilson	*Palace of the Peacock* (Guyanese 1960)
Head, Bessie	*The Collector of Treasures* (Botswanan 1977)
Heinlein, Robert A.	*The Moon Is a Harsh Mistress* (American 1967)
Heller, Joseph	*Catch-22* (American 1955)
Helprin, Mark	*A Winter's Tale* (American 1983)
Hijuelos, Oscar	*The Mambo Kings Play Songs of Love* (American 1989)
Himes, Chester	*Pinktoes* (American 1965)
Hoffman, Alice	*At Risk* (American 1988)
Hogan, Linda	*Mean Spirit* (American 1990)
Hulme, Keri	*The Bone People* (New Zealand 1985)
Icaza, Jorges	*The Villagers* (Ecuadorian 1951)
Ihimaera, Witi	*The Matriarch* (New Zealand 1986)
Irving, John	*The Water Method Man* (American 1972)
Isherwood, Christopher	*Berlin Stories* (British 1945)
Jhabvala, Ruth Prawer	*Heat and Dust* (Indian 1975)
Johnson, Charles	*The Middle Passage* (American 1989)
Jolley, Elizabeth	*The Well* (Australian 1987)
Jones, James	*From Here to Eternity* (American 1951)
Kawabata, Yasunari	*Thousand Cranes* (Japanese 1959)
Kazantzakis, Nikos	*Zorba the Greek* (Greek 1946)
Keillor, Garrison	*Lake Wobegon Days* (American 1985)
Keneally, Thomas	*The Chant of Jimmy Blacksmth* (Australian 1972)
Kennedy, William	*Ironweed* (American 1983)
Kerouac, Jack	*On the Road* (American 1955)
Kesey, Ken	*One Flew Over the Cuckoo's Nest* (American 1962)

Kim, Richard E.	*The Martyred* (Korean-American 1964)
Kincaid, Jamaica	*Annie John* (American 1985)
Kinsella, W.P.	*Shoeless Joe* (Canadian 1982)
Knowles, John	*A Separate Peace* (American 1959)
Lamming, George	*In the Castle of My Skin* (Barbadan 1954)
Lampedusa, Giuseppe di	*The Leopard* (Italian 1960)
Laurence, Margaret	*The Diviners* (Canadian 1974)
Lee, Harper	*To Kill A Mockingbird* (American 1960)
Le Guin, Ursula	*The Left Hand of Darkness* (American 1969)
Lem, Stanislaus	*Solaris* (Polish 1961)
Lessing, Doris	*The Golden Notebook* (British 1962)
Lodge, David	*Souls and Bodies* (British 1980)
Lovelace, Earl	*The Dragon Can't Dance* (Trinidadian 1979)
Lowry, Malcolm	*Under the Volcano* (British 1947)
MacLennan, Hugh	*Two Solitudes* (Canadian 1945)
Mahfouz, Naguib	*Palace Walk* (Egyptian 1956)
Mailer, Norman	*The Naked and the Dead* (American 1948)
Mais, Roger	*Brother Man* (Jamaican 1954)
Malamud, Bernard	*The Fixer* (American 1966)
Malouf, David	*Remembering Babylon* (Australian 1993)
Mason, Bobbie Ann	*In Country* (American 1985)
McCarthy, Cormac	*All the Pretty Horses* (American 1992)
McMurtry, Larry	*Lonesome Dove* (American 1985)
McPherson, James Allen	*Hue and Cry* (American 1969)
Miller, Walter	*A Canticle for Liebowitz* (American 1959)
Mishima, Yukio	*The Sailor Who Fell from Grace with the Sea* (Japanese 1965)
Moore, Brian	*Lonely Passion of Judith Hearne* (Irish-Canadian 1973)
Moravia, Albert	*Two Women* (Italian 1958)
Morris, Wright	*Love Among the Cannibals* (American 1957)
Morrison, Toni	*Beloved* (American 1987)
Mudrooroo (Colin Johnson)	*Doctor Wooreddy's Prescription for Enduring the End of the World* (Australian 1983)
Murdoch, Iris	*Under the Net* (French 1954)
Nabokov, Vladimir	*Lolita* (Russian-American 1953)

Naipaul, V.S.	*A House for Mr. Biswas* (Anglo-Indian-Trinidadian 1961)
Narayan, R.K.	*The Man-Eater of Malgudi* (Indian 1961)
Ngugi wa Thiong'o	*Weep Not, Child* (Kenyan)
Oates, Joyce Carol	*Them* (American 1969)
O'Brien, Tim	*Going After Cacciato* (American 1975)
O'Connor, Edwin	*The Last Hurrah* (American 1956)
O'Connor, Flannery	*The Violent Bear It Away* (American 1955)
Oe, Kenzabura	*A Personal Matter* (Japanese 1964)
Okri, Ben	*The Famished Road* (Nigerian 1991)
Olsen, Tillie	*Tell Me a Riddle & Other Stories* (American 1971)
Ondaatje, Michael	*The English Patient* (Canadian 1992)
Orwell, George	*1984* (British 1949)
Oz, Amos	*My Michael* (Israeli 1968)
Ozick, Cynthia	*Levitation: Five Fictions* (American 1983)
Paley, Grace	*Enormous Changes in Last Minute* (American 1960)
Pasternak, Boris	*Doctor Zhivago* (Russian 1958)
Paton, Alan	*Cry, the Beloved Country* (South African 1948)
Pekar, Harvey	*Our Cancer Year* (American 1994)
Percy, Walker	*The Moviegoer* (American 1960)
Piercy, Marge	*Gone to Soldiers* (American 1987)
Plath, Sylvia	*The Bell Jar* (American 1971)
Porter, Katherine Anne	*Pale Horse, Pale Rider* (American 1939)
Potok, Chaim	*My Name is Asher Lev* (American 1972)
Powers, J.F.	*Morte D'Urban* (American 1956)
Powers, John R.	*The Last Catholic in America* (American 1973)
Pritchett, V.S.	*Collected Stories* (British 1981)
Proulx, E. Annie	*The Shipping News* (American 1993)
Puig, Manuel	*Kiss of the Spider Woman* (Argentinian 1979)
Purdy, James	*Malcolm* (American 1959)
Pym, Barbara	*Quartet in Autumn* (British 1980)
Pynchon, Thomas	*Gravity's Rainbow* (American 1973)
Quiriga, Horacio	*South American Jungle Tales* (Uruguayan 1959)
Rao, Raja	*The Serpent and the Rope* (Indian 1960)
Read, Piers Paul	*A Married Man* (British 1980)

Richler, Mordecai	*The Apprenticeship of Duddy Kravitz* (Canadian 1969)
Robbe-Grillet, Alain	*Jealousy* (French 1987)
Robbins, Tom	*Even Cowgirls Get the Blues* (American 1976)
Robinson, Marilynne	*Housekeeping* (American 1981)
Roth, Philip	*Goodbye, Columbus* (American 1959)
Rhys, Jean	*Wide Sargasso Sea* (British 1966)
Rulfo, Juan	*Pedro Páramo* (Mexican 1955)
Rushdie, Salman	*Midnight's Children* (Indian 1980)
Russ, Joanna	*The Female Man* (American 1975)
Russo, Richard	*Nobody's Fool* (American 1993)
Sábato, Ernesto	*The Tunnel* (Argentinian 1948)
Sagan, Françoise	*Bonjour Tristesse* (French 1954)
Salinger, J.D.	*The Catcher in the Rye* (American 1945)
Seals, David	*Powwow Highway* (American 1990)
Selvon, Sam	*The Lonely Londoners* (Trinidadian 1956)
Shaara, Michael	*Killer Angels* (American 1974)
Sheed, Wilfred	*People Will Always Be Kind* (American 1973)
Shields, Carol	*The Stone Diaries* (Canadian-American 1993)
Silko, Leslie Marmon	*Ceremony* (American 1977)
Sillitoe, Alan	*Saturday Night and Sunday Morning* (British 1958)
Simon, Claude	*The Grass* (French 1958)
Singer, Isaac Bashevis	*The Collected Stories* (American 1981)
Singh, Kushwant	*Train to Pakistan* (Indian 1956)
Smiley, Jane	*A Thousand Acres* (American 1991)
Solzhenitsyn, Alexander	*One Day in the Life of Ivan Denisovich* (Russian 1963)
Sontag, Susan	*I, Etcetera* (American 1978)
Soyinka, Wole	*Interpreters* (Nigerian 1965)
Spark, Muriel	*The Prime of Miss Jean Brodie* (British 1966)
Spiegelman, Art	*Maus I & II* (American 1986)
Stead, Christina	*The Man Who Loved Children* (Australian 1940)
Stone, Robert	*Dog Soldiers* (American 1974)
Styron, William	*Lie Down in Darkness* (American 1951)
Tanizaki, Junichiro	*Some Prefer Nettles* (Japanese 1965)
Taylor, Peter	*A Summons to Memphis* (American 1986)

Thomas, D.M.	*The White Hotel* (British 1981)
Tolkien, J.R.R.	*The Lord of the Rings* (British 1954-55)
Toole, John Kennedy	*A Confederacy of Dunces* (American 1980)
Tutuola, Amos	*My Life in the Bush of Ghosts* (Nigerian 1954)
Tyler, Anne	*Dinner at the Homesick Restaurant* (American 1982)
Updike, John	*Rabbit, Run* (American 1960)
Valenzuela, Luisa	*Strange Things Happen Here* (Argentinian 1979)
Vargas Llosa, Mario	*Green House* (Peruvian 1965)
Vidal, Gore	*Creation* (American 1981)
Vonnegut, Kurt	*Slaughterhouse Five* (American 1969)
Wain, John	*Hurry on Down* (British 1953)
Walker, Alice	*The Color Purple* (American 1982)
Wallant, Edward Louis	*The Pawnbroker* (American 1962)
Warren, Robert Penn	*All the King's Men* (American 1946)
Welch, James	*Winter in the Blood* (American 1974)
Welty, Eudora	*Collected Stories* (American 1980)
White, Patrick	*The Aunt's Story* (Australian 1946)
White, T.H.	*The Once and Future King* (British 1958)
Wiesel, Eric	*A Beggar in Jerusalem* (Romanian 1968)
Williams, John A.	*The Man Who Cried I AM* (American 1967)
Woiwode, Larry	*Beyond the Bedroom Wall* (American 1976)
Wolff, Tobias	*In the Garden of North American Martyrs* (American 1981)
Yourcenar, Marguerite	*Memoirs of Hadrian* (French 1951)

Drama

(Note: Date indicates century)

	Everyman (British 15th)
	The Second Shepherds' Play (British 15th)
Aeschylus	*Agamemnon* (Greek 5th B.C.)
Albee, Edward	*Who's Afraid of Virginia Woolf?* (American 20th)
Anouilh, Jean	*Antigone* (French 20th)
Aristophanes	*Lysistrata* (Greek 5th B.C.)
Baldwin, James	*Blues for Mister Charlie* (American 20th)

Baraka, Imamu	*Dutchman* (American 20th)
Barnes, Peter	*The Ruling Class* (British 20th)
Beaumarchais, Pierre de	*The Marriage of Figaro* (French 18th)
Beckett, Samuel	*Waiting for Godot* (Irish-French 20th)
Brecht, Bertolt	*The Caucasian Chalk Circle* (German 20th)
Büchner, Georg	*Woyzek* (German 19th)
Calderon, Pedro	*Life Is a Dream* (Spanish 17th)
Camus, Albert	*Caligula* (French 20th)
Chekhov, Anton	*The Cherry Orchard* (Russian 19–20th)
Chikamatsu	*Chusinguia: Treasury, Royal Retainers* (Japanese 17th)
Cocteau, Jean	*The Infernal Machine* (French 20th)
Congreve, William	*The Way of the World* (British 17th)
Corneille, Pierre	*The Cid* (French 17th)
Dryden, John	*All for Love* (British 17th)
Dumas, Alexandre (fils)	*The Lady of the Camellias* (French 19th)
Dürrenmatt, Friedrich	*The Physicists* (Swiss 20th)
Eliot, T.S.	*Murder in the Cathedral* (American-British 20th)
Euripides	*The Bacchae* (Greek 5th B.C.)
Frisch, Max	*The Firebugs* (Swiss 20th)
Fry, Christopher	*The Lady's Not for Burning* (British 20th)
Fugard, Athol	*Master Harold and the Boys* (South African 20th)
Gay, John	*The Beggar's Opera* (British 18th)
Genet, Jean	*The Balcony* (French 20th)
Giraudoux, Jean	*Tiger at the Gates* (French 20th)
Goethe, Johann W. von	*Faust* (German 18–19th)
Gogol, Nikolai	*The Gamblers* (Russian 19th)
Goldsmith, Oliver	*She Stoops to Conquer* (British 18th)
Hansberry, Lorraine	*A Raisin in the Sun* (American 20th)
Hellman, Lillian	*The Little Foxes* (American 20th)
Hochhuth, Rolf	*The Deputy* (German 20th)
Hugo, Victor	*Hernani* (French 19th)
Ibsen, Henrik	*Hedda Gabler* (Norwegian 19th)
Inge, William	*Picnic* (American 20th)
Ionesco, Eugene	*Rhinoceros* (French 20th)

Jonson, Ben	*Volpone* (British 17th)
Kalidos	*Skakuntala* (Indian 5th)
Kennedy, Adrienne	*Funnyhouse of a Negro* (American 20th)
Kipphardt, Heinar	*In the Matter of J. Robert Oppenheimer* (Greek 20th)
Kramer, Larry	*Faggot* (American 20th)
Kushner, Tony	*Angels in America* (American 20th)
Lorca, Federico Garcia	*The House of Bernarda Alba* (Spanish 20th)
MacLeish, Archibald	*J.B.* (American 20th)
Maeterlinck, Maurice	*The Blue Bird* (Belgian 20th)
Mamet, David	*American Buffalo* (American 20th)
Marlowe, Christopher	*Dr. Faustus* (British 16th)
McCullers, Carson	*Member of the Wedding* (American 20th)
Miller, Arthur	*Death of a Salesman* (American 20th)
Molière	*Tartuffe* (French 17th)
Montherland, Henri de	*La Reine Morte* (French 20th)
O'Casey, Sean	*Juno and the Paycock* (Irish 20th)
Odets, Clifford	*Waiting for Lefty* (American 20th)
O'Neill, Eugene	*Long Days Journey into Night* (American 20th)
Orton, Joe	*What the Butler Saw* (British 20th)
Pinter, Harold	*The Birthday Party* (British 20th)
Pirandello, Luigi	*Six Characters in Search of an Author* (Italian 20th)
Plautus, Titus	*Amphitryon* (Roman 3rd–2nd B.C.)
Racine, Jean	*Phaedra* (French 17th)
Rice, Elmer	*The Adding Machine* (American 20th)
Rostand, Edmond	*Cyrano de Bergerac* (French 19th)
Sanchez, Florencio	*Down the Gully* (Argentinian 20th)
Sartre, Jean Paul	*No Exit* (French 20th)
Scholler, Friedrich	*Maria Stuart* (German 18th)
Shaffer, Peter	*Amadeus* (British 20th)
Shakespeare, William	*Macbeth* and *A Midsummer Night's Dream* (British 16th–17th)
Shange, Ntozake	*for colored girls who have considered suicide when the rainbow is enuf* (American 20th)
Shaw, George Bernard	*Major Barbara* (Irish 20th)
Solorzano, Carlos	*The Hands of God* (Guatemalan 20th)

Sophocles	*Oedipus the King* (Greek 5th B.C.)
Soyinka, Wole	*A Dance of the Forests* (Nigerian 20th)
Stoppard, Tom	*Rosencrantz and Guildenstern Are Dead* (British 20th)
Strindberg, August	*Miss Julie* (Swedish 19–20th)
Synge, John Millington	*Playboy of the Western World* (Irish 20th)
Terence (Publius Terentius Afer)	*The Eunuch* (Roman 2nd B.C.)
Tsuchi	*Sukeroku: Flower of Edo* (Japanese)
Usigli, Rodolfo	*El Gesticulador* (Mexican 20th)
Webster, John	*The Duchess of Malfi* (British 17th)
Weiss, Peter	*Marat/Sade* (*The Assassination of Marat as Performed by the Inmates of Charenton Asylum under the Direction of the Marquis de Sade*) (German 20th)
Wilde, Oscar	*The Importance of Being Earnest* (British-Irish 19th–20th)
Wilder, Thornton	*Our Town* (American 20th)
Williams, Tennessee	*A Streetcar Named Desire* (American 20th)
Wilson, August	*Ma Rainey's Black Bottom* (American 20th)
Wycherley, William	*The Country Wife* (British 17th)
Yeats, William Butler	*The Countess Cathleen* (Irish 20th)

You recognize that each person you know speaks with a distinctive voice, rhythm, intonation, and vocabulary. Perhaps you've noticed yourself modeling some of your speech patterns on those of people you know (and admire). It should come as no surprise, then, that writers are the same—and the best writers can create a personality (their own and those of the characters they create) on paper with the same clarity and recognizability as anyone speaking.

To develop an appreciation of this miracle of communication, you need to expose yourself to as wide a variety of writing as you can manage. "Wide variety" doesn't mean just different genres (news reportage, novels, non-fiction, technical writing, essays, letters). Go beyond that, and read the works of writers who use British, South African,

Australian, and other national varieties of English. (Accessible British writers I frequently recommend include Julian Barnes and David Lodge.) Don't limit yourself to contemporary works alone; expand your horizons to include works of previous generations of writers. (Earlier American authors whose works are easily enjoyed include S.J. Perelman, James M. Cain, and James Thurber.) Developing an appreciation of the variety of literature will increase your ability to enjoy all good writing, and it will greatly improve your own writings in later life, whether creative works or daily office memos.

Michael Agnes
Editor in Chief
Webster's New World Dictionaries

Yale University
New Haven, CT 06520
(203) 432-4771
http://www.yale.edu

Yale College freshmen are offered a variety of introductory English courses to improve their skills as prose writers and interpreters of literature. Brief descriptions of some of those courses follow:

In "Introduction to Literary Study," readings vary from section to section, but most sections read at least one play by **Shakespeare**. Other authors studied have included **Samuel Beckett, Charles Dickens, Frederick Douglass, James Joyce**, **Toni Morrison, Mary Shelley**, **Walt Whitman**, and **Virginia Woolf.**

Readings in another course, which introduces the study of the epic tradition, include

Cervantes, Miguel de	*Don Quixote*
Dante	*Inferno*
Homer	*The Odyssey*
Vergil	*The Aeneid*

and one or more modern novelists such as **George Eliot**, **James Joyce**, **Virginia Woolf**, and **Derek Walcott.**

In the course "The European Literary Tradition," students read **Homer**'s *Iliad* and the Greek dramatists **Aeschylus**, **Aristophanes**, **Euripides**, and **Sophocles**. They also study plays by **Samuel Beckett**, **Bertolt Brecht**, **Georg Büchner**, **Anton Chekhov**, **Caryl Churchill**, **Henrick Ibsen**, **Molière**, **Jean Racine**, **Ntozake Shange**, **Geoffrey Chaucer**, **John Milton**, and **Alexander Pope**.

Edmund Spenser and a Renaissance lyric poet, a Romantic poet, and a modern poet are read in "Major English Poets."

Texts for a course on nature writing include

Austin, Mary	*Land of Little Rain*
Dillard, Annie	*Teaching a Stone to Talk*
Finch and Elder, eds.	*The Norton Anthology of Nature Writing*
Kincaid, Jamaica	*At the Bottom of the River*
Leopold, Aldo	*Sand County Almanac*
Maclean, Norman	*A River Runs Through It*
Oliver, Mary	*House of Light* (poems)
Stoppard, Tom	*Arcadia* (a play)
Thoreau, Henry David and Ralph Waldo Emerson	*Nature: Walking*

Yeshiva University
Main Campus
500 West 185th Street
New York, NY 10033-3201
(212) 960-5400
http://www.yu.edu

Each summer first-year undergraduate students entering Yeshiva College and Sy Syms School of Business at the University are sent a book and supporting material as part of the College's annual summer reading project. A semester-long discussion based on the book takes up such issues as identity, race, and cultural conflict. The issues are discussed during freshman orientation and explored more thoroughly in regular course work and through special events.

Books read have included

Conrad, Joseph	*Heart of Darkness*
Brecht, Bertold	*Galileo*
Kaplan, Robert D.	*Balkan Ghosts*

In Freshman Honors Seminars, some of the works studied have been

	Beowulf
	"Caedmon's Hymn"
	The Second Shepherd's Play of the Wakefield cycle
	Sir Gawain and the Green Knight
	"The Wanderer"
Beckett, Samuel	*Waiting for Godot*
Blake, William	Poems
Browning, Robert	Poems
Chaucer, Geoffrey	*The Canterbury Tales*
Conrad, Joseph	*Heart of Darkness*
Donne, John	Poetry
Freud, Sigmund	*Civilization and Its Discontents*
Goethe, Johann W. von	*Faust,* part I, translation
Hacker, Diana	*A Writer's Reference*
Hoffer, Eric	*The True Believer*
Hopkins, Gerard Manley	Poems
Jefferson, Thomas, et al.	*The Declaration of Independence*
Kant, Immanuel	*On Perpetual Peace*
Keats, John	Poems
King, Martin Luther, Jr.	"Letter from Birmingham Jail"
Marcuse, Herbert	*One Dimensional Man* (excerpt)
Marlowe, Christopher	*Dr. Faustus*
Marx, Karl	*The German Ideology* (excerpt)
Milton, John	*Paradise Lost*; "Areopagitica"; *Samson Agonistes*
Mirandola, Pico della	*Oration on the Dignity of Man*
Orwell, George	"Shooting an Elephant"

Paley, Grace	"The Loudest Voice"
Pericles	"Funeral Oration" (Thucydides)
Plato	*Crito*
Pope, Alexander	"An Essay on Man"
Shakespeare, William	*King Henry IV, Part* I; *King Lear, The Merchant of Venice*; sonnets and lyrics
Shelley, Mary	*Frankenstein*
Sieyès, Emmanuel, et al.	*The Declaration of the Rights of Man*
Sophocles	*Antigone*
Swift, Jonathan	"A Modest Proposal," *Gulliver's Travels*
Tennyson, Alfred Lord	*In Memoriam*
Tocqueville, Alexis de	*Democracy in America* (excerpt)

CHAPTER 5

Special Interest Lists and Major Literary Awards

At the turn of the century, we have become a very list-oriented society. There are hundreds of books of lists published every year. We can find books that list the most indispensable inventions, most popular movies, best dog breeds, most profitable companies, hottest new stars, and on and on. And we make lists in our daily lives to help us accomplish our goals and keep us organized. In Chapter 2 of this book, you were encouraged to make your own personal reading list.

There are some other reading lists that you should have at your fingertips as you plan your pre-college reading. In this chapter, you will find two types of lists. The first are lists centered around certain disciplines. The books on those lists are suggestions that reflect some basic works for that field of knowledge. Some are old, some contemporary, some are broad overviews, some rather technical, but all are merely points of departure and should lead you to other works in that area. Following those are lists of awards given for literary works. If an author has been awarded a Nobel Prize, perhaps you should make yourself familiar with his works. Or if you notice that a certain book won a Pulitzer and a National Book Award, you may want to add it to your reading list.

Special Interest Lists

If You Plan to Study Science…

Physics

Bloomfield, Louis A.	*How Things Work: The Physics of Everyday Life*
Bohr, Niels	*Atomic Physics and Human Knowledge*
Bronowski, Jacob	*Science and Human Values*
Cohen, I. Bernard	*The Birth of a New Physics*
Duhem, Pierre	*To Save the Phenomena: An Essay on the Idea of Physical Theory from Plato to Galileo*
Dyson, Freeman	*Disturbing the Universe*
Einstein, Albert	*Meaning of Relativity; Relativity: The Special and the General Theory*
Feynman, Richard P.	*Feynman Lectures on Physics; The Character of Physical Law*
Genz, Henning	*Nothingness: The Science of Empty Space*
Hawking, Stephen	*A Brief History of Time: From the Big Bang to Black Holes*
Heisenberg, Werner	*Physics and Philosophy; Across the Frontier; Physics and Beyond*
Hersey, John R.	*Hiroshima*
Petroski, Henry	*Invention by Design: How Engineers Get from Thought to Thing*
Rhodes, Richard	*The Making of the Atomic Bomb*

Biology

Attenborough, David	*Life on Earth: A Natural History; The Living Planet*
Bronowski, Jacob	*The Ascent of Man; Science and Human Values*
Darwin, Charles	*Origin of Species*
Diamond, Jared	*Guns, Germs, and Steel: The Fates of Human Societies*
Gould, Stephen Jay	*Ontogeny and Phylogeny; The Panda's Thumb*
Keller, Evelyn	*A Feeling for the Organism: The Life and Work of Barbara McClintock*

Storer, John H.	*The Web of Life*
Stringer, Christopher	*African Exodus: The Origins of Modern Humanity*
Thomas, Lewis	*The Lives of a Cell: Notes of a Biology Watcher; The Medusa and the Snail*
Weiner, Jonathan	*Time, Love, Memory: A Great Biologist and His Quest for the Origins of Behavior*
Zinsser, Hans	*Rats, Lice and History*

Astronomy

Galilei, Galileo	*Dialogue Concerning the Two Chief World Systems, Ptolemaic and Copernican*
Kaufman, William J. and R.A. Freedman	*Universe: Magnificent Cosmos*
Kolb, Rocky	*Blind Watchers of the Sky: The People and Ideas that Shaped Our View of the Universe*
Kuhn, Thomas S.	*The Copernican Revolution*
Pagels, Heinz	*The Cosmic Code*
Sagan, Carl	*Cosmos; Broca's Brain: Reflections on the Romance of Science*

Chemistry

Glasstone, Samuel	*Sourcebook on Atomic Energy*
Green, Bill	*Water, Ice, and Stone: Science and Memory on the Antarctic Lakes*
Kuhn, Thomas S.	*The Structure of Scientific Revolutions*
MacDonald, Malcolm M. and Robert E. Davis	*Chemistry and Society*
Pauling, Linus	*The Architecture of Molecules; The Nature of the Chemical Bond*
Schrodinger, Erin C.	*Science, Theory, and Man*
Snyder, Carl H.	*The Extraordinary Chemistry of Ordinary Things*
Weinberg, Alvin M.	*Reflections on Big Science*
Watson, James D.	*The Double Helix: A Personal Account of the Discovery of the Structure of DNA*

Earth Sciences

Carson, Rachel	*Silent Spring; The Sea Around Us*
Eisley, Loren	*The Immense Journey*
Leopold, Aldo, et al.	*A Sand County Almanac* and *Sketches Here and There*
Leopold, Luna Bergere	*Water, Rivers, and Creeks*
McPhee, John	*In Suspect Terrain*
Peterson, Roger Tory	*A Field Guide to the Birds*
Zebrowski, Ernest Jr.	*Perils of a Restless Planet: Scientific Perspectives on Natural Disasters*

Behavioral Sciences

Achebe, Chinua	*Things Fall Apart*
Addams, Jane	*Twenty Years at Hull-House*
Baars, Bernard J.	*In the Theater of Consciousness: the Workspace of the Mind*
Berger, Peter L. and T. Luckmann	*The Social Construction of Reality*
DeBeauvoir, Simone	*The Second Sex*
Douglas, Mary	*Purity and Danger*
Dubos, René	*Mirage of Health: Utopias, Progress, and Biological Change*
Freud, Sigmund	*A General Introduction to Psychoanalysis; Civilization and its Discontents; Interpretation of Dreams*
Gould, Stephen Jay	*The Mismeasure of Man*
Harris, Thomas A.	*I'm OK, You're OK*
Hudson, Liam	*The Cult of the Fact*
Jung, Carl Gustav	*The Psychology of the Unconscious*
Marriott, Alice	*The Ten Grandmothers*
Maslow, Abraham	*Toward a Psychology of Being*
May, Rollo	*Existence*
Mead, George Herbert	*Mind, Self, and Society*
Meade, Margaret	*Coming of Age in Samoa*
Mitford, Jessica	*The American Way of Death Revisited*

Neisser, Ulric — *Memory Observed*

Penfield, Wilder — *The Mystery of the Mind*

Pinker, Steven — *How the Mind Works*

Sagan, Carl — *The Dragons of Eden: Speculations on the Evolution of Human Intelligence*

Sacks, Oliver — *The Man Who Mistook His Wife for a Hat and Other Clinical Tales*

Schneider, David — *American Kinship*

Skinner, B.F. — *About Behaviorism; Beyond Freedom and Dignity; Walden Two*

Mathematics

Beckmann, Petr — *A History of Pi*

Davis, Phillip and R. Hersh — *The Mathematical Experience*

Hardy, G.H. — *A Mathematician's Apology*

Huff, Darrell — *How to Lie with Statistics*

Kline, Morris — *Mathematical Thought from Ancient to Modern Times*

Newman, James R. — *The World of Mathematics*

Paulos, John Allen — *Innumeracy: Mathematical Illiteracy and Its Consequences*

Pollya, George — *Mathematics and Plausible Reasoning*

Singh, Simon — *Fermat's Enigma: The Epic Quest to Solve the World's Greatest Mathematical Problem*

Sobel, Dava — *Longitude: The True Story of a Lone Genius Who Solved the Greatest Scientific Problem of His Time*

Tufte, Edward R. — *The Visual Display of Quantitative Information*

Whitehead, Alfred North and B. Russell — *Principia Mathematica to 56*

Whitehead, Alfred North — *An Introduction to Mathematics; Science and the Modern World*

If You Plan to Study Business…

Badaracco, Joseph L. Jr. — *Defining Moments: When Managers Must Choose Between Right and Right*

Bolles, Richard Nelson — *What Color Is your Parachute? 2000*

Carnegie, Dale, et al.,	*How to Win Friends and Influence People*
Chernow, Ron	*Titan: The Life of John D. Rockefeller, Sr.*
Covey, Stephen R.	*The Seven Habits of Highly Effective People: Powerful Lessons in Personal Change*
Galbraith, John Kenneth	*Affluent Society*
Graham, Ben	*Security Analysis*
Griffin, Jack	*How to Say It at Work: Putting Yourself Across with Power Words, Phrases, Body Language and Communication*
Keynes, John Maynard	*The General Theory of Employment, Interest, and Money*
Machiavelli, Niccolò	*The Prince*
McCormack, Mark H.	*What They Don't Teach You at Harvard Business School*
Molloy, John T.	*John T. Molloy's New Dress for Success; New Women's Dress for Success*
Musashi, Miyamoto	*A Book of Five*
Packard, Vance	*The Hidden Persuaders*
Peters, Thomas and R. Waterman	*In Search of Excellence: Lessons from America's Best-Run Companies*
Smith, Adam	*The Wealth of Nations*
Taylor, Frederick Winslow	*The Principles of Scientific Management*

If You Plan to Study Education...

Adams, Henry	*The Education of Henry Adams*
Bloom, Allan	*The Closing of the American Mind*
Braithwaite, Edward R.	*To Sir With Love*
Codell, Esme Raji	*Educating Esme: Diary of a Teacher's First Year*
Dewey, John	*Democracy and Education*
Freedman, Samuel	*Small Victories: The Real World of a Teacher, Her Students, and Their High School*
Gardner, Howard	*Frames of Mind: The Theory of Multiple Intelligences*
Hayden, Torey L.	*Somebody Else's Kids*
Hilton, James	*Goodbye, Mr. Chips*
Jensen, Eric	*Teaching with the Brain in Mind*
Kane, Pearl Rock	*My First Year as a Teacher*

Kaufman, Bel	*Up the Down Staircase*
Kluger, Richard	*Simple Justice: The History of Brown v Board of Education and Black America's Struggle for Equality*
Kozol, Jonathan	*Savage Inequalities: Children in America's Schools*
Montessori, Maria	*The Secret of Childhood*
Palmer, Parker J.	*The Courage to Teach: Exploring the Inner Landscape of a Teacher's Life*
Sadker, Myra	*Failing at Fairness: How Our Schools Cheat Girls*
Sizer, Theodore and Nancy Sizer	*The Students Are Watching: Schools and the Moral Contract*
Wagner, Walter W. and Robert Gagne	*Principles of Instructional Design*

If You Plan to Study Art, Architecture, Music, Dance, or Theater…

Adams, Ansel	*The Camera; The Negative; The Print*
Andrew, Geoff	*The Director's Vision: A Concise Guide to the Art of 250 Great Filmmakers*
Arnason, H. Harvard	*History of Modern Art: Painting, Sculpture, Architecture, and Philosophy*
Arnheim, Rudolf	*Art and Visual Perception*
Belloli, Andrea	*A Day in the Country; Impressionism and the French Landscape*
Bernstein, Leonard	*The Joy of Music*
Boorstin, Jon	*Making Movies Work: Thinking Like a Filmmaker*
Byron, Robert	*The Appreciation of Architecture*
Ching, Frank D.K. and Frances D. Ching	*Architecture: Form, Space, and Order*
Cooke, Deryck	*The Language of Music*
Cooke, Mervyn	*The Chronicle of Jazz*
Copland, Aaron	*Music and Imagination*
Copland, Aaron	*What to Listen for in Music*
Cross, Milton	*The Story of the Opera*
Cumming, Robert	*Annotated Art*
Curtis, William J.R.	*Modern Architecture Since 1900*
Finn, David	*How to Look at Sculpture*

Garfunkel, Trudy	*On Wings of Joy: The Story of Ballet from the 16th Century to Today*
Gombrich, E.H.	*The Story of Art*
Grosser, Maurice	*The Painter's Eye*
Jonas, Gerald	*Dancing: The Pleasure, Power, and Art of Movement*
Kendall, Elizabeth	*Where She Danced: The Birth of American Art Dance*
Kerner, Mary	*Barefoot to Balanchine: How to Watch Dance*
McLaughlin, Jack	*Jefferson and Monticello: The Biography of a Builder*
Murray, Albert	*Stomping the Blues*
O'Gorman, James	*ABC of Architecture*
Panofsky, Erwin	*Meaning in the Visual Arts*
Rand, Ayn	*The Fountainhead*
Read, Sir Herbert	*The Art of Sculpture*
Rybcznski, Witold	*The Most Beautiful House in the World*
Sessions, Roger	*The Musical Experience of Composer, Performer, Listener*
Sontag, Susan	*On Photography*
Strickland, Carol	*The Annotated Mona Lisa: A Crash Course in Art History from Prehistoric to Post-Modern*
Weitz, Morris	*Philosophy of the Arts*
Zevi, Bruno	*Architecture as Space*

If You Plan to Study Philosophy…

Aristotle	*Nicomachean Ethics*
Berlin, Isaiah	*Russian Thinkers*
Buber, Martin	*I and Thou*
Descartes, René	*Meditations on First Philosophy*
Dewey, John	*Reconstruction in Philosophy*
Durant, Will	*The Story of Philosophy; Ideas and Opinions*
Einstein, Albert	*Meaning of Relativity*
Erasmus	*In Praise of Folly*
Frankl, Viktor	*Man's Search for Meaning*
Gandhi, Mohandas K.	*An Autobiography: The Story of My Experiments with Truth*
Hallie, Phillip P.	*Lest Innocent Blood Be Shed*

Hardy, Henry, ed.	*The Proper Study of Mankind: An Anthology of Essays*
Heidegger, Martin	*Being and Time*
Heilbroner, Robert	*The Worldly Philosophers*
Hofstadter, Douglas R.	*Gödel, Escher, Bach: An Eternal Golden Braid*
Hughes, Robert	*The Shock of the New*
James, William	*The Varieties of Religious Experience*
Karnos, David and R. Showmaker	*Falling in Love with Wisdom: American Philosophers Talk about their Calling*
Locke, John	*An Essay Concerning Human Understanding*
Machiavelli, Niccolò	*The Prince*
Mill, John Stuart	*On Liberty*
Moore, G.E.	*Principia Ethica*
More, Thomas	*Utopia*
Nietzsche, Friedrich	*Thus Spake Zarathustra*
Persig, Robert	*Zen and the Art of Motorcycle Maintenance*
Plato	*Dialogues (Apology; Phaedo; The Republic)*
Russell, Bertrand	*The Problems of Philosophy*
Sartre, Jean-Paul	*Being and Nothingness*
Saint Augustine	*City of God; Confessions*
Thoreau, Henry David	*Disobedience and Other Essays; Walden*

If You Plan to Study History or Political Science…

Aristotle	Ethics; Politics
Bullock, Alan	*Hitler: A Study in Tyranny*
Catton, Bruce	*This Hallowed Ground*
Churchill, Winston	*My Early Life: 1874–1904*
Dangerfield, George	*The Strange Death of Liberal England*
Diamond, Jared	*Guns, Germs, and Steel: The Fates of Human Societies*
Gandhi, Mohandas K.	*An Autobiography: The Story of My Experiments with Truth*
Goldman, Emma	*Living My Life*
Guevara, Ernesto "Che"	*Guerrilla Warfare*
Hamilton, Alexander et al.	*The Federalist Papers*

Herman, Edward S. and N. Chomsky	*Manufacturing Consent: The Political Economy of the Mass Media*
Hofstadter, Richard	*The American Political Tradition*
Lukacs, John	*The Last European War: September 1939–December 1941*
Malcolm X and Alex Haley	*The Autobiography of Malcolm X*
Marx, Karl and Friedrich Engels	*Communist Manifesto*
Mattingly, Garrett	*The Armada*
Moorhead, Alan	*Gallipoli*
Plato	*The Republic*
Schlesinger, Arthur	*The Crisis of the Old Order*
Thompson, Edward P.	*Making of the English Working Class*
Tocqueville, Alexis de	*Democracy in America*
Tuchman, Barbara	*The Guns of August*
White, Theodore	*The Making of the President 1960*
Wiesel, Elie	*Night*
Williams, Juan	*Eyes on the Prize: America's Civil Rights Years, 1954–1965*

If You Plan to Take Advanced Placement English Classes…

In her guide *AP English Literature and Composition* (ARCO), Dr. Laurie Rozakis recommends a number of works that you should read to prepare for the AP English exams. These works also comprise a good list for pre-college reading by all students whether AP or not.

Suggested Reading List (Novels)

Austen, Jane	*Pride and Prejudice; Emma*
Baldwin, James	*Go Tell It on the Mountain*
Bellow, Saul	*Seize the Day*
Brontë, Charlotte	*Jane Eyre*
Brontë, Emily	*Wuthering Heights*
Buck, Pearl	*The Good Earth*
Camus, Albert	*The Stranger*
Chopin, Kate	*The Awakening*

Conrad, Joseph	*Heart of Darkness*
Crane, Stephen	*The Red Badge of Courage*
Defoe, Daniel	*Moll Flanders*
Dickens, Charles	*David Copperfield; A Tale of Two Cities*
Dostoevski, Fyodor	*Crime and Punishment; The Brothers Karamazov*
Dumas, Alexander	*The Count of Monte Cristo*
Eliot, George	*Silas Marner*
Ellison, Ralph	*Invisible Man*
Faulkner, William	*The Sound and the Fury; As I Lay Dying*
Fielding, Henry	*Joseph Andrews*
Fitzgerald, F. Scott	*The Great Gatsby*
Flaubert, Gustave	*Madame Bovary*
Forster, E.M.	*Passage to India*
Fowles, John	*The French Lieutenant's Woman*
Golding, William	*The Lord of the Flies*
Greene, Graham	*The Power and the Glory*
Hardy, Thomas	*The Return of the Native*
Hawthorne, Nathaniel	*The Scarlet Letter; The House of Seven Gables*
Hemingway, Ernest	*The Sun Also Rises; For Whom the Bell Tolls*
Howells, William D.	*The Rise of Silas Lapham*
Huxley, Aldous	*Brave New World*
James, Henry	*The Turn of the Screw*
Joyce, James	*A Portrait of the Artist as a Young Man*
Knowles, John	*A Separate Peace*
Lawrence, D.H.	*Sons and Lovers*
London, Jack	*Call of the Wild*
Lee, Harper	*To Kill a Mockingbird*
Mailer, Norman	*The Naked and the Dead*
Malamud, Bernard	*The Fixer*
Maugham, W. Somerset	*Of Human Bondage*
Melville, Herman	*Moby-Dick; Billy Budd; Foretopman*
Morrison, Toni	*Song of Solomon*
Norris, Frank	*The Octopus*
Orwell, George	*1984; Animal Farm*
Roth, Philip	*Goodbye, Columbus*

Shelley, Mary	*Frankenstein*
Steinbeck, John	*The Grapes of Wrath; Of Mice and Men*
Stowe, Harriet Beecher	*Uncle Tom's Cabin*
Swift, Jonathan	*Gulliver's Travels*
Tan, Amy	*The Joy Luck Club*
Thackeray, William	*Vanity Fair*
Turgenev, Ivan	*Fathers and Sons*
Twain, Mark	*The Adventures of Huckleberry Finn*
Updike, John	*Rabbit, Run*
Walker, Alice	*The Color Purple*
Warren, Robert Penn	*All the King's Men*
West, Nathanael	*Miss Lonelyhearts*
Wharton, Edith	*Ethan Frome*
Woolf, Virginia	*To the Lighthouse; Mrs. Dalloway*
Wright, Richard	*Native Son*

Suggested Reading List (Drama)

	Everyman
	The Second Shepherd's Play
Aeschylus	*Agamemnon*
Albee, Edward	*Who's Afraid of Virginia Woolf?; Zoo Story*
Aristophanes	*The Frogs*
Beckett, Samuel	*Endgame; Waiting for Godot*
Bolt, Robert	*A Man for All Seasons*
Brecht, Bertold	*The Caucasian Chalk Circle*
Capek, Karel	*R.U.R*
Chekhov, Anton	*The Cherry Orchard; The Sea Gull*
Congreve, William	*The Way of the World*
Eliot, T.S.	*Murder in the Cathedral*
Euripides	*Medea*
Gibson, William	*The Miracle Worker*
Gilbert, W.S.	*The Mikado*
Goldsmith, Oliver	*She Stoops to Conquer*
Hansberry, Lorraine	*A Raisin in the Sun*
Hellman, Lillian	*The Little Foxes*

Ibsen, Henrik	*A Doll's House; Ghosts; The Enemy of the People; The Wild Duck*
Ionesco, Eugene	*The Lesson*
Lerner and Loewe	*My Fair Lady*
MacLeish, Archibald	*J.B.*
Marlowe, Christopher	*Dr. Faustus*
Miller, Arthur	*The Crucible; Death of a Salesman*
Molière	*Tartuffe; The Physician in Spite of Himself*
O'Casey, Sean	*Juno and the Paycock; The Plough and Stars*
O'Neill, Eugene	*The Emperor Jones; The Hairy Ape; Mourning Becomes Electra*
Pinter, Harold	*The Birthday Party*
Pirandello, Luigi	*Six Characters in Search of an Author*
Rostand, Edmond	*Cyrano de Bergerac*
Sartre, Jean-Paul	*No Exit*
Shakespeare, William	*Hamlet; King Lear; Othello; Julius Caesar; As You Like It; Macbeth; Romeo and Juliet; The Tempest*
Shaw, George Bernard	*Arms and the Man; Man and Superman; Major Barbara; Saint Joan; Pygmalion*
Sheridan, Richard	*The Rivals; The School for Scandal*
Sophocles	*Antigone; Oedipus Rex*
Stoppard, Tom	*Rosencrantz and Guildenstern Are Dead*
Synge, John Millington	*Playboy of the Western World*
Wilde, Oscar	*The Importance of Being Earnest*
Wilder, Thornton	*Our Town*
Williams, Tennessee	*The Glass Menagerie; Cat on a Hot Tin Roof*
Wilson, August	*Fences*

Major Literary Awards

The Nobel Prize for Literature

Since 1901, the Nobel Prize has been awarded annually to an individual based on the body of his published work. Here are the winners (and their countries).

1999	**Günter Grass** (Germany)
1998	**Jose Saramago** (Portugal)

1997	**Dario Fo** (Italy)
1996	**Wislawa Szymborska** (Poland)
1995	**Seamus Heaney** (Ireland)
1994	**Kenzaburo Oe** (Japan)
1993	**Toni Morrison** (USA)
1992	**Derek Walcott** (Caribbean)
1991	**Nadine Gordimer** (South Africa)
1990	**Octavio Paz** (Mexico)
1989	**Camilo Jose Cela** (Spain)
1988	**Naguib Mahfouz** (Egypt)
1987	**Joseph Brodsky** (USA)
1986	**Wole Soyinka** (Nigeria)
1985	**Claude Simon** (France)
1984	**Jaroslav Seifert** (Czechoslovakia)
1983	**William Golding** (England)
1982	**Gabriel García Márquez** (Columbia)
1981	**Elias Canetti** (Bulgaria)
1980	**Czeslaw Milosz** (USA)
1979	**Odysseus Elytis** (Greece)
1978	**Isaac Bashevis Singer** (USA)
1977	**Vincente Aleixandre** (Spain)
1976	**Saul Bellow** (USA)
1975	**Eugenio Montale** (Italy)
1974	**Eyvind Johnson** (Sweden) and **Harry Martinson** (Sweden)
1973	**Patrick White** (Australia)
1972	**Heinrich Böll** (Germany)
1971	**Pablo Neruda** (Chile)
1970	**Aleksandr Solzhenistyn** (USSR)
1969	**Samuel Beckett** (France)
1968	**Yasunari Kawabata** (Japan)
1967	**Miguel Angel Asturias** (Guatemala)
1966	**Samuel Yosef Agnon** (Israel) and **Nelly Sachs** (Sweden)
1965	**Mikhail Sholokhov** (Russia)

1964	**Jean-Paul Sartre** (France)
1963	**Giorgos Seferis** (Serferiades) (Greece)
1962	**John Steinbeck** (USA)
1961	**Ivo Andric** (Yugoslavia)
1960	**St-John Perse** (France) (Alexis St. Léger)
1959	**Salvatore Quasimodo** (Italy)
1958	**Boris Pasternak** (USSR)
1957	**Albert Camus** (France)
1956	**Juan Ramón Himénez** (Spain)
1955	**Halldór Kijan Laxness** (Iceland)
1954	**Ernest Hemingway** (USA)
1953	**Sir Winston Churchill** (England)
1952	**François Mauriac** (France)
1951	**Pär Lagerkvist** (Sweden)
1950	**Bertrand Russell** (England)
1949	**William Faulkner** (USA)
1948	**Thomas Stearns Eliot** (England)
1947	**André Gide** (France)
1946	**Hermann Hesse** (Switzerland)
1945	**Gabriela Mistral** (Chile)
1944	**Johannes V. Jensen** (Denmark)
1940–1943	No Award
1939	**Frans Eemil Sillanpää** (Finland)
1938	**Pearl S. Buck** (USA)
1937	**Roger Martin Du Gard** (France)
1936	**Eugene O'Neill** (USA)
1935	**Luigi Pirandello** (Italy)
1934	**Ivan G. Bunin** (Russia)
1933	**John Galsworthy** (England)
1932	**Erik A. Karlfeldt** (Sweden)
1931	**Sinclair Lewis** (USA)
1930	**Thomas Mann** (Germany)
1929	**Sigrid Undset** (Norway)
1928	**Henri Bergson** (France)
1927	**Grazia Deledda** (Italy)

1926	**George Bernard Shaw** (Great Britain)
1925	**Wladyslaw Reymont** (Poland)
1924	**William B. Yeats** (Ireland)
1923	**Hacinto Benavente** (Spain)
1922	**Anatole France** (France)
1921	**Knut Hamsun** (Norway)
1920	**Carl Spitteler** (Switzerland)
1919	**Karl Gjellerup** (Denmark) and **Henrick Pontoppidan** (Denmark)
1918	**Verner Von Heidenstam** (Sweden)
1917	**Romain Rolland** (France)
1916	**Rabindranath Tagore** (India)
1915	**Gerhart Hauptmann** (Germany)
1914	**Maurice Maeterlinck** (Belgium)
1913	**Paul von Heyse** (Germany)
1912	**Selma Lagerlöf** (Sweden)
1911	**Rudolf Euken** (Germany)
1910	**Rudyard Kipling** (England)
1909	**Giosue Carducci** (Italy)
1908	**Henryk Sienkiewicz** (Poland)
1907	**Frédéric Mistral** (France) and **José Echegaray** (Spain)
1906	**Bjørnsterne Bjørnson** (Norway)
1905	**Theodor Mommsen** (Germany)
1904	**René F.A. Sully Prudhomme** (France)

The Pulitzer Prizes

The Pulitzer Prize is given each year for fiction, non-fiction, biography, history, drama, and poetry by an American author.

Fiction

2000	**Jhumpa Lahiri**	*Interpreter of Maladies*
1999	**Michael Cunningham**	*The Hours*
1998	**Philip Roth**	*American Pastoral*

1997	**Steven Millhauser**	*Martin Dressler: The Tale of an American Dreamer*
1996	**Richard Ford**	*Independence Day*
1995	**Carol Shields**	*The Stone Diaries*
1994	**E. Annie Proulx**	*The Shipping News*
1993	**Robert Olen Butler**	*A Good Scent from a Strange Mountain*
1992	**Jane Smiley**	*A Thousand Acres*
1991	**John Updike**	*Rabbit at Rest*
1990	**Oscar Hijuelos**	*The Mambo Kings Play Songs of Love*
1989	**Anne Tyler**	*Breathing Lessons*
1988	**Toni Morrison**	*Beloved*
1987	**Peter Taylor**	*A Summons to Memphis*
1986	**Larry McMurtry**	*Lonesome Dove*
1985	**Alison Lurie**	*Foreign Affairs*
1984	**William Kennedy**	*Ironweed*
1983	**Alice Walker**	*The Color Purple*
1982	**John Updike**	*Rabbit is Rich*
1981	**John Kennedy Toole**	*A Confederacy of Dunces*
1980	**Norman Mailer**	*The Executioner's Song*
1979	**John Cheever**	*The Stories of John Cheever*
1978	**James Alan McPherson**	*Elbow Room*
1977	No Award	
1976	**Saul Bellow**	*Humboldt's Gift*
1975	**Michael Shaar**	*The Killer Angels*
1974	No Award	
1973	**Eudora Welty**	*The Optimist's Daughter*
1972	**Wallace Stegner**	*The Angle of Repose*
1971	No Award	
1970	**Jean Stafford**	*Collected Stories*
1969	**N. Scott Momaday**	*House Made of Dawn*
1968	**William Styron**	*The Confessions of Nat Turner*
1967	**Bernard Malamud**	*The Fixer*
1966	**Katherine Anne Porter**	*Collected Stories of Katherine Anne Porter*
1965	**Shirley Anne Grau**	*The Keepers of the House*

1964	No Award	
1963	**William Faulkner**	*The Reivers*
1962	**Edwin O'Connor**	*The Edge of Sadness*
1961	**Harper Lee**	*To Kill a Mockingbird*
1960	**Allen Drury**	*Advise and Consent*
1959	**Robert Lewis Taylor**	*The Travels of Jamie McPheeters*
1958	**James Agee**	*A Death in the Family*
1957	No Award	
1956	**Mackinlay Kantor**	*Andersonville*
1955	**William Faulkner**	*A Fable*
1954	No Award	
1953	**Ernest Hemingway**	*The Old Man and the Sea*
1952	**Herman Wouk**	*The Caine Mutiny*
1951	**Conrad Richter**	*The Town*
1950	**A.B. Guthrie**	*The Way West*
1949	**James Gould Cozzens**	*Guard of Honor*
1948	**James A. Michener**	*Tales of the South Pacific*
1947	**Robert Penn Warren**	*All the King's Men*
1946	No Award	
1945	**John Hersey**	*A Bell for Adano*
1944	**Martin Flavin**	*Journey in the Dark*
1943	**Upton Sinclair**	*Dragon's Teeth*
1942	**Ellen Glasgow**	*In this Our Life*
1941	No Award	
1940	**John Steinbeck**	*The Grapes of Wrath*
1939	**Marjorie Kinnan Rawlings**	*The Yearling*
1938	**John Phillips Marquand**	*The Late George Apley*
1937	**Margaret Mitchell**	*Gone With the Wind*
1936	**Harold Davis**	*Honey in the Horn*
1935	**Josephine Winslow Johnson**	*Now in November*
1934	**Caroline Miller**	*Lamb in his Bosom*
1933	**T.S. Stribling**	*The Store*
1932	**Pearl S. Buck**	*The Good Earth*
1931	**Margaret Ayer Barnes**	*Years of Grace*
1930	**Oliver LaFarge**	*Laughing Boy*

1929	**Julia Peterkin**	*Scarlet Sister Mary*
1928	**Thornton Wilder**	*The Bridge of San Luis Rey*
1927	**Louis Bromfield**	*Early Autumn*
1926	**Sinclair Lewis**	*Arrowsmith*
1925	**Edna Ferber**	*So Big*
1924	**Margaret Wilson**	*The Able McLaughlins*
1923	**Willa Cather**	*One of Ours*
1922	**Booth Tarkington**	*Alice Adams*
1921	**Edith Wharton**	*The Age of Innocence*
1920	No Award	
1919	**Booth Tarkington**	*The Magnificent Ambersons*
1918	**Ernest Poole**	*His Family*

Non-Fiction

2000	**John Dower**	*Embracing Defeat*
1999	**Jared Diamond**	*Guns, Germs, and Steel: The Fates of Human Societies*
1998	**John McPhee**	*Annals of the Former World*
1997	**Richard Kluge**	*Unabashed Triumph of Philip Morris*
1996	**Tina Rosenberg**	*The Haunted Land: Facing Europe's Ghosts After Communism*
1995	**Jonathan Weiner**	*The Beak of the Finch*
1994	**David Remnick**	*Lenin's Tomb*
1993	**Garry Wills**	*Lincoln at Gettysburg*
1992	**Daniel Yergin**	*The Prize: The Epic Quest for Oil, Money and Power*
1991	**Bert Holldobler and Edward O. Wilson**	*The Ants*
1990	**Dale Maharidge and M. Williamson**	*And Their Children After Them*
1989	**Neil Sheehan**	*A Bright Shining Lie: John Paul Vann and America in Vietnam*
1988	**Richard Rhodes**	*The Making of the Atomic Bomb*
1987	**David K. Shipler**	*Arab and Jew: Wounded Spirits in a Promised Land*
1986	**J. Anthony Lukas**	*Common Ground*

Biography

2000	**Stacy Schiff**	*Véra (Mrs. Vladimir Nabokov)*
1999	**A. Scott Berg**	*Lindbergh*
1998	**Katharine Graham**	*Personal History*
1997	**Frank McCourt**	*Angela's Ashes*
1996	**Jack Miles**	*God: A Biography*
1995	**Joan D.Hedrick**	*Harriet Beecher Stowe: A Life*
1994	**David Levering Lewis**	*W.E.B. DuBois*
1993	**David McCullough**	*Truman*
1992	**Lewis B. Puller Jr.**	*Fortunate Son*
1991	**Steven Smith and G.W. Naifeh**	*Jackson Pollock*
1990	**Sebastian DeGrazia**	*Machiavelli in Hell*
1989	**Richard Ellmann**	*Oscar Wilde*
1988	**David Herbert Donald**	*Look Homeward: A Life of Thomas Wolfe*
1987	**David J.Garrow**	*Bearing the Cross*
1986	**Elizabeth Frank**	Louise Bogan: A Portrait

History

2000	**David Kennedy**	*Freedom from Fear*
1999	**Edwin G. Burrows and Mike Wallace**	*Gotham: A History of New York City to 1898*
1998	**Edward J. Larson**	*Summer for the Gods: The Scopes Trial and America's Continuing Debate over Science and Religion*
1997	**Jack N. Rakove**	*Original Meanings: Politics and Ideas in the Making of the Constitution*
1996	**Alan Taylor**	*William Cooper's Town*
1995	**Doris Kearns Goodwin**	*No Ordinary Time*
1994	No Award	
1993	**Gordon S. Wood**	*The Radicalism of the American Revolution*
1992	**Mark E. Neely Jr.**	*The Fate of Liberty: Abraham Lincoln and Civil Liberties*
1991	**Laurel Thatcher Ulrich**	*A Midwife's Tale*

1990	**Stanley Karnow**	*In Our Image: America's Empire in the Philippines*
1989	**Taylor Branch**	*Parting the Waters: America in the King Years 1954–63*
1989	**James M. McPherson**	*Battle Cry of Freedom: The Civil War Era*
1988	**Robert Bruce**	*The Launching of Modern American Science, 1846–1976*
1987	**Bernard Bailyn**	*Voyagers to the West*
1986	**Walter A. McDougall**	*The Heavens and the Earth: A Political History of the Space Age*

Drama

2000	**Donald Margulies**	*Dinner with Friends*
1999	**Margaret Edson**	*Wit*
1998	**Paula Vogel**	*How I Learned to Drive*
1997	No Award	
1996	**Jonathan Larson**	*Rent*
1995	**Horton Foote**	*The Young Man From Atlanta*
1994	**Edward Albee**	*Three Tall Women*
1993	**Tony Kushner**	*Angels in America*
1992	**Robert Schenkkan**	*The Kentucky Cycle*
1991	**Neil Simon**	*Lost in Yonkers*
1990	**August Wilson**	*The Piano Lesson*
1989	**Wendy Wasserstein**	*The Heidi Chronicles*
1988	**Alfred Uhry**	*Driving Miss Daisy*
1987	**August Wilson**	*Fences*

Poetry

2000	**C.K. Williams**	*Repair*
1999	**Charles Wright**	*Black Zodiac*
1998	**Mark Strand**	*Blizzard of One*
1997	**Lisel Mueller**	*Alive Together: New and Selected Poems*
1996	**Jorie Graham**	*The Dream of the Unified Field*
1995	**Philip Levine**	*The Simple Truth*

1994	**Yusef Komunyakaa**	*Neon Vernacular*
1993	**Louise Gluck**	*The Wild Iris*
1992	**James Tate**	*Selected Poems*
1991	**Mona VanDuyn**	*Near Changes*
1990	**Charles Simic**	*The World Doesn't End*
1989	**Richard Wilbur**	*New and Collected Poems*
1988	**William Meredith**	*Partial Accounts*
1987	**Rita Dove**	*Thomas and Beulah*
1986	**Henry Taylor**	*The Flying Change*

National Book Award: Fiction

This award established in 1950 is given to honor American books of the highest literary merit.

1999	**Ha Jin**	*Waiting: A Novel*
1998	**Alice McDermott**	*Charming Billy*
1997	**Charles Frazier**	*Cold Mountain: A Novel*
1996	**Andrea Barrett**	*Ship Fever Stories*
1995	**Philip Roth**	*Sabbath's Theater*
1994	**William Gaddis**	*A Frolic of His Own*
1993	**E. Annie Proulx**	*The Shipping News*
1992	**Cormac McCarthy**	*All the Pretty Horses*
1991	**Norman Rush**	*Mating*
1990	**Charles Johnson**	*Middle Passage*
1989	**John Casey**	*Spartina*
1988	**Pete Dexter**	*Paris Trout*
1987	**Larry Heinemann**	*Paco's Story*
1986	**E.L. Doctorow**	*World's Fair*
1985	**Don DeLillo**	*White Noise*
1984	**Ellen Gilchrist**	*Victory over Japan: A Book of Stories*
1983	**Alice Walker**	*The Color Purple*
1982	**John Updike**	*Rabbit is Rich*
1981	**Morris Wright**	*Plains Song*

1980	**William Styron**	*Sophie's Choice*
1979	**Tim O'Brien**	*Going After Cacciato*
1978	**Mary Lee Settle**	*Blood Tie*
1977	**Wallace Stegner**	*The Spectator Bird*
1976	**William Gaddis**	*JR*
1975	**Robert Stone**	*Dog Soldiers*
1975	**Thomas Williams**	*The Hair of Harold Roux*
1974	**Thomas Pynchon**	*Gravity's Rainbow*
1973	**John Barth**	*Chimera*
1972	**Flannery O'Connor**	*The Complete Stories*
1971	**Saul Bellow**	*Mr. Sammler's Planet*
1970	**Joyce Carol Oates**	*Them*
1969	**Jerzy Kosinski**	*Steps*
1968	**Thornton Wilder**	*The Eighth Day*
1967	**Bernard Malamud**	*The Fixer*
1966	**Katherine Anne Porter**	*The Collected Stories of Katherine Anne Porter*
1965	**Saul Bellow**	*Herzog*
1964	**John Updike**	*The Centaur*
1963	**J.F. Powers**	*Morte D'Urban*
1962	**Walker Percy**	*Moviegoer*
1961	**Conrad Richter**	*The Waters of Kronos*
1960	**Philip Roth**	*Goodbye, Columbus*
1959	**Bernard Malamud**	*The Magic Barrel*
1958	**John Cheever**	*The Wapshot Chronicle*
1957	**Morris Wright**	*The Field of Vision*
1956	**John O'Hara**	*Ten North Frederick*
1955	**William Faulkner**	*A Fable*
1954	**Saul Bellow**	*The Adventures of Augie March*
1953	**Ralph Ellison**	*Invisible Man*
1952	**James Jones**	*From Here to Eternity*
1951	**William Faulkner**	*The Collected Stories of William Faulkner*
1950	**Nelson Algren**	*The Man With the Golden Arm*

The National Book Critics Circle Awards

Fiction Awards

Berriault, Gina	*Women in Their Beds*
Cheever, John	*The Stories of John Cheever*
Doctorow, E.L.	*Billy Bathgate*
Elkin, Stanley	*George Mills*
Elkin, Stanley	*Mrs. Ted Bliss*
Erdrich, Louise	*Love Medicine*
Fitzgerald, Penelope	*The Blue Flower*
Flanagan, Thomas	*The Year of the French*
Gaines, Ernest J.	*A Lesson Before Dying*
Gardner, John	*October Light*
Hazzard, Shirley	*The Transit of Venus*
Kennedy, William	*Ironweed*
Lethem, Jonathan	*Motherless Brooklyn*
McCarthy, Cormac	*All the Pretty Horses*
Morrison, Toni	*Song of Solomon*
Mukherjee, Bharati	*The Middleman and Other Stories*
Munro, Alice	*The Love of a Good Woman*
Price, Reynolds	*Kate Vaiden*
Roth, Philip	*The Counterlife*
Shields, Carol	*The Stone Diaries*
Smiley, Jane	*A Thousand Acres*
Tyler, Anne	*The Accidental Tourist*
Updike, John	*Rabbit at Rest*

General Non-Fiction Awards

Bate, Walter Jackson	*Samuel Johnson*
Branch, Taylor	*Parting the Waters: America in the King Years 1954–63*
Caro, Robert	*The Path of Power: The Years of Lyndon Johnson*
Donner, John W.	*War Without Mercy: Race and Power in the Pacific War*
Dorris, Michael	*The Broken Cord*

Dyson, Freeman	*Weapons and Hope*
Fadiman, Anne	*The Spirit Catches You When You Fall Down*
Faludi, Susan	*Backlash: The Undeclared War Against American Women*
Gould, Stephen Jay	*The Mismeasure of Man*
Gourevitch, Philip	*We Wish to Inform You That Tomorrow We Will Be Killed with our Families*
Harr, Jonathan	*A Civil Action*
Hersch, Seymour M.	*The Price of Power: Kissinger in the Nixon White House*
Howard, Maureen	*Facts of Life*
Kingston, Maxine Hong	*The Woman Warrior: Memories of Girlhood Among Ghosts*
Lomax, Alan	*The Land Where the Blues Began*
Lukas, J. Anthony	*Common Ground: A Turbulent Decade in the Lives of Three American Families*
Maclean, Norman	*Young Men and Fire*
Nicholas, Lynn H.	*The Rape of Europa: The Fate of Europe's Treasures in the Third Reich and the Second World War*
Raban, Jonathan	*Bad Land*
Rhodes, Richard	*The Making of the Atomic Bomb*
Steel, Ronald	*Walter Lippmann and the American Century*
Steele, Shelby	*The Content of Our Character: A New Vision of Race in America*
Taylor, Telford	*Munich: The Price of Peace*
Weiner, Jonathan	*Time, Love, Memory: A Great Biologist and His Quest for the Origins of Behavior*

The PEN/Faulkner Award

The PEN/Faulkner Award is given by writers to honor their peers for works of American fiction. It was established in 1980 and is named in honor of William Faulkner because he used his Nobel Prize money to establish an award for young writers.

Ha Jin	*Waiting*
Abish, Walter	*How German is It?*

Berriault, Gina	*Women in Their Beds*
Boyle, T. Coraghessan	*World's End*
Bradley, David	*The Chaneysville Incident*
Cunningham, Michael	*The Hours*
DeLillo, Don	*Mao II*
Doctorow, E.L.	*Billy Bathgate*
Ford, Richard	*Independence Day*
Guterson, David	*Snow Falling on Cedars*
Olson, Toby	*Seaview*
Proulx, E. Annie	*Postcards*
Roth, Philip	*Operation Shylock*
Salter, James	*Dusk*
Taylor, Peter	*The Old Forest*
Wideman, John Edgar	*Philadelphia Fire; Sent for You Yesterday*
Wiley, Richard	*Soldiers in Hiding*
Wolff, Tobias	*The Barracks Thief*
Zabor, Rafi	*The Bear Comes Home*

The Whitbread Awards

The Whitbread Novel Award

The Whitbread Novel Award is given for the best work of fiction by an author who has lived in Ireland or Great Britain for over three years. It is administered by the Booksellers Association of Great Britain and Ireland.

Ackroyd, Peter	*Hawksmoor*
Bainbridge, Beryl	*Everyman for Himself*
Brady, Joan	*Theory of War*
Cartwright, Justin	*Leading the Cheers*
Clarke, Lindsay	*The Chymical Wedding*
Crace, Jim	*Quarantine*
Gardam, Jane	*The Queen of the Tambourine*
Gray, Alasdair	*Poor Things*
Hope, Christopher	*Kruger's Alp*
Ishiguro, Kazuo	*An Artist of the Floating World*
Johnston, Jennifer	*The Old Jest*

Leitch, Maurice	*Silver's City*
Lodge, David	*How Far Can You Go*
McEwan, Ian	*The Child in Time*
Mosley, Nicholas	*Hopeful Monsters*
Rushdie, Salman	*The Moor's Last Sigh*
Rushdie, Salman	*The Satanic Verses*
Theroux, Paul	*Picture Palace*
Trevor, William	*Felicia's Journey; Fools of Fortune*
Wain, John	*Young Shoulders*

The Whitbread First Novel Award

The Whitbread First Novel Award is given to the writer of a first novel who has lived in Ireland or Great Britain for more than three years.

Atkinson, Kate	*Behind the Scenes at the Museum*
Boyd, William	*A Good Man in Africa*
Buchan, James	*A Parish of Rich Women*
Burn, Gordon	*Alma: A Novel*
Chatwin, Bruce	*On the Black Hill*
Crace, Jim	*Continent*
Cusk, Rachel	*Saving Agnes*
D'Aguiar, Fred	*The Longest Memory*
Foden, Giles	*The Last King of Scotland*
Fuller, John	*Flying to Nowhere*
Kureishi, Hanif	*The Buddha of Suburbia*
Lancaster, John	*A Debt to Pleasure*
Melville, Pauline	*The Ventriloquist's Tale*
Paterson, James Hamilton	*Gerontius*
Sayer, Paul	*The Comfort of Madness*
Torrington, Jeff	*Swing Hammer Swing!*
Winterson, Jeanette	*Oranges Are Not the Only Fruit*